Socialism

Socialism examines socialist ideals and realities from a variety of anthropological perspectives. Although socialism as a radical critique of capitalist industrial society may appear to be defunct, no one can doubt that it will leave behind powerful cultural legacies in countries all over the world, as well as conceptual legacies within anthropology and other social sciences.

The contributors reveal the factors which have given socialism such a profound worldwide impact, and which helped socialist societies to reproduce themselves for so long. They develop theories and analyses of socialism both in relation to 'primitive communism' and as a modern form of social organization with revolutionary aspirations. Case studies are drawn not only from the non-European countries with which anthropology is most commonly associated, but also from both Western and Eastern Europe. Recurring themes include the links with ethnic and national conflicts, with 'traditional' cultures and religious practices, and with gender relations. A number of contributors also illuminate the mechanisms of the recent changes which have removed socialists from power in many countries.

The first book to present a sustained and wide-ranging investigation of socialism by social anthropologists, this volume will do much to help us comprehend the experiences of 'ordinary people' under socialism and their responses to new post-socialist dilemmas. As well as opening up new fields of investigation for political anthropology, it makes an important contribution to our understanding of some of the most central and far-reaching events of contemporary history.

Socialism

Ideals, ideologies, and local practice

Edited by C.M. Hann

London and New York

First published in 1993
by Routledge
11 New Fetter Lane, London EC4P 4EE

Simultaneously published in the USA and Canada
by Routledge

Typeset in Palatino by Michael Mepham, Frome, Somerset
Printed and bound in Great Britain by
Biddles Ltd, Guildford and King's Lynn.

British Library Cataloguing in Publication Data
A catalogue record for this book is available from the British Library.

Library of Congress Cataloging in Publication Data
Socialism: ideals, ideologies, and local practice/edited by C.M. Hann.
    p. cm. — (ASA monographs; 31)
    Includes bibliographical references and indexes.
    1. Socialism and culture—Congresses. 2. Socialism—Cross-
    cultural studies—Congresses. 3. Ethnology—Congresses.
    I. Hann, C.M., 1953–   . II. Series: A.S.A. monographs; 31.
HX523.S5715   1992
306.3'45—dc20   92-15337
                                                                    CIP

ISBN 0–415–08322–2

Contents

Contributors

Ray Abrahams is Lecturer in Social Anthropology and Fellow of Churchill College, University of Cambridge.

Alan Barnard is Senior Lecturer in Social Anthropology at the University of Edinburgh.

Sufian Bukurura is a research student in the department of Social Anthropology, University of Cambridge.

Pat Caplan is Professor and Head of the Department of Anthropology and Community Studies, Goldsmiths' College, University of London.

Angela Cheater is Professor of Sociology and Social Anthropology at the University of Waikato, Hamilton, New Zealand.

Tamara Dragadze is Research Fellow at the School of Slavonic and East European Studies, University of London, and Assistant Director of the Centre for Caucasian and Central Asian Studies.

Grant Evans is Senior Lecturer in Anthropology, Department of Sociology, University of Hong Kong.

Ernest Gellner is William Wyse Professor of Social Anthropology, University of Cambridge, and Professor in Residence at the Central European University, Prague.

Ralph Grillo is Professor of Social Anthropology and Dean of the School of African and Asian Studies, University of Sussex.

Chris Hann is Professor of Social Anthropology, University of Kent at Canterbury. He was formerly Lecturer in Social Anthropology, University of Cambridge.

Ladislav Holy is Professor of Social Anthropology, University of St Andrews.

Joanna Overing is Senior Lecturer in Social Anthropology, London School of Economics, University of London.

Frances Pine is Post-Doctoral Research Associate, Department of Social Anthropology, University of Cambridge.

Jack M. Potter is Professor of Anthropology, University of California at Berkeley.

Peter Skalník was until recently Lecturer in Social Anthropology at the University of Cape Town; he is now Lecturer at the Charles University, Prague, and is shortly to become his country's ambassador to the Lebanon.

Jonathan Spencer is Lecturer in Social Anthropology, University of Edinburgh.

Michael Stewart is Post-Doctoral Research Associate, Department of Anthropology, London School of Economics.

Katherine Verdery is Professor and Chair of Anthropology, The Johns Hopkins University, Baltimore.

Susan Wright is Lecturer in Social Anthropology, School of Cultural and Community Studies, University of Sussex.

Editor's preface

The 1991 Conference of the Association of Social Anthropologists was convened 9–12 April in Cambridge. Meetings were held at the University Centre, whilst accommodation and meals – including a splendid celebration of the ninetieth birthday of Sir Raymond Firth, an active conference participant – were provided by Corpus Christi College. Supporting facilities were provided by the Department of Social Anthropology, where the convenor would not have survived without the secretarial assistance of Mrs Margaret Story and Mrs Mary MacGinley. He is especially grateful to Dr Frances Pine, who undertook all the responsibilities of local organizer with great efficiency.

Further thanks must be extended to Ernest Gellner, William Wyse Professor of Social Anthropology in Cambridge, who has done much to pioneer the anthropological study of socialism, both in theory and in practice. He played a full part in the conference, and has kindly contributed a Foreword to this volume in his own inimitable style.

The convenor/editor is also indebted to many other ASA members who chaired sessions and contributed to three days of fascinating exploration; and especially to Keith Hart and David Parkin, who provided stimulating summaries at the closing session.

Finally, he wishes to place on record his thanks to the following organizations for grants which enabled a substantial number of Soviet and East European scholars to take an active part in the conference: the British Academy, the British Council, the Royal Anthropological Institute, and the Wenner-Gren Foundation for Anthropological Research.

Foreword

Ernest Gellner

Editor's preface

Since the Middle Ages, Europe has twice been bifurcated ideologically. The first time, it was the Reformation which in the end divided those parts of Europe which were neither Orthodox nor occupied by a Muslim power between itself and those left to the Counter-Reformation. The so-called Enlightenment was, in a way, an attempt to explain and disseminate the achievements of the Reformed part of Europe – economic prosperity, political liberty – to the rest of Europe. The second major bifurcation arose between the liberal and the Marxist parts of the continent. As an ideological conflict, it began of course in the nineteenth century, but the contest only acquired territorial, political incarnation after 1917. For a time after 1945, the Great Contest, as it was called by a writer who was clear in his mind that victory would and should go to socialism, looked fairly evenly balanced.

By 1989, however, it was all over. As in the previous great bifurcation of Europe, victory went to the more liberal, pluralist, and individualist of the two contestants, and the outcome was decided by an economic rather than a military struggle. The victory of the liberals over the Marxists was much quicker and more total and convincing than that of the Protestants over the Counter-Reformation. The victory was overtly recognized and in the end loudly trumpeted by the leaders of the defeated system themselves. This is historically unprecedented: as far as I can recall, there has never been a case of an ideocracy, a Caesaro-Papist regime, hauling down the flag and conceding defeat, without being compelled to do so by either a violent uprising or a foreign military force. Never before has a previously charismatic and total faith been disavowed by its own sacerdotal-political leadership.

In Central Europe, the dominant feeling may be expressed by the motto I have devised for any newly revived Danubian federation: *Better Franz Josef than Josef.*

The demise of Marxist socialism does not of course automatically invalidate all other forms of socialist theory. But it would be comic for the socialist Old Believers to pretend that nothing has happened, that no thinking is required. For a long time they had claimed, when they were not whitewashing Bolshevism altogether, that it was merely a distortion or perversion of something good, and that when purged of these distortions it would revert to being the fulfilment of a pure ideal. Isaac Deutscher, who coined the 'Great Contest' phrase and used it as a title for one of his books, also believed that there was a 'contradiction' between the base of the Soviet social order, with its absence of private property, and its unattractive political and cultural superstructure, so that the latter were bound to go fairly soon. But by the late 1980s, most of those condemned to live under the system were clear in their minds that its defects were not in contradiction with, but *consequences of* the basic principles of its socio-economic organization. Advanced industrial society must in any case be centralized politically: the maintenance of order must be in the hands of a single agency or cluster of agencies with a single apex. A society of this kind simply cannot leave peace-keeping in the hands of its sub-units, as happens in, say, segmentary tribal organizations. But precisely for this reason, if such a society is to have the benefits of pluralism and countervailing forces at all, they must be located in the economic and ideological spheres. It cannot afford to unify all three aspects of life internally, and with one another. The consequences of so doing have been shown to be disastrous both morally and economically. But if there are to be independent centres of economic power as a precondition of civil society – and that is the widespread and urgent intuition of most of those who actually had to endure communism – it follows that the ideal of complete social control over material resources must not be implemented. A proportion of resources at least must remain under the control of parts of society rather than society as a whole. In other words, socialism in a full sense must be avoided.

The pre-eminence of Marxism within the socialist tradition was all in all well deserved. Marxism spelt out, systematized, codified the central intuition of socialists. Before industrialism, Europeans had lived in a social order dominated by specialists in coercion who controlled land. They were replaced by specialists in commerce and production, who also substituted a relatively pacific ethos of productive activity over the glorification of the exercise of violence and the possession of land. This showed there was nothing eternal about social systems.

The new order had a number of defects. It engendered, especially at its beginning, very great inequality, an individualism verging on a psychically crippling isolation, and a great waste of resources: inequality led to the inability of purchasing power to keep up with productive power. Was it not possible that a further social order was on the horizon, one which combined the economic power of capitalism with the cooperativeness of a very early social order, allegedly demonstrated by anthropology as prevailing at the beginnings of human history? This is where anthropology first helped Marxism. The new socialist order, based on the abolition of the key institution of capitalism (private property) proved catastrophic. Russians these days sometimes wryly observe that their role is to demonstrate to mankind the unviability of certain ideological options. They shouldn't really flatter themselves: their own experience might not have been conclusive. One could always blame Byzantine theology, the Tartar whip, Chayanovian work-aversion, or Muscovite centralism, and so on. But it won't do. Communism was tried in countries with centralist and with pluralist traditions, in countries docile to Moscow and others insolent to it, in countries with a good industrial tradition and those entirely lacking it, in countries in which communist power emerged endogenously and in countries in which it was brought by the Red Army, in ethnically plural ones and in homogeneous ones, some in Europe and some in the Third World, in democratic-egalitarian cultures and in authoritarian-hierarchical ones, in countries with almost every available religion, and so all possible combinations were tried in an exceptionally thorough experiment, and the results did not vary much, ranging only from the unspeakable to the very unattractive. This cannot be shrugged away. Our socialist Bourbons, who have forgotten nothing and learnt nothing, would have us do so, but that would be totally wrong. The order set up by the French Revolution was destroyed by its enemies, but that set up by the Russian Revolution was dismantled by the members of the very movement created for its protection. This is historically unique and we must try to learn the lesson contained in it.

For those for whom 'socialism' was a sacred and heart-warming word, it meant a society in which private control of resources was absent, *and* which was good. That still doesn't quite capture the intuition underlying the idea: what these people really felt, with great intensity, that such a society would be good *because* private ownership of the means of production was absent from it. Now this is simply false: it isn't merely that this inference is not valid. The absence of private control of resources, the concentration of control over them in the hands of the political institutions of that society, is compatible with a vast range of possible social orders, some perhaps good, some indifferent, and unquestionably, some of them appalling. Once this is clearly realized, it also becomes evident that any positive evaluation of the social order attaches not to the abolition of private ownership as such (accompanied by the socialist intuition that this will automatically lead, unless there are dreadful 'distortions', to a meritorious society), but to the selection of the *type* of political institution in the society in question.

Moreover, in the light of actual socialist experience, it seems manifest that a measure of economic decentralization is a precondition of a free society. So the whole problem needs reformulation. It cannot remain in that naïve stage in which it was when socialism was conceived as a self-justifying correction of the acquisitiveness, competitiveness, ruthlessness, inequality, and unnecessary poverty of industrial capitalism. And the reformulation of the problem needs the kind of data and ideas found in this collection of essays.

This does not mean, of course, that the other extreme, the ideal of a pure market society, must automatically be endorsed. For a time, it is inevitable that it should seem to be desirable, at any rate in regions which had to endure up to seven decades of coercive and mendacious imposition of the socialist vision. But for various reasons, it is exceedingly unlikely that an advanced industrial society can live by the market alone. It is quite certain that it cannot live by socialism, but it is at least unlikely that it can manage on the unaided market. In an age of very powerful technology, uncontrolled private pursuit of gain would be ecologically disastrous (though the secrecy of monolithic government proved to be even more harmful in this respect). In an age of very complex science, it is impossible to disaggregate the contribution of various elements to the latest advance, and market rewards are arbitrary and inequitable. In an age when all life depends on a lumpy, indivisible infrastructure, the strategies of political collectivities are more vital than the economic decisions of individuals. In an age of affluence, the toleration of pockets of deprivation and squalor is morally unacceptable. For all these reasons, it is likely that an advanced industrial society will once again display that pre-eminence of the political over the economic which has been the normal condition of mankind. That pre-eminence was suspended for a time during the early part of the transition from the idiocy of agrarian life to the affluence of effective industrialism, at a time when, miraculously, the technology was just strong enough to bribe away discontent but not strong enough to destroy society and the environment, and when one society was fortunate enough to possess the right infrastructure without much help from central government. But that time is now over.

If one takes socialism to mean the dominance of political-cultural considerations over purely economic ones, then it will yet prevail. But of course this minimal, and morally neutral, definition does not give the socialist Old Believer what his heart desires. What he has in his mind's eye is a society which is cooperative, free of the opportunity for greed and acquisitiveness, and yet efficient and free of oppression. Recent decades would seem to have demonstrated conclusively that the latter two aims cannot be achieved in an organizationally and ideologically monolithic society, and that a pre-condition of not having this monster is a measure of private control over resources. Once this is admitted, 'socialism' ceases to be a magical password to a self-authenticating, legitimate social order. If what is at issue is merely the reaffirmation of the control of the political over the economic, then this formula on its own does not yet give us anything inherently good or bad. It is, on the contrary, compatible with an extremely wide range of social possibilities, as we have already noted. The question then becomes just what kind of political control there is to be, how much leeway must be granted for the private deployment of economic power in order to avoid the possibility of dictatorship. The correct formulation seems to me to be this: political dominance over the economic is inevitable and in itself neither good nor bad, but the idea that this will in itself automatically produce a unique and a good social form is simply absurd. (The idea *was* contained in Marxism, in as far as it taught that the obliteration of private property would eliminate classes, and this in turn would obliterate political domination, so that a desirable, or an actually non-existent – because redundant – form of polity was guaranteed.) Whatever merit there is in any given alternative will not be a corollary of the constraints of the economic as such, but of the particular form and extent of those constraints.

There is, of course, not the slightest reason for supposing that the pattern to emerge will be the same throughout Eastern Europe and the territories of the erstwhile Soviet Union, let alone in other parts of the world which have experimented with socialism. We shall most probably witness great diversity, and this will contribute to our understanding of how political and economic institutions interact. The transition from the feudal or absolutist variants of a command economy to a modern production-orientated free society was long, often painful, and, in the main, unplanned. The transition from an over-centralized socialist absolutism to something new will inevitably be rapid, it *is* intended, and it will certainly be painful and probably turbulent. We do not know the outcome, or range of possible outcomes. We need not expect a repetition of the classical pattern, the slow emergence of a new bourgeois ethos. There is no evidence of the emergence of a new breed of Forsytheskis or Buddenbrookovs. On the contrary, there are some grounds to fear the emergence of a Lumpenbourgeoisie composed of the old black marketeers and the old opportunist aparatchiks, and a widespread criminalization of society. One can only hope that the new, and expanded, intelligentsia with its longing for a genuine civil society, made numerous by the occupational transformation, and no longer insulated in Chekhovian ghettos, will prevent such a collapse, and find the political clout to impose its own values.

These questions will now have to be pondered. In order to get anywhere, we need data and we need ideas. We need to know what actually happened under so-called 'actually existing socialism' (the insinuation contained in the phrase was – this is the best you can have, so you'd better like it). We need to know how socialist ideology and aspirations actually operated in the real world. Social anthropology has a good record for realism: its practitioners are trained to distinguish between the manifest and the latent elements in social institutions. They possess a good technique for locating the latter, and a fine sense for both the interrelatedness of things and the tensions liable to arise between various strands in the life of any one society. The present volume assembles an outstanding collection of inquiries into what has gone on and continues to go on in the world of socialist reality and aspiration. It makes a splendid contribution to a debate which is supremely important and which will go on for a long time.

Introduction
Social anthropology and socialism

C.M. Hann

Much has been written about socialism, for it and against it, from every conceivable political and academic vantage point. The contributions of social anthropology have hitherto been sparse, and for good reasons. The subject has long been associated with the study of the 'exotic' and the 'primitive', and with the persistence of small-scale 'traditional cultures' in the contemporary world. How could this discipline cast light on the large-scale upheavals brought about by the European intellectuals, radical social engineers and leaders of disciplined party organizations, who have been the principal agents of the most significant modernizing experiments of the industrial era? Many answers emerged in the papers and discussion during the three days of the ASA's 1991 conference, and the selection published in this volume bears testimony to the vitality and diversity of contemporary anthropology.[1] The papers should be accessible to a wide audience, both inside the discipline and outside it, and this introduction is an attempt to sketch a context which does not assume any prior familiarity with academic anthropology.

Readers should be aware that the conference was held in April 1991, after the collapse of socialist governments in Eastern Europe but before the disintegration of the Soviet Union. (At the time of writing in November 1991 it remains premature to speak of any collapse of socialist power in China.) The conference theme was in fact determined in spring 1989, before all the recent convulsions in Eurasia. The resulting papers consequently differ greatly in their emphases. Some of the papers on Eastern Europe offer analyses of apparently well-established socialist systems, with little direct reference to recent political developments (for example, the chapters by Pine and Stewart). Others present diachronic accounts from the perspective afforded by recent developments, though even then the author may place greater emphasis upon political and cultural continuities at the local level (for instance, Skalník). Ladislav Holy writes about the revolutionary moment itself in Czechoslovakia, whilst other authors address specific aspects of the transition to a post-socialist future, including ethnicity and nationalism (Verdery) and religion (Dragadze). All of the Eurasian papers are based on recent or continuing fieldwork, and they show how anthropology can contribute both in understanding those societies as they were before 1989, and in assessing the transitions to non-socialist futures and the full implications of socialist legacies.

But the original conference proposal, under the same title as this volume, deliberately cast a wider net. It was recognized that anthropologists would wish to identify a plurality of socialisms in the contemporary world and to explore socialist ideas in a wide variety of settings in space and in time. Approximately half the papers are not concerned directly with the Eurasian heartland of socialism. They include accounts of local politics and gender relations in Tanzania and North-east England, discussions of Islam and Buddhism as well as Marxist-Leninist orthodoxy, and the production of national as well as supra-national ideologies in several post-colonial states. Two papers represent another important theme of the conference. Both Alan Barnard and Joanna Overing examine deeply problematic links between socialist ideas and anthropological analyses in the fields with which the discipline is most commonly associated, the study of 'hunter-gatherers' and 'tribal' peoples. Ralph Grillo, on the other hand, highlights the use made of social anthropology itself by the leading theoreticians of 'African socialism'. Apart from this set, grouped together in the next three chapters, most papers are concerned with specific political and economic manifestations of socialism as institutionalized within modern states. They are concerned not so much with socialism or communism as abstract ideals, but with their concrete realization in 'actually existing' societies.[2]

The encounter between anthropology and socialism may be rich in dividends for the future of the discipline as well as for the understanding of socialism. Towards the end of this Introduction I put forward some specific suggestions concerning the concepts available to anthropologists in studying contemporary social life, and above all its political aspects, in conditions which socialist systems have illustrated with great clarity. It should be emphasized that these remarks reflect my particular interests and enthusiasms. They were not elaborated at the conference, and it is unlikely that they would receive much support from colleagues, including the other contributors to this volume. In his Foreword, Ernest Gellner mocks those he terms 'socialist Old Believers', and it was pointed out at the conference (by Paul Stirling) that anthropologists studying socialism may find themselves in a more complex relationship with both their subjects and their readers than colleagues writing about traditional belief systems or political practices among remote peoples. Of course, there are few if any peoples in today's world who remain unaffected by the impact of socialism, both as a political force and as a set of ideas; and there can be few ethnographic accounts of 'primitive societies' entirely uncontaminated by those same ideas. All I can say is that, though responsibility for this Introduction is mine alone and partiality inevitable, I hope my summary treatment here of some very complex themes is judged free of any simplistic prejudice.

SOCIALISM AND 'PRIMITIVE SOCIETY'

Anthropology means, literally, the study of mankind. The word has been used in many ways, but one central focus (linking, for example, authors as diverse as the early Karl Marx and Pope John Paul II) is a concern with 'human nature', with the essence of what it means to be human. One of the achievements of modern social anthropology and cognate disciplines has been to bring forward many new kinds of data for approaching such questions, previously addressed for the most part by philosophers and theologians. Of particular interest here is the use made of anthropological materials by early socialists, above all Engels in his *History of the Family, Private Property and the State* (1884). Anthropology was called upon to provide part of the validating charter of the most influential strand of socialism for, if it could be shown that human beings had once before in their evolution lived in conditions of 'primitive communism', then it might become more difficult to dismiss the prospect of a communist future for industrial societies as mere Utopian fantasy.

But if anthropology was called upon to legitimate socialism, it is also important not to lose sight of the influence of socialist ideas and theories upon anthropology itself. This has remained strong down to the present day. Some anthropologists (perhaps under-represented in this volume) may choose to approach socialist and post-socialist societies in theoretical terms which are themselves derived from Marxian theory (or at least from one of the many available versions of neo-Marxism).[3] It has taken anthropology a long time to appreciate fully the extent to which the questions asked of primitive society were in fact questions generated by the specific conditions and intellectual traditions of the West. The answers obtained have sometimes been more revealing of the sympathies of an author and the ideological climate prevailing in the countries of the anthropologists than of the ostensible subjects of inquiry.[4] For example, well into the twentieth century some Western anthropologists were still busy documenting communal property ownership among savage peoples. Nowadays it seems reasonable to suggest that this approach was strongly influenced by the ascendancy of private property rights in their own North Atlantic culture, and by a socialist critique of that system. Alan Barnard's chapter in this volume shows how starkly opposed positions within a modern Western debate between socialism (collectivism) and capitalism (individualism) could claim support from the investigation of one and the same primitive people (in this case the Bushmen of Southern Africa).

Similar points emerge in Joanna Overing's chapter. Karl Marx's notion of 'original proprietorship' is shown to be inadequate for understanding Guianese collectivities. Yet it is nearer the mark and contains more insight that the 'Protestant ethic' judgements of one of the most influential of contemporary anthropologists, Marshall Sahlins. The latter saw himself as working within a Marxist tradition, but Overing shows through drawing upon her own and other ethnography that his emphasis upon individualist anarchy is overdrawn: Piaroa *do* have communities, and 'their freedom in work is a political fact' (p.56). She points to the concept of *sociality* as a way out of the ethnocentric trap into which so many anthropologists have fallen. For Amazonian Indians, as for Bushmen, it should be possible for us to acknowledge *both* the autonomy of persons and small groups *and* the political realization of common identities among larger collectivities.[5]

The field of peasant studies has long been characterized by a comparable tension between scholars who emphasize the collectivist bases of social behaviour in small rural communities and, on the other hand, those who emphasize individualist motivations.[6] The chapter by Grant Evans in this volume cuts through this ultimately sterile argument through a careful analysis of 'merit-making' under practical Buddhism in the context of the socialist state of Laos. In this case the failure of socialist cooperatives can be explained, at least in part, by the inability of socialist powerholders to grasp the importance of personal and familial autonomy which had existed alongside the main 'communal' institutions of the pre-socialist period, the monasteries. Essentially the same problem is also well documented by Pat Caplan in a chapter which outlines repeated attempts by Tanzanian state officials to promote communal cultivation in the name of *ujamaa*. Whatever the collective character of life in agrarian communities (Evans speaks of 'reciprocity', Jonathan Spencer speaks of 'mutuality' in Sri Lanka, as do the African socialists discussed by Ralph Grillo), it was not conducive to the imposition of large-scale farms with joint cultivation and bureaucratic organization. Massive force was required for such imposition to proceed, and this is indeed how it was accomplished in most of Eurasia. Even there, village cultivators would resist such imposition with whatever means at their disposal – and sometimes succeed, as in the Polish case discussed in this volume by Frances Pine.

Barnard establishes that Western anthropologists frequently report in the ethnographic evidence what they have been predisposed to find by their own basic assumptions about the world. Does this mean that all past and present research among non-Western societies is futile? Must the socialist dogma of primitive communism remain a question of faith, of theology, not susceptible to empirical investigation? It is important to recognize the ideological dimension of anthropology itself, and most anthropologists have in recent years adopted a more critical stance towards the texts of their discipline. These ideological elements were nowhere stronger than in the former Soviet Union, where ingenious and elegant work was carried out within the orthodox Engels tradition. Gellner has shown how one Soviet anthropologist found a sophisticated answer to the riddle of mankind's essence, an answer consistent with the collectivist assumptions of social life in the pre-Gorbachev Soviet Union.[7] He also suggested that Yuri Semenov's theory could be empirically refuted if the 'communistic primordial community' were shown as a result of further anthropological and archaeological research to have been hierarchical and not egalitarian at all (1988: 38). But in the light of the chapters by Barnard and Overing this opposition too must seem suspect. It remains to be seen whether further exploration of the concept of *sociality* will enable researchers to move permanently beyond the familiar Western dichotomies which 'socialism' has done so much to sustain throughout the history of modern anthropology.

IDENTITY AND CULTURE, CONTINUITY AND CHANGE

The study of 'ruling classes' and political elites under socialism has exercised other disciplines for many years, and although a good case might be made for more ethnographic work in this field, little was in evidence at the conference. However the role of cultural elites was much in evidence, and this is a theme which takes us at once to the changing character of social anthropology in recent decades. There was a time when anthropologists were almost exclusively preoccupied with non-literate societies and abstained from any attempt to study historical changes in those societies, let alone changes consciously planned and implemented by an elite. But if anthropologists wish to engage the contemporary world and come to terms with all its interconnectedness they certainly cannot afford to ignore the role of intellectuals in shaping – and occasionally perhaps inventing – new cultural traditions. Holy's portrayal of the actors who, as the voices of the Czech nation, precipitated that country's 'Velvet Revolution' is the most dramatic of a number of illustrations provided in this volume, several of which deal with Africa.[8]

The work of educated African elites in forging the concept of 'African socialism' is the main subject of Ralph Grillo's chapter. Among the pioneers was Jomo Kenyatta, who had studied social anthropology under Malinowski at the London School of Economics in the 1930s (and was well remembered from this period by Sir Raymond Firth). Other significant strands identified by Grillo led back to Fabian and social-democratic thought in Europe in the 1950s, and particularly the British Labour Party. It is curious that some of the most influential formulations of African socialism were made in Kenya, a country later much maligned by other self-styled socialists for its pursuit of capitalist roads of development. Other African socialists, notably Julius Nyerere in Tanzania in his development of the concept of *ujamaa*, were similarly concerned to find roots for the new types of collectivity which they promoted in their overwhelmingly rural economies in 'traditional' African ideals of working together. It is difficult to know how far African elites succeeded in legitimating their policies by such appeals to tradition, but it would be uncharitable to assume that they promoted these policies for reasons other than the strength of their socialist convictions. Whatever its wider impact throughout African societies, Grillo argues persuasively that socialism provided many educated Africans with a powerful and positive source of *identity* in the late colonial and early post-colonial periods.

Perhaps because she is dealing with leaders and events of a later generation, when socialist backsliding was already familiar in many parts of the continent of Africa, Angela Cheater is highly critical of the ways in which allegedly socialist Zimbabwean elites have promoted the creation of 'traditional culture'. Noting the vaguely 'Western' enthusiasms of many disaffected young Zimbabweans (for example, in dress and musical tastes), Cheater shows how Robert Mugabe's government has pursued highly artificial pseudo-socialist alternatives, not any longer on a pan-African scale but strictly within the context of an ethnically diverse state. Many of the alleged continuities with pre-socialist traditions are evidently spurious, such as the way in which the President came to expect deferential kneeling in his presence from young Shona women. (Such dubious appeals to tradition may also be made by local groups themselves, as shown by Ray Abrahams and Sufian Bukurura in their account of how reliance upon traditional weaponry may have helped to protect village vigilante groups from suppression by Tanzanian state bureaucracy.) One reason for such manipulation of tradition in the Zimbabwean case appears to lie in the leader's need to bolster his personal supremacy (though Cheater does not pursue comparisons with the 'cult of personality' surrounding other socialist leaders, in Albania, China, Cuba and elsewhere) in the course of establishing a one-party, Marxist-Leninist style of political system in Zimbabwe. In this, as in the other African examples, much more work is needed to assess how successful these 'cultural' policies have been in meeting their legitimation objectives. Cheater's account is pessimistic and points to a mass of contradictions. As in other socialist countries, liberal and enlightened legal codes have been enacted to eliminate sex discrimination; for instance, in many areas of family law. Yet despite official condemnation of 'bad customs', the Zimbabwean government has tacitly condoned the subversion of new laws which threaten traditional patriarchal controls.[9] Recently it has apparently abandoned its nominal commitment to socialism altogether.

Cheater's case study takes us into another very complex area for investigation, that of the links between socialism and nationalism, its major rival ideology in the political history of the twentieth century. It is an area in which many anthropologists have already been active, and a previous ASA

Conference considered examples of the role played by intellectuals in providing appropriate versions of history to support the claims and aspirations of ethnic groups and nations.[10] Contrary to the 'internationalist' expectations both of the European founding fathers of the nineteenth century and of the African socialists of the mid-twentieth, the discourses and practices of socialism and nationalism have often proved compatible. Powerholders in some very old nation-states as well as in comparatively new ones such as Zimbabwe and Romania have found the idea of belonging to a common nation more potent in mobilizing support than any other.[11]

The recent demise of socialism in many parts of the world has led numerous commentators to predict a strengthening of nationalism. This is already happening in many places, but as the chapter by Katherine Verdery shows it would be a mistake to imagine that ethnic and national conflicts were simply suspended or held in 'cold storage' under socialism. On the contrary, regardless of whether frequent recourse to the symbols of nationalism does actually enhance their legitimacy, socialist powerholders may well have encouraged certain kinds of ethnic conflict through their economic and bureaucratic organization. Citing the Romanian case as an example, Verdery suggests that the shortages of consumer goods caused by socialist economic planning accentuated ethno-national allegiances, as access to goods came to depend more and more upon personalistic ties and networks.

Both socialism and nationalism are often nominated as 'secular religions'.[12] Undoubtedly for some followers, 'the faithful', this interpretation of socialism had some plausibility over a long period (it is doubtful if it is anywhere very plausible for significant numbers of people today). Communism was able to provide an image of the promised land, ample compensation for the indignities one has to suffer here and now. Marx, Lenin, and a few others provided the scriptures, and the Communist Party supplied some of the institutional trappings of a church. Human needs for affectivity were met through the adaptation of many old rituals as well as the invention of some new ones. Aidan Southall has drawn upon classic anthropological theories, particularly the work of Victor Turner, in accounting for the impact of socialism in the formative period of the Soviet Union.[13] It would seem that wherever socialist political parties have achieved popular support, in Western Europe as well as further east, rational, atheistic principles have been supported by a range of symbols and ritual practices, at least some of which have probably had considerable success in broadening popular acceptance of the new religion. This is another important area in which anthropologists have already begun to make a distinctive contribution to the study of socialism.[14]

Anthropological investigations of socialism do not on the whole confirm its ability to overcome and substitute for traditional forms of religion. Realities have proved more complex, as shown, for example, in the chapters by Grant Evans and Jonathan Spencer in this volume. The icons of socialism and nationalism will have to coexist and compete with other symbols, more deeply rooted in centuries of social interaction which preceded the intrusion of modern ideologies. This third set, if indeed they form a coherent set, may be systematically plundered by the other two. It may disappear from view during the apogee of Marxism-Leninism, when the old temples are likely to be sacked (though only Albania and Cambodia went so far as formally to ban traditional religion *per se*). When the wave of militant atheism passes and conditions permit the expression of grassroots identities once again, traditional religion may reappear with undiminished strength. Alternatively, it may appear in some modified form. Tamara Dragadze's chapter presents some evidence from various parts of the former Soviet Union, and focuses upon shifts in the boundary between sacred and profane. She suggests that the pre-socialist religious system does undergo major changes during the periods of repression and later uneasy coexistence with the doctrines of rational scientific Marxism; it is then likely to be further transformed when called upon to provide the key symbols for nationalist movements.

The survival of traditional forms is more unambiguously emphasized in the chapter by Jack Potter, who shows how the 'liberalization' which has taken place in China since the late 1970s has allowed the re-emergence of many rituals suppressed for more than a generation.[15] Indeed, Potter's emphasis upon continuity goes further than this (and too far to be credible to some other conference participants). He finds many ways in which pre-socialist patterns (particularly local kinship organization) were insidiously effective throughout the Maoist period, undermining all attempts 'from above' to create a new society on a *tabula rasa* (see also Stewart, this volume). As he and S.H. Potter have phrased it elsewhere, the 'cunning of structure' (1990: 268) behind Chinese rural culture was maintained throughout successive socialist transformations and continues to determine life conditions now that many elements of socialism have been modified or abandoned.

There is another view, however, according to which socialism does achieve a revolutionary break with the past, a rupture which cannot be masked by apparent continuities in such fields as folk rituals. For example, working in an adjacent region of South China to Potter, Helen Siu (1989) finds that many people performing such rituals today have lost any sense of their traditional meaning. According to Siu, the political context has changed so radically under the monoply of power exercised by the Communist Party that one must place greater emphasis upon discontinuity: survivals are more apparent than real, a genuine revolutionary transformation has occurred.

Essentially the same debate could be rehearsed for most other socialist societies.[16] Probably the majority of anthropologists have been inclined, at the end of the day, to place greater emphasis upon the cultural continuities. These have had a significant impact upon the forms that socialism has taken locally, and sometimes they have given people resources with which to resist alien impositions (for a very interesting case study from Romania, see Kligman 1988). This should come as no surprise, and the basic point has long been conceded by most political scientists. For example, despite the relative uniformity of socialist institutions among Soviet allies in Eastern Europe before 1989, the actual implementation of socialist programmes varied enormously, in ways that could to some extent be explained by reference to differences in pre-socialist history and 'political culture'.[17] Is this, then, to be the main thrust of anthropology's contribution to the comparative study of contemporary socialism? Is the task best seen as one of *micro* cultural investigations, designed to illustrate how core ideas and institutions (such as class struggle, public ownership, the centrally planned economy, or the democratic-centralist party) may be modified in particular instances?

The importance of this micro-scale ethnographic work should not be under-estimated. Most anthropologists still rely upon 'participant observation' as their most important method of data collection. They typically live in a small community, or if the settlement is a large one they nevertheless aim to achieve a close acquaintance with particular groups and networks within it (and, as we have noted, these groups and networks nowadays may include intellectuals as well as 'ordinary people'). The qualitative evidence and extended case studies which distinguish most anthropological accounts from those of other social scientists can usefully complement the type of understanding achieved in other disciplines. At its best, the anthropological approach can offer a fully satisfying account of 'how the system really works', the *pays réel* as opposed to the *pays légal*, including the influence of specific cultural traditions upon its operation. Perhaps even more valuably, the anthropologist should be able to convey a sense of what it *feels* like to live in such a system.

Among the papers which achieved this goal most satisfactorily at the conference, several were concerned to highlight the disadvantaged position of women under very different sorts of socialist conditions (Caplan and Cheater for Africa, Pine and Wright for Eastern and Western Europe respectively). There were some striking similarities in the materials presented: male disregard for the views of women at 'public' meetings does not seem to vary much between Mafia Island, Tanzania, and Teesside, England. Susan Wright's chapter offers insights into competing versions of socialism in a depressed region of Britain where the Labour Party has frequently found it more convenient to impose its own models of development (modernization) than to heed the wishes of local people. This paper met with a particularly enthusiastic response from the (mainly British) conference audience, and showed – if any further proof were needed – that anthropological methods can be used to great advantage in one's own society.[18]

It is often objected that the community which the anthropologist has chosen to study may not be typical, a criticism which is almost always accurate but beside the point. Wright is able through her local study to illuminate changes taking place in images of socialism in many other parts of Britain, and perhaps much further afield. Similarly, although the Vlach Gypsies studied by Michael Stewart in Hungary are rather atypical of other Gypsies, let alone the dominant Magyar population of the country, his study of them none the less brings out some of the most frequently recurring features of socialism, such as the ideological emphasis placed upon regular wage-labour and the intolerance of cultural difference. The 'typicality' of the setting for anthropological investigations has little or no bearing on the extent to which they can illuminate the wider systems and processes of socialism.

A second answer suggested by some of the papers offered at the conference, perhaps most explicitly in the paper by Verdery, is that, if socialist societies provide the best examples of a new type of political system, a new type of economic organization, and a new type of belief system, none of them known before the twentieth century, then it is worth paying systematic attention to *discontinuities* and to *macro* levels of investigation in an effort to provide a theoretical understanding of this form of social organization. Many scholars of socialism, including most of the contributors to this volume, have given priority to the sphere of politics. More precisely, they have sought to ground their understanding of socialism in terms of state power. For most commentators, the state stands opposed to society, resembling – at least superficially – the pattern identified in some classic studies of primitive societies (Clastres 1977; cf. Barnard, this volume).

I would like to question the use of these concepts of state and society and also to consider further another problematic term which I have already used several times, that of legitimation. How, if at all, has power been legitimated in socialist conditions? One hypothesis from a long-term historical perspective would be that socialism achieved a wide measure of legitimacy because it gave priority to social control , as opposed to formal economic rationality.[19] As such, it was a dialectical response to the rapid and largely uncontrolled expansion of North Atlantic capitalism. The system which subordinates formal economic rationality to substantive political rationality is in disarray at the present time, in Sri Lanka no less than Siberia, in large measure because capitalist systems have performed better in terms of providing the goods people wish to consume. But if the recent revolutions which have displaced socialism in many countries do not deliver the goods for everyone, then problems of legitimation will remain, and further dialectical shifts are likely. In the remainder of this Introduction I would like to consider these problems with particular reference to Eastern Europe, the region which I know best myself, whilst simultaneously attempting to draw out some general implications for political anthropology.

LEGITIMACY, MORALITY, AND 'MUDDLING THROUGH'

Western fieldworkers in most socialist countries before the recent revolutions faced a variety of difficulties. In addition to the usual problems which anthropologists tend to face everywhere, such as gaining acceptance among the people they wish to study and access to information, they were liable to run into difficulties when they disseminated their results in the West. Let me give a personal example. When I reported, after some three years' residence in Hungary, including one spent in a small village, that the country's socialist authorities enjoyed a high degree of legitimacy, I was taken to task by an American colleague.[20] Michael Sozan advised me that the term was not used in American anthropology (see also Verdery, this volume). He clearly found it especially inappropriate in Eastern Europe, where all socialist regimes enjoyed 'Leninist legitimacy', or in other words, whatever the party did was by definition right and good for the people. My point was not to deny the absence of pluralist democratic freedoms in Eastern Europe, but to suggest that by the 1970s the extent to which socialist political domination had become popularly accepted among 'ordinary people' varied considerably within the region. Hungary, where I had been doing fieldwork from 1975 onwards, was a distinctive case: despite being run by a political regime installed by a foreign power amidst the bloodshed and repression of 1956, these same authorities had been unusually successful in meeting the economic aspirations of citizens, and I found these positive aspects recognized and appreciated by large numbers of the villagers among whom I lived.[21]

Most of the chapters in this volume outline a more depressing picture: for example, in Central Europe the state was apparently hated as much by peasants (Pine) as by intellectual elites (Holy). Yet there can be little doubt that at least some of the twentieth-century socialist systems of Eurasia enjoyed substantial measures of popular support. They cannot all be dismissed as repressive aberrations, in the present euphoria of capitalist triumphalism. For some Westerners the fact that communist or socialist parties performed for the most part rather badly as soon as competitive elections were held in their countries is sufficient to prove that socialism was always illegitimate; but, as both Holy and Skalník would agree in the Czechoslovak case, an anthropological analysis must dig deeper than this.

Many East Europeans themselves rejected their regimes as uncompromisingly as they dared before 1989. There were also substantial numbers of people who gave enthusiastic support to socialist powerholders. But in most countries, most of the time, most 'ordinary people' simply took the system for granted, accommodated to it and got on with their lives without joining either the Communist Party or a dissident group. In other words they 'muddled through', just as people do in other kinds of society.[22]

A contrary view tends to be put forward by intellectuals within Eastern Europe. For example, Elemér Hankiss has argued that, precisely because of the 'disabling' of society under socialism, people in Eastern Europe have enjoyed a kind of 'ironical freedom'. They are better able to think in alternatives than Westerners, who tend to 'accept things, and their lives, as they are', whilst Easterners could experience 'the freedom of living outside the system in which they lived' (1990: 7). These suggestions are to my mind highly plausible for artists and writers, but in Hankiss' view East European socialism 'made philosophers *malgré eux* even out of the men and women in the street' (1990: 7). Anthropological investigations can put this claim to the test. It can certainly be granted that socialist systems made some demands upon all their citizens which would be unusual in other systems, and these demands must be carefully examined. But these distinctive features of socialist political systems may not provide sufficient grounds for Western anthropologists to emphasize only the features which are *not* common to other systems, let alone to proceed rapidly on this basis to classify the socialist systems as illegitimate.

Perhaps anthropologists would do better to avoid the idea of legitimacy altogether, given that levels of political awareness vary enormously and even the same person may have very flexible and ambiguous attitudes to powerholders. We might instead make the arguably less controversial claim that, however imperfectly, for a long time socialist political systems *worked*. It is easy to see with hindsight that central planning is inherently incapable of meeting rapidly expanding consumer expectations, and that many other tensions were at work in socialist systems. But it is foolish to insist that there was anything inevitable about their demise. If one can understand the basis of their reproduction before 1989, one may reach a better understanding of their legacies and avoid repetition of the disasters, not only of Marxist-Leninist socialism, but of other systems which made socialist messages attractive to so many in the first place.

It goes without saying that coercion was all too frequently invoked to establish and maintain socialists in power, and the effects of this form of power (even when exercised for very limited periods) have been far-reaching. The economic dimension has already been mentioned, and is well explored in this volume by Verdery and Stewart, among others. Socialists generally sought to establish greater central control over all areas of economic life than their predecessors. Only in those few cases such as Hungary, where policy emphasis on production (especially in heavy industry) was tempered with the encouragement of elements of the market and individual initiative, did socialist regimes succeed in making themselves attractive to their citizens through their economic performance. In terms of political life in the narrower sense, the socialist regimes of Eurasia generally secured the elimination of all serious rivals to the Communist Party, usually organized according to Leninist principles of 'democratic-centralism'. This party could claim to represent the entire working class, but whatever this theory pretended, it is doubtful whether the power and privileges associated with party membership did much to enhance the legitimacy of socialist powerholders among either members or non-members.

When due account has been taken of all other dimensions, the military, the economic, the party-political, and so on, I want to hypothesize that socialists were able to sustain themselves in power in considerable part through their ability to win and maintain a significant degree of moral endorsement. The concept of 'legitimacy' may indeed be, as Verdery suggests, an over-simplification, a Western social-science concept with a long pedigree, but far too crude to be of much help to anthropologists. But what can never be left out of the picture entirely, it seems to me, is how far the exercise of political power can enjoy moral endorsement. 'Ordinary people' may muddle through but, in socialist Eurasia as elsewhere, they also maintain their own concepts of what is just and what is unjust. It seems to me that many have been persuaded to accept that socialism embraces extensive welfarism and the restoration of a moral component to economic life, from which morality was effectively expunged following the rapid expansion of European industrial capitalism (cf. the definition put forward by John Dunn, cited by Jonathan Spencer in this volume, pp. 120–1). In this sense the socialist venture has a profoundly conservative meaning concealed behind its more visible emphasis upon revolutionary radicalism. I suggest that the readiness with which so many citizens of even the most corrupt socialist countries have found excuses for their rulers and professed their continued commitment to socialist ideals testifies to their conservatism, and to the continued failure of the available alternatives to satisfy this basic moral criterion by embedding economic life in a humane social framework.

Many accounts of the demise of socialism have already paid some attention to this moral dimension. The sociologist Runciman (1985) identified the failure of socialists to command this ethical respect as central to the support gained by Solidarity in Poland in 1980–81. More recently Hankiss (1990), Chirot (1991), and Clark and Wildavsky (1991) have all used similar terms whilst exploring the downfall of socialist regimes throughout the region, and Holy does so in his chapter on the Czech revolution in this volume. In the Czech case, as in some other socialist countries, so-called dissidents founded their political opposition on an attempt to reclaim the moral high ground from socialist powerholders. Perhaps the most talented writer as well as the most successful politician was Czechoslovakia's Vaclav Havel, who railed against 'living a lie' and and sought to show how the survival of the system depended upon the complicity of millions of ordinary people, prepared to march on May Day and to display appropriate slogans and flags in their windows when required (1985: chap. 1). Steven Sampson has called recently for much closer anthropological study of what he terms 'collaboration' (1990). But how deep is this complicity, and is this collaboration really so different from what we find in other, non-socialist political conditions?

INTELLECTUALS, ANTHROPOLOGISTS, AND ORDINARY PEOPLE

There can be no doubting the vital role played by intellectuals in the recent upheavals in Eastern Europe, hardly less significant in Warsaw, where an electrician became the first post-socialist President, than in Prague, where the job went directly to the playwright. But one should enter a note of caution here. Intellectuals such as Havel created a rhetorical framework which no doubt has itself influenced the course of recent history, but can we trust these intellectuals to provide conclusive accounts of the phenomenology of socialism? It is also worth recalling that many intellectuals whose spontaneous migrations to the West triggered revolutions in their native countries did so unashamedly for pragmatic, materialist reasons. As Zygmunt Bauman has noted,

> Well fed and clad, educated and cosseted young East German professionals stampeding to the West did not pretend to be running away from disliked political philosophy; . . . they admitted that what they were after . . . was a wider assortment of goods in the shops and wider selection of holidays.
>
> (1990–91: 188)

Unfortunately, as Peter Skalník brings out clearly, many among the non-migrants and ordinary citizens of all the countries which have recently (and with good reason) abandoned the fetters of orthodox central planning will find the 'truth' of capitalist market economies no more palatable than the alleged 'lies' of socialism. Many will find themselves much worse off materially under the new slogans of 'market economy' and 'joining the West'; and they will recall the original moral critique which socialism offered. Indeed, Havel might do well to recall that an earlier generation of East European intellectuals was once just as confident that it had discovered 'truth' – in socialism itself.[23]

Havel's conceit is a very significant one, and I think it can direct us towards the role political anthropology should play in the study of these societies. In much of Eastern Europe in 1989 there was a sense, carefully fostered by opposition intellectuals over many years, of 'people power'.[24] The word 'society' was by no means just a technical term used in academic analyses. Rather, society was an active collective agent embarked upon the heroic task of emancipating itself from the socialist state. According to this 'Manichean' (Hankiss 1990) perspective, state and society are viewed as diametrically opposed players in a zero-sum game. Socialism is construed as the apotheosis of artificial, 'top-down', bureaucratic, etatist social engineering, whilst (civil) society is presented as a 'natural', organic entity composed of autonomous individuals and groupings who generate solidarity and consensus 'from below', together with the values and identities conducive to a fully human existence.

Many people, and above all anthropologists, with their vaguely populist sympathies, will be tempted to enter into this Manichean game with gusto on the side of 'society'. But a little reflection should enable them to see that this very opposition should be approached very warily. It is, of course, itself the product of centuries of Western political theory. The extent to which certain ideas associated with the singular noun 'state' and the collective noun 'society' have been popularized in socialist (and now ex-socialist) political systems is a matter for empirical investigation, as are the channels by which the ideas have been disseminated. Anthropologists can play a part, along with other intellectuals, in tracing the genealogies of such ideas, but their more distinctive contribution lies in documenting the significance of the ideas in concrete social contexts. Perhaps it is time that anthropologists recalled the conclusions of Fortes and Evans-Pritchard in their 1940 manifesto for political anthropology: *African Political Systems*, they found, could not be usefully illuminated by Western political theory.[25] The complication today is that, unlike the African cases considered by those authors, the 'worn coinage' of Western political philosophy and its concern for morality in the abstract is widely disseminated among many of the people anthropologists wish to study. Thus the concepts of state and society may be prominent in the arguments and self-understandings of some East Europeans, but such data do not necessarily take us very far in the search for explanations of how actual socialist political systems have operated.

It may be useful to go back briefly to the African papers in this volume, in order to pursue this point about intellectual elites and the question of what should take priority in anthropological research. Ralph Grillo is concerned with intellectual genealogies of 'African socialism', and his 'ethnography' comprises a study of the texts produced by leading politicians. The essential anthropological counterpoint is provided in the chapters by Caplan and Abrahams and Bukurura, which are concerned with how villagers experienced socialist policies and adapted to them. Like most chapters in this volume these are concerned *both* with a general exposition of ideas *and* specific local evidence. It is not my purpose here to argue that any one type of approach is better than another, and indeed the conference proved that sharply opposed styles of anthropology may all have a useful contribution to make. But it did seem to be generally agreed that anthropology cannot afford to lose its direct engagement with 'ordinary people' (or even, in socialist parlance, 'the masses'). Of course the very notion of 'ordinary people' may itself be manipulated and contested by opposed groups of political activists, as Susan Wright demonstrates for Teesside; but she also gives space to the voices of village women in a valuable case study which complements the more general sections of her chapter.

Certainly, it is a valid and important task for anthropologists to study the intellectual producers of new cultures and historiographies, and to criticize the texts of dead politicians as well as dead anthropologists. But it is at least as vital to document the actual life experiences of other people as studied during fieldwork, and we need to be especially careful in trusting the intellectuals themselves to provide authentic accounts of the systems in whose creation and maintenance they are deeply implicated.

Related questions concerning the anthropologist's own political commitments and ethical responsibilities punctuated the conference throughout. Jonathan Spencer argued at one point that the past dominance of evolutionary and positivist frameworks had linked the discipline itself to the projects of social engineers; and this history made it very difficult for anthropologists today to become engaged in debate on political and economic issues of concern to those they study. In response, Ray Abrahams acknowledged the ethical and other difficulties involved in representing the interests of the local groups we study, but pointed out that alternatives might sometimes be worse. For if anthropologists eschewed such engagement, other, less modest self-styled scientific experts would step forward, with much greater likelihood of disastrous practical outcomes. Some young African participants seemed to go further, notably Abrahams' co-author Sufian Bukurura, in arguing that indigenous anthropologists, as intellectuals themselves, could not content themselves with offering interpretations of their social worlds: they also had an obligation to change them. This commitment was not elaborated in specifically socialist terms, and would certainly entail paying more respect to local interests and genuine participation than has been in the case in socialist development hitherto; but these and other exchanges in the discussion did, I think, serve to remind the conference audience again of the common ground that may exist between anthropology and the emancipatory political projects launched by the pioneers of socialism.

STATE AND SOCIETY IN EASTERN EUROPE – AND ELSEWHERE

The last two decades have seen a number of valuable anthropological studies of Eurasian socialist societies. Little appreciated for the most part, either within anthropology or within the other academic subjects dealing with the region, some of this work I suggest, may point the way towards more satisfactory understandings of other varieties of socialism as well. I also think it has implications for the study of many non-socialist societies.

Of course by no means all fieldworkers in socialist countries have been concerned explicitly to address contemporary socialist conditions. Sometimes they may have experienced practical constraints, in other cases their intellectual interests have lain elsewhere. For example, a good deal of work has been carried out by Western anthropologists in various parts of Yugoslavia in the socialist period. Much of this was historically orientated (for example, Halpern and Halpern 1972; Winner 1971) or it was concerned primarily with the distinctive cultural traditions of specific ethnographic contexts (Lockwood 1975; Rheubottom 1971). But starting in the 1970s, the era of East European *détente*, a number of researchers began to confront head-on the 'problems of socialism' (c.f. Cole 1985) and this is the work I wish to highlight here. Of course, political conditions dictated that certain countries would figure much more prominently in this work than others: those most intensively studied in Eastern Europe have been the very diverse cases of Hungary, Poland, and Romania.[26]

Much of this work has concentrated upon the kind of case study that would offer the closest approximation to the ususal scope of a fieldwork project in a more 'exotic' setting. Thus the anthropologists studied the survival or disintegration of peripheral groups, such as certain ethnic minorities (for instance, McArthur 1976 on Transylvanian Saxons; Stewart 1987 and Williams 1992 on Gypsies). Not only did they choose to work in bounded communities, but they often selected villages in very remote mountain locations which inevitably reflected socialist changes in different ways from settlements closer to the centres of urban development (for example in Poland, Pine and Bogdanowicz 1982, Hann 1985; in Romania, Beck 1976, Randall 1976). A few researchers, however, studied villages in which the more general lines of socialist transformation emerge very clearly: examples would include the work of Peter Bell on the Great Hungarian Plain (1984) and David Kideckel (forthcoming) on Transylvania. All of these studies provide valuable documentation of how socialism was experienced at local levels. They bring out the compromises that were struck in the actual implementation of government policies, and the ambiguities in the position of local officials, charged on the one hand to implement directives received from outside ('from above') but also required to observe the norms of social interaction with kinsmen and neighbours in their communities. (These ambiguities were by no means confined to Eastern Europe, as Pat Caplan makes clear in her analogy between the officials of TANU in Tanzania and the earlier predicament of 'the proverbial headman in British Central Africa' (p. 77).) Not even collectivization, as the work of Kideckel in particular illustrates, can be understood simply as the imposition of state power upon helpless villagers. Villagers were able to influence its implementation, and in Hungary they were able eventually to subvert and transform it to their own advantage (cf. Elek 1991; Hann 1980; Szelényi 1988).

Other anthropological studies of socialism have moved beyond the conventional framework of the community study. Steven Sampson (1984a) has argued in favour of taking a 'vertical slice' approach, by which he means that the anthropologist should select a specific theme in social life (in Sampson's case the subject was settlement policy in Ceauşescu's Romania) and pursue it at many levels, from individuals and families in small communities to the highest governmental decision-takers. Equally ambitious is the work of Janine Wedel (1986; see also Wedel (ed.) 1992) in Poland, which is undoubtedly one of the countries where the 'state versus society' arguments have been most prominent (for reasons which have much to do with historical discontinuities in Polish political history). Wedel's anthropology ties in with a good deal of work by Polish social scientists as well as 'dissident' intellectuals throughout Eastern Europe. A 'private' domain, is argued to be more significant than the 'public' domain which is dominated by the socialist state. Citizens have created their own networks not merely to help them cope with economic shortage but also to provide them with positive values and identities lacking in socialism. Wedel writes of 'a more vital Poland that operates underneath the surface of the state, sometimes limiting it, sometimes, without its gratitude, enabling it to function' (1992: viii).

Although much of her work would seem to confirm the usefulness of the 'state versus society' dichotomy, Wedel also goes on to question the rhetorical construction of such a simple adversarial relationship. As the quotation above already hints, an alternative interpretation of the evidence which she and other anthropologists have gathered in socialist Eastern Europe would emphasize the 'interpenetration' and 'entwining' of the allegedly separate spheres of state and society, public and private, formal and informal. The administrative apparatus of socialist states is large; apart from the large civil service, most economic enterprises are state controlled, likewise the academies and universities. Just as the staff of all these 'state' bodies cannot be arbitrarily detached from their positions in 'society', so there is not much in socialist 'society' (consider for a moment the provision of welfare services and education) that can be understood without careful reference to agencies associated with 'the state'.

In short, it may be much too simple to argue (as so many intellectuals have, both Eastern and Western) that under socialism 'society' was squashed by a more or less totalitarian form of state power, and that now in the aftermath we may expect the 'vacuum' to be filled by a Western-style 'civil society'. The actual patterns are more complex. For example, in the Tanzanian case Abrahams and Bukurura show that the notion of a monolithic 'party-state' is misleading, given the differences which exist between the TANU party and the state bureaucracy. In the Romanian case Verdery discusses competition within and between bureaucracies by adapting the old anthropological concept of 'segmentation'. In Poland too, as Wedel has shown, the 'vacuum' metaphor is quite unhelpful. Here an unusually chaotic form of socialism provided conditions in which intellectuals were able to deploy 'society' as a concept to create the illusion of an integrated and unified populace, with very diverse groups being drawn together through their common opposition to perceived powerholders. A system of power usually theorized in terms of a strong state dominating, penetrating, or colonizing a weak society actually generated the converse, a weak state and a much stronger sense of a coherent 'society' than one normally expects to find in capitalist conditions. Of course this unity and 'solidarity' proved difficult to sustain when socialist powerholders were defeated or withdrew, at which point nationalist aspirations often provided the only alternative rallying slogans.

It is obvious, then, that informal, 'non-public networks' play a vital role in the actual social organization of socialist societies. They are particularly well demonstrated in Pine's chapter, which shows the influence of kinship, neighbourhood, and the domestic division of labour upon the myriad of new economic activities in which Polish women are now engaged. This 'second economy' under socialism closely resembles phenomena already well-known to anthropologists and sociologists from studies of many other complex societies, where people do not have to march on May Day and display slogans in their windows. From crowded slums in African cities (Hart 1973) to contemporary Britain (Pahl 1984), the importance of this dimension of social life has been well documented. Researchers have also shown that it must never be artificially detached from the 'formal' or 'public' dimension (Harding and Jenkins 1989; cf. Hart forthcoming), and that it can be reliably investigated only through intensive ethnographic research. As research into the actual social and working lives of ordinary people proceeds, the similarities between basic organizational characteristics of socialist Eurasia and modern conditions in the so-called First and Third Worlds may come to seem much more compelling than the differences. It follows that the chances of anything radically different emerging in post-socialist Eurasia must be considered rather slim. Poles will march on 3 May (a national holiday commemorating the bourgeois constitution of 1791) instead of May Day, and the slogans in shop windows will be different; or they may not march at all, and political slogans may disappear from shops altogether. But, as Janine Wedel concludes, 'the continuities of the środowisko ['social circle'] will be critical in shaping Poland' (1992: 18).

If this analysis is correct, more radical conclusions may follow. Ironically, it seems to me, not only do the strong states in which socialist societies are supposed to specialize turn out to be much weaker than was supposed, but a closer examination of the socialist cases undermines the continued application of the whole discourse of state and society as this has evolved in Western theorizing since pre-industrial times. Whatever their popularity among East Europeans themselves, the concepts of state and society are so 'entwined' as to be unhelpful in contemporary social science investigations. Anthropologists have recently made a start in this direction, when a majority voted after a public debate in favour of declaring the concept of society 'obsolete'.[27] An equally critical look at the concept of the state is now surely overdue.

Having already jettisoned much of the available theoretical baggage (note again that hardly a single anthropologist in this volume uses the hallowed Marxist concepts of class and exploitation), political anthropologists may not find it easy to drop these terms as well. They may fear some intellectual impoverishment of their subject if they are unable to come up with neat synthetic alternatives. I would argue that it is unfair to expect this of them. This volume contains a number of chapters which ask searching questions about definitions of the political and the implied scope of political anthropology (see especially chapters by Overing, Holy, and Spencer). In the case of socialism, we can expect anthropological work to bring out *both* significant differences in its reception by different peoples with distinctive cultural traditions, *and* the striking similarities which its derivatives have generated all over the contemporary world. Investigations may also reveal that socialist societies have much more in common with many non-socialist societies than is usually supposed, a point noted by several contributors.

CONCLUSION

Twentieth-century socialisms may be viewed as the most distinctive and systematic attempts to humanize the allegedly 'disembedded' economies of capitalism, and thereby to create good societies in the modern world. The demise of Stalinism has little bearing on the continuing urgency of this fundamental moral imperative. But it is undeniable that in practice, and in spite of many rhetorical efforts to demonstrate the contrary, socialist ideals and ideologies – such as materialist rationality and development planning – have often proved incompatible with local traditions, with the established values, religious idioms and authentic aspirations of real human communities. For the most part, of course, socialisms have been pursued not in mature capitalist conditions, but among peoples whose experience of modern industrial society has been slight or non-existent. The study of the social and cultural characteristics of these peoples has been the speciality of anthropology, a discipline which has itself been profoundly influenced by socialist ideals. The full legacies of the many varieties of socialism, short term and long term, practical and theoretical, will only become clear through further investigations. For this to happen, we may need a *perestroika* (but not necessarily a revolution, still less disintegration) in actually existing political anthropology!

NOTES

1 The absence of almost half the original conference papers from this volume is a source of deep regret to me the editor. Although the quality of the materials was uniformly high, to publish the full proceedings would have required a second volume – and unfortunately there is no precedent for such a step in the ASA Monographs series. A number of papers were excluded from the final selection because arrangements had already been made for their publication elsewhere, and I am aware that several people had good reasons for preferring this course (this applies in particular to two papers dealing with the contemporary trans-formation of the Soviet Union; see Humphrey 1991; Vitebsky 1992). Those which remain reflect a consciously eclectic policy designed to ensure representation not only of as many countries and ethnographic contexts as possible, but also of the many styles and approaches available within contemporary anthropology worldwide.

2 The phrase 'actually existing socialism' (*Realsozialismus*) originates among East German dissidents in the 1970s. They were critical of their socialist regime but loyal to Marxian ideals; see Bahro 1978.

   For concise introductions to Marx and central themes in Marxist theory see McLellan 1973, Kolakowski 1978, Bottomore (ed.) 1983. Clearly, it was not the business of anthropologists at this conference to make a contribution to 'Marxology', or to take sides in the continuing debates within and between socialist traditions.

   As far as the difference between 'socialism' and 'communism' is concerned, the former has generally been taken to refer to a more or less protracted transitional stage in progress towards the latter, the classless, ultimate destination of human societies. Most of the countries discussed in this volume have described them-selves as socialist rather than communist. (Of course, according to one theoretical strand they should be classified as 'state-capitalist', thereby allowing one to hail the revolutions of 1989 as the possible resurrection of socialism rather than its demise – see, for example, Callinicos 1991.) In the West, at least until recently, 'communist' political parties were obliged to use this name in order to distin-guish themselves from other parties of a social-democratic type. In everyday life in Eastern Europe in recent decades the term 'communist' has been used, along with the term 'Bolshevik', for the most part with emphatic derogatory intent. A similar nuance may be detected in the chapters in this volume, with some authors preferring to write about communism, while others prefer socialism; the editor has not attempted to impose overall consistency.

3 For a wide-ranging sympathetic review of the main ideas of Marx and Engels in the light of modern ethnographic evidence and of neo-Marxist work, see Bloch 1983.

4 One reason for this state of affairs has been a low level of interest in the history of the discipline during most of the twentieth century. This is now being remedied: on this particular topic see Kuper 1988.

5 In addition to references provided by Overing in her chapter, the concept of 'innate' sociality is explored by Carrithers 1989.

6 For influential examples of these approaches, see Scott 1976, Popkin 1979.

7 Gellner presented Semenov's theory at the conference, in the same session as the papers of Barnard and Overing. See Gellner 1988.

8 In addition to the Africanist papers published in this volume the conference benefited from hearing a sensitive assessment by Dr Susan Fleming of the International Development Centre of the University of Manchester of rural development in Angola ('Peasants and peasant associations in Angola; a look at

policy and practice'). In this example too, the attempt to impose Marxist-Leninist institutions had failed to meet its objectives, but Fleming held out some hope that a looser form of 'peasant association' would leave greater scope for local initiative and 'bottom-up' development. On the negative side, gender bias seemed as strong here as in the Tanzanian and Zimbabwean cases reported to the conference, and there remained strong pressures to create a central organization which would give elite groups more effective power to control grassroots action.

9 A comparable pattern can be observed in China in the 1980s where the authorities had to face an upsurge of what they termed 'feudal customs' in the wake of economic liberalization, particularly decollectivization. They attempted to counter such customs with ideological emphasis upon the values of 'socialist spiritual civilization'; but it is doubtful whether they have been any more successful in such campaigns than the authorities in Zimbabwe, as a paper presented at the conference by Kwang-ok Kim of the College of Social Sciences, Seoul National University suggested, with the help of some fascinating examples ('Socialist civilization and the resurgence of tradition in China').

10 See Tonkin *et al.* (eds) 1989.

11 An excellent example of socialist ideology in an 'old' nation-state was provided at the conference by Zdzisław Mach of the Department of Social Anthropology of the Jagiellonian University, Cracow. In his paper, 'The construction of national identity and nationalistic ideology in a socialist state: the case of Poland', Mach analyzed history textbooks to show how the authorities have sought to adjust their version of the past to suit the needs of a present in which Warsaw must be allied with Moscow. He also showed how the emphasis given to national symbols left little room for recognition of the other ethnic groups and nations who have lived alongside and among Poles in the past, and in smaller numbers even today: the suppression of political pluralism under socialism is matched by the suppression of ethnic diversity (see also Mach 1989). A still more extreme case is that of Ceauşescu's Romania: see Verdery's chapter in this volume, and for more detailed treatment, Verdery 1991.

12 In the case of nationalism, this is close to the position of Anderson 1983; for socialism as a faith, see Gellner 1990.

13 In the paper he presented at the conference, 'Marx, Lenin and the problems of socialism for anthropological theory', Southall also gave a very good example of the way in which some anthropologists have been able to *empathize* with certain moments of socialist history (see also Southall 1992).

14 For the Soviet case, see Binns (1979–80) and Lane (1981). In Western contexts the case of Italian communism is the most intensively studied to date: see Kertzer 1980, Shore 1990. At the conference Cris Shore examined the term 'socialism' itself as a symbol, before going on in his paper to present a fascinating account of the dilemmas faced recently by the British Communist Party in its attempts to reform and shed some of its Leninist heritage ('What's in a name? "Socialism" and the British Communist Party').

15 Broadly similar patterns have also been identified following recent fieldwork in Northern China by Kwang-ok Kim (see note 9 above).

16 They could be rehearsed also for many other populations which have been exposed to comparable political pressures from non-socialist governments: for example, Fascist regimes in Europe, or the Kemalist tradition in Turkey. But as Steven Sampson has pointed out, things will normally be more complicated than a simple problematic of 'change' versus 'continuity': 'Several distinct processes seem to be at work: the *survival* of cultural forms which the state has been unable

to suppress, the state's *resuscitation* and *manipulation* of local cultural expressions, and the popular *reinvention* of traditions in new contexts' (1991: 17).

17 See Brown and Gray (eds) 1979, Rothschild 1989; but on the concept of political culture see also the strictures of Spencer, this volume.

18 Another rich and ambitious ethnographic study of socialism in the context of a capitalist state by an indigenous anthropologist was presented to the conference by Italo Pardo (Department of Anthropology, University College, London) under the title, 'Socialist visions: Naples and the Neapolitans'. Many of the more general issues raised by the practice of 'anthropology at home' were discussed at a previous ASA conference: see Jackson (ed.) 1987. Some of the more specific problems concerning 'insider' accounts by intellectuals of their own socialist societies are discussed further below.

19 This vocabulary derives from Max Weber and Karl Polanyi, two of the key figures in modern Western social science.

20 Michael Sozan was of Hungarian descent (unlike myself) and had also carried out fieldwork in Hungary. Sadly, he died of leukaemia in 1988. See the articles which appeared in the *Newsletter of the East European Anthropology Group*, under the general heading 'Western anthropologists in Eastern Europe', in 1986, 5(1): 3–4; 5(2): 2–3; and 1987, 6: 1–2, 2–3.

21 But see Michael Stewart's chapter in this volume for a more sombre assessment of legitimacy in the Hungarian case. I fully accept that the reasons why I tend to take a more positive view may have much to do with the timing and location of my original fieldwork: in the mid–1970s the Hungarian 'economic miracle' was still at its peak, and I chose to work in the county where agricultural policies had been unusually flexible, where villagers had for the most part evaded the ills of collectivization, and yet benefited enormously from government support and incentives. For further discussion of the successful cooperatives of this region, see Hann 1992.

22 Both the general argument and the specific phrasing here owe much to Steven Sampson: see, for example, 1984b.

23 The Hungarian Georg Lukács is perhaps the most distinguished of the intellectuals who gave the socialist project eventual unconditional endorsement. In my experience, ordinary people in the region are more familiar with John Lennon's version of the same basic refrain, 'All I want is the truth, just gimme some truth' (from the 'Imagine' album, very popular among East European youth; see Ryback 1990). Lennon remains one of the biggest culture heroes among East European youth.

24 For a typical account of this climate of opinion and the revolutions of 1989 see Ash 1990. Many of this author's writings on Eastern Europe, all extremely unsympathetic to socialism, have been translated into Eastern European languages, sometimes subsidized by the new post-socialist governments.

25 As has been pointed out recently, these authors were not particularly successful in following through the implications of their own advice. Not only did their primary means of classifying African political systems reflect a very Western concern with the presence or absence of centralized government, but a careful reading, particularly of Evans-Pritchard's work on the acephalous Nuer, also shows the authors to be under the influence of a particular, 'folk' version of British political history. See Stocking (ed.) 1984, especially the essay by Kuklick.

26 It is impossible to offer a full review here of all previous Western anthropological work on socialist societies, and my bias towards particular parts of Eastern Europe is very obvious. Mention must be made, however, of pioneering work in the Soviet Union by Humphrey (1983) and Dragadze (1988). Anthropological

fieldwork was all but impossible in mainland China until the 1980s, by which time socialist institutions in the countryside had already undergone sweeping changes. For some sharply contrasting results of recent work see Mosher 1983, Siu 1989, Potter and Potter 1990.
27 See Ingold (ed.) 1990. It may be worth adding here that the popular use of the term 'society' by progressive movements throughout socialist Eurasia was cited in this debate (by J.D.Y. Peel) as one reason why anthropologists should hesitate to discard the concept as 'obsolete'. In my view its continued use as a 'benchmark' in anthropological work is unfortunate, even (or perhaps especially) when we are dealing with nation-state structures which leave no stone unturned in their efforts to instil some sense of allegiance into all members of the collectivity. Similar conclusions have already been reached by some sociologists (for example, Mann 1986).

REFERENCES

Anderson, B. (1983) *Imagined Communities; Reflections on the Origin and Spread of Nationalism*, London: Verso.
Ash, T.G. (1990) *We the People*, Cambridge: Granta Books.
Bahro, R.F. (1978) *The Alternative in Eastern Europe*, London: Verso.
Baumann, Z. (1990–91) 'Communism: a post-mortem', *Praxis International*, 10(3–4): 185–92.
Beck, S. (1976) 'The emergence of the peasant-worker in a Transylvanian mountain community', *Dialectical Anthropology*, 1: 365–75.
Bell, P.D. (1984) *Peasants in Socialist Transition: Life in a Collectivized Hungarian Village*, Berkeley: University of California Press.
Binns, C.A.P. (1979–80) 'The changing face of power: revolution and accommodation in the development of the Soviet ceremonial system', *Man*, 14–15: 585–606 and 170–87.
Bloch, M. (1983) *Marxism and Anthropology: The History of a Relationship*, Oxford: Clarendon Press.
Bottomore, T. (ed.) (1983) *A Dictionary of Marxist Thought*, Oxford: Blackwell.
Brown, A. and Gray, J. (eds) (1979) *Political Culture and Political Change in Communist States*, London: Macmillan.
Callinicos, A. (1991) *The Revenge of History: Marxism and the East European Revolutions*, Cambridge: Polity Press.
Carrithers, M. (1989) 'Sociality, not aggression, is the key human trait', in S. Howell and R. Willis (eds) *Societies at Peace: Anthropological Perspectives*, London: Routledge.
Chirot, D. (ed.) (1991) *The End of Leninism and the Decline of the Left: The Revolutions of 1989*, Seattle: University of Washington Press.
Clark, J. and Wildavsky, A. (1991) *The Moral Collapse of Communism: Poland as a Cautionary Tale*, San Francisco: Institute for Contemporary Studies.
Clastres, P. (1977) *Society against the State*, Oxford: Blackwell.
Cole, J.W. (1985) 'Problems of socialism in Eastern Europe', *Dialectical Anthropology*, 9: 233–56.
Dragadze, T. (1988) *Rural Families in Soviet Georgia: A Case Study in Ratcha Province*, London: Routledge.
Elek, S. (1991) 'Part-time farming in Hungary: an instrument of tacit decollectivization', *Sociologia Ruralis*, 31(1): 82–8.
Engels, F. (1972 [1884]) *The Origin of the Family, Private Property and the State*, New York: Pathfinder Press.
Fortes, M. and Evans-Pritchard, E.E. (eds) (1940) *African Political Systems*, Oxford: Clarendon Press.

Gellner, E. (1988) *State and Society in Soviet Thought*, Oxford: Blackwell.
—— (1990) 'Introduction' in O. Glebov and J. Crowfoot (eds) *The Soviet Empire: Its Nations Speak Out*, London: Harwood Academic Publishers.
Halpern, J.M. and Halpern, B.K. (1972) *A Serbian Village in Historical Perspective*, New York: Holt, Rinehart & Winston.
Hankiss, E. (1990) *East European Alternatives*, Oxford: Clarendon Press.
Hann, C.M. (1980) *Tázlár: a Village in Hungary*, Cambridge: Cambridge University Press.
—— (1985) *A Village Without Solidarity: Polish Peasants in Years of Crisis*, New Haven, CT: Yale University Press.
—— (1992) 'Property relations in the new Eastern Europe; the case of specialist cooperatives in Hungary', in M. De Soto and D.G. Anderson (eds) *The Curtain Rises: Rethinking Culture, Ideology and the State in Eastern Europe*, New York: Humanities Press.
Harding, P. and Jenkins, R. (1989) *The Myth of the Hidden Economy: Towards a New Understanding of Informal Economic Activity*, Milton Keynes: Open University Press.
Hart, K. (1973) 'Informal income opportunities and urban employment in Ghana', *Journal of Modern African Studies*, 11(1): 61–89.
—— (forthcoming) 'State and market after the Cold War', in Roy Dilley (ed.) *Contesting Markets*, Edinburgh: Edinburgh University Press.
Havel, V. (with others) (1985) *The Power of the Powerless: Citizens Against the State in Central-Eastern Europe*, London: Hutchinson.
Humphrey, C. (1983) *Karl Marx Collective: Economy, Society and Religion in a Siberian Collective Farm*, Cambridge: Cambridge University Press.
—— (1991) 'Icebergs, barter and the mafia in provincial Russia', *Anthropology Today*, 7(2): 8–13.
Ingold, T. (ed.) (1990) *The Concept of Society is Theoretically Obsolete*, Manchester: Group for Debates in Anthropological Theory.
Jackson, A. (ed.) (1987) *Anthropology at Home* (ASA Monograph 25), London: Routledge.
Kertzer, D.I. (1980) *Comrades and Christians: Religion and Political Struggle in Communist Italy*, Cambridge: Cambridge University Press.
Kideckel, D.A. (forthcoming) *The Solitude of Collectivism: a Romanian Region before the Revolution*, Ithaca, NY: Cornell University Press.
Kligman, G. (1988) *The Wedding of the Dead: Ritual, Poetics and Popular Culture in Transylvania*, Berkeley: University of California Press.
Kolakowski, L. (1978) *Main Currents of Marxism: Its Rise, Growth and Dissolution*, Oxford: Clarendon Press (3 Vols).
Kuper, A. (1988) *The Invention of Primitive Society: Transformations of an Illusion*, London: Routledge.
Lane, C. (1981) *The Rites of Rulers: Ritual in Industrial Society – The Soviet Case*, Cambridge: Cambridge University Press.
Lockwood, W.G. (1975) *European Moslems: Economy and Ethnicity in Western Bosnia*, New York: Academic Press.
McArthur, M. (1976) 'The Saxon Germans: political fate of an ethnic identity', *Dialectical Anthropology*, 1: 349–64.
McLellan, D. (1973) *Karl Marx: His Life and Thought*, London: Macmillan.
Mach, Z. (1989) *Symbols, Conflict and Identity*, Cracow: Jagiellonian University.
Mann, M. (1986) *The Sources of Social Power* (vol.1), Cambridge: Cambridge University Press.
Minnich, R.G. (1979) *The Home-Made World of Zagaj: An Interpretation of 'Practical Life' among Traditional Peasant-farmers in West Haloze – Slovenia*, Bergen: Universitetet i Bergen.
Mosher, S.W. (1983) *Broken Earth: The Rural Chinese*, New York: Free Press.
Pahl, R. (1984) *Divisions of Labour*, Oxford: Blackwell.

Pine, F.T. and Bogdanowicz, P.T. (1982) 'Policy, response and alternative strategy: the process of change in a Polish highland village', *Dialectical Anthropology*, 7: 67–80.

Popkin, S.L. (1979) *The Rational Peasant: the Political Economy of Rural Society in Vietnam*, Berkeley: University of California Press.

Potter, H.S. and Potter, J.M. (1990) *China's Peasants; The Anthropology of a Revolution*, Cambridge: Cambridge University Press.

Randall, S.G. (1976) 'The family estate in an upland Carpathian village', *Dialectical Anthropology*, 1: 277–85.

Rheubottom, D. (1971) 'A structural analysis of conflict and cleavage in Macedonian domestic groups', Unpublished Ph.D. dissertation, University of Rochester.

Rothschild, J. (1989) *Return to Diversity: A Political History of East Central Europe since World War II*, New York: Oxford University Press.

Runciman, W.G. (1985) 'Contradictions of state socialism: the case of Poland', *The Sociological Review*, 33(1): 1–21.

Ryback, T, (1990) *Rock Around the Bloc: The Influence of Western Popular Music in the Soviet Union and Eastern Europe*, Oxford: Oxford University Press.

Sampson, S.L. (1984a) *National Integration through Socialist Planning: An Anthropological Study of a Romanian New Town*, Boulder, CO: East European Monographs.

—— (1984b) 'Muddling through in Romania: why the mamaliga doesn't explode', *International Journal of Romanian Studies*, 3(1–2): 165–85.

—— (1990) 'Towards an anthropology of collaboration in Eastern Europe', *Culture and History* (Copenhagen: Akademisk Forlag) No.8: 107–18.

—— (1991) 'Is there an anthropology of socialism?' *Anthropology Today*, 7(5):16– 19.

Scott, J.C. (1976) *The Moral Economy of the Peasant: Rebellion and Subsistence in Southeast Asia*, New Haven, CT: Yale University Press.

Shore, C. (1990) *Italian Communism: The Escape from Leninism: An Anthropological Perspective*, London: Pluto Press.

Siu, H.F. (1989) *Agents and Victims in South China: Accomplices in Rural Revolution*, New Haven, CT: Yale University Press.

Southall, A. (1992) 'Marx, Engels, Lenin and the anthropology of change', in M. De Soto and D.G. Anderson (eds) *The Curtain Rises: Rethinking Culture, Ideology and the State in Eastern Europe*, New York: Humanities Press.

Stewart, M. (1987) 'Brothers in song: the persistence of (Vlach) Gypsy identity and community in socialist Hungary', Unpublished Ph.D. dissertation, London School of Economics, University of London.

Stocking, G.W. (ed.) (1984) *Functionalism Historicized: Essays in British Social Anthropology*, Madison: University of Wisconsin Press.

Szelényi, I. (with others) (1988) *Socialist Entrepreneurs; Embourgeoisement in rural Hungary*, Cambridge: Polity Press.

Tonkin, E., McDonald, M. and Chapman, M. (eds) (1989) *History and Ethnicity* (ASA Monograph 27), London: Routledge.

Verdery, K. (1991) *National Ideology under Socialism: Identity and Cultural Politics in Ceauşescu's Romania*, Berkeley: University of California Press.

Vitebsky, P. (1992) 'Landscape and self-determination among the Eveny: the political environment of Siberian reindeer herders today', in E. Croll and D. Parkin (eds) *Bush Base: Forest Farm. Culture, Environment and Development*, London: Routledge.

Wedel, J. (1986) *The Private Poland*, New York: Facts on File.

—— (ed.) (1991) *The Unplanned Society: Poland During and After Communism*, New York: Columbia University Press.

Williams, A. (1992) 'Literacy and ethnicity among Polish Gypsies', Unpublished doctoral dissertation, University of Cambridge.

Winner, I. (1971) *A Slovenian Village, Zerovnica*, Providence, RI: Brown University Press.

Chapter 1

Primitive communism and mutual aid
Kropotkin visits the Bushmen[1]

Alan Barnard

> But still we know that when the Europeans came, the Bushmen lived in
> small tribes (or clans), sometimes federated together; that they used to
> hunt in common, and divided the spoil without quarrelling; that they
> never abandoned their wounded, and displayed strong affection to their
> comrades.
>
> Peter Kropotkin (1987a [1902]: 83)

Concepts such as 'anarchist', 'communist', 'socialist', and even 'Bushman',
are artificially constructed. This does not mean that they have no meaning.
On the contrary, it means that their meanings are contingent on the anthropological and sometimes the political perspectives of the commentators.
Each ethnographer's understanding of the 'Bushmen' is mediated through
a desire to represent them within a larger theory of society.

For the last seventy years or so, 'primitive communism' has erroneously
been equated with either 'revolutionary communism' or 'Marxism'. My
intention in this chapter is to provide an alternative, very much non-
Marxist view of primitive communism – namely that of Peter Kropotkin,
anarchist Russian prince, geographer, and an early mentor of A.R.
Radcliffe-Brown. Whereas Marx and Engels perceived history as a se-
quence of stages, Kropotkin saw it in terms of a continuity of fundamental
human goodness. His own contribution on 'Anarchism' in the eleventh
edition of the *Encyclopaedia Britannica* (1910; reprinted in Kropotkin 1987c:
7–22) is a classic summary of the historical setting for his social theory. After
hearing a lecture entitled 'On the law of mutual aid' by the Russian
zoologist Karl Fredorovich Kessler in 1880, and reading *The Descent of Man*
(Darwin 1871) in 1883, Kropotkin resolved to put forward his own version
of Darwinism (Kropotkin 1987a: 13–14; see also 1988a [1899]: 298–301). The
result was *Mutual Aid* (Kropotkin 1987a [1902]). This was conceived as an
answer to the Social Darwinists, who saw in nature a *mutual struggle* which
validated the aims of capitalism.

Among other noteworthy writings are Kropotkin's influential comments on 'Anarchist Communism' (1987b [1887]) and 'The state' (1987d
[1897]). The former was originally published in *The Nineteenth Century* as

two separate articles – 'The scientific bases of anarchy' and 'The coming anarchy'. The titles are revealing, for they reflect Kropotkin's twin concerns: the theoretical understanding of society, and the practical solution to its problems. The practical solution was much the simpler aspect, as abolition of the state was seen as the easy answer. The state, in its turn, was a problematic concept. For many, including some anarchists in Kropotkin's day, the *state* and *society* were synonymous. Yet Kropotkin (for example, 1987d [1897]: 9–16) argued strongly against this assumption. For Kropotkin, society predates the state, and his notion includes both animal societies and human, 'primitive communist' societies.

AUTHORITY AND SHARING AMONG THE BUSHMEN

Two specific concerns in Bushman ethnography have been the degree of *authority* in the hands of leaders, and the extent of *sharing* as a mechanism for redistributing wealth and preventing the development of a social hierarchy.

Among the earliest true ethnographers of Bushmen was Dorothea Bleek. In 1920 and 1921 she conducted field research with the Nharo (whom she called Naron) and the Southern !Kung or ≠Au//eisi (Auen), who lived along the Bechuanaland–South West Africa border. Her comments are interesting because she implies a change, in the time not long before her fieldwork, from hierarchical to egalitarian organization among those she classified as Northern and Central Bushmen.

> Both Naron [Central Bushmen] and Auen [Northern Bushmen] had chiefs when the old men were young. The middle-aged men just remember them. . . . Among Southern Bushmen there were no chiefs and they had no name for chieftainship. . . . There are no class distinctions among Naron and Auen, nor, excepting the medicine men, are there any trades.
> (Bleek 1928: 36, 37)

Contrast this statement with the comments of a more recent ethnographer George Silberbauer on the G/wi, a Central group who live east of the Nharo in what became (at Silberbauer's own instigation) the Central Kalahari Game Reserve of Botswana:

> There are no chiefs or headmen and every adult member of the band has rights equal to those of all the other members who reside in the band's territory. . . . In the regulation of the band's affairs, none has any more authority than any other by reason of superior status and, except for the obligations within his or her kinship group toward senior kin. . . , no man or woman yields to the superior authority of any other member.
> (Silberbauer 1965: 73)

Silberbauer, like most of his contemporaries, has emphasized the lack of hierarchy. Elsewhere (1982: 31, 34), he proposes *consensus* as the basis of Bushman political power. Power, he suggests, lies not in the ability of individuals to *force* a consensus, but in their perceiving the mood of the band and compromising and creating opportunities to have their goals realized when the time is appropriate.

Has Bushman social organization really changed, or has its perception, by Bushmen themselves or by Europeans, changed? Is there really a north/south difference in this issue, as Bleek's statement suggests, or is the difference dependent on the respective insights of northern and southern ethnographers? In my view, when Bleek argued that there were chiefs in the past, even placing the statement in the mouths of her Bushman informants, she was trying to counter potential claims arising from the descriptions of Bushmen common in her day. Kropotkin's (1987a [1902]: 83–4) understanding of the Bushmen hails from the same writings known to Bleek.[2] Yet he perceived them as representatives of a primitive communist and not a hierarchical social structure. He also perceived Bushman society as in a state of decline from its high degree of mutual aid, a point I shall return to later.

Bushman society is commonly characterized in late twentieth-century sources as being based on *sharing*. These statements by Tanaka, on the G//ana and G/wi, and Marshall, on the Zu/'hoãsi or Central !Kung, are typical.

> The integrating and governing principles of egalitarian San society are the principles of sharing and cooperation. . . . For outsiders, the San ideology of equal sharing is very difficult to comprehend, and its practice is even more difficult. It was this point that gave me the most trouble when I began living among the San.
>
> (Tanaka 1980: 95–6)

> They lived in a kind of material plenty. . . . They borrow what they do not own. With this ease, they have not hoarded, and the accumulation of objects has not become associated with status.
>
> (Marshall 1961: 243–4)

Sahlins (1974: 9–10) quotes this last passage, from Marshall's 'Sharing, talking, and giving' (1961), as a keynote to his theory of the 'original affluent society'. In reprints of her paper, Marshall has amended the last sentence to read: 'I believe that for these reasons they have not developed permanent storage, have not hoarded, and the accumulation of objects has not become associated with admirable status' (for example, 1976: 308–9). In the original version she goes on to say: 'they mitigate jealousy and envy, to which they are prone, by passing things on to others' (1961: 244). In the later versions, she specifies: 'by passing on to others objects that might be coveted' (1976: 309). Although I doubt whether these alterations mark any significant changes in Marshall's thinking, much less any transformations in !Kung society itself, they nevertheless display subtle changes in emphasis, first with reference to storage, and secondly with reference to the reasons why an individual might want to pass objects on to others. In mentioning storage, Marshall in fact amplifies Sahlins' theory, which, of course, is built on her *own* ethnography. In mentioning coveting, she not only clarifies her original statement but also gives emphasis to the point, made in the meantime by Lee (for instance, 1965 *passim*; cf. Lee 1979: 370–400; Draper 1978), that !Kung society is fraught with dispute and violence.

Marshall's addition on coveting is a far cry from Sahlins' reading of her original statement, or from Tanaka's, which gives emphasis to *sharing* in its positive sense by coupling it with *cooperation*. 'Sharing' is an emotive word, and one must be careful not to misconstrue its ethnographic meanings. Marshall's amplified description has grown simultaneously towards and away from that of Sahlins, while Tanaka here has picked up on only one aspect of her discussion – one which concerned him especially in his role as fieldworker. It is perhaps worth further reflection that the groups studied by Tanaka – the G//ana and the G/wi (Central Kalahari Bushmen) – lack any notion of formalized, delayed-reciprocal giving on non-consumable property. Their 'sharing' is less formal than that found among the !Kung.

According to Schapera (1930: 147): 'The economic life of the [Bushman] band, although in effect it approaches a sort of communism, is really based on a notion of private property.' He does go on to point out that land is held in common ownership, but movable property is individually owned, as are meat, vegetable food, and water (1930: 147–9). Lee (1979: 333–400) places particular emphasis on relations of production as determinants of !Kung politics. Although they do have words to express notions of leadership and authority (for example, *kx'au n!a*, headman or 'great owner'), !Kung have no formal political structures. Rights to land and resources are inherited bilaterally, and kinship bonds provide a framework for both production and political organization. The core group of kinsmen within each band are known as the *kx'ausi* (owners) of the *n!ore* (band territory). Membership of the core group, seniority of residence, age, and personal qualities are all factors in ascribed leadership, but boastfulness and attempts to dominate are strongly discouraged.

Virtually all Bushman groups possess systems of universal kin categorization (Barnard 1978; 1981). This ideology of classifying everyone as a member of some kin category affords them the mechanism for distributing both movable property and rights over natural resources (cf. Keenan 1981: 16–18). Other forms of social classification, either kinship based or non-kinship based, define the social limits of particular arenas of distribution. Marshall (for instance, 1976: 156–312) emphasizes the significance of both kinship and sharing for maintaining cooperation within the band, and between bands. In particular, !Kung society is characterized by strict rules of meat-sharing. Hunters lend arrows to one another, and the 'owner' of the kill is the owner of the killing arrow even though it will have been shot by another hunter. The owner shares his meat with the other hunters, with his affines, with the members of his band, and often with members of other, nearby bands too. Those who receive meat then distribute it to their families, to name relatives, and to others.

Some twenty years after Marshall's fieldwork, Wiessner took up in more detail the problem of the formalized giving of non-consumables and succeeded in uncovering a wide network (Wiessner 1977; 1982; 1986). This has come to be known by the !Kung term *hxaro*, which means roughly 'giving in formalized exchange'. By the time of marriage, the average !Kung will have between ten and sixteen *hxaro* partners, including both close kin and distant relatives and friends (Wiessner 1982: 72–4). Underlying the *hxaro* system of delayed, balanced reciprocity is an assumption that these gift-giving partners exist in a state of mutual generalized reciprocity of rights to water and plant resources (1982: 74–7).

In addition to exchange within !Kung society, there has long been trade contact between !Kung and other peoples (see, for example, Wilmsen 1986). The evidence is extensive: all of Zu/'hoã (Central !Kung) country and beyond 'seems to have been crisscrossed with well-developed trading networks' (Gordon 1984: 207). Implicit in the accounts of Gordon and Wilmsen is an assumption that other recent ethnographers have been blinded by their desire to see the !Kung as isolated remnants of primitive purity untouched by wider economic structures. But does this mean that they, or their even more 'acculturated' southern neighbours, have long since lost their primitive communism and mutual aid?

COMMUNISM, CAPITALISM, AND 'ACCULTURATED BUSHMEN'

In his definition of primitive communism, Lee (1988) recognizes a relative egalitarianism and emphasizes the communal ownership of land, rather than specifically the lack of hierarchical institutions. For Lee (1988: 254–5), even chiefly societies qualify as retaining primitive communist principles in a 'semi-communal' social structure (cf. Testart 1985; Flanagan 1989; Gulbrandsen 1991).

But to what extent are the Bushmen communistic? This dilemma lies at the root of the quarrel in the mid-1970s between Elizabeth Wily and H.J. Heinz. Wily argued (for example, 1973a; 1973b; 1976) that Bushman social organization exemplified principles of *collective* ownership and *communal* will, while Heinz argued (1970; 1973; 1975) that on the contrary it exhibited the incipient *capitalist* principles of private ownership and free enterprise. Each had interpreted their respective experiences at the !Xõ settlement at Bere, where Wily had served as teacher and Heinz as benefactor and development planner, as evidence for the equation of Bushman ideology with their own.

Heinz established livestock-rearing at Takathswaane, on the main road across the Kalahari, in 1969. By 1971 he had moved a number of Takath-swaane families to a new settlement at Bere, a few miles to the west. At Heinz's instigation, !Xõ families from Okwa were invited to join the scheme too. The only requirement was that they should each own at least one cow. At that point, with two bands of different geographical origin, Bere was declared a 'closed' settlement. Early on in the project a shop and a school were built. Each was a success in some sense, but each also marked the onset of unanticipated difficulties. The shop was run by Heinz's !Xõ wife, who because of her status and her financial skills soon found herself in a difficult position in the community. The school became the preserve of Liz Wily, who proved to be an excellent teacher but whose ideas were at odds with those of Heinz. The latter had explicitly set up Bere on capitalist principles, while Wily was said to have espoused at least some of the principles of Maoist China. Their well-publicized quarrel resulted in Wily leaving the scheme and taking up a post as Botswana's first Basarwa (Bushman) Development Officer.

Today Bere is run by the Botswana government. It is fair to say that the !Xõ are neither successful capitalists nor Maoists, though they may be, in Kropotkin's loosest sense, 'anarchist communists'. The greatest problem with the Bere scheme has always been the reluctance on the part of the !Xõ residents to invest the time required to keep herds of animals. The small scale of livestock ownership also militated against subsistence by herding. Heinz was right to maintain that Bushman economics is predicated on individualism as much as on collectivism, but individual ownership of very small herds (often one beast per family) does not permit sufficient sales of livestock for the accumulation of capital, much less the maintenance of a fully fledged capitalist system.

In an earlier paper (Barnard 1986: 49–50), I noted the tendency towards buying and selling meat, rather than exchanging or sharing it, between Nharo groups at Hanahai, another government settlement scheme to the north of Bere. It is significant, however, that despite such new buying and selling arrangements between social groups previously defined spatially as 'band clusters', these Nharo give meat freely, in the traditional manner, within the bands that make up a given band cluster. There is a temptation to regard buying/selling relationships as indicative of social change, simply because they have not occurred before. Yet it could well be that they define age-old divisions between social and territorial units – units which would not previously have had any contact at all with one another. It is hence not surprising that they buy and sell meat, and it would be more surprising if they *did* give meat freely across band cluster boundaries. If

Bushmen are communists, then their communism is confined to the 'commune'.

PRIMITIVE COMMUNISM AND THE FORAGING ETHOS

One element in a complex debate which has recently graced the pages of *Current Anthropology* (Solway and Lee 1990; Wilmsen and Denbow 1990) is the question of a primitive communist mode of production. The main protagonists in the wider, more implicit, debate are Richard Lee (for example, 1979; 1984), Lorna Marshall (1976), George Silberbauer (1981), and the many others who have described Bushman society as an entity in itself (the 'isolationists' or 'traditionalists'); and Edwin Wilmsen (for instance, 1983; 1989), Carmel Schrire (1980), James Denbow (1984), Robert Gordon (1984), and others who have emphasized historical contacts between Bushmen and non-Bushmen (the 'integrationists' or 'revisionists'). Jacqueline Solway and Richard Lee (1990) have bent considerably towards the revisionists in recognizing historical links, yet they nevertheless reject the radical criticisms of those who deny the existence of a mode of production based on foraging or sharing. Wilmsen and Denbow (1990) also accuse Lee in particular of a shift from describing Bushmen as exemplars of a 'foraging' (Lee 1981), to a 'communal' (Lee 1988; 1990) mode of production. This seems to be unacceptable to Wilmsen and Denbow because of their emphasis on external trade, but the simple existence of trade need not undermine Lee's position. The key point, as Solway and Lee (1990: 119) imply, is that foraging and communalism generally do go together. I prefer instead to think of a foraging *mode of thought*, which is linked to communal as well as individual interests. This mode of thought persists after people cease to depend on hunting and gathering as their primary means of subsistence.

Foraging remains very much in the ethos of Bushman society, even where groups look after boreholes and livestock, keep their own animals, and grow crops. The Bushmen on the margins of the larger, non-Bushman society are essentially foragers. To them wage-labour and seasonal changes in subsistence pursuits are but large-scale foraging strategies (Guenther 1986a; Motzafi 1986; Barnard 1988a). If the concept of 'mode of production' makes any sense at all, it makes sense as a broad characterization of all these activities. Bushman are 'foragers' in many ways. Kin classification and gift-giving involve social 'foraging', for relatives and for relationships of exchange (cf. Barnard 1978; Wiessner 1977). Their religious ideology is characterized as 'foraging' for ideas (cf. Guenther 1979; Barnard 1988b). Even the Khoekhoe word *saan* or *san*, so popular as an ethnic label for 'Bushmen', means simply 'foragers' – with all the negative as well as the positive connotations 'foraging' conjures (cf. Guenther 1986b).[3]

Kropotkin used the splendidly sympathetic and detailed account of

Peter Kolb (Kolben 1731) as his main source on the Khoekhoe or 'Hottentots' (Kropotkin 1987a [1902]: 84–5). Kropotkin describes the Khoekhoe as
being the same in 'social manner', but 'a little more developed than the
Bushmen' (1987a [1902]: 84). Indeed, he generalizes from Kolb's description
of the 'Hottentots' to 'savages' almost universally in one crucial regard –
food sharing.

> If anything is given to a Hottentot, he at once divides it among all present
> – a habit which, as is known, so much struck Darwin among the
> Fuegians. He cannot eat alone, and, however hungry, he calls those who
> pass by to share his food. And when Kolben expressed his astonishment
> thereat, he received the answer: 'That is Hottentot manner.' But this is
> not Hottentot manner only: it is an all but universal habit among the
> 'savages'.
>
> (Kropotkin 1987a [1902]: 84)

Kropotkin goes on to quote at length Kolb's views of Khoekhoe morality.
For example: 'One of the greatest Pleasures of the *Hottentots* certainly lies
in their Gifts and Good Offices to one another' (Kolben 1731: 89–90). From
the 'Hottentots', Kropotkin goes on to tell of the 'natives of Australia', the
'Papuas', the 'Eskimos', and others. The 'Eskimos' receive special commen-
dation for their 'communism' (Kropotkin 1987a [1902]: 88–9), which, like
'communism' among the Bushmen, Kropotkin thought was fast disappearing as a result of foreign influence.

There are two related problems here. First, there is the problem of the
disappearing culture. Secondly, there is the problem of hunter-
gatherer/herder divide, so significant in modern anthropology that it
overrides the more obvious unity of what later came to be called *Khoisan*
culture. The first problem is simple. Cultures are always 'disappearing', just
after they are studied. The phenomenon occurs consistently across the
globe, with much the same frequency as, say, that cannibals are always
found on the other side of the hill and not among one's own kind (Arens
1979). The second problem concerns the failure of modern anthropologists
to take in the idea of the unity of the Khoisan culture area. This unity seems
to have been obvious to Kolb, and, I think, also to Kropotkin, but it is sadly
lacking in recent work on both sides of the current 'Great Bushman Debate'.

THE GOLDEN AGE OF SHARING

Price (1975) and Bird-David (1990) have drawn attention to the differences
between 'sharing' and 'reciprocity'. 'Sharing' is defined as an internal,
integrative process of giving without the expectation of return, and resembles Sahlins' notion of 'generalized reciprocity'. It is frequently found
within small groups such as bands. Beyond that, it 'may be found universally, to varied extents and in varied realms, just as [balanced and negative

reciprocity] are' (Bird-David 1990: 195). Indeed, it could well be 'the most universal form of human economic behavior, distinct from and more fundamental than reciprocity' (Price 1975: 3). Price and Bird-David define 'reciprocity'as giving with the expectation of return – 'the gift' in Mauss's (1990 [1925]) sense.

It is commonplace to regard hunter-gatherers as having distinctive political and especially economic forms of organization, and sharing is often seen as especially significant in hunting and gathering societies. Yet, while some of these typically hunter-gatherer features of social structure (for example, egalitarianism) are much more applicable to Khoisan foragers than to Khoisan herders, there are nevertheless similarities which have until now escaped notice. In Khoekhoe and Damara society, institution-alized gift-giving and meat-sharing are as important as in some Bushman societies (Barnard 1992: 169, 189–91, 203–5). Likewise, marital exchanges involving the transfer of goods, often cited as a typical feature of pastoralist societies, are found among Kalahari hunter-gatherers (Barnard 1980: 120–2; Lee 1984: 74–7). The existence of 'sharing' practices among the Khoekhoe and 'reciprocity' among Bushmen should cause us to rethink our notions of what constitutes a typical 'hunting' or 'herding' society, and indeed to consider the notion of a pan-Khoisan constellation of economic institutions. Kropotkin grasped this, and expressed this view accurately in his very brief discussion of mutual aid among the Bushmen and Khoekhoe.

Most modern attempts to draw boundaries between 'our kind of society' and 'other kinds' have placed the boundary right down the middle – between 'hunter-gatherers' and 'others', between 'Khoe' and 'San' (for example, Lee and DeVore 1968). However, attempts to temper classification on the basis of means of subsistence with a closer look at the ideology of sharing and reciprocity have yielded different results. Thus the Golden Age of Sharing can be defined either more narrowly than the hunter-gatherer (for instance, Woodburn 1980, 1982; Testart 1981; 1982, Lee 1981, 1988, 1990), or more widely (Sahlins 1974). I prefer to see the notion of 'sharing' defined in cultural, ideological terms. My vision of a *foraging ethos* is not far from Lee's, except that, unlike him, I do not conceive of such an ethos as dependent in any sense on the mode of production of the larger society. It could apply just as well, and with positive associations, to the *san* of any society, including the urban homeless of modern Western societies. Figure 1.1 illustrates, very loosely (with a double line), the relative extent of the Golden Age of Sharing according to each of the various theorists who have commented on the question.

I suggest that the idea of 'foraging' can help us to identify the central characteristics of Bushman society, not quite in the literal sense of Ingold (1986: 79–100, 101–29; 1988), who emphasizes non-deliberate action, but in a sense which connotes a lack of concern about the specific result of the activity. When a Bushman man goes 'hunting', he will almost certainly stop

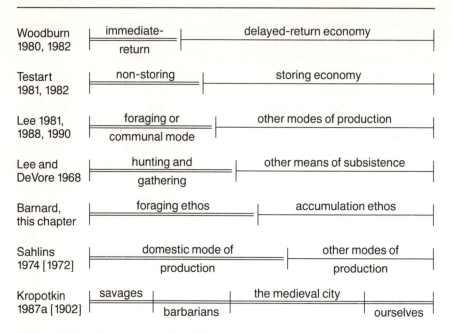

Figure 1.1 The Golden Age of Sharing

to pick berries or nuts (cf. Barnard 1980: 116–17). He might even bring some home, especially if the hunt proper is unsuccessful. His wife, in her turn, may go off to collect firewood and come back with some roots to roast. I find the term 'foraging' is useful as a description of these kinds of activity, and even more useful in designating the ethos and ideology of Bushman society.[4]

A SUMMARY OF CHARACTERIZATIONS OF BUSHMAN SOCIETY

Bushman society has been characterized in any number of ways. The following list represents only a few of the characterizations which have been made since Kropotkin's time:

1 primitive communism, or
2 incipient capitalism;

3 mutual aid, or
4 anarchy (in its negative sense);

5 universal kinship, or
6 immediate-return economies;

7 foraging mode of production, or
8 domestic mode of production;

9 natural purity and a mystical awareness of nature, or
10 technological simplicity, but with an ingenuity associated with a foraging ethos;

11 isolation from the wider regional politico-economic system of Southern Africa, or
12 integration into that system, as traders, labourers, and servants.

Some of these are contradictions of others. Indeed, I have deliberately paired a number of characterizations which can be taken as opposites, though not all pairings are really opposed in quite this manner. Nevertheless, characterizations emerge which highlight alternative understandings of Bushman society. Are they poor or rich? Violent or peaceful? Practical or mystical? Traditionally isolated from their neighbours or integrated in a network of widespread trade links? In a sense, each of these oppositions expresses a contradictory truth about Bushman society. They are poor because their wants are many; rich because their needs are few. They are violent because of the relatively high incidence of homicide; peaceful because of the lack of warfare in living memory. They are practical because of their successful adaptation to both the natural environment and changing social conditions; mystical because their adaptation to nature expresses a harmony lacking in 'advanced' societies. They are traditionally isolated, in the sense that both they and outsiders define them in terms of their relation to nature; yet they are integrated, in the sense that they have long traded and shared their land and resources with members of other ethnic groups. Each characterization identifies a different aspect of the same society.

This does not mean that the Bushmen are not really anarchists or communists. They are simultaneously both and neither. They are communists because they hold land in common. They are non-communists because they each own movable property as individuals. They are anarchists because they possess no form of indigenous overlordship. They are non-anarchists because they recognize, and have long recognized, the overlordship of the neighbouring tribal chief, the colonial state, or the nation-state.

CONCLUSION

The descriptions available to Schapera when compiling his magnificent *Khoisan Peoples of South Africa* (1930) suggested that both the Khoekhoe and the Bushmen had a system of communal ownership over land. Neverthless, Schapera (1930: 319, 321) rejected the idea that either this system or the widespread systems of sharing and exchange of food, livestock, and material culture, indicated a form of true 'communism', whereas earlier writers (such as von François 1896: 222) had suggested it did. Schapera's position seems to be part of a wider phenomenon. As Lee (for example, 1990: 231–5) and Leacock (1983) have at least hinted, anthropologists writing in the decades following the Bolshevik Revolution had quite a different notion of 'primitive communism' than did those writing before it. Generally speaking, the term seems to have carried few political overtones before that time, whereas afterwards only Marxists have seen fit to use it at all. Not only did the authoritarian communists appropriate the state, they appropriated the word 'communist' too. Their intellectual descendants jealously guard it to this day, while others refrain from using it lest they be branded 'Marxists' or worse.

Kropotkin's *Mutual Aid* was at the same time primitivist and evolutionist. Mutual aid is found in all human societies and in nature; that is, in animal societies. Yet, at the end of the day, Kropotkin's understanding of Bushman society actually approaches the 'revisionist' view more closely than it does that of Lee, Marshall, Tanaka, and Silberbauer. In a speech to English anarchists in 1888, Kropotkin (1988a [1888]: 102) described 'Anarchist-Communism' simply as a combination of the 'two great movements' of the nineteenth century: 'Liberty of the individual' and 'social co-operation of the whole community'. It is worth some reflection that Kropotkin's descriptions of societies *he* considered 'communist' might still serve as models of ethnographic generalization, if not as charters for political action.

NOTES

1 I would like to thank Chris Hann, Adam Kuper, and Ed Wilmsen for their comments on earlier drafts.
2 Kropotkin's knowledge of Bushmen was entirely second-hand. In contrast, Dorothea Bleek grew up with Bushmen. Her father, Wilhelm Bleek, was the world's foremost authority on Bushman languages and folklore. After his untimely death in 1875, his work was continued by Dorothea's aunt Lucy Lloyd, and ultimately by Dorothea herself. Kropotkin's main source on the Bushmen seems to have been Volume 2 of Theodor Waitz's six-volume survey, *Anthropologie der Naturvölker* (Waitz 1860). Among primary sources he cites Lichtenstein (1811–12), Fritsch (1872 [1863]; 1868) and W. H. I. Bleek (1875), and mentions in passing Philip (1828), Burchell (1822–24) and Moffat (1842), all cited by Waitz. Kropotkin also refers to Elisée Reclus's nineteen-volume *Géographie universelle* (1878–94). Like Kropotkin, Reclus was both a geographer and an anarchist, and the two had worked closely together in France in the 1870s.
3 It is a peculiar irony that this term is the one favoured by both Lee (who calls these people 'San') and Wilmsen (who calls them 'San-speaking peoples'), when most other specialists have returned to other labels – most commonly 'Bushmen'. The subject of what to call 'Bushmen' is also an ongoing debate, and one with a grand history. The first recorded usage seems to have been in 1682, in the journal

of Olof Bergh (Wilson 1986: 257). In the early days of Dutch settlement at the Cape, *Soaqua* or *Sonqua* (the Cape Khoekhoe masculine plural form; *San* is common gender plural) seems to have been more common, but *Bosjesmans*, *Bushmen*, and other variants gained predominance by the late eighteenth century. Peter Kolb (or Kolben), for example, referred to 'a Sort of *Hottentot Banditti* . . . call'd *Buschies* or High-way Men' (Kolben 1731: 89–90). Kolb's account was probably far better known in the eighteenth than it has been in the twentieth century. From the seventeenth to the nineteenth centuries, Bushmen were frequently described as part of 'Hottentot' society, and indeed late twentieth-century work by some of the revisionists (such as Schrire 1980) suggests a return to this view.

4 Ingold shares with Kropotkin the idea of a continuity between animal and human societies, though the modern scholar also points to a number of significant contrasts. I share many of the specific views Ingold espouses, but disagree with his restriction of the term 'foraging' to non-human activities alone. In my view this places undue emphasis on the *intentionality* of human activities.

REFERENCES

Arens, W. (1979) *The Man-eating Myth: Anthropology and Anthropophagy*, Oxford: Oxford University Press.

Barnard, A. (1978) 'Universal systems of kin categorization', *African Studies*, 37: 69–81.

—— (1980) 'Sex roles among the Nharo Bushmen of Botswana', *Africa*, 50: 115–24.

—— (1981) 'Universal kin categorization in four Bushman societies', *L'Uomo*, 5: 219–37.

—— (1986) 'Rethinking Bushman settlement patterns and territoriality', *Sprache und Geschichte in Afrika*, 7(1): 41–60.

—— (1988a) 'Cultural identity, ethnicity and marginalization among the Bushmen of southern Africa', in R. Vossen (ed.) *New Perspectives on Khoisan*, Hamburg: Helmut Buske Verlag (Quellen zur Khoisan-Forschung 7).

—— (1988b) 'Structure and fluidity in Khoisan religious ideas', *Journal of Religion in Africa*, 18: 216–36.

—— (1992) *Hunters and Herders of Southern Africa: A Comparative Ethnography of the Khoisan Peoples*, Cambridge: Cambridge University Press.

Bird-David, N. (1990) 'The giving environment: another perspective on the economic system of gatherer-hunters', *Current Anthropology*, 31: 189–96.

Bleek, D.F. (1928) *The Naron: A Bushman Tribe of the Central Kalahari*, Cambridge: Cambridge University Press.

Bleek, W.H.I. (1875) *A Brief Account of Bushman Folklore and Other Texts*, Cape Town: Juta.

Burchell, W.J. (1822–24) *Travels in the Interior of Southern Africa* (2 vols), Glasgow: MacLehose.

Darwin, C. (1871) *The Descent of Man, and Selection in Relation to Sex* (2 vols), London: John Murray.

Denbow, J.R. (1984) 'Prehistoric herders and foragers of the Kalahari: the evidence of 1500 years of interaction', in C. Schrire (ed.) *Past and Present in Hunter Gatherer Studies*, Orlando, FL: Academic Press.

Draper, P. (1978) 'The learning environment for aggression and anti-social behavior among the !Kung', in A. Montagu (ed.) *Learning Non-aggression: The Experience of Non-literate Societies*, New York: Oxford University Press.

Flanagan, J.G. (1989) 'Hierarchy in simple "egalitarian" societies', *Annual Review of Anthropology*, 18: 245–66.

François, H. von (1896) *Nama und Damara. Deutsch Süd-West Afrika*, Magdeburg: Baensch.

Fritsch, G. (1868) *Drei Jahre in Süd-Afrika*, Breslau: Ferdinand Hirt.

—— (1872 [1863]) *Die Eingeborenen Süd-Afrikas*, Breslau: Ferdinand Hirt.

Gordon, R. (1984) 'The !Kung in the Kalahari exchange: an ethnohistorical perspective', in C. Schrire (ed.) *Past and Present in Hunter Gatherer Studies*, Orlando, FL: Academic Press.

Guenther, M.G. (1979) 'Bushman religion and the (non)sense of anthropological theory of religion', *Sociologus*, 29: 102–32.

—— (1986a) 'From foragers to miners and bands to bandits: on the flexibility and adaptability of Bushman band societies', *Sprache und Geschichte in Afrika*, 7(1): 133–59.

—— (1986b) '"San" or "Bushmen"?', in M. Biesele, with R. Gordon and R. Lee (eds) *The Past and Future of !Kung Ethnography: Critical Reflections and Symbolic Perspectives, Essays in Honour of Lorna Marshall*, Hamburg: Helmut Buske Verlag (Quellen zur Khoisan-Forschung, 4).

Gulbrandsen, Ø. (1991) 'On the problem of egalitarianism: the Kalahari San in transition', in R. Grønhaug, G. Henriksen, and G. Haaland (eds) *Ecology of Choice and Symbol: Essays in Honour of Fredrik Barth*, Bergen: Alma Mater.

Heinz, H.J. (1970) *Experiences Gained in a Bushman Pilot Settlement Scheme (Interim Report)*, Johannesburg: Dept. of Pathology, University of the Witwatersrand (Occasional Paper No. 1).

—— (1973) *Bere: A Balance Sheet*, Johannesburg: Dept. of Pathology, University of the Witwatersrand (Occasional Paper No. 4).

—— (1975) 'Acculturation problems arising in a Bushman development scheme', *South African Journal of Science*, 71: 78–85.

Ingold, T. (1986) *The Appropriation of Nature: Essays on Human Ecology and Social Relations*, Manchester: Manchester University Press.

—— (1988) 'Notes on the foraging mode of production', in T. Ingold, D. Riches, and J. Woodburn (eds) *Hunters and Gatherers*, Vol. 2: *Property, Power and Ideology*, Oxford: Berg Publishers.

Keenan, J. (1981 [1977]) 'The concept of the mode of production in hunter-gatherer societies', in J.S. Kahn and J.R. Llobera (eds) *The Anthropology of Pre-capitalist Societies*, London: Macmillan.

Kolben [Kolb], P. (1731) *The Present State of the Cape of Good-Hope*, Vol. I (trans. G. Medley), London: W. Innys.

Kropotkin, P. (1910) 'Anarchism', *Encyclopaedia Britannica* (11th edn), Vol. 1, pp. 914–19. (Also reprinted in Kropotkin 1987c.)

—— (1987a [1902]) *Mutual Aid: A Factor of Evolution*, London: Freedom Press.

—— (1987b [1887]) *Anarchist Communism: Its Basis and Principles*. (In Kropotkin 1987c: 23–60.)

—— (1987c) *Anarchism and Anarchist Communism*, N. Walter (ed.), London: Freedom Press.

—— (1987d [1897]) *The State: Its Historic Role* (translated from the French), London: Freedom Press.

—— (1988a) *Act for Yourselves: Articles from Freedom, 1886–1907*, N. Walter and H. Becker (eds) London: Freedom Press.

—— (1988b [1899]) *Memoirs of a Revolutionist*, London: The Cresset Library.

Leacock, E. (1983) 'Primitive communism', in T. Bottomore (ed.) *A Dictionary of Marxist Thought*, Oxford: Blackwell Reference.

Lee, R.B. (1965) 'Subsistence ecology of !Kung Bushmen', Unpublished Ph.D. dissertation, University of California at Berkeley.
—— (1979) *The !Kung San: Men, Women, and Work in a Foraging Society*, Cambridge: Cambridge University Press.
—— (1981 [1980]) 'Is there a foraging mode of production?', *Canadian Journal of Anthropology*, 2(1): 13–19.
—— (1984) *The Dobe !Kung*, New York: Holt, Rinehart & Winston.
—— (1988) 'Reflections on primitive communism', in T. Ingold, D. Riches, and J. Woodburn (eds), *Hunters and Gatherers*, Vol. 1: *History, Evolution and Social Change*. Oxford: Berg Publishers.
—— (1990) 'Primitive communism and the origins of social inequality', in S. Upham (ed.) *The Evolution of Political Systems: Sociopolitics in Small-scale Sedentary Societies*, Cambridge: Cambridge University Press.
Lee, R.B. and DeVore, I. (1968) 'Problems in the study of hunters and gatherers', in R.B. Lee and I. DeVore (eds), *Man the Hunter*, Chicago: Aldine.
Lichtenstein, M.H.C. (1811–12) *Reisen im südlichen Afrika in dem Jahren 1803, 1804, 1805 und 1806* (2 vols), Berlin: C. Salfeld.
Marshall, L. (1961) 'Sharing, talking, and giving: relief of social tensions among !Kung Bushmen', *Africa*, 31: 231–49. (Reprinted with amendments in Marshall 1976.)
—— (1976) *The !Kung of Nyae Nyae*, Cambridge, MA: Harvard University Press.
Mauss, M. (1990 [1925]) *The Gift: The Form and Reason for Exchange in Archaic Societies*, London: Routledge.
Moffat, R. (1842) *Missionary Labours and Scenes in Southern Africa*, London: Snow.
Motzafi, P. (1986) 'Whither the "true Bushmen": the dynamics of perpetual marginality', *Sprache und Geschichte in Afrika*, 7(1): 295–328.
Philip, J. (1828) *Researches in South Africa, Illustrating the Civil, Moral and Religious Condition of the Native Tribes* (2 vols), London: Duncan.
Price, J.A. (1975) 'Sharing: the integration of intimate economies', *Anthropologica* (n.s.), 17: 3–27.
Reclus, E. (1878–94) *La Nouvelle géographie universelle, la terre et les hommes* (19 vols), Paris: Librairie Hachette et Cie.
Sahlins, M. (1974 [1972]) *Stone Age Economics*, London: Tavistock Publications.
Schapera, I. (1930) *The Khoisan Peoples of South Africa: Bushmen and Hottentots*, London: George Routledge & Sons.
Schrire, C. (1980) 'An inquiry into the evolutionary status and apparent identity of San hunter-gatherers', *Human Ecology*, 8: 9–32.
Silberbauer, G.B. (1965) *Report to the Government of Bechuanaland on the Bushman Survey*, Gaberones [Gaborone]: Bechuanaland Government.
—— (1981) *Hunter and Habitat in the Central Kalahari Desert*, Cambridge: Cambridge University Press.
—— (1982) 'Political process in G/wi bands', in E. Leacock and R. Lee (eds) *Politics and History in Band Societies*, Cambridge: Cambridge University Press.
Solway, J.S. and Lee, R.B. (1990) 'Foragers, genuine or spurious? Situating the Kalahari San in history', *Current Anthropology*, 31: 109–46.
Tanaka, J. (1980) *The San, Hunter-gatherers of the Kalahari* (trans. D.W. Hughes), Tokyo: University of Tokyo Press.
Testart, A. (1981) 'Pour une typologie des chasseurs-cueilleurs', *Anthropologie et Sociétés* 5(2): 177–221.
—— (1982) *Les chasseurs-cueilleurs ou l'origine des inégalités*, Paris: Société d'Ethnographie.

—— (1985) *Le communisme primitif*, I: *Economie et idéologie*, Paris: Editions de la Maison des Sciences de l'Homme.

Waitz, T. (1860) *Anthropologie der Naturvölker*, Vol. II: *Die Negervölker und ihre Verwandten*, Leipzig: G. Gerland.

Wiessner, P.W. (1977) 'Hxaro: a regional system of reciprocity for reducing risk among the !Kung San' (2 vols), Unpublished Ph.D. dissertation, University of Michigan, Ann Arbor.

—— (1982) 'Risk, reciprocity, and social influence on !Kung San economics', in E. Leacock and R. Lee (eds) *Politics and History in Band Societies*, Cambridge: Cambridge University Press.

—— (1986) ' !Kung San networks in a generational perspective', in M. Biesele, with R. Gordon and R. Lee (eds) *The Past and Future of !Kung Ethnography: Critical Reflections and Symbolic Perspectives, Essays in Honour of Lorna Marshall*, Hamburg: Helmut Buske Verlag (Quellen zur Khoisan-Forschung 4).

Wilmsen, E.N. (1983) 'The ecology of an illusion: anthropological foraging in the Kalahari', *Reviews in Anthropology*, 10: 9–20.

—— (1986) 'Historical process in the political economy of San', *Sprache und Geschichte in Afrika*, 7(2): 413–32.

—— (1989) *Land Filled with Flies: A Political Economy of the Kalahari*, Chicago and London: University of Chicago Press.

—— and J.R. Denbow (1990) 'Paradigmatic history of San-speaking peoples and current attempts at revision', *Current Anthropology*, 31: 489–524.

Wilson, M.L. (1986) 'Notes on the nomenclature of the Khoisan', *Annals of the South African Museum*, 97(8): 251–66.

Wily, E.A. (1973a) 'An analysis of the Bere Bushman settlement scheme', Unpublished report to the Ministry of Local Government and Lands, Gaborone, Botswana.

—— (1973b) 'Bere as a prototype for further development', Unpublished report to the Ministry of Local Government and Lands, Gaborone, Botswana.

—— (1976) 'Bere and Ka/Gae', Unpublished report to the Ministry of Local Government and Lands, Gaborone, Botswana.

Woodburn, J. (1980) 'Hunters and gatherers today and reconstruction of the past', in E. Gellner (ed.) *Soviet and Western Anthropology*, London: Duckworth.

—— (1982) 'Egalitarian societies', *Man* (n.s.), 17: 431–51.

Chapter 2

The anarchy and collectivism of the 'primitive other'

Marx and Sahlins in the Amazon[1]

Joanna Overing

'Primitive communalism' and 'primitive anarchy' are Western constructs about imaginary others. They are categories much more telling of Western evaluations and political desires than of the understandings and practice of peoples to whom they have been applied. From the ethnography on the tropical forest groups of South America, we see that for many of these peoples the choice between 'collectivism' and 'anarchy' is inappropriate: for them sociality is premised upon an assumption of personal autonomy, and thus 'unity' and 'freedom' are not opposed as valuations in their own political philosophies. However, in many analyses of so-called primitive or pre-capitalist economies and polities the reader has been given the either/or choice of 'the tribal' *either* as herd animal *or* as anarchist, intractable to social control.

There are strong political undertones to such classifications, and the application of them is often a means for making subtle and complicated judgements about the West, and what *it* should or should not be. Apparently straightforward labels become multi-layered, rich in evaluative connotations and chains of associations that can be difficult to unravel because they are part and parcel of specific understandings about what is natural or good in the world. Marx, for example, in his essay on pre-capitalist economic formations, makes the obvious factual generalization that capitalist society is marked by productive progress in a way that the pre-capitalist world is not. He then makes a leap that links productive progress, through the division of labour, with the growth of individualism. This conclusion leads him to expand his original distinction (societies involved in productive progress and those which are not) to include the contrast of individualism and communalism – and of maturity and immaturity. For Marx, productive progress and the individualism that grew with it entailed a maturity, an elaboration of the 'creative disposition' (albeit 'vulgar and mean' in its bourgeois manifestation), that the 'childlike world of the ancients' with its attachment to the communal form could not attain (1965 [1857–58]: 84–5).

Since such labels as 'collectivity', 'communalism', 'individualism', 'freedom', and 'order' are all loaded ones within our own history of debates, the question of their relevance to the political understanding of, say, the peoples of the South American rainforest is yet another matter. It can be as difficult to make a fit between the Amazonian valuation of the social and anthropological discussions of 'collectivity' as it is to find any common ground between the personal autonomy they value in daily life and Western ideals of individualism. Moreover, the very contrast of 'priority upon collectivity' versus 'priority upon the individual' belongs to the domain of Western discourse and as such is basic to tensions within our own political heritage.

Because any classification of the pre-capitalist world as 'anarchic' or 'collectivist' is to a certain extent based upon constructs emerging from our own distinctions of worth, it is not surprising that interpretations through them of ostensibly similar ethnographic facts can be highly contradictory. Marx places pre-capitalist production firmly on the side of community, while Sahlins argues for its anarchic and therefore asocial base. It is therefore worthwhile comparing the logic of Marx, in *Precapitalist Economic Formations*, with that of Sahlins, in *Stone Age Economics*, in their respective discussions of pre-capitalist production and sociality. Their analyses are of particular interest because of the influence both have had on anthropological interpretations.

Marx stresses the importance of the relation between work and community in pre-capitalist production, but he over-states the hold of community over its members, and therefore speaks of the 'sheeplike' nature of the tribal consciousness.[2] In contrast, there is no community in Sahlins' pre-capitalist society until its anarchic domestic mode of production is transcended through non-economic strategy. While Marx classifies 'the tribal' as free (in work) and social, but unproductive, uncreative, pre-political and not very bright, Sahlins categorizes those living in conditions of the 'domestic mode of production' as free, affluent and leisurely, but basically asocial, under-productive and therefore irrational from a narrow economic point of view.

Although Sahlins states clearly (1972: 76) that his analysis of primitive economy is meant to be *'chez* Marx', the conclusions of Marx and Sahlins are irreconcilably opposed, in particular those concerning the relation between the economy and the community. Marx's emphasis is first and foremost upon the social nature of his category of original proprietorship, while unity, or the social relations of community life, far from being a precondition in Sahlins' 'domestic mode of production', becomes a feature that stands opposed to it. Why, we may ask, the difference? In part it is because both interpretations carry evaluative judgements, positive and negative, about the 'pre-capitalist' and about us. They are judgements that are ultimately structured by specific views about what the author thinks should hold in general about 'good work', 'good sociality', and 'the adult life'. They are, in other words, judgements about the nature of 'proper' power, 'proper' production, 'proper' freedom, and, indeed, 'proper' rationality.

The peoples of tropical forest South America also make their own judgements about work, sociality, adulthood, power, freedom, and rationality. Although Marx had little ethnography available to him through which to understand tribal production, he was nevertheless able to make an imaginative leap into the 'tribal' world that led him to grasp some of its values better than Sahlins was able to do. The reason for this is that Marx's own judgements about 'proper sociality', 'proper power', and certainly 'proper work', are closer to those of the Amerindian than are those of Sahlins. Marx's complex sketch of 'original proprietorship' is subtle and powerful. Nevertheless, there is much in it that remains unclear, and modern ethnographic work among Amazonian peoples has not yet teased out the answers, yea or nay, to many of the more interesting questions he raises concerning proprietorship and production.

Both Sahlins and Marx stress personal autonomy in work as being a characteristic of the 'tribal' world. This freedom from being coerced or commanded to work is reported time and again in the ethnography of lowland South America, and the case can also be made with relative ease for the high valuation by Amerindians of personal autonomy in other areas of their life. More troublesome, especially for the 'loosely structured' and relatively egalitarian native peoples of the Guianas, is the notion of 'collectivity'. The structure of the Guianese community, its order, has been very difficult to capture through ordinary anthropological vocabulary, because the very notion of 'collectivity' is so often predicated in anthropological use upon principles of coercion, hierarchy, and difference. For the native peoples of the Guianas, 'collectivity' as a value, far from being predominantly associated with the constraints of relations of domination and subordination, is in contrast – and this will be central to my argument – a 'collectivity of the intimate and the informal'.

If the very description of Guianese social order taxes ethnographic ingenuity, one would think that the Marxist notion of the 'community' as a force of production would be even more problematic. Yet once the Amerindian understanding of proper sociality is unfolded, it becomes clear that 'collectivity' – but not in the Western sense of constraint and hierarchy – is in fact a force of production in lowland communities. The 'puzzle' of Guianese collectivity will be examined further below. Before turning to the ethnography, I shall discuss in more detail aspects of Marx's notion of 'original proprietorship' and Sahlins' construction of 'the domestic mode of production'. Of specific interest will be the way Sahlins departs in understanding from Marx on the relation between production and community in tribal economies. A related question concerns how personal autonomy in work fits in with the ties of community. What will become clear through the data on Amazonia is that the principle of informality so salient in the ordering of their production and their community life is often associated with a highly egalitarian political creed. Any classification of this creed will inevitably be influenced by the analyst's own particular distinctions of worth.

'ORIGINAL PROPRIETORSHIP' AND THE PRECONDITIONS OF PRE-CAPITALIST APPROPRIATION

In 'Precapitalist economic formations', a chapter of *Grundrisse*, the primary concern of Marx is to understand the capitalist formation and to specify its strengths and weaknesses by contrasting it with pre-capitalist modes of production from their foundation in the tribal community. He stresses the unity of pre-capitalist modes of production in order to highlight their radical discontinuity with capitalism and wage labour.[3] In Marx's view, pre-capitalist modes of production have two distinct advantages over the capitalist which have to do with the relationship of the individual first to his own labour, and secondly to social collectivity. Thus his emphasis when describing them is upon proprietorship as a right *and* as a social relationship. He claims, for instance, that the tribal regards the land – its raw materials, its soil – as his own, and therefore labours as its proprietor. Thus each person's access to the use of natural resources, their appropriation, is taken for granted, as too it is taken for granted that one has mastery over one's own labour in such appropriation (see 1965 [1857–58]: 67,97).[4] This assumption of access was how Marx defined property in the tribal community.

The *pre*condition of such property is, however, collectivity. In Marx's scheme of the history of production, the community, based upon a communality of blood, language, and customs, is the primordial prerequisite of all pre-capitalist appropriation, and, as such, a force of production (1965 [1857–58]: 68–9). In his understanding, one could be a proprietor in pre-capitalist modes of production *only* by virtue of being a member of a community, where at the same time people labour only in so far as they participate in the community. The purpose of such labour, Marx says, 'is not the *creation of value*', but 'the maintenance of the owner and his family as well as of the communal body as a whole' (1965 [1857–58]: 68, his italics).

Marx also argued that in pre-capitalist formations labour is not at the origin of property, but rather property is a precondition of labour: rights of possession and use are given 'naturally' and not through the process of labour. On this point the Amazonian understanding of personal possessions would confound him. The preconditions of appropriation for the native peoples of lowland South America are complex, but, very briefly, the following four principles of proprietorship are usually recognized: (1) no person and no group of people can own basic resources, neither of the forest nor of the rivers; (2) everyone has access to these resources for the purpose of providing for self and others; (3) it is open to everyone to acquire the skills for transforming the earth's resources for use; and finally, (4) the individual, and not the group, possesses the products of his or her labour. Despite the last principle of proprietorship, the point that Marx was emphasizing – that the individual as one who is given the status and identity of *worker*, is a product of history – could not be disputed.[5]

Although Marx understands tribal proprietorship to be superior to the capitalist in the two respects mentioned, he sees the 'childlike world of the ancients' as falling short in its possibilities for progress – progress both in humankind's capabilities for the domination of nature and for the development of the individual. For Marx the 'free and full development of individual or society' is inconceivable in the ancient world. Such evolution, allowing for the elaboration of creative dispositions, stands in contradiction to the original relation of the individual to community (1965 [1857–58]: 83–5). The individual, though free in work, originally 'appears as a *generic being, a tribal being, a herd animal*'; and it is the development of exchange, Marx argues, that makes the herd animal superfluous and dissolves the links that 'chain' one to community (1965 [1857–58]: 96, his italics). Thus the historic process that dissolves the ancient forms, where 'the labourer is an owner and the owner labours' (1965 [1857–58]: 97), is ironically the same as that which allows for the freedom and full development of the individual – and for productive progress.

Because of later interpretations that stress the coerciveness of social unity for individuals in tribal societies, it is important to state what Marx does *not* mean. His 'tribal herd being' is not chained politically to the community. Indeed, Marx tends to view the 'tribal' as both naïve and apolitical, or pre-political. He does not state the mastery the individual has over time and labour as political freedom. On the other hand, he does not equate the high valuation of community in tribal life with submission to authority and hierarchy, but with an existence that is very restricted. For Marx it is not the coerciveness of community in pre-capitalist formations that prevents both the forces of production and individualism from taking off, but the attachment to the particular social structure and the desire for its preservation. His rhetoric about the brutish and naïve 'herd animal' of the tribal commune reflects his ethnocentric belief that the full development of individual and societal powers, with respect to any sort of knowledge or capabilities, could only be achieved within societies where priority was placed upon productive progress.

SAHLINS ON UNITY AND THE AUTONOMOUS HOUSEHOLD

While Marx understands the community to be a force of production in tribal societies, Sahlins argues that the primary unit of tribal production is the autonomous household, and *not* a community of relations. Indeed, any unity the community establishes stands opposed to the independence of the household unit (his primary unit of production) and to its centrifugal relations with other domestic units (Sahlins 1972: 77). In Sahlins' interpretation, political and kinship ties beyond the primary domestic unit of production enter the economic scene surreptitiously, so to speak, and through non-economic means they create a unity and social order that is in contradiction to the anarchy of the original 'domestic mode of production'. In his view, it is because of the economic autonomy of the household unit that tribal production is at its base unpoliticized. The aspects of the 'domestic mode of production' that Sahlins ostensibly views with a positive eye are, however, similar to those that Marx also noted in his sketch of 'original proprietorship'. Production is for livelihood, with a view toward domestic contentment. It is for the benefit of the producers only. The members of the household have freedom over work: they retain primacy of appropriation in its relation to productive resources and priority in the disposition of the products of their work (1972: 93). Because the purpose of such a 'domestic mode of production' is for use, it is also sparing of labour power (1972: 77,84).

Sahlins comes then to the highly significant conclusion that in tribal societies 'the economic' is a *'modality of the intimate'* (1972: 77) – but it is one of which he clearly disapproves.[6] Although he makes the case, and strongly so, that this modality leads to an affluent life from a social point of view (the individual has both freedom and leisure), Sahlins nevertheless scolds. The 'domestic mode of production' is at once too simple and *too* leisurely. His is a 'Protestant ethic' judgement: primitives just do not work hard enough; they value their leisure too highly. Production in 'the domestic mode', he complains, 'has all the organization of the so many potatoes in a certain famous sack of potatoes' (1972: 95). As a type of production, it is 'anti-surplus' (1972: 82) and therefore has a 'profound' tendency to *under*-produce. Because labour power is 'unexploited' there are 'wasteful' limits to production (1972: 88). In short, Sahlins argues that as a system the 'domestic mode of production' is predicated upon the 'underuse of labour', the 'underexploitation' of resources, and an uncertain household base (1972: 82, 98–9). As a result, tribal economies 'do not realize' their own economic capacities (1972: 41). The basis for his judgement would seem to be determined by his own high evaluation of the economic organization of state societies, which is predicated upon a principle of hierarchy that incorporates relations of domination and subordination in both economic and political life.

Reminiscent of Freud's laments about the childishness of human nature with respect to work in *The Future of an Illusion*, Sahlins remarks that the greatest political challenge in tribal societies is that of 'getting people to work more, or more people to work' (1972: 82). The reason for this is that the 'domestic mode' is 'refractory to the exercise of political power and the enlargement of production' (1972: 42), and in itself provides no mechanisms for holding a growing community together. It is Sahlins' conclusion that economically primitive society is founded on anti-society. As such, it is flawed, and unless the 'domestic mode' is forced beyond itself, the 'entire Society' does not survive (1972: 86, 97). Thus the problem for the polity is to achieve the public economic goal, which is always over and against the 'petty, private self concerns' of the household economy (1972: 131).

In Sahlins' view, society is achieved among tribal peoples only in so far as the 'economic defects' of the 'domestic mode of production' are overcome. In effect, what this means is that the economic values of autonomy and equality must be undermined before the social can be created (1972: 130–4), a job basically to be done by the political leader. It is he who is able to encroach 'upon the domestic system to undermine its autonomy, curb its anarchy, unleash its productivity' (1972: 130). According to Sahlins, not only is political action a necessary stimulus to production, but chiefly 'liberality' and rhetoric of reciprocity (all in line with the primary economic values of domestic intimacy) are but a cloak for what is in fact (a necessary) exploitation.

At this point in his argument, on the subject of mystification, Sahlins sets aside his original contrast of the tribal and the capitalist modes of production, and moves instead to a position that cites exploitation as a universal of the human condition:

> the conjunction of a norm of reciprocity with a reality of exploitation would not distinguish the primitive political economy from any other: everywhere in the world the indigenous category for exploitation is 'reciprocity'.
>
> (Sahlins 1972: 134)

Sahlins *must* take this position on the universality of the political economy. For him social order, and thus the state of sociality itself, is only possible through the action forthcoming from institutions of hierarchy. It is only through exploitation that people can be pushed beyond the original asocial and anarchic domestic mode. Sahlins (1972: 132ff.) thus looks with a cynical eye at the observations by Lévi-Strauss on the plight of the generous chief among the Nambikwara of Brazil who was at the mercy of collective greed. In his article on Nambikwara chieftainship, Lévi-Strauss (1967[1944]) had concluded that it was a relation of reciprocity, and not one of subordination/domination, that bound the group as a recognized collectivity to its chief.[7] Given the data presented by Lévi-Strauss, it is difficult to detect chiefly exploitation. Sahlins does not quote passages from Lévi-Strauss where he details the ways in which the chief had to *work* harder than anyone else, and how it was through his own personal labour that he provided in times of economic disaster (see Lévi-Strauss 1967[1944]). The chief's skills and initiative were greater than those of other people. At the same time he had no power to order the labour of members of his group, nor could he reprimand disorderly conduct or laziness. In sum, he had no coercive power at his disposal (1967[1944: 53). Lévi-Strauss explains that for the Nambikwara consent was at the origin of leadership and the only measure of its legitimacy. Indeed, the difficulties of leadership were so great, the duties of the leader so exacting and tiresome, that Lévi-Strauss wonders why anyone accepted the role of leader in Nambikwara society – was the prize worth the trouble?

It is easy, on the other hand, to see why the Nambikwara group, given its own conditions for leadership, wanted a leader. The weight of the welfare of the group was on his shoulders. It was also because of *its desire for collectivity* that the group desired the leader. Sahlins, on the other hand, writes as if leadership is *imposed* upon the group, and for the sake of the collectivity so acquired household units must sacrifice their autonomy and their leisure – they must bow to exploitation. It is difficult to understand why people would accept political leadership under such conditions. The Nambikwara, far from displaying any acceptance of relations of subordination for the sake of collectivity, would have left any leader whom they understood to be using coercive techniques. They did, however, recognize leadership as a force that brings about collectivity. Lévi-Strauss tells us that their word for chief, *Uilikande*, seemed to mean 'the one who unites' or 'the one who joins together'. He concludes that 'the leader appears as the cause of the group's willingness to aggregate rather than as the result of the need for a central authority felt by a group already constituted' (1967: 53). The critical question is the *nature* of this collectivity that the Nambikwara desired. What was it for? Lévi-Strauss gives us a good clue when he states that a major duty of leadership was to create high morale within the group: 'the chief must be a good singer and dancer, a merrymaker always ready to cheer up the band and to brighten the dullness of daily life' (1967: 55).

To summarize briefly, for Marx *all* modes of production are social ones, with community the hallmark of all pre-capitalist production. For Sahlins, tribal social order is achieved to the degree that exploitative political forces through the means of mystification overcome the asocial structure of production. His argument depends in part upon a rather arbitrary separation of 'the domestic' from 'the public'. Although such a split clearly fits our own understanding of the relation between family and state or civil society, its saliency is not always so clear-cut for the indigenous peoples of Amazonia. Moreover, given the stress that they often place on the freedom of the *individual* in work, the primary unit of production could just as well be, not the household, but the individual person, male or female, adult or child. It can equally be said (somewhat *chez* Marx) that the community itself, especially for the peoples of the Guianas, constituted a basic unit of production.

COLLECTIVITY AS A MODALITY OF THE INTIMATE AND THE INFORMAL: THE GUIANESE EXAMPLE

The social unity valued by the indigenous peoples of the Guianas bears little resemblance to the 'collectivity' envisaged as necessary to their well-being by Sahlins. It is also a type of social linkage that can be difficult for the ethnographer to describe. Rivière has recently argued (in press) that the community, a settlement of people that typically dwelt within a single multi-family communal dwelling, was the basic social unity in the Guianas. He states that as a unit this community was politically autonomous, and in ideal socially and economically self-sufficient. He stresses, however, the ephemerality of these communities and the fluidity of their social arrangements. Thomas, who writes on the Pemon of Venezuela (1982), similarly emphasizes the difficulty of seeing 'collectivity' as a strong factor in the social organization of this Guianese people. He comments that in the Pemon case, order and solidarity were not associated, for their emphasis was so strongly upon the principles of personal autonomy and egalitarianism. Thus Pemon attachment to community was not to a concrete solidary entity; nor did the settlement in any convincing way impinge upon its members as 'the community as a whole' (1982: 235–6). The Pemon were a peaceful people – a peacefulness, Thomas suggests, that was to a large extent a function of 'the community' having a minimal constraining effect, in structural terms, upon the individual. Each person, beyond the level of nuclear family and sibling set, defined his or her own unique social field for both work and residence. The first response of a Pemon to insult, injury, or personal friction was *to move*; the response to dissension was felt to be *in one's own hands*. Because the community was not a decision-making body, it could not achieve hegemony over the individual in concrete economic or political terms. Yet at the same time Thomas comments that for the Pemon 'autonomy is not being alone' (1982: 236). Thus, we return to my opening comments about sociality for the tropical forest peoples of South America being predicated upon the principle of personal autonomy. For them, autonomy is a highly social state, and this seems to be the puzzle for the Western analyst.

Collectivity of a very important type did obviously characterize life in a Pemon settlement, and the order for which they strove was not simply a figment of the tropical imagination. Settlements did have physical existence on one site over a twenty-year time span. Thomas, almost inadvertently, places his finger upon the primary characteristic of Amazonian collectivity when he stresses the intimacy achieved between members of a settlement. He notes that 'the conditions of constant interaction and solidarity within the Pemon household and settlement are conducive to a heightened awareness of others' moods and needs and of the necessity of adapting oneself to them' (1982: 235). The persistent destabilization of hierarchy in Pemon social relationships – as, for example, might hold between father-in-law and son-in-law – is another lead that should guide us to their understanding of sociality. The institutionalization of hierarchy is not conducive to informality, nor to relations of intimacy, and the *only* collectivity with which Pemon individuals were comfortable was that conducive to the establishment of the intimate and the informal.

As already mentioned, Sahlins describes his 'domestic mode of production' as a 'modality of the intimate', which from his point of view embodies the anarchy of nature. The indigenous peoples of the Guianas, on the other hand, understand such a modality as a highly desirable *social* state to be achieved. It is my argument that sociality for them was the *accomplishment* of the principles of intimacy and informality through the everyday activities of community life. In contrast to peoples who believe that their communities have temporal existence through such mechanisms as the corporate ownership of property and the jural rules of such corporation, the Guianese community had existence through time as a political, economic, and social unit to the extent that its members were able to achieve, on a daily basis, the goals of intimacy and informality. Community for them was a process of existence that had to be *daily* achieved by individuals through both tact and work (see Overing 1989). The question remains of how a collectivity based upon such principles might also be conducive to production.

THE COMMUNITY AS 'A FORCE OF PRODUCTION'

Many of the attributes of Sahlins' 'domestic mode of production' – leisure, affluence, the freedom to choose how and when one works – can be dependent upon community. For a large number of indigenous peoples of the Amazon, the community is an obvious unit of production.[8] When I conducted fieldwork among the Piaroa, the local group was usually composed of six to seven families living together within a large communal house. Informal work organization that cross-cut household boundaries typified the rhythm of daily work. A husband and wife were careful to discuss with each other their daily plans. But, although they jointly owned their garden plots, or shared the ownership of such plots with another couple, daily production and consumption patterns did not closely conform to the family unit. A woman could be accompanied to her field by daughter, daughter-in-law, mother, sister, sister-in-law, and female visitors. Young girls worked with mother, father's sister, mother's sister, brother, sister, potential sister-in-law, and father. A boy could choose to work with his father, his mother's brother, his sister or his mates – or not at all. Men went hunting alone or with whomsoever they pleased. If large peccary were sighted, a man would join a hunting party comprised of all the men in his community. Collecting parties were frequently spontaneous affairs that cross-cut family units. The household, although a hearth-owning unit, was no more a primary unit of consumption than it was for production. Because each game species was subject to specific culinary rules, consumption patterns within the community could be complicated. Depending upon age and gender, people could eat certain parts of an animal, but not others. Thus for some meals young men might cook and eat together, while women and children ate separately from a common pot, as too might the adult men as a group.

As these examples indicate, daily production and consumption for the Piaroa was loosely organized, and work usually reflected the personal moods and preferences of the individuals involved. As with the Pemon, right of preference referred both to the personal choice of co-residents with whom one found it most congenial to spend time and to the type of task itself. The Piaroa stated explicitly that the affluent community was the one that could take into account on a daily level both flexibility in schedules of work and right to individual preference. Affluence was a matter of achieving personal comfort in work. The achievement of such wealth demanded the establishment of a community that had both the high morale and the size to allow for flexibility and fluid patterns of cooperation.

The Piaroa repeatedly stated the correlation between personal affluence and community size. A very small community of fifteen people simply did not have the membership resources to allow for personal choice and a positive everyday state of mood and health in the carrying out of all the duties required for daily survival – the fishing, the hunting, the collecting of food and firewood, the gardening, the preparation of game and garden produce, the making of tools and clothing, and the conducting of ritual necessary for daily protection. The size of a community and thus its affluence was related to the qualities of its leader, for it was his job to attract into his community a large number of people who could also amiably cooperate on a daily basis (see Overing Kaplan 1975). While the leader of a Piaroa community had no powers of coercion over work, and little weight in the daily organization of economic activities, it *was* his duty (as it was for the Nambikwara chief) to maintain the high morale of his community so that work, and existence generally, remained comfortable for its members.

As Goldman has noted for the Cubeo of the North-west Amazon (1963: 88), the critical difference between the wealthy and the poor community was not a matter of productive accumulation, but of morale. This makes good sense if a primary value of a people is upon personal autonomy and personal comfort in work, a value encompassing the idea that work must cater to individual desires, talents, and dispositions. The important point that Goldman understood about Amazonian social and political organization, and the philosophy of sociality that supported it, was that the very fact of people living together in a community was dependent upon the *daily* creation of high morale among its members. Since linkage to others for both the Piaroa and the Cubeo remained (insistently) on a relatively informal plane and to a large extent subject to personal preference, the group stayed together only so long as its members and its leader achieved and maintained geniality of relationships (Goldman 1963: 279–83; Overing 1989: 164). It was through the construction of high morale that collective activities, and indeed all work, could be smoothly carried out. In this respect the community could be viewed as a force of production. As Goldman points out, collectivity and the political work required to create and maintain community were more a matter of the 'politics of mood management', than the establishment of institutions of hierarchy incorporating command/obedience relations.

It is important to be even clearer on the relations between community, wealth, and personal autonomy. Wealth for the Piaroa was assessed from the point of view of the individual, and not of the community. Both the capacity to create materially and to act socially were aspects of personal autonomy: the power for both social and material action was in the hands of the individual. Each person was responsible for developing within the self the capacities that allowed for his or her own social and material existence. Individuals were truly wealthy only if their 'thoughts were awakened' (ta'kwa poiaechi), and therefore the 'life of the mind' (ta'kwarü) well developed. It was the well-developed 'life of the mind' that gave one the powerful means to act materially in the world. The stress in the Piaroa theory of power was upon the agent's knowledge, capabilities, and will: these qualities, which together formed a person's ta'kwarü, were the source of materially good things in life.

Nevertheless, wealth was a social notion. A wealthy individual by definition lived with many people and enjoyed a certain quality of life that gave both leisure and abundance. The wealthy person had the powers to live tranquilly with others. Tact, the recognition of the personal autonomy of others, was clearly considered to be an aspect of productive knowledge.[9] Although the stress in the Piaroa theory of power and wealth was upon personal autonomy and creativity, it was also a theory firmly based upon the ideal of sociality and not that of property.

Personal possession as we know it is very different from the Piaroa understanding of it, and several observations about their views are pertinent. Products of work were possessed by the individual, and not the group. They were recognized as manifestations of the particular individual's thoughts, and ownership or personal possession was often expressed through reference to the person's life of the mind (see Overing 1992). The owner also had the privilege of disposal, but not necessarily privileged use. Generosity in sharing (the disposing and distributing of the products of one's labour) was an important social principle for the Piaroa, and in some areas an obligation, such as all products brought back to the house from the jungle. In hunting, fishing, and collecting a person appropriated in large part on behalf of the collectivity. Possession also denoted a relationship of nurture, as with a kinsman. It is significant that the use of kinship terms was in the possessed form. This is logical, for one created kinsmen not only through reproductive capacity, but also through work freely chosen through personal decision. To create kinsmen demanded personal responsibility in a form not so different from that required in the caring for other products of one's work. Kinsmen, as other possessions, required nurturing and protecting. In short, the notion of personal possession among the Piaroa emphasized ownership as a social relationship.

The community as a collectivity of kinsmen living and therefore working together was ideally a community of nurture.[10] The Piaroa, in referring to the membership of their communal house, most often used the phrase '*tutae itsotu*', which literally meant 'the collectivity of like beings to which I belong'. According to the Piaroa, people became physically 'of a kind' through the process of living together. Thus those who were not originally close kinsmen became so over time through proximity. The process of 'becoming of a kind' included working and eating together, and mutual caring for one another through daily work. The work of each adult, and especially that of the leader who possessed the greatest productive skills, contributed to the daily achievement of community, its relatedness, and well-being. Through physical contact, the food one ate affected everyone with whom one lived, as too did one's own personal powers (see Overing 1986). Moreover, the food one ate was usually as much a result of the work of others as of self – and as such a product of *their* thoughts as well as one's own.

It is clear that work, conducted through the modality of the intimate and the informal, was not alienated from the personal relationships of community and their morality. The Piaroa did not distinguish 'work' as a category separable from human living in general. Work, as far as possible, was to be pleasurable. Both intensely personal and social, it was ideally both a product of pleasurable social relationships and a creator of them.[11] As Gow (1991) has described work for the indigenous peoples of the Lower Urubamba in Peru, it was action that fulfilled the desire to provide for self and the desires and lives of others – of children, spouse, and other members of the community. Only through such work could a proper community and linkage with others be created and maintained. Thus personal work and social linkage were constitutive of each other. Without the tranquil relationships of good community life, one could not work. Without work, one had no community. In other words, work, understood as the daily maintenance of life, was the way in which linkage with others could be achieved.

CONCLUSION

What was notable about Piaroa production, within the framework of community, was the informality of its organization and the personal autonomy that such informality allowed. Their vision of the good life was in sharp contrast to Sahlins' understanding of the productive and therefore social community, where through relations of hierarchy resources, labour, and their products could be exploited to their fullest. His yardstick is capitalism: the economic defects of 'the domestic mode of production' must be overcome so that tribal peoples can become workers. But should this occur, as when the indigenous peoples of Amazonia become involved in wage-labour, they are no longer operating within a modality of the intimate and the informal. As Marx understood, the change from one form of sociality (with its attachment to community) to the next (with its focus upon productive progress) was a radical step in general in the history of humankind.

Sahlins, although he captures well the principles of autonomy and intimacy so characteristic of tribal economies, does not give these principles either social or political value. They do have both, and they were values often and vehemently expressed in daily life by individual Piaroa. The *political* choice of the Piaroa was to opt for daily physical and emotional comfort rather than for, let us say, the more abstract stability provided by the rules and regulations ordering past and future inheritance. The primary political goal of the Guianese community was the achievement of the social, but such sociality was dependent upon both the economic autonomy of the individual members of the community and the creation of high morale among them.

It tends to go against the grain in Western analysis to ascribe political freedom to the tribal, or to label as 'political' the freedom that such peoples as those of the Guianas demand in work and their everyday decisions. As already mentioned, Marx tends not to grant political status to such freedom for 'the tribal'. Lefort (1986: 153), however, construes Marx's interpretation of the primitive commune to be, in implication at least, no less political than economic. With capitalism, Marx understands the workers' lack of freedom (lack of property) as a political fact. Where people do have mastery over their own labour and the products of it (where they *are* property owners in more or less the original sense), would these people in Marx's understanding be politically free? Probably not, but in the light of modern ethnography we can claim they are – or at the very least we can argue that their freedom in work is a political fact.

NOTES

1 I give warm thanks to the Leverhulme Foundation who, in awarding me a

Research Grant for the academic year of 1989/90 gave me the time to work on many of the issues of this paper. I also thank Peter Rivière and Eduardo Viveiros de Castro for their comments on an earlier draft of it.
2 For example see Marx and Engels (1970 [1845–46]: 51).
3 See the discussion by Lefort (1986: 142).
4 The discussion of Marx and Engels in *German Ideology* (Part 1: Feuerbach) on gender relations makes clear that Marx in his discussion of original property was referring especially to one's freedom in disposing of one's own labour. However, they also maintained that women never had such autonomy (see 1970 [1845–46]: 44, 52).
5 See also the discussion of Lefort (1986: 143).
6 Sahlins conflates throughout most of his discussion in *Stone Age Economics* what in ordinary anthropological parlance would be separated as 'hunters and gatherers' and 'horticulturalists'. I am not opposed to such conflation.
7 Sahlins quotes only from *Tristes Tropiques* (1961), and not from Lévi-Strauss's article on Nambikwara chieftainship, which was first published in 1944.
8 For some Amazonian groups, such as the Achuar of Ecuador, demographic factors make the household a fairly literal unit of production. See Descola (1986).
9 See Thomas (1982) and Goldman (1963) on the same theme.
10 The observations of Ingold (1986: chap. 9) on collectivity and personal possession in band societies bear many similarities to my own on the Piaroa. See also Ingold (1986: 227) on the 'community of nurture' among hunters and gatherers.
11 See Overing (1989), where I describe the Piaroa 'aesthetics of production' which entails a particular relation between morality, the beauty of a person, and productive knowledge.

REFERENCES

Descola, P. (1986) *La Nature domestique: symbolisme et praxis dans l'ecologie des Achuar*, Paris: Fondation Singer-Polignac.
Freud, S. (1957 [1927]) *The Future of an Illusion*, Garden City, NY: Doubleday.
Goldman, I. (1963) *The Cubeo*, Urbana: University of Illinois Press.
Gow, P. (1991) *Of Mixed Blood: Kinship and History in Peruvian Amazonia*, Oxford: Clarendon Press.
Ingold, T. (1986) *The Appropriation of Nature*, Manchester: Manchester University Press.
Lefort, C. (1986) *The Political Forms of Modern Society*, Cambridge: Polity Press.
Lévi-Strauss, C. (1961) *Tristes Tropiques*, New York: Atheneum.
—— (1967) 'The social and psychological aspects of chieftainship in a primitive tribe: the Nambikuara of Northwestern Mato Grosso', in R. Cohen and J. Middleton (eds) *Comparative Political Systems*, pp. 45–62, Garden City, NY: The Natural History Press. First published in 1944 in *Transactions of the New York Academy of Sciences*, 7.
Marx, K. (1965 [1857–58]) *Pre-capitalist Economic Formations*, Introduction by Eric J. Hobsbawm, New York: International Publishers.
—— and Engels, F. (1970 [1845–46]) *The German Ideology*, C.J. Arthur (ed.), London: Lawrence & Wishart.
Overing, J. (1986) 'Men control women? the "Catch 22" in the analysis of gender', *International Journal of Moral and Social Studies*, 1 (2): 135–56.
—— (1989) 'The aesthetics of production: the sense of community among the Cubeo and Piaroa', *Dialectical Anthropology*, 14: 159–75.
—— (1992) 'Wandering in the market and the forest: an Amazonian theory of

production and exchange', in Roy Dilley (ed.) *Contesting Markets*, Edinburgh: University of Edinburgh Press.

Overing Kaplan, J. (1975) *The Piaroa, a People of the Orinoco Basin*, Oxford: Clarendon Press.

Rivière, P. (in press) 'Houses, places and people: community and continuity in Guiana'.

Sahlins, M. (1972) *Stone Age Economics*, London: Tavistock.

Thomas, D. (1982) *Order Without Government: The Society of the Pemon Indians of Venezuela*, Urbana: University of Illinois Press.

Chapter 3

The construct of 'Africa' in 'African Socialism'

Ralph Grillo

THE AFRICAN SOCIALISM OF SESSIONAL PAPER NO. 10

In spring 1965,[1] the Kenya Government published its long-awaited policy statement, 'Sessional Paper No. 10, African Socialism and its application to planning in Kenya' (Republic of Kenya 1965). It is this document, which one observer thought 'sounded as if it had been drafted by neither an African nor a socialist' ('Critic' in Nationalist of Tanzania, 28 June 1965, cited in Odinga 1967: 310), which is at the core of this chapter.

Though African Socialism's socialist credentials were integral to the debate surrounding Sessional Paper No. 10, and I will address them, the emphasis of this chapter falls rather on its conception of 'Africa'. For what is distinctive about African Socialism (and the Paper is only one convenient example) is the way its proponents sought to identify certain traditions, cultural practices, and modes and principles of organization as inherently or essentially socialist. I wish therefore to explore the construction of Africa within African Socialism. This will entail looking backwards (and forwards) from 1965, through writing of the 1930s, by Africans and others, examining how and why 'African' socialism was such an attractive concept and to whom, its purpose and function, and its meaning for those who embraced it.

African Socialism was not primarily or even significantly a Kenyan concept. During the decade preceding the Paper's publication, it had become diffused throughout Africa through the advocacy of Nkrumah, Nyerere, Senghor, Sékou Touré, and many others. By the 1960s, says Mohiddin (1981: 13) 'to espouse "African Socialism" was one of the most respectable things for any leader to do' (cf. Brockway 1963: 14). None the less there were local contributions, most obviously from Jomo Kenyatta and Tom Mboya, and a socialist tendency could also be identified within 'Mau Mau' or the 'Kenya Land and Freedom Army' – the anti-colonial movement of the 1950s.

Kenyatta, an associate of George Padmore and C.L.R. James in the International African Service Bureau, founded in 1937, and of Padmore, Nkrumah, and others in the Fifth Pan-African Congress of 1945 (Hooker

1967; Nelkin 1964; Padmore 1956), could not himself, due to his imprison-ment in the 1950s, contribute to a doctrine which became central to the programme of the Kenya African National Union (KANU) (Kenyatta's Party). KANU's 1963 Manifesto offered the electorate 'a democratic African socialist Kenya', but in such vague terms as to leave considerable room for debate, particularly over nationalization and, crucially, land (Mohiddin 1981: 39ff.). To end the confusion (and allay foreign fears) the Government decided to 'pronounce its own official definition of socialism' (Mohiddin 1981: 40). Hence Sessional Paper No. 10, and let me begin with an outline of its contents (summaries in Goldsworthy 1982: 235; Leys 1975: 222ff.; and Mohiddin 1981: 67–81; extracts in Minogue and Molloy 1974: 129–41).

Following a presidential Preface (see also Kenyatta 1965), Part I focuses on basic principles:

> The word 'African' [in African Socialism] is not introduced to describe a continent to which a foreign ideology is to be transplanted. It is meant to convey the African roots of a system that is itself African in its characteristics. African socialism is a term describing an African political and economic system that is positively African (Section 7). The main features of African Socialism include – (i) political democracy; (ii) mutual social responsibility; (iii) various forms of ownership; (iv) a range of controls to ensure that property is used in the mutual interests of society and its members; (v) diffusion of ownership to avoid concentration of economic power; (vi) progressive taxes to ensure an equitable distribu-tion of wealth and income (Section 48).

The first two of these represent 'African traditions' which 'form an essential basis for African Socialism' (Section 8), in which,

> every member of society is important and equal; every mature citizen can belong to the party without restriction or discrimination; and the party will entertain and accommodate different points of view. African Socialism rests on full, equal and unfettered democracy. Thus African Socialism differs politically from communism because it ensures every mature citizen equal political rights and from capitalism because it prevents the exercise of disproportionate political influence by economic power groups. Another fundamental force in African traditional life was religion which provided a strict moral code for the community. This will be a prominent feature of African Socialism (Section 10).

However, 'progress cannot be achieved by reverting to pre-colonial condi-tions. The best of Kenya's African social heritage and colonial economic legacy must be re-organized and mobilized' (Section 2). Thus, while draw-ing on African tradition, African Socialism should be flexible and efficient, 'designed to be a working system in a modern setting, fully prepared to adapt itself to changing circumstances and new problems' (Section 22).

Well, was it socialism? This question, awkward for an anthropologist, much exercised proponents and opponents of the Paper. A second is more manageable: What kind of socialism was it? African socialism can be described as 'a potpourri of ideas having little coherence' (Friedland and Rosberg 1964: 1; cf. Cox 1966: 19, 70; Kilson 1966: 18). Sessional Paper No. 10 is, however, relatively coherent, and the strategy of sustained growth (see Section 98), with the state as planner and facilitator of economic goals and the welfare which their achievement would enable, makes it relatively easy to 'place' its socialism and identify its origins. It is European demo-cratic socialism of the post-war years, the socialism of the German SPD's Bad Godesberg Programme, of the British Labour Party of Attlee and Gaitskell, of Swedish social democracy.

A focus on the views of the Paper's principal author, Tom Mboya is revealing.[2] A frequent visitor to Europe, Mboya had important contacts with the British Labour movement. Of Mboya's year at Ruskin College (1955–56), where he drew up a 'Plan for a Socialist Political Party in Kenya', Goldsworthy (1982: 54) says: 'Mboya described himself as a democratic socialist. His political thinking was basically pragmatic . . . in a thoroughly "British" mould' (cf. Rake 1962: 109). In 1960, it was Mboya who was chosen to go to London 'to allay the fears aroused in British business circles' (p. 171) about the approaching independence of Kenya (Rake entitles chapter 12 of his book 'A socialist in a city suit').

Goldsworthy comments:

> Mboya's distinctly non-revolutionary approach to the economic future . . . was wholly of a piece with the seven years' work he had already done . . . in his capacity as labour leader. Mboya the advocate of economic continuity was the same Mboya who had always sought the workers' advancement by incremental means within existing structures.
>
> (1982: 171; cf. Leys 1975: 60)

In many ways a technician concerned with practical matters of planning (see, for example, 1964: 254–7), Mboya was, according to Goldsworthy (1982: 204–5), 'a concerned developmentalist whose broad ideas were very typical of the time and culture. The language of "growth" and "modern-ization" came readily to him.' His emphasis on a mixed economy, with 'centralized planning, Israeli-style workers' enterprises, producer and con-sumer co-operatives, state distribution networks' (ibid.), enables us to identify African Socialism, as its proponents identified it, with other major strands of socialist thought and practice. One might debate whether policy and practice were consistent, or whether any of this theory should have been applied to the Kenyan case, but it seems fruitless to argue whether or not this is 'really' socialism according to some universal touchstone.

WHAT THE CRITICS SAID

Gertzel (1970: 54) identifies two factions in KANU in 1964–65: the pro-Eastern 'Radicals', and the pro-Western 'Conservatives', with opposing views on the economy, land policy, and nationalization. Mboya, like Kenyatta (1964: 79), was against nationalization and dissociated himself from British Labour Party 'Clause Four Socialists' (Mboya 1963: 169). Gertzel suggests that Sessional Paper No. 10 was integral to a campaign against the Radicals, defining African socialism 'in terms to which [they] could not logically take exception' (Gertzel 1970: 69).

Speaking in the Parliamentary debate, Bildad Kaggia, a key figure in 'Mau Mau' and undoubtedly one of the 'Radicals', not least for his views on land reform (cf. Odinga 1967: 263–9), gave the Paper a guarded welcome:

> I do not mind calling our socialism African socialism, Kenya socialism, Kikuyu socialism, or even Luo socialism, but I believe that whatever prefixes we use, it must be socialism and not capitalism, and I believe that the Government is really intending to implement socialism as applied to our own conditions and environment, but not to bring capitalism under the cover of socialism.
>
> (in Gertzel *et al*. 1969: 139)

Kaggia, however, soon joined the ranks of the opponents, chief of whom was Oginga Odinga, then the Vice-President of Kenya. Odinga, a complex figure – teacher, businessman, ethnic leader of the Luo – with many contacts in the Eastern bloc, resigned from the Government in April 1966, and founded the radical Kenya Peoples Union (KPU). His resignation statement (in Gertzel *et al*. 1969: 143), called for policies which would bring about 'complete economic, social and political independence', and the Manifesto of the KPU argued:

> In the mouths of the Government and KANU leaders, 'African Socialism' has become a meaningless phrase. What they call African socialism is neither African nor socialism. It is a cloak for the practice of total capitalism. To describe the policies of the present Government as 'African Socialism' is an insult to the intelligence of the people. . . The KPU condemns the Government's and KANU's capitalist policies: it is opposed to the creation of a small class of rich people while the masses live in poverty. It will pursue truly socialist policies to benefit the wananchi. It will share out the nation's wealth equitably among the people, extend national control over the means of production and break the foreigners' grip on the economy.
>
> (in Gertzel *et al*. 1969: 150)

In his autobiography, Odinga declared: 'Only the political and economic content of independence can reveal whether it will have any real meaning for the mass of the people' (1967: 255). He attacks 'opportunist or career politicians . . . manipulating office for self interest'; who 'want to build a capitalist system in the image of Western capitalism but are too embarrassed or dishonest to call it that' (1967: 250, 302). In similar vein, the *Journal of African Marxists* (1982) praised the 1963 KANU Manifesto ('a testament to what might have been', p. 18), but considered the 'puffed-up African middle class [which] emerged to rule us in 1963 were, in many cases those who had betrayed our freedom fighters' (p. 11).

The rejoinder of Mboya and Kenyatta was sharp. In 1963 Mboya had attacked 'so-called "socialists" [who] peddle and parrot foreign slogans' (1964: 251), and later he declared: 'There are those in the East and in the West who have tried to tell us what we mean by African socialism, and there are those at home who twist the phrase to their own petty uses' (1970: 73). Similarly Kenyatta: 'There are some persons who suggest that our African Socialism is of no account. They would have Kenya surrender to external interests and put what they call 'scientific socialism' in its place. Such people are traitors to the cause of Kenya nationalism' (1968: 313).

Academics too have dealt severely with African Socialism. Ahmed Mohiddin called it 'a mere rationalisation and Africanisation of the existing socioeconomic institutions [which] promotes and encourages class divisions' (1981: 79); its basis is 'not traditional African values but the profit motive' (1981: 196). The 1972 ILO Report offered a mildly phrased, though no less damning assessment ('dynamic factors tending to perpetuate and intensify inequalities may be operative in the Kenyan social and economic system' – ILO 1972: 97), and called for policies 'in line with the philosophy underlying Sessional Paper No. 10' (p. 12). Leys claimed that references to socialism in the Paper should be taken as nothing more than the 'homage vice pays to virtue' (Leys 1975: 262–3). Kenyatta's and Mboya's African Socialism 'was a pure statement of "bourgeois socialism". . . a formulation of "comprador" ideology' (p. 208). Odinga's and Kaggia's socialism, Leys added, 'was of a petty-bourgeois variety', thus putting everyone firmly in their place.

There is little evidence for what any of this meant on the ground, but events surrounding the 'Little General Election' of 1966 are instructive. Following the formation of the KPU, the KANU Government obliged former MPs of their party to resign. There were twenty-nine by-elections of which KANU won twenty on a 33 per cent turnout (Gertzel 1970: 83ff.). Gertzel (1970, chap. 4) contains an account, largely by John Okumu (see also Okumu 1969) of the by-elections in the Nyanza area of western Kenya, Odinga's homeland, where the KPU won most of its seats. Okumu (1969: 113) describes how the KPU, adopting the bull (a potent Luo image) as their logo, campaigned through 'clan heads and other local notables' with many small meetings in their homes. For such elders, 'and for most others the election was about Odinga's position and therefore the position of the Luo themselves' (1969: 108). Certainly the KPU campaign had 'strong egalitarian overtones', and an 'appeal to traditional Luo ideas of equality and to the strong attachment to community characteristic of Luo social organization' (1969: 119). But the main issues were fears of Kikuyu dominance and the dominance of the centre over regions and localities (1969: 120, 123). In Nyanza at least, therefore, the split between KANU and the KPU was seen essentially in 'ethnic' rather than ideological terms. Parkin, who observed that during the late 1960s the KPU became 'almost exclusively' a (Luo) ethnic political party, suspects that its left-wing identification was essentially 'rhetorical' (1978: 220, 224; but see Buijtenhuis 1973: 35ff.).

COMMUNITY, FAMILY, LAND, LABOUR

What, then, of the 'African' in 'African Socialism'?

'Tradition' is a word used frequently throughout Part I of Sessional Paper No. 10, and usages may be grouped around two main headings which the Paper itself identifies: 'Mutual social responsibility' – the association of African tradition with the 'co-' words: cooperation, community, corporateness, co-ownership, and so on; and 'Political democracy' – the democratic and classless nature of traditional African society. I link these themes from the Paper with the wider discourse in which they are located – discourse, like 'networks' (Barnes 1969: 66ff.), is finite but unbounded.

Nyerere wrote that he was 'brought up in tribal socialism' (1964: 245). In the construction of this socialism the 'co-' words are crucial, and they are linked directly with 'Ujamaa', a word of Arabic origin implying 'gathered together'. Kenyatta explained as follows:

> We must create a sense of togetherness, of national familyhood. In Swahili we express this by the word 'ujamaa', which can also be roughly translated as socialism. . . . We shall make use of those attitudes of selfhelp, good-neighbourliness and communal assistance, which are such an important feature of our traditional societies.
>
> (1964: 8)

A belief in the 'communitarian' values of traditional society was widely shared in Anglophone Africa (cf. Onuoha 1965: 19), and in Francophone Africa too (cf. Andrain 1964; 1966; and, for example, Mamadou Dia, in Friedland and Rosberg 1964: 248–9). Within East Africa, an influential statement of principle was Nyerere's Kivukoni speech of 1962 (Nyerere 1964). In this address, originally given in Swahili, Nyerere argued that in

> traditional African society. . . nobody starved . . . he could depend on the wealth possessed by the community of which he was a member. That was socialism. That is socialism. . . . We were individuals within a com-

munity. We took care of the community, and the community took care of us. We neither needed nor wished to exploit our fellow men.

(Nyerere 1964: 240)

For Nyerere (1964: 246), the foundation was the extended family; for Kenyatta it was 'the sense of brotherhood' (1968: 308). Thus 'mutual social responsibility' (a key tenet of African Socialism, and a significant phrase in the whole discourse) was seen as an 'extension of the African family spirit to the nation as a whole' (Mboya 1970: 78; cf. Mboya 1963: 256; 1970: 171).

Central to community are land and labour. For Padmore: 'Our starting point must be the land, with its communal ownership and production and its element of co-operative self-help' (1964 [1959]: 231). Kenyatta wrote: 'I love the soil, and I love those who love the soil. . . . I go back to the soil every morning of my life' (1964: 62). Mboya suggested that 'in the African tradition' the idea that 'we are all sons (and daughters) of the soil' gave rise to the 'logic and practice of equality', and 'the practice of the communal ownership of the vital means of life – the land' (Mboya 1964: 253; cf. Mboya 1963: 163). For Nyerere: 'To us in Africa, land was always recognized as belonging to the community. . . the African's right to land was simply the right to use it' (1964: 242; cf. Mboya 1963: 165). Hence, the Government's intolerance of large under-developed landholdings was 'in keeping with African socialism or traditions in which the concept of ownership and property rights was never the inalienable right it was in Europe' (Mboya 1970: 84).

Mboya continues:

This single unifying African principle has been that no matter who owned or managed land or other productive resources, they were expected to be used, and used for the general welfare. No individual family or clan could treat productive assets as private property unless the uses to which those assets were put were regarded as consonant with general welfare . . . no person could treat a piece of land as his own with the freedom to use it or not to use it as he chose.

According to Odinga, 'the tribe as a whole was the proprietor of all the land in its area'; animals were 'community property', and 'common ownership of the land was accompanied by a system of communal cultivation' (1967: 13). Hence there was antipathy towards consolidation of land into individual plots, and Odinga argued that, under Luo land tenure, individual land ownership was not entrenched, and cooperation was a spirit in which the people were deeply steeped. It might be said that this traditional Luo farming was halfway to socialism (1967: 14).

'The spirit of self-help and co-operation will have to be encouraged', said Padmore, whilst warning simultaneously, 'idleness will have to be condemned as a social evil' (1964 [1959]: 234). Kenyatta, in his 'Back to the land' speech (1964: 60–2; 1968: 232–4), asserted: 'Whereas we believe in African Socialism, we do not believe in loitering and idleness. We believe in co-operatives, but not in promoting a state of affairs in which some people try to live on the sweat of others.' 'In traditional African society', said Nyerere (1964: 240), 'everybody was a worker' (meaning 'not idle'). 'Parasitism' was avoided. Nyerere quoted a Swahili proverb 'Mgeni siku mbili; siku ya tatu mpe jembe' ('Treat your guest as a guest for two days; on the third day give him a hoe!'), and adds: 'In actual fact, the guest was likely to ask for the hoe even before his host had given him one – for he knew what was expected of him, and would have been ashamed to remain idle' (1964: 241). (The same proverb is cited by Mboya 1963: 163, Onuoha, 1965: 34; and Brockway 1963: 29.) Describing how cooperative labour would be employed in the building of a hut, Mboya concluded that 'if someone refused to take part, then he would find that when his time came few people would come to help him and he might be completely boycotted' (1963: 166). Thus,

> the African structure of interdependence within the community, where each man knows he has certain responsibilities and duties and where there are certain sanctions against those who do not fulfil expectations . . . provides the discipline, self-reliance and stability needed in new nations.
>
> (Mboya 1963: 68–9)

DEMOCRACY AND CLASS

Padmore had commented extensively on the democratic traditions of pre-colonial society in Nigeria and Ghana, where chiefs 'derived their authority from the common peoples delegated through elders and counsellors' (1949: 112). 'We, in Africa', said Nyerere (1964: 246), 'have no more need of being "converted" to socialism than we have of being "taught" democracy. Both are rooted in our own past – in the traditional society which produced us.' This theme was taken up in chapter IX of Kenyatta's *Facing Mount Kenya*, where he sought to show how at successive levels of Kikuyu organization (family, village, district, nation – his terms) a senior male was 'president', presiding over council meetings and representing the council at the next higher level. He continued:

> In the whole governmental organisation there was no inheritable position, everything depending on personal merit. . . . The group had the right to recall and dismiss or suspend any of its representatives whose behaviour was contrary to the well-established rules of conduct. In fact, it was the voice of the people or public opinion that ruled the country. . . . The spirit of collectivism was . . . ingrained in the mind of the people.
>
> (1961 [1938])

According to Kenyatta, 'An elder. . . renders his services freely . . . . In 'recognition he receives public tributes ceremonially, and is regarded specifically as the father and officiating priest of the community' (1961 [1938]: 265). One finds a similar notion in chapter 1 of Odinga's autobiography, entitled *At the Feet of the Village Elders*: 'The [hut] in the centre [of the compound] was the duol or office of the Jaduong Dala, or chief elder. . . . He had to consult with the other elders, and they formed themselves into a kind of village cabinet to regulate village life and maintain discipline' (1967: 6).

Similarly, Mboya believed that political systems in Kenya traditionally 'assured every mature member of the tribe a voice or at least an influence in tribal decisions, such influence or voice depending more on age grouping rather than wealth' (1970: 171); elsewhere he extends this claim to include the Baganda (1963: 72). Consequently, it was

> a true reflection of African thought and tradition that the chosen leader of the nation should have his home and his roots in a locality where, also, he is the chosen leader of his kinsmen and his neighbours. . . . We have no tradition of kingship in this country. . . . Our people have always governed their affairs by looking to a council of elders elected and headed by their own chosen leader, giving them strong and wise leadership. That tradition – which is an Africanism – will be preserved in this new constitution.
>
> (in Gertzel *et al.* 1969: 195)

If traditional African society was democratic, it was also classless. Sessional Paper No. 10 set out the reasons why Marxism was not applicable in Africa, concluding that:

> The sharp class divisions that once existed in Europe have no place in African Socialism and no parallel in African society. No class problem arose in the traditional African society and none exists today among Africans (Section 36).

Where elders were only 'guardians' of wealth (Nyerere 1964: 241), 'everyone was a worker', albeit perhaps in different senses. (Others were not so sanguine: for Senghor (1964: 265; cf. Nkrumah 1966: 5), traditional African societies were 'community-based', but not without hierarchy.) Moreover, the community basis of pre-colonial African society undermined the applicability of a Marxist conception of class. Thus, 'the whole African social system arising out of and resting upon the basis of the tribal communal or common ownership in the means of living – the land – shaped itself in agreement with that basis into a form of 'primitive communism' (Padmore 1964 [1959]: 223).

THE MAKING OF A MYTH

> There is a kind of socialism which is still unknown in England and in the Continent of Europe, but which prevails in all African communities not under the rule of Europe, and that is, the principle of hospitality. This is socialism pure and simple.
>
> > (*Sierra Leone Weekly News*, May 1913, in Ayo Langley 1979: 506–7)

In sum, then, there is a vision of affinity between socialism and the traditions of African society: no classes, common ownership, or at any rate control, of the means of production, cooperation in labour, and a fundamental form of democracy. Socialism was Africa's 'pristine condition' (Abraham 1962: 182).

It is easy to dismiss all this, to argue (1) that Africa was never thus; or (2) if it once was, colonialism has long since changed it; or (3) if it still was, tradition could not coexist with modernity; or (4) if traditional Africa was as 'communitarian' as believed, its attributes were not essentially 'African', but 'human', reflecting the values of societies 'at a certain level of productive capacity' (Babu 1981: 57); or (5) that whatever the nature of traditional African society, socialism is universal and scientific (cf. Cox 1966: 71, 105, and elsewhere).[3] It will be observed, too, that a striking feature of the discussion is a complete silence on questions of gender.

On (2), Kaggia's speech in the debate on Sessional Paper No. 10 cast doubt on the extent to which

> the old African society which was here before the British came . . . is still in existence . . . . We must agree that most of this has been completely destroyed and there is very little that is left, unless we suggest here that we are going to demolish everything that we have here, that we go back to our old traditions and we start building our socialism on that.
>
> > (in Gertzel *et al*. 1969: 139)

His doubts were shared by Potekhin, who argued that private ownership of land had long been a feature of much of Africa (Potekhin 1964: 109). Furthermore, Potekhin, like the *Journal of African Marxists*, thought that recent African society was distinctly not classless. Cox (1966: 32) accepted that the view of Africa as an 'early communal society' which 'embodied the principles of socialism' was correct, and in accordance with Engels. However, he argued that much of Africa had already achieved a feudal stage before the colonial era, and that colonialism had led to further decay of communal systems of ownership (cf. Babu 1981: 589; Nkrumah 1966). Policies followed by independent African governments would lead to their further deterioration.

On (1), Mboya himself had reservations (1970: 100). Much earlier, Malinowski in his preface to *Facing Mount Kenya* (Kenyatta 1961 [1938]: xi) had expressed, guardedly, his doubts about Kenyatta's argument, and criticized 'such antitheses as "collective" v. "individual" in opposing the native outlook as "essentially social" to the European as "essentially personal"'. The counter-argument was, however, put most fully by the American anthropologist Igor Kopytoff, who through an account of Suku agriculture disputed the notion that it was characterized by 'co-operation' (Kopytoff 1964: 56ff.; cf. Morse 1964: 49–50).

Against this, Sprinzak (1973) believed that Kopytoff paid insufficient attention to what the proponents of African socialism had actually said. He proposed to treat the notion of a communitarian basis of African society as an ideal type construct. 'The dominant feature of social life before the advent of the Europeans was the kinship group with its special social interactions' and its 'non-individualistic thinking' (1973: 634, 635). Drawing on Horton, he claimed that 'the structure of social thinking of the traditional society in Africa was communal', meaning 'no individual or group ... develops a counter ideology' (1973: 642); cf. Nkrumah's argument (1966: 5) that African socialism was about the 'spirit' of traditional African society, not its 'structure'.

Sprinzak may be guilty of special pleading, of trying to rescue an idea from its contradictions, but his point that African socialist ideas should be treated seriously is well taken. But whose myth was it, and how was it constructed?

By the time of Nkrumah, Nyerere, and Mboya, many of the themes were commonplace, and I will briefly examine their sources.[4] The influence of George Padmore is the most conspicuous (Hooker 1967; Nelkin 1964; Padmore 1949, 1956). Padmore was a communist expelled from the Comintern for 'petty bourgeois nationalist deviation' (Hooker 1967: 32), but he had remained of the Left, associating with the British Independent Labour Party, and he retained an affection for Lenin (Padmore 1956: 290ff.). Concerned with the position of subordinate races under colonialism, he advocated a socialist stance for that great unifying conception of the post-war period in Africa: Pan-Africanism. But disillusionment with Third and Second Internationals led him to a socialism which was neither capitalist nor communist (Padmore 1956: 229; see also 148–51 passim, and p. 319 for his praise of Mao and Tito).

It is easy in retrospect to see how Padmore and others arrived at an independent, non-aligned socialism, but African socialism implies more than this. So whence the idea that traditional African society was socialistic? A key source was, I believe, *Facing Mount Kenya*, which Padmore must have read (he mentions it – 1956: 150) but does not obviously use in any of his accounts of Kenya (for example, 1949, 1956). Throughout, Kenyatta emphasizes doing things together: 'partnership', 'co-operation', 'reciprocal obligations', 'mutual help and the tribal solidarity'; 'mutual help, extending from the family group to the tribe' (p. 174), 'corporate effort'. Indeed there is considerable continuity in the discourse through which African society is constructed from *Facing Mount Kenya* to Sessional Paper No. 10, and indeed far beyond.

But Kenyatta's construction of African tradition (which makes it available for the discourse of African socialism) did not depend on any specifically socialist or, rather, Marxist philosophy. The case for the existence of primitive communism in pre-colonial Africa is not one that is generally made (though see Cox 1966, chap. 4; and also Padmore's remark cited above). There are, rather, two other, related, ways of framing Africa which seem to have been influential. The first is the liberal, missionary perspective. In *Facing Mount Kenya*, Kenyatta (1961 [1938]: 123) refers to a review by Oldham (of a book by the German writer Knak) which obviously made a strong impression on him. Oldham/Knak had argued that 'full recognition should be given to the spiritual values in African society [which were] in many respects nearer to the true meaning and Christian understanding of life than western civilization' (Oldham 1931: 549, 550). What Kenyatta drew from this was the key phrase 'sense of mutual obligation and responsibility', which Oldham's review employed on several occasions (1931: 551–2). The significance of this perspective requires further investigation, but note that Onuoha (1965) provides another example of religious intervention in the debate when he interprets the already formed discourse of traditional African socialism in the language of post-Vatican II Catholicism.

The second is, perhaps not surprisingly, social anthropology. The discipline has several times appeared in this story, though mainly as a source of material and ideas for critics of the idea of African socialism. This is obviously so in the case of Kopytoff, but Cox, for example, makes great use of *African Political Systems* (see Fortes and Evans-Pritchard 1940) as well as Marxist sociologists/anthropologists such as Suret-Canale, Potekhin, and Worsley in his defence of the 'scientific' viewpoint. More difficult to substantiate is the influence of anthropology on the other side. Certainly there is Malinowski and Kenyatta, but beyond that? One problem is that anthropology or anthropological evidence was rarely cited explicitly. Thus Odinga, Mboya, Nyerere (and indeed Kenyatta) were usually inclined to draw more on personal experience. Yet what they said often read like anthropology; it is presented in the anthropological register. It is anthropological at the discursive level. The anthropological influence stemmed from the way that the discipline shaped discussion of traditional African society and represented it, or at any rate some aspects of it; for instance, acephalous lineage systems. It wrote about Africa in such a way as to make its results 'available' for the discourse of African socialism (just as 'ordered anarchy' makes the Nuer available for another political tradition). In his 1966 paper Nkrumah associates an emphasis on the 'structural', as opposed to 'spiritual', basis of African socialism with the 'anthropological' approach (pp. 5–6).

Reviewing early sources for the idea of a collectivist basis for African societies, Kopytoff concludes that African socialism reflected 'the building by the elite of a Pan-African social mythology whose vocabulary remains essentially Western' (1964: 55). He also wondered whether 'the categories of Western mythology [have] influenced the social sciences in their analyses of [African] societies' (1964: 59). Ranger (1983: 261) has referred to 'two ambiguous legacies' bequeathed to African politicians: traditions transplanted from Europe to Africa; and the 'whole body of reified "tradition" invented by colonial administrators, missionaries, "progressive nationalists", elders and anthropologists' (1983: 261–2); cf. Hopkins' concept (1973: 10) of 'Merrie Africa'. He points out that the novelist Ngugi, who rejects the one, is in danger of succumbing to the other. This might be illustrated by the passage in *Petals of Blood* (pp. 120ff.), in which Ngugi portrays 'Ilmorog' (Kenya, Africa) before the fall, so to say, in terms strongly reminiscent of the discourse of which I have been speaking.

'A PHILOSOPHY OF OUR OWN'

Why the myth? Why the appeal of African Socialism?

The attractiveness of the idea is frequently explained by reference to its political 'function'. Kopytoff himself (1964: 62) found in it a device for mobilizing support for the socialist policies it proclaimed – see also Mushkat (1975: 86). In fact it was more usually asserted that its function was diametrically opposite: the 'most likely and attractive label to promote a capitalist model of Kenya' (Mohiddin 1981: 203); 'to formulate a "developmental" ideology adapted to "comprador" interests' (Leys 1975: 270). Dissident pamplets put it more bluntly. Thus the 'People's Front of East Africa', opposing Sessional Paper No. 10, announced: 'It is only a fool who can support the theories which go under the name of "African Socialism". . . . So-called "African socialist" ideologies are nothing but a dishonest smokescreen for capitalism. . . . The only Socialism valid the world over is Scientific Socialism' (cited in Andrain 1966: 43). In similar vein, the *Journal of African Marxists*, concluded:

> Many African regimes have sought to disguise class antagonisms by declaring themselves to be 'African Socialist'. They then go on to glorify a mythical African past where, in theory, all people were nice to each other and all shared communally the wealth produced communally. . . . In practice African Socialism generally protects and nourishes a neo-colonial dependency with imperialist-oriented economies. . . . The word 'socialism' – detached from its social and economic moorings – is merely

bandied about by these regimes to cover their innate inadequacies with a cloak of morality.

(1982: 88–9)

This journal condemned Sessional Paper No. 10 as 'full of dubious concepts and ambiguities', such as the message that 'there need be no class struggle in Kenya because Kenyans – true to their mythical African heritage – form one big united family. . . . Ruling class ideology thus projects an imaginary relationship which blurs the real and deep divisions in our society' (1982: 27, 38).

Remarks such as that attributed to one MP ('An African socialist is by nature a capitalist', in Gertzel *et al.* (1969: 83)), perhaps illustrate Mohiddin's point that to describe Kenya's policies as African Socialism is 'simply an exercise in linguistic gymnastics' (1981: 194).

Burke commented that the metaphysical nature of the concept of *ujamaa* enabled it 'to provide justification or explanation for almost any govern-ment policy' (1964: 219). Certainly in Kenya, the rhetoric of African Socialism was used to justify policies which might otherwise have been unpalatable, such as wage-restraint (Mboya 1970: 71), or the one-party state which Kenyatta defended by reference to the assumed absence of a class struggle in Africa (1964: 24), and the existence of 'the traditional Tribal Council' and other mechanisms which provided the opportunity for 'con-structive opposition from within' (cf. Kenyatta 1968: 230). As Onuoha (1965: 64) put it: 'Ancient tribal government was democratic without an opposi-tion party. It would, therefore, seem more African to continue in that tradition.'

Be that as it may, like Sprinzak, I still think there is something to be gained by taking what African leaders have said at face value. What was the meaning (rather than the function) of African socialism? Friedland and Rosberg (1964: 4–5) stress the importance for African socialism of discus-sions of Négritude and the African Personality, and thus of rediscovering roots. A wide range of writers, including 'radicals' such as Kaggia, Odinga, and Babu, alluded to the need to repair 'damaged ego or loss of identity' (Burke 1964: 205), incurred through the colonial experience. 'Liberation of the mind was to pave the way for liberation from the colonial government', said Kaggia (1975: 74). 'The African', said Odinga, 'was made ashamed of the traditions of his own society' (1967: 63). He described how he encour-aged his own nickname of 'Jaramogi' (1967: 133), and cultivated the use of 'traditional' dress when speaking in the Legislative Council, as a means of demonstrating the falsity of the view that 'civilized meant European and that anything traditional was inferior' (1967: 141–2; cf. Parkin 1978: 219, 239, *passim*). This is a constant motif of Kenyatta's, but the Kenyan politician who developed the theme most fully was Mboya:

We are immersed in a massive transition in which we are seeking new identities at personal, national and international levels. Africans are struggling to build new societies and a new Africa and we need a new political philosophy – a philosophy of our own – which will explain, validify (*sic*), and help to cement our experience.

(Mboya 1964: 250)

That 'philosophy of our own' was African socialism, which referred to

proved codes of conduct in the African societies which have, over the ages, conferred dignity on our people and afforded them security regardless of their station in life ... to universal charity which characterized our societies and ... to the African's thought processes and cosmological ideas which regard man, not as a social means, but as an end and entity in the society.

(Mboya 1964: 251)

(Cox's comment on this is: 'What a lot of meaningless phrases' (1966: 76).)

In a speech on 'Africa and Afro-Americans', Mboya (1970: 228) explained that it was at this level that 'African-ness' was to be found:

Some [black Americans] think that to identify with Africa one should wear a shaggy beard or a piece of cloth on one's head or a cheap garment on one's body. I find here a complete misunderstanding of what African culture really means. An African walks barefoot or wears sandals made out of old tyres not because it is his culture, but because he lives in poverty. We live in mud and wattle huts and buy cheap Hong Kong fabrics not because it is part of our culture, but because these are the conditions imposed on us today by poverty. . . . Our culture is something much deeper. It is the sum of our personality and our attitude toward life. The basic qualities that distinguish it are our extended family ties and the codes governing relations between old and young, our concept of mutual social responsibility and communal activities, our sense of humour, our belief in a supreme being and our ceremonies for birth, marriage and death. These things have a deep meaning for us, and they pervade our culture, regardless of tribe or clan. They are qualities that shape our lives, and they will influence the new institutions that we are now establishing.

What started as a chapter on socialism must end as one on person and identity. African Socialism, says Onuoha, is 'an expression of the desire of all Africans to find themselves, be themselves, and assert themselves' (1965: 30). The point, I think, is not the success or failure of the enterprise, but what it was trying to do. African Socialism was attempting to address not just the economic or political problems of independence, but also the cultural, and indeed spiritual ones. In this respect, the African authors of African Socialism and (perhaps with the exception of those who espoused full-blooded 'scientific socialism') their African critics shared much common ground. Even when they disagreed about the socialism, they usually agreed about the African. And it is understandable why they did so.

NOTES

1 Researching the labour force of the then East African Railways and Harbours (see Grillo 1973; 1974), I was in Nairobi when Sessional Paper No. 10 appeared, and queued, in the rain, for an early copy. As in Mohiddin (1981), African Socialism (capitalized) refers to the doctrines set out in Kenya's Sessional Paper No. 10, and socialism (uncapitalized) to the wider doctrines. I thank Sussex colleagues Richard Brown, Saul Dubow, and Bill Epstein for their advice and help.

2 The authorship is debated. Leys (1975: 208) says: 'According to people who should know it was largely drafted by an American economist in Mboya's ministry' – Professor Edgar O. Edwards of Rice University (an expatriate adviser to the Ministry of Economic Planning and Development, see Edwards 1968: 6, 12). Goldsworthy's bibliography (1982: 296) notes: 'Mboya acted more as supervisor and editor than as writer. However, the pamphlet bears the stamp of his thinking and he more than once defended it in print.' Mboya's own account (1970: 74) of its drafting shows it was a collective product, and the product of a collective discourse. As Leys suggests, 'it does not really matter who drafted it' (Leys 1975: 208).

3 On (3) Mboya himself pointed out the drawbacks of the extended family – joint ownership of land, and the system of supporting dependants – which 'can be detrimental in . . . the modern, monetary exchange economy' (1970: 171), a view shared by the radical Tanzanian, A.R.M. Babu who argues that even if traditional African practice were collectivist, the forms of organization of that epoch were 'backward' and hence a 'hindrance to progress' (1981: 58, cf. Cox 1966: 32). On (4) and (5), I. I. Potekhin, the leading Soviet Africanist of the 1950s, the British communist Idris Cox, Babu, and the *Journal of African Marxists* all oppose the idea of a specifically 'African' socialism. Onuoha (1965: 89–92) described a seminar at Nairobi in 1964 at which John Kakonge, Secretary-General of the Uganda Peoples' Congress, argued that 'there was only one type of true Socialism', namely 'Scientific Socialism', and that 'African Socialism' was to be rejected as a 'call for us to return to the past and to reject all mankind's achievements' (p. 89). (See Mushkat 1975 for a review of the socialist bloc's position.)

4 There are two lines of descent: one Francophone, traceable through discussions of Négritude and the African Personality, at times very philosophical, even 'mystical'; the other Anglophone, more rooted in an account of social practice (though see Nkrumah 1964). I concentrate on the latter. Mushkat (1975) and Mudimbe (1988) provide good accounts of the former.

REFERENCES

Abraham, W.E. (1962) *The Mind of Africa*, London: Weidenfeld.
Africa Report (1963), Special issue on African Socialism (May 1963).
Andrain, C. (1966) 'Patterns of African socialist thought', *African Forum*, 1(3): 41–60.
Andrain, C.F. (1964) 'Guinea and Senegal: contrasting types of African Socialism', pp. 131–59 in W.H. Friedland, and C.G. Rosberg (eds) *African Socialism*, Stanford, CA: Stanford University Press.

Ayo Langley, J. (ed.) (1979) *Ideologies of Liberation in Black Africa, 1856–1970*, London: Rex Collings.

Babu, A.R.M. (1981) *African Socialism or Socialist Africa?*, London: Zed Press.

Barnes, J.A. (1969) 'Networks and political process', pp. 51–76 in J.C. Mitchell (ed.) *Social Networks in Urban Situations*, Manchester: Manchester University Press

Brockway, Fenner (1963) *African Socialism*, London: Bodley Head.

Buijtenhuis, R. (1973) *Mau Mau Twenty Years After*, The Hague: Mouton.

Burke, F.G. (1964) 'Tanganyika: the search for Ujamaa', pp. 194–219 in W.H. Friedland and C.G. Rosberg (eds) *African Socialism*, Stanford, CA: Stanford University Press.

Cox, I. (1966) *Socialist Ideas in Africa*, London: Lawrence & Wishart.

Edwards, E.O. (1968) 'Development planning in Kenya since independence', *East African Economic Review*, 4(2): 1–15.

Fortes, M. and Evans-Pritchard, E.E. (eds) (1940) *African Political Systems*, Oxford: Oxford University Press.

Friedland, W.H. and Rosberg, C.G. (eds) (1964) *African Socialism*, Stanford, CA: Stanford University Press.

Gertzel, C. (1970) *The Politics of Independent Kenya, 1963–68*, London: Heinemann.

Gertzel, C., Goldschmidt, M. and Rothchild, D. (eds) (1969) *Government and Politics in Kenya*, Nairobi: East African Publishing House.

Goldsworthy, D. (1982) *Tom Mboya: the Man Kenya Wanted to Forget*, London: Heinemann.

Grillo, R.D. (1973) *African Railwaymen*, Cambridge: Cambridge University Press.

—— (1974) *Race, Class and Militancy: an African Trade Union, 1939–1965*, New York: Chandler Publishing Co.

Hooker, J.R. (1967) *Black Revolutionary: George Padmore's Path from Communism to Pan-Africanism*, London: Pall Mall Press.

Hopkins, A.G. (1973) *An Economic History of West Africa*, London: Longman.

ILO (1972) *Employment, Incomes and Equality: A Strategy for Increasing Productive Employment in Kenya*, Geneva: International Labour Office.

Inukai, I. (1974) 'African socialism and agricultural development strategy – comparative study of Kenya and Tanzania', *Developing Economies*, 12(1): 3–22.

Journal of African Marxists (1982) *Independent Kenya*, London: Zed Press.

Kaggia, B. (1975) *Roots of Freedom, 1921–1963*, Nairobi: East African Publishing House.

Kenyatta, Jomo (1961 [1938]) *Facing Mount Kenya*, London: Mercury Books.

—— (1964) *Harambee! The Prime Minister of Kenya's Speeches, 1963–1964*, Nairobi: Oxford University Press.

—— (1965) 'African socialism and African unity', *African Forum*, 1(1): 23–37.

—— (1968) *Suffering without Bitterness*, Nairobi: East African Publishing House.

Kilson, M. (1966) 'Politics of African Socialism', *African Forum*, 1(3).

Knak, S. (1931) *Zwischen Nil und Tafelbai*, Berlin: Heimatdienst-Verlag.

Kopytoff, I. (1964) 'Socialism and traditional African societies', pp. 53–62 in W.H. Friedland and C.G. Rosberg (eds) *African Socialism*, Stanford, CA: Stanford University Press.

Leys, C. (1975) *Underdevelopment in Kenya*, London: Heinemann.

Mboya, Tom (1963) *Freedom and After*, London: André Deutsch.

—— (1964 [1963]) 'African Socialism', pp. 250–8 in W.H. Friedland and C.G. Rosberg (eds) *African Socialism*, Stanford, CA: Stanford University Press.

—— (1970) *The Challenge of Nationhood*, London: André Deutsch.

Minogue, M. and Molloy, J. (eds) (1974) *African Aims and Attitudes: Selected Documents*, Cambridge: Cambridge University Press.

Mohiddin, Ahmed (1981) *African Socialism in Two Countries*, London: Croom Helm.
Morse, C. (1964) 'The economics of African Socialism', pp. 35–52 in W.H. Friedland and C.G. Rosberg (eds) *African Socialism*, Stanford, CA: Stanford University Press.
Mudimbe, V.Y. (1988) *The Invention of Africa: Gnosis, Philosophy and the Order of Knowledge*, Bloomington: Indiana University Press.
Mushkat, M. (1975) 'Figure du socialisme africain', *Mondes en Developpement*, 9: 57–86.
Nelkin, D. (1964) 'Socialist sources for Pan-African ideology', pp. 63–79 in W.H. Friedland and C.G. Rosberg (eds) *African Socialism*, Stanford, CA: Stanford University Press.
Ngugi wa Thiongo, (1977) *Petals of Blood*, London: Heinemann.
Nkrumah, K. (1964) *Consciencism*, London: Heinemann.
—— (1966) 'African socialism revisited', *African Forum*, 1(3): 3–9.
Nyerere, J. (1964 [1962]) 'Ujamaa: the basis of African Socialism, pp. 238–47 in W.H. Friedland and C.G. Rosberg (eds) *African Socialism*, Stanford, CA: Stanford University Press.
Odinga, Oginga, (1967) *Not Yet Uhuru*, London: Heinemann.
Okumu, J. (1969) 'The by-election in Gem: an assessment', *East African Journal*, 6(6): 9–17.
Oldham, J.H. (1931) 'Dr Siegried Knak on the Christian task in Africa', *International Review of Missions*, 80 (Oct.): 547–55.
Onuoha, Bede (1965) *The Elements of African Socialism*, London: André Deutsch.
Padmore, G. (1949) *Africa: Britain's Third Empire*, New York: Negro Universities Press.
—— (1956) *Pan-Africanism or Communism? The Coming Struggle for Africa*, London: Dennis Dobson.
—— (1964 [1959]) 'A guide to Pan-African Socialism', pp. 223–227 in W.H. Friedland and C.G. Rosberg (eds) *African Socialism*, Stanford, CA: Stanford University Press.
Parkin, D.J. (1978) *The Cultural Definition of Political Response: Lineal Destiny among the Luo*, London: Academic Press.
Potekhin, I.I. (1964) 'On African Socialism: a Soviet view', pp. 97–112 in W.H. Friedland and C.G. Rosberg (eds) *African Socialism*, Stanford, CA: Stanford University Press.
Rake, Alan (1962) *Tom Mboya: Young Man of New Africa*, New York: Doubleday.
Ranger, T. (1983) 'The invention of tradition in colonial Africa', pp. 211–62 in E. Hobsbawm and T. Ranger (eds) *The Invention of Tradition*, Cambridge: Cambridge University Press.
Republic of Kenya (1965) 'African socialism and its application to planning in Kenya', Sessional Paper No. 10, Nairobi: Government Printer.
Senghor, L. (1964 [1961]) 'African-style Socialism', pp. 264–6 in W.H. Friedland and C.G. Rosberg (eds) *African Socialism*, Stanford, CA: Stanford University Press.
Sprinzak, E. (1973) 'African traditional socialism – semantic analysis of political ideology', *Journal of Modern African Studies*, VII(4): 629–47.

Chapter 4

Socialism from above in Tanzania
The view from below

Pat Caplan

THE PROBLEM OF SOCIALISM IN TANZANIA

It has been frequently pointed out that Tanzania has suffered from many shortages, but the study of its political economy is not one of them.[1] This introduction outlines a few of the themes and debates with which observers – both Tanzanian and Western – have concerned themselves.

First, there is a debate around the meaning of socialism, and whether or not Tanzania is, or ever was or intended to be, a truly socialist country. Prominent in this discussion is Nyerere's vision of African socialism (*ujamaa*) and its relationship to other forms of socialism (see also Grillo, this volume). One facet of this debate is the extent to which the reality has lived up to the rhetoric.

Secondly, there has been much discussion concerning ends and means. The Arusha Declaration in 1967 was designed to prevent the formation of a capitalist class in Tanzania – to eliminate the *'wabenzi'* (those who ride in Mercedes Benz cars). Yet some have claimed to identify capitalist farmers, indeed an emerging class of kulaks as well as growing differences between men and women[2] and between rural and urban dwellers. More recently, the debate has turned on the extent to which market forces should be allowed to guide the economy, and the degree to which the government should accommodate its policies to fit in with the International Monetary Fund.

While Nyerere's own writings emphasize equality, they have also shown concern with raising production in order to improve living standards. It has been argued that the expanding 'bureaucratic bourgeoisie' of the state was obliged to concur in this process, since its very existence as a class was threatened by the mounting economic disasters of the 1970s and 1980s. Many have suggested that as a result of the apparent failure of the peasants to grow more crops for sale, the state and its officials had increasing recourse to the methods formerly utilized by the colonial regime – threats and force.

Since Nyerere's departure from the Presidency in 1985, there has been further discussion about a number of major policies which characterized his regime. Should food production have been given so much priority and does this explain the poor performance of export crops (Sender and Smith 1990)? Would all production have improved if farmers had not been continually pressurized first into *ujamaa* villages, then nucleated villages? Would they have produced more if they had been offered better prices – paid regularly – or if there had been more to buy with the money they earned? Was the answer to efficient marketing of cash crops cooperatives or parastatals? These questions and many more have been raised in the literature, sometimes from a theoretical viewpoint, sometimes through empirical studies of particular areas of the country. The latter are of varying quality, and very few of them are anthropological – Abrahams (ed.) 1985 is a notable exception. In the body of this chapter, I shall consider the impact of the state and its policies upon one village over a twenty-year period and cite information collected during three fieldwork trips – mid-1960s, mid-1970s, and mid-1980s.

I am concerned first to show how policies from above are acted upon by local officials who are still, in many ways, like the proverbial headman in British Central Africa, behaving as they do because of the structural situation in which they find themselves. Many of them are dedicated and hard-working, but their implementation of government policies may nevertheless vary greatly from that intended by the policy-makers. Secondly, I discuss how the words and actions of local officials are perceived and interpreted by peasant villagers, most of whom are at the bottom of the socio-economic heap. Yet they are agents too – they have their ways of resisting policies they do not like, and taking advantage where they can. Finally, I consider the gap between rhetoric and reality. Social differentiation is growing, in spite of *ujamaa*/socialism – especially in terms of the relative wealth and well-being of men and women.

THE 1960s: *MAENDELEO* (DEVELOPMENT) AND *KUJITOLEA* (SELF-HELP)

In traditional African society, *everybody* was a worker. There was no other way of earning a living for the community . . . . I do not use the word 'worker' simply as opposed to 'employer' but also as opposed to 'loiterer' or 'idler'. . . . There is no such thing as socialism without work. . . .

The foundation, and the objective, of African Socialism is the Extended Family. The true African Socialist does not look on one class of men as his brethren and another as his natural enemies. . . . He rather regards *all* men as his brethren. That is why the first article of TANU's creed is 'BINADAMU WOTE NO NDUGU ZANGU NA AFRIKA NI MOJA' ('all human beings are my brothers and sisters and Africa is one').

'UJAMAA', then, or 'Familyhood' describes our Socialism. It is opposed to Capitalism . . . . and it is equally opposed to doctrinaire

Socialism. . . . We in Africa have no more need of being 'converted' to socialism than we have of being 'taught' democracy. Both are rooted in our own past.

(Nyerere 1966: 165)

It is therefore obvious that the foreign currency we shall use to pay back the loans used in the development of the urban areas will not come from the towns or the industries. Where, then, shall we get it from? We shall get it from the villages and from agriculture. . . .

Everybody wants development; but not everybody understands and accepts the basic requirements for development. The biggest requirement is hard work.

(Nyerere 1968: 242)

The site of my fieldwork has been the village of Kanga, situated in the north of Mafia, a large island lying off the Rufiji Delta some 80 miles south of Dar-es-Salaam. The southern part of the island was largely transformed into coconut and cashewnut plantations during the period of Arab rule of the coast and islands, utilizing slave labour imported from the interior. The north, however, where the soil was less suitable, remained the preserve of the indigenous peoples variously known as Washirazi, Wambwera, Wapokomo – all of them Muslim Swahili-speakers practising subsistence cultivation of crops such as rice (both wet and dry-land), millet, beans, sweet potatoes, and, more recently, maize. Coconuts, and to a lesser extent cashewnuts, were none the less introduced into the north during the German period and are today the chief cash crop for all Mafians. Coconut trees, unlike the bush land adjacent to the northern villages, are individually owned, may be bought and sold for cash, and are inherited according to Islamic law. Both women and men inherit trees from parents and spouses, but women inherit at only half the rate of men.

Kanga village in the mid-1960s had a population of around 1,000 people. Although, like most coastal villages, it was largely a nucleated settlement, some of its hamlets were spread out to the south and east. The village centre consisted of the dispensary, a couple of small shops, and a mosque, while the local primary school, which at that time had only classes 1–4, lay some distance to the north of the village, as it served both Kanga and its northern neighbour, Bweni. Kanga, like all other villages at that period, had a Village Development Committee (VDC) of some twenty members. It rapidly became plain to me that the workings of the VDC was a form of 'mosque politics'; membership was dominated almost entirely by those of higher socio-religious status – that is, Wambwera rather than Wapokomo – and particularly those closely related to the village Sheikh. The Chairman was a Gunya Sharif (descendant of the Prophet), the Diwan (representative to the District Council) was a cousin and brother-in-law to the Sheikh, and so on. Members of the Wapokomo ethnic group, on the other hand, especially those deeply involved in the spirit possession cults, were conspicuous by their absence on the VDC at this stage even though some of them, especially shamans, were among the wealthier members of the village (cf. Caplan 1975, chap. 7).

The political rhetoric of the Tanganyika Africa National Union (TANU) in this period was concerned with the values of hard work and self-reliance.[3] In speeches by Nyerere and other leaders, it was emphasized that Tanzania was a poor country whose main resource was its people. For socialism to be achieved, people had to rely on themselves instead of expecting handouts, whether from foreign governments or from the state. Accordingly, in each village there was at least one self-help project to which all able-bodied adult villagers were supposed to contribute labour. In Kanga, the project was the building of a teacher's house. Villagers were less than enthusiastic about this work, and heads of 'ten-house cells' were often hard put to it to recruit labour when it was their turn to do so.

Most of the exhortations for communal labour came from the government-appointed and salaried VEO (Village Executive Officer). For the first few months, the incumbent was a youth from the south of the island, and it was obvious that adult villagers resented being told what to do by one whom they regarded not only as an outsider, but a mere stripling at that. After a few months, this youth was replaced by another southerner, a much older man who had already served in this capacity in the south of the island. Far from improving matters, relations between the villagers and the VEO became even more seriously strained. The new official constantly called meetings at which he berated the villagers for their lack of understanding or enthusiasm for what the Government was trying to do, and threatened them with dire consequences. At one meeting, he called the people of Kanga, especially the women, 'ignorant' (wajinga – a serious insult).

After a few months, this official was transferred, much to everyone's relief, and a new VEO was brought in. This man was a Kanga villager, brother of the Diwan, and also a more tactful person. For most of the rest of my stay tensions were lessened, and the self-help project made some slight progress. Even this VEO, however, completely failed to persuade the villagers that another proposed self-help scheme – a communally culti-vated field of cotton – was a good idea. At meeting after meeting visiting government officials tried to convince the villagers who resisted on the grounds that cotton was a labour-intensive crop whose peaks coincided with peak labour demand for food crops. Furthermore, they declared themselves uninterested in communal cultivation.

It was apparent during much of this period that the way the villagers saw 'progress' (maendeleo) differed considerably from the view of government officials. When questioned (and I must confess here that I posed this question mainly to men during this period), people said that the major problems (mashida) in the village were first, the appalling state of the road, and secondly, the lack of water. The road, which runs from north to south linking the northern villages to the central large village of Kirongwe, and thence to the district capital Kilindoni, was and still is for much of its length a dirt track which becomes impassable in the rains. At that time, there was no regular transport north of Kirongwe; indeed, villagers usually walked across the mangrove flats, which took about two and a half hours. If they were lucky, they would get a lift on one of the few lorries which ran between Kirongwe and Kilindoni some 12 miles to the south. Kilindoni had a wide variety of (relatively) large shops selling cloth and other goods. It also housed the magistrate's court, the district hospital, and a variety of government offices, including that of the Area Commissioner, the most important government official on the island. For most of the northern villagers Kilindoni was their metropolis, and they needed better access to it. Most were convinced that if the road were improved, everything else in terms of development would follow. The second problem, the lack of water, was exacerbated by a drought during 1965, when many of the existing wells in the village ran dry. Women had to walk long distances to fetch water, often resorting to going in the cool of the night, when some wells which were dry during the day had a little water.

In the numerous meetings called when visiting government officials arrived in their Land Rovers, these problems were rarely addressed, and if raised by villagers, tended to be brushed aside by officials. The latter had their own agenda, which included communal cotton-growing, cleaning the coconut plantations and planting additional acreages of cassava. They also wanted the villagers to dig and use pit latrines and to send their children to school. None of these proposals met with much enthusiasm from the villagers. Some children, almost all boys, did attend school, but campaigns to persuade or coerce parents into sending girls were relatively unsuccessful. Parents argued that girls should be secluded at puberty and married off as soon as possible afterwards. The school attendance campaign waged by the VEO received a considerable set-back when the Headmaster was arraigned before the VDC, accused of beating a child too severely in a case brought by the boy's father. The campaign to dig pit latrines was totally unsuccessful – they were thought to be 'dirty' and 'smelly', although villagers usually told officials that they would do as requested provided that the Government supplied the materials. Efforts by the Agricultural Officer to persuade the villagers to grow more cassava did meet with somewhat more success. Cassava was recognised as both drought- and locust-resistant, and therefore a useful crop, although it was still thought locally to be inferior to rice, the preferred staple (to which it is indeed nutritionally much inferior). A large area of bush land was set aside by the Agricultural Officer, and a number of men began to cultivate fields there.

A difference, then, between pre- and post-colonial periods is that the penetration by the state into even such areas as northern Mafia, formerly considered to be a remote backwater, intensified after independence. During the mid-1960s, people were constantly being urged to pay their dues and join TANU. *'Tanu, Tanu yajenga nchi'* ('TANU, TANU is building the country') was heard not only on the radio but became the song most frequently sung at gatherings in the village. Despite this, people were in the main not too interested in TANU, regarding it as a part of 'government' (*serikali*). Moreover, there was a curious continuity about the campaigns run during the colonial period, and those of the post-colonial period. Not only were the exhortations similar, but so was the method of communication; namely, from the top down. So too was the response – to listen politely to the visiting officials, to try and squeeze some resources out of them if possible, and then to watch them go and return to business as usual.

During my year in Kanga I attended numerous meetings of the VDC, but I only once heard the villagers being asked to set their own agenda for *maendeleo*. This was at a meeting at which no non-villagers (except myself) were present. They came up with a list of things they thought were needed including (inevitably) improvements to the road and to the wells, and help with cultivation in the form of coconut seedlings and traps for pests like pigs and monkeys. They also wanted the school to be upgraded to Standard 5, and asked for a proper TANU office to be built. A letter was duly conveyed to the higher authorities by the VEO but it seemed to have little effect.

If villagers and officials did not always agree on what 'progress' really meant, there was even less agreement on how it should be achieved. For the officials it meant self-help, whereas for the villagers it meant the Government providing at least part of whatever was needed. Since government officials found it difficult to convince the villagers to provide labour for self-help schemes, they resorted to threats: usually to call in the next level of authority. One VEO told me frankly, 'My job is to frighten people', a statement which squared ill with contentions that TANU was the people's party.

People had their own ways of getting back at those in power. One was stubborn silence. Another was effusive agreement in meetings, and lack of action afterwards. But a third was purveying gossip about them, and this was disseminated particularly effectively in songs sung by women at public events as in the following examples:

Hogo la M. [the Area Commissioner] nilidhania kigoma, lakini imenitia homa.
I had thought that M's penis was only a little cassava tuber, but (in fact) it has given me a fever [a reference to his reputation for fornication].

Mwalimu S. kajitia kinuni, na yeye si mtwanzi.
Teacher S. [a TANU secretary on the island] has put himself at the mortar, but he is no pounder!

(Here the *double entendre* lies in the metaphor of pounding, which is both sexual and also refers to the exercise of power.)

Ulisema we utapiga kilemba, taifa nitajenga.
You said you would put on a turban and go and build the country. ('Putting on a turban' not only means 'taking up an office', it is also slang for 'having a man'. The song refers to a woman politician.)

THE 1970s: THE VILLAGIZATION CAMPAIGN

In a socialist Tanzania, then, our agricultural organization would be predominantly that of cooperatives living and working for the good of all. This means that most of our farming would be done by groups of people who live as a community and work as a community.
   . . . A nation of such village communities would be a socialist nation. For the essential element in them would be equality of all members of the community, and the members' self-government in all matters which concerned only their own affairs.
   . . . Yet socialist communities cannot be established by compulsion. . . . For a farmer may well be suspicious of the Government official or Party leader who comes to him and says, 'Do this'; he will be more likely to listen to the one who says 'This is a good thing to do for the following reasons and I am myself participating with my friends in doing it'. . . . [I]t is vital that whatever encouragement Government and TANU give to this type of scheme, they must not try to run it; they must help the people to run it themselves.
   . . . What is here being proposed is that we in Tanzania should move from being a nation of individual peasant producers who are gradually adopting the incentives and the ethics of the capitalist system. Instead we should gradually become a nation of ujamaa villages where the people cooperate directly in small groups and where these small groups cooperate together for joint enterprises.

(Nyerere 1968: 351–65)

I returned to Kanga nine years after my first fieldwork to find a number of small but significant changes in the village. Both the dispensary and the school had been upgraded somewhat, and almost all children, including girls, attended school on a more or less regular basis. Water was less of a problem, mainly due to more plentiful rainfall and not to any improvement in the village wells, but the road remained in its original state and people still complained that 'travel is our biggest problem'. However, the major clashes with the Government during this period came from the villagization policy. The Arusha Declaration in 1967 had urged the setting up of socialist villages in Tanzania, but progress towards this goal had been extremely slow. In 1973, TANU decided that it must be hastened, and during 1974, the villagization campaign (*Operation Sogeza*) was carried out. In the space of twelve months, a large part of Tanzania's rural population was moved from scattered settlements into nucleated villages of around 250 households each.

Kanga, in spite of being a nucleated coastal village, had, like other northern Mafian villages, gone through this process. People had been forced to move, sometimes long, sometimes short distances, and were vociferous in their complaints about the situation. At a meeting which was filmed by the camera team acompanying me on this occasion, visiting officials exhorted the villagers to accept the new situation and to rebuild their houses properly, instead of trying to return to their old house sites under the guise of building field huts (a common practice during the agricultural season). A second matter of concern to the officials on this occasion was the level of food production. Although it appeared that Kanga had suffered rather less from the villagization campaign than other areas, and food production had not dropped very much as a result, party and government representatives complained that their inspection of fields had shown that many people were not cultivating cassava. The Area Commissioner then spoke:

> From now on, if any able bodied man over 18 has not at least one acre of cassava, he will be sent to the school (chuo) which has just been opened at Kilombero to teach people who do not know how to cultivate to do so. From now on there will be no more fines – we know that people come and pay their fines and think nothing of it. Everyone who doesn't cultivate will get a month either at Kilombero or another similar place.

In short, then, villagers in Kanga, as elsewhere in the country, had not only been moved by force, but were also being told to increase their cultivation or face unpleasant consequences.

THE 1980s: PROGRESS/NO PROGRESS?

> The most fundamental principle of our socialist policy is equality among all citizens . . . equality means equal access to basic social services. It also means equality in decision making on matters of interest and importance to society. It means, above all, equality in personal incomes.
>
> . . . By providing free education Tanzania has made remarkable achievments in the struggle against one of our enemies, ignorance. At the time of independence in 1961, only 486,000 children went to primary school. Today 3.7 million go. In 1961, only 11,832 pupils were enrolled in public secondary school. In 1984, 40,617 were enrolled.
>
> . . . The number of hospitals has increased from 98 at independence to 149 today. The number of dispensaries has increased from 978 to more than 2,600. . . . Infant mortality has fallen from 225 babies for every 1,000

children born to 137. . . . In 1961, only about 11 per cent had access to clean water. Today it is estimated that over 10 million people or just under 50 per cent of the population have access to clean water within 400 metres of their homes.

The policy of socialism has enabled us to prevent the growth of gross inequalities in incomes between Tanzanians. For example in 1962, the ratio of urban personal income after tax was estimated to be 18.8 to 1. . . . In 1984 the ratio was 4.9 to 1. This progress towards equality in personal incomes has been made possible through deliberate fiscal, monetary and income policies. These policies have helped us to prevent the growth of a class society.

(President Mwinyi, Dec. 1986 at a
conference on the Arusha Declaration)

A further nine years on, when I returned again in 1985, it was to concentrate on precisely those areas in which Tanzania claimed to have made most progress – food production, health, and education. Tanzania was in a state of economic crisis. The oil price rises, the war with Uganda, and a series of droughts had played havoc with development planning. Inflation was astronomical and was accompanied by an acute shortage of all goods. In the village, people still complained about the problem of travel and the lack of good water, but they now spoke also about prices, making comparisons with the 'good old days'.

I asked if they did not think any progress had taken place – no, none they said. I persisted, suggesting education and health, much stressed in state rhetoric, as areas in which great improvements had taken place in the twenty years since I had first come to the village. What about the fact that all the children now attended the local school, which had been extended up to standard 6? Yes, but hardly any went to secondary school, and there were no jobs locally. I visited the local primary school on several occasions – absenteeism was rife and there were few textbooks or writing materials for those children present. The books they had often failed to reflect the reality of their lives. For example, basic readers introduced school children to Mr Juma, a farmer, and 'Mrs Juma', a 'housewife' who was pictured arranging flowers. The reality was that, as Nyerere had pointed out in the Arusha Declaration, village women worked very hard every day of their lives. Indeed, the fact that their children now attended school for most of the day increased their own work-loads, as older children were no longer available to help with younger ones, or be sent on errands.

What about the upgrading of the dispensary to clinic? People replied that often there were no medicines, and the staff 'did not always treat people properly'. The paramedic in the clinic was from Moshi, and was used to a somewhat higher standard of living than he found in northern

Mafia. He had an uneasy relationship with the villagers, and towards the end of my stay was arrested for selling medicines illegally.

Did they not think that the Mother and Child Health Centre which had been set up offered useful facilities? I sat in for several days at the MCH centre, staffed by a young midwife from the south of the island. She actually appeared to get on very well with village women, who were keen to bring their babies for weighing and for vaccinations and arrived in large numbers. But throughout the two months of my stay there was no kerosene for the clinic fridge, and therefore no drugs requiring this facility could be stored, including vaccinations. Many women, who had come from neighbouring villages carrying heavy toddlers, were angry to find that they could not get them vaccinated when they arrived.

When I attended a meeting called to hear two visiting Health Officers, I discovered that not much had changed in the way state functionaries communicated with villagers. Unusually, it was attended by a handful of women. They had been specially summoned and sat on the side, almost too far away to hear the speeches, which were in any case almost identical to ones the villagers and I had been hearing for the past twenty years. The Health Officer intoned:

> There has been a lot of diarrhoea and vomiting, and this is not the first time. There are three reasons: people don't use latrines – there are 300 houses here and only 3 latrines – they don't boil drinking water, and they don't clear the weeds and brush from around their houses. Nor do they always wash their hands before eating.

The villagers replied that they needed help with materials to carry out the officials' instructions, but this was ignored. As the meeting continued, the villagers were harangued by their village manager, their paramedic, and the two visiting health officers. No one asked for their views of the situation, they were simply told what to do, until finally the villagers' response became a mixture of apparent acquiescence and annoyance:

Villager: Let's close the meeting. We will dig latrines, and ask the women to clear around the houses, and we will send our children to the clinic . . . let's close the meeting.

Health Officer: There is another problem – people don't take their children to be vaccinated. . . . You women – what about taking your children to the clinic for vaccinations?

The women did not respond at all. Nobody mentioned that the clinic had been without kerosene for the fridge, and therefore without vaccine for months. The men may well not have known this, and the women would not speak in public.

SOCIALISM FOR WHOM? GENDER AND 'DEVELOPMENT'

It would be appropriate to ask our farmers, especially the men, how many hours a week and how many weeks a year they work. Many do not even work for half as many hours as the wage-earner does. The truth is that in the villages, the women work very hard. At times they work for 12 or 14 hours per day. They even work on Sundays and public holidays. Women who live in the villages work harder than anybody else in Tanzania. But the men who live in villages (and some of the women in towns) are on leave for half of their life.

(Nyerere 1968: 244–5)

Although the cultivation of cassava had continued to expand, it was apparent that by the 1980s locally grown food supplies had dropped, and people were more reliant upon purchasing to meet their daily needs. Vagaries of the weather aside, a major reason for this was the fact that men were playing even less part in subsistence farming than before, and were concentrating their energies on planting coconut trees. Coconuts were no longer sold to the cooperatives, nor was copra being produced. Instead, nuts were exported by dhow directly to Dar-es-Salaam, where they fetched high prices in the local markets. Men were not only planting new trees themselves as fast as they could, they were even hiring the labour of upcountry immigrants to so so. This situation had increased the local wealth disparities between women and men – it was male labour that was replaced by hired labour, and it was men who were likely to profit from increased cash cropping. At the same time, male labour was withdrawn from subsistence production, leaving women with yet heavier workloads.

In spite of these conditions, the local branch of the UWT (Tanzania Women's Organization), organized by the (male) village manager (*Katibu Kata*), had made more attempts to persuade the women to cultivate communally. Although the women's communal field had not been at all successful the previous year, the *Katibu Kata* called a meeting of the village women:

Manager:	What about the cassava field? We must plan for the rains. We will use the same field as last year.
Chairwoman of UWT:	Let those who want to come, come, and I will be among them.
Manager:	We need a committee for this.
Women:	We'll just go, even if there are only a few of us.
Manager:	No, *all* women must turn up on Wednesday.
Chairwoman:	Those who want to can come and those who don't . . .
Manager:	Never mind that, no more democracy, *everyone* come at 8 a.m.

Woman:	So that's a government decree? Then we'll *have* to go.
Manager:	Now we're going to start afresh. Never mind who was in last year. Let's have someone from each area to spread the word. I want you all here at 8 a.m. with your bill-hooks and hoes. You won't find any kohl or face powder there!
Women (indignantly):	You think we're using make-up at this time of year? But if we get access to sweet potato seeds, we'll have to give that priority over cassava.
Manager (resignedly):	Better let ten women who have no work come than none at all.
Women (angrily):	*Are* there are any women who don't have work?

In this dialogue, the Manager attempts to impose on the women not only an idea (communal organization), but also a schema for organizing it (a committee), and a precise timetable. The women attempt to point out that it should be voluntary, and that cassava cultivation, which is not very seasonal, is less important than planting sweet potatoes, which depends upon the short rains, but he is not listening; indeed, he belittles them by suggesting that their main concern is their make-up. Thus the main function of this officially supported women's organization seemed to be to extract yet more work out of women, and to impose another agenda on them. It is no wonder that they resisted involvement in such schemes.[4]

Another scheme in which women signally refused to participate involved the acquisition of a lorry by Kanga village, although, in this case, most men were enthusiastic. I first heard about this project when I arrived in Dar-es-Salaam in 1985 and visited some Kangans living there. A number of other villagers appeared who were visiting the capital to negotiate with the island's MP and other officials about the purchase of a British Leyland lorry. I was amazed that the villagers could contemplate raising the kind of money involved (£18,000). Soon afterwards I was back in the village, where a meeting was called to discuss this question. The Mafia MP, who was holding the funds, had come to collect the balance of about £6,000. He reported that out of the 629 adults in the village, only 182 people had so far contributed and few of these were women:

| Mafia MP: | The women are not in there. Yet they have the ability (*nguvu*). All the women here make mats and sell raffia – I counted three loads of it just now. And many women buy 'Mombasa' *kanga* at 900 shillings each. Maybe some can't afford to contribute, but many could find ways of raising the money. The women in Baleni (another village) gave 50,000 shillings. If 44 women from that village can pay, others here could too. And where are the women anyway? |

| | I wanted them to come to this meeting. Are they looking after the fields or what? |
| *Villager*: | They are harvesting. |

It was finally decided to adopt the suggestion made originally by the MP. People who had cattle would offer them instead of cash, so that they could be slaughtered and the meat sold. For the rest of my stay, several animals a week were butchered – a process which took most of the day, and occupied the time of a large number of men while the women continued their harvesting. The money was finally raised, but largely without the participation of the women. Soon after my departure, the lorry was ordered.

Why was there such a divergence of interests between men and women in this matter? At first I thought that the men's desire for a lorry was to bring the 'cargo' of development to the village. This was partly true, but I later realized that they did not want the lorry so much in order to bring in goods as to get themselves to the District capital. Their main desire was to be able to visit the government offices, the shops, the law court, and the hospital. They wanted to be able to participate more fully in the political life there, to go and transact business themselves, rather than have to wait passively for the state to intervene in their lives in the form of visiting officials. In this respect, having a lorry and being mobile meant a diminution of the inequality between themselves and government officials.

Women, on the other hand, were much less interested in acquiring a lorry because they did not travel nearly as much as men. They were usually too busy, and they rarely had the cash for fares. Few of them had sufficient cash to buy shares in the lorry, a project about which they had not been consulted since they were not invited to attend village meetings.

CONCLUSION

This chapter covers two decades of Tanzanian history in which some form of socialist ideology was dominant at the state level. What effect has this ideology and the policies associated with it had on one village in a relatively remote area?

Villagers have undoubtedly benefited from improved health and educational facilities, but not to the extent which they had hoped and which they felt had been promised. More villagers are now involved in local government, but beyond the village level people still experience the government as 'them' not 'us', as instructions not consultation. Paradoxically, then, in spite of the rhetoric of socialism in the post-independence era, continuities exist between this and the period of colonial rule in terms of the methods of communication, the state's requirements of the peasants, and the structural position of party/state bureaucrats. The socialist state in

Tanzania did not succeed in changing the top-down flow of information and decision-making. Nor did the state tackle increasing gender asymmetry very seriously. The gap between men and women in wealth, cash income, work-load/leisure, education, and morbidity has widened (Caplan 1989). Women not only remain excluded from village government, but also the organization which is supposed to represent their interests is seen, with some justice, as an agent of government, designed to extract from them yet more in terms of work and money.

So did the fact that Tanzania chose to practise a form of socialism make any difference? Much depends upon the basis for comparison. People in northern Mafia compare their standard of living today with that of ten, twenty, or thirty years ago, particularly in terms of prices, and complain. They compare what they have with what they had hoped to have, or what they feel they were promised by independence and *ujamaa*, and find it lacking. We, however, may compare Tanzania with other parts of Africa, ravaged by war and famine, and decide that it has not, after all, done too badly. Tanzanian socialism has not achieved equality, but there is less inequality than in most other African countries. Furthermore, throughout the post-colonial period, there has been reasonably open, even critical debate about government policies. We might even conclude that what was needed was more, rather than less socialism.

NOTES

1 The following is a small (and rather arbitrary) selection of the material available on these debates: Cliffe and Saul 1972; Coulson 1979 and 1982; Fortmann 1980; Hyden 1980; Kahama *et al.* 1986; Kim *et al.* 1979; Mwansasu and Pratt 1979; Raikes 1978; Shivji 1976; Von Freyhold 1979; Yeager 1989.
2 The most important source for gender relations in Tanzania is Mascarenhas and Mbilinyi 1983. Other useful references are Oomin-Myin 1981; Swantz 1985; and Vuorela 1987.
3 At the time of my first fieldwork, begun in 1965, Tanzania had been independent for only a few years and the union with Zanzibar was only twelve months old. The respective ruling parties of each, however, remained separate – TANU for the mainland, and the ASP (Afro-Shirazi Party) for the islands – until 1977.
4 See Geiger 1982 for further information on the UWT.

REFERENCES

Abrahams, R. (ed.) (1985) *Villagers, Villages and the State in Modern Tanzania*, Cambridge: Cambridge African Studies Centre Monograph 4.
Caplan, A.P. (1975) *Choice and Constraint in a Swahili Community*, Oxford: IAI/OUP.
—— (1982) 'Development policies in Tanzania: some implications for women', in N. Nelson (ed.) *African Women in the Development Process*, London: Frank Cass, 1982, pp. 98–108.
—— (1989) 'Perceptions of gender stratification', *Africa* 59: 196–208.

Cliffe, L. and Saul, J.S. (1972) *Socialism in Tanzania*, Nairobi: East African Publishing House.

Coulson, A. (1979) *African Socialism in Practice: The Tanzanian Experience*, Nottingham: Spokesman Press.

—— (1982) *Tanzania: A Political Economy*, Oxford: Clarendon Press.

Fortmann, L. (1980) *Peasants, Officials and Participation in Rural Tanzania: Experience with Villagization and Decentralization*, Ithaca, NY: Cornell University (mimeo).

Freyhold, M. von (1979) *Ujamaa Villages in Tanzania: Analysis of a Social Experiment*, London: Heinemann.

Geiger, S. (1982) 'Umoja wa Wanawake and the needs of the rural poor', *African Studies Review*, XXV (2 and 3): 45–65.

Hodd, M. (ed.) (1988) *Tanzania after Nyerere*, London and New York: Pinter Publishers.

Hyden, G. (1980) *Beyond Ujamaa in Tanzania: Underdevelopment and an Uncaptured Peasantry*, London: Heinemann.

Kahama, C.G., Maliyamkono, T.L. and Wells, S. (1986) *The Challenge for Tanzania's Economy*, London and Dar-es-Salaam: James Currey, Heinemann, and Tanzania Publishing House.

Kim, S., Mabeke, R.B. and Schultheis, M.J. (1979) *Papers on the Political Economy of Tanzania*, London: Heinemann.

Mascarenhas, O. and Mbilinyi, M. (1983) *Women in Tanzania: An Analytical Bibliography*, Uppsala and Stockholm: Scandinavian Institute of African Studies and SIDA.

Mwansasu, B.U. and Pratt, C. (1979) *Towards Socialism in Tanzania*, Toronto: University of Toronto Press.

Oomin-Myin, M.A. (1981) *Involvement of Rural Women on Village Development in Tanzania: A Case Study in Morogoro District*, University of Dar-es-Salaam (mimeo).

Nyerere, J.K. (1966) 'Ujamaa – the basis of African Socialism 1962', in J.K. Nyerere, *Freedom and Unity: Uhuru na Umoja*, Oxford: Oxford University Press.

—— (1968) 'The Arusha Declaration, 1967' and 'Ujamaa Vijijini: Socialism and Rural Development 1967', both in Nyerere *Freedom and Socialism: Uhuru na Ujamaa*, Oxford: Oxford University Press.

Raikes, P. (1978) 'Rural differentiation and class-formation in Tanzania', *Journal of Peasant Studies*, 5(3): 285–325.

Sender, J. and Smith, S. (1990) *Poverty, Class and Gender in Rural Africa: A Tanzanian Case Study*, London and New York: Routledge.

Shivji, I. (1976) *Class Struggles in Tanzania*, London: Heinemann.

Swantz, M.L. (1985) *Women in Development, a Creative Role Denied? The Case of Tanzania*, London and New York: St Martin's Press, Hurst & Co.

Vuorela, U. (1987) *The Women's Question and the Modes of Human Reproduction: An Analysis of a Tanzanian Village*, Helsinki: Finnish Society for Development Studies.

Yeager, R. (1989) *Tanzania: An African Experiment*, Boulder, CO: Westview Press.

Chapter 5

Party, bureaucracy, and grassroots initiatives in a socialist state

The case of Sungusungu village vigilantes in Tanzania

Ray Abrahams and Sufian Bukurura[1]

Socialism has many faces. At the ideological level, it is clearly a system for the sharing of control and ownership of a society's resources, and this is commonly taken also to imply a substantial degree of sharing in policy-making and the management of public affairs. At the level of action, this ideal of popular participation has been often tempered by a number of real or asserted practical constraints. In many socialist regimes, 'socialism from above', sometimes in quite oppressive forms, has been deemed necessary for the sake of efficiency and, at least temporarily, for the control and/or re-education of recalcitrant and unenthusiastic groups still burdened by their bourgeois aspirations.

At a structural level, government under such regimes frequently involves a readily recognizable and to some extent predictable combination of institutions. The institutions themselves are found in many other systems, and it is the form of their mixture which is special. A common pattern includes a single party, which may be varyingly populist or elitist, a governmental and bureaucratic structure, and an elected chamber. There is also typically a military whose role varies greatly from one period and one country to another. There is commonly a substantial overlap between the party leadership and that of other institutions, and this can sometimes make it difficult to distinguish them in practice, but there are also tendencies to divisions of interest and often struggles for power between them. The party tends to assert the ideology of the system, and demand its dominance in the formulation and implementation of policy. Governmental staff and bureaucrats are likely to be much more sensitive to practicalities of administration and to the demands of their own inherited norms and *modus operandi*.[2] They are also likely to be the most highly educated element in the system. An elected chamber may perhaps be expected to exhibit a special respect for the demands of an electorate, but this is not always the case, and such a chamber rarely has the same amount of power and influence as the other major structures we have mentioned. Of course, the ideals of the system stress that all the organs we have mentioned should work together for the enhancement of the interests of the people as a whole, but just as this does not prevent their quarrelling among themselves, it also often fails to stop their using domination and control as the main media of public service.

This chapter deals with a development in Tanzania which highlights some of the paradoxes and contradictions in a system of this sort. It is more directly concerned with the polity than the economy of socialist Tanzania. Much of the general configuration of a socialist regime as outlined above applies to the Tanzanian case. Since the early years of independence, Tanzania has been a single-party state whose stated aim has been the development of socialism and participatory democracy.[3] Over the years, the party leadership has strongly asserted its constitutional predominance, often at the expense of the elected Parliament. Early military unrest was suppressed, and since then there has been little overt trouble from that quarter. Party and bureaucracy have had an uneasy relationship, which, as we shall see, is sometimes difficult to unravel.

At the same time, the country also reveals several special features which are closely connected with objective and subjective elements of its history as an East African country. A linked series of divisions between centre and periphery, town and country, party and governmental leadership and populace, and national and local culture have all had an important role in shaping Tanzanian society. In addition, the vision of an African socialism developed by its first President, Julius Nyerere, has also been extremely influential, and indeed his influence has spread well beyond the country's own immediate boundaries. As has been described in several publications, this vision has involved a substantial misreading of many features of traditional African society, but this does not mean that it has simply been a 'mystifying' charter for manipulation and control. It has served – if not always successfully – to support the view that socialism can be achieved in Tanzania without violent imposition from above or violent revolution from below, and it has more generally stressed the idea, which again has not always been honoured, that the country's villagers possess a range of social and cultural resources which the state needs to treat with respect.[4]

THE RISE OF SUNGUSUNGU

The main ethnographic background to the present chapter has been presented in a number of earlier publications (Abrahams 1967; 1981; 1987; 1989). Sungusungu is a system of village (and more recently also urban) vigilante groups. It started in the early 1980s as a grassroots response to perceived high levels of disorder in the Nyamwezi and Sukuma area, where there is a long history of many forms of neighbourhood collaboration. The groups were first established in a few villages on the edges of Kahama, Nzega, and Shinyanga Districts, and new ones were then rapidly founded throughout the area and eventually well beyond its boundaries, including in some towns. They initially arose to combat increasing levels of well-armed brigandage and cattle theft, and there has also been an anti-witchcraft element in their activities in some villages. The groups typically consist of all the able-bodied men within a community, and in some places there is also a women's wing. Members are armed with whistles which can only be used in an emergency, and there are very heavy penalties against those failing to respond and against false alarms. The whistling apparently spreads very rapidly over wide areas from one village to another, so that rustlers and others are quite likely to be intercepted as they flee. A remarkable feature of the groups has been their determination – with some very recent exceptions – to rely only on 'traditional' weaponry; namely, bows and (poisoned) arrows, as opposed to firearms. This has probably been crucial for their ability to develop alongside formal party and state institutions, despite considerable disquiet about them in some quarters. They appear to have been successful in restoring a good level of security and order to the countryside, though this has sometimes been achieved at the cost of rough justice and the harassment and alleged torture and murder of some suspects. Although such behaviour has worried the authorities, within their own communities the groups have enjoyed wide, if not necessarily universal, support, since those they have attacked are generally perceived as criminals. Recently, the system has been formally incorporated by legislation into the framework of the country's law enforcement system. We shall discuss some aspects of this legislation later in the chapter. It may be noted here, however, that the legal recognition and incorporation of the Sungusungu vigilante groups has followed several years of argument about their status and much understandable anxiety about the challenges which they appear to pose to the authority and legitimacy of the state's own machinery of law and order. In his 1987 paper, Abrahams noted briefly that the response to the groups' activities from party leaders tended to be more supportive than that of bureaucracy and law enforcement agencies. This difference of response and the problems of its interpretation form a main focus of this chapter.

PARTY AND BUREAUCRACY

In trying to understand the differences between the responses of the party and those of other agencies to Sungusungu, it seems useful to consider elements of ideology and competition in the situation. At the level of ideology, the party – under Nyerere's leadership – has clearly been committed to the creation and development of a socialist participatory democracy. The other institutions of the system, including the bureaucracy, are perceived from this vantage point as subordinate to that end, and bureaucratic tendencies to hinder such developments have received sharp criticism on a number of occasions beyond the confines of the present issue.

It is therefore not surprising that a development like Sungusungu should have some appeal for party leaders. It has been a genuinely grassroots initiative, and its aim in general terms – of improving communal security and well-being through an attack on criminals who seek wealth and power at the expense of others – is admirable, even though not everyone would agree about the detailed definition of this task.

Nyerere himself has been one of the most outspoken supporters of the new development. While still President (and also chairman of the party), he described the groups as a 'revolutionary force' within the villages which should be encouraged, and not harassed, by bureaucracy. A number of group members had been arrested for their activities and he said that they should be released. Later, in 1986, while still chairman but no longer President, he condemned continuing attempts to prosecute them. He was reported to have said that the law under which they were charged was a bad law since it worked against the people's interests and created conflict between them and the state, and he is also said to have argued that the groups were in a better position than the police and courts to know the identity of thieves and other criminals. In comparable vein, the party's secretary-general, Rashidi Kawawa, spoke warmly of the groups in 1983 and again in early 1984 at a national youth rally. Like Nyerere, he described them as a revolutionary force voluntarily working for the safety and security of their communities, and he encouraged young people every-where to follow their example. Significantly, however, he described the groups – by no means wholly accurately – as working under the guidance of the party. 'Sungusungu are', he claimed, 'young CCM members who are fulfilling the party's call for mass action to maintain "security".'

As the above implies, some of the most overt hostility to the groups was displayed by police and courts. Many group members were prosecuted, and some were initially condemned to death for their more violent actions. Early police statements described the groups as unlawful and bent on harassing and torturing people. As Abrahams (1987) has described, it is clear that the groups constituted a serious criticism of and competitive threat to these established instruments of law and order. Villagers were often overtly cynical about the ability and even the will of police and courts to combat cattle theft and other rural crime, and their perceived failure to do so was undoubtedly a major stimulus to the establishment of the groups. It is initially tempting to interpret the situation mainly in this light. Party ideology can be seen as struggling along well-worn tracks (cf. TANU *Party Guidelines* 1971) against the inefficiency of a bureaucratic legal system which is anxious to retain its own monopoly of policing power and juris-diction.

It seems clear that this was a major element in the situation, but there was also much more to it than this. First, the element of competition was by no means wholly lacking from party responses. This was most clear at the ward and village levels, where local party leaders complained quite early on that the groups were undermining their authority. One issue here was the adoption of the title *'ntemi'* (chief) by the local leaders of the groups, since this was interpreted (quite wrongly) as an attempt to resuscitate traditional chiefship in the area. Another source of contention had been an initial decision by the groups to describe themselves as *'Chama cha busalama'* or Security *'chama'*. The word *'chama'* is the standard Swahili term for any form of association, but it is also the normal word for *'party'*, and this appears to have caused anxiety to local leaders. The worry also seems to have been shared at higher levels, and it appears to have formed part of the background to Kawawa's above-quoted insistence that Sungusungu and the party were one in both personnel and spirit.

It would also clearly be mistaken to ignore ideological elements in the opposition to the groups. The respect for 'due process' is important here, and most party leaders themselves seem to have been less willing than their chairman to cast this to the winds in their positive pronouncements on the groups. The need to collaborate in an ordered way with police and courts was often stressed by them, and it is not altogether surprising if members of the legal profession, and at least some of the police, were strongly committed to the maintenance of such norms in themselves rather than as a source simply of their own power and authority. The roots of such commitment are at least in part 'colonial', and it is arguable that, for better or for worse, this is part of a more general link which persists between the legal worlds of Tanzania and Britain. The attitudes in question are interestingly apparent in a student dissertation on the Sungusungu groups, written by two Tanzanian lawyers (Sabasaba and Rweyemamu 1984). Their main focus is straightforwardly the formal legality or illegality of the groups' actvities. They argue, plausibly enough, that the groups were in fact illegal at the time of writing, and they are highly critical on these grounds of party support for them. They also express strong disapproval of the methods used by groups to detect and interrogate their suspects. At the same time, they show little interest in the more practical issues of effective crime prevention, which gave rise to the groups' establishment, and they are not fired with any enthusiasm for the element of grassroots initiative which clearly caught Nyerere's imagination and which fitted well with party guidelines on security. It should of course be recalled here that a number of people seem to have died violently at the groups' hands, and that only some of these were cattle rustlers caught red-handed. Others included individuals suspected of such thievery, and also some suspected witches.

So far, we have tried to document in outline a broad contrast between party and what we might loosely call 'bureaucratic' or 'administrative' approaches to the development of Sungusungu. We have argued that there was an ideological element in both responses. The party line stressed the importance of popular participation in political life, and the bureaucrats and law enforcement agencies stressed the importance of legality and due process. In both cases also, the groups' activities were seen to involve an element of competition to the formal structures of the state. The threat to the police and the judiciary was most immediate and obvious, since it highlighted their failure to solve a series of pressing law and order problems. At the same time it is arguable that the threat to the party was also serious though less immediately critical. Party membership was much less widespread than leaders' rhetoric suggested, and Sungusungu – with its inclusive and enthusiastic membership – seemed in danger of providing an enriched sense of community sentiment and commitment from below which the party had tried but failed to generate from above. One interesting aspect of this was the wildfire success of Sungusungu as opposed to the earlier failure of party-led 'people's militia' units to engender popular participation and support.

Before moving away from the question of the ideological components in the situation, it is necessary to add a third such element to the analysis. This is of course the value system of the Sungusungu members. This can only be sketched in the broadest brush-strokes here, and much of it has been documented in detail elsewhere (cf. Abrahams 1981; 1987; 1989). The existence of a gap between such local interests and values and those of the state extends well beyond the present setting of a socialist Tanzania, and it has been argued that such a gap has, in one form or another, been a persistent feature of relations between Nyamwezi villagers and their various pre-colonial, colonial, and post-colonial rulers (Abrahams 1989). The world of Nyamwezi villagers has of course been deeply influenced by government and the state, but it also has its own internal driving force. It is a world of 'ordinary' people concerned to secure the health, and the moral and material prosperity of themselves, their families, and at times their neighbours, against real and culturally constructed enemies. For them, all governments, despite variations, tend to be above and outside many of their everyday concerns, and the legitimacy of government is to a considerable degree dependent upon its ability to satisfy their needs. This ability is, moreover, typically measured against the substantial fund of organizational skills which the people themselves possess in many different spheres of life, including that of law and order maintenance.

FROM VILLAGERS' RESPONSE TO NATIONAL INSTITUTION

Sungusungu, as a Nyamwezi and Sukuma village system, still persists in 1991. From its beginnings as a grassroots reaction to real and perceived deterioration in the broad area of 'law and order', it has developed into a legally recognized organization which has spread to several other areas, including major towns. Legislation was passed in 1989 recognizing the groups, and conferring on them powers of arrest equal to those of the police constabulary. The law provides for compensation for them for injury arising in the course of duty, and the Minister of Home Affairs is entitled to introduce regulations from time to time to ensure the proper functioning of the system. All this is not without its problems. In Dar-es-Salaam, for example, regular night-watches are kept, and each household has to provide a member to join such watches on a rota basis. Some people complain that it is hard to take part in activities of this sort, and then go on to do a day's work afterwards. Others complain of harassment by Sungusungu groups when moving after dark on perfectly legitimate business. The groups, both rural and urban, are, however, supposed to receive training, and they are also supposed to collaborate fully with the police and courts. It is hoped that this will permit them to work effectively while limiting the damage which can all too easily arise through over-enthusiasm.

How effectively the system will continue to persist and satisfy the needs of villagers is hard to say. Much will depend on how far they are able to continue their activities without undue interference, and it seems possible – especially with the recent relaxation of control over settlement patterns – that many village-level activities will pass unnoticed by officialdom. In 1987, Abrahams suggested that enthusiasm would be likely to wane if the government hijacked the system. There are some subsequent reports supporting this, but a recent brief visit to northern Unyamwezi suggests that the groups are still alive and well in their home area at village level and that collaboration with the police and courts so far presents few problems.[5]

The development of Sungusungu from village-level to national institution raises several issues for an understanding of the Tanzanian polity. First, it is important to recognize that there was nothing automatic about the persistence of the system through the 1980s. There were many cries from local party officials, and serious attempts by police and courts to suppress the new development, and it seems clear that Nyerere's and others' strongly populist pronouncements on the groups, and his intervention in the legal process of their prosecution in some cases, were of vital importance. In this case at least, the dominant position of the party *vis-à-vis* bureaucracy, which is an ideal feature of the Tanzanian system, has been confirmed. At the same time, it is also clear, as we have noted earlier, that the groups' own insistence from the start upon using only 'traditional weaponry' was a critical survival aid. This allowed them and their allies to argue that they were a traditional cultural and social phenomenon, rather than a subversive 'modern' political form, and it seems to have effectively blurred the debate about their legal status until legislation was eventually promised by the Attorney-General in 1987 and then passed in 1989.

The world of political motivation is, of course, notoriously an uncertain one, and it would be excessively naïve to see the process of incorporation of Sungusungu as simply the realization of a populist ideal. Government and party officials, for example, clearly wished to take pragmatic advantage of the new development in the mid-eighties when they called upon the groups to collect taxes in the villages and to come into towns like Mwanza and Tabora to seek out violent criminals and black marketeers. And there cannot be any serious doubt that both party and bureaucracy were anxious ultimately to bring the groups under control. It would seem to be unnecessarily cynical to suggest a conspiracy between them, of the hard and soft policeman kind, but it is clear that once assimilation and control rather than abolition began to emerge out of the political process as the most practical possibility for control, all sides began to move to implement that aim.

In presenting the above material, we have been conscious of the problem of determining how much of it is special to a 'socialist society'. Vigilantism is a widespread phenomenon both spatially and historically, and its milder forms – of suburban neighbourhood watch or rural farm watch – coexist reasonably amicably with the police and courts of numerous countries, including Britain. The problems of political control from above, and the potential for conflict between 'due process' and effective 'crime prevention', emerge in a wide range of political and social settings. Also the kind of cultural diversity and local-level specificity of Tanzania is a common feature of all sorts of 'new nations'. None the less, it does seem that a vital ingredient in the present case has been the influential and positive ideological reaction of ex-President Nyerere and his close party associates, such as Kawawa, to the groups' emergence. Without this, the chances of a violent confrontation between them and the state, and of their ultimate suppression, appear likely to have been much greater. It may be noted here that such a possibility was foreseen for the Tanzanian system in more general terms by Ghai (1976: 80), who noted that a broad ideological orientation may be more adaptive in situations of rapid change than a rigid and narrowly defined rule structure.[6]

There are also further features of the situation which seem worth a mention here, though it is difficult at this stage of our knowledge to pronounce authoritatively on them. No evidence exists at present to suggest that Sungusungu activities represent the kinds of political and/or economic factions and divisions with which vigilantism seems to be connected in countries such as Kenya and South Africa, or in some of its American manifestations.[7] The cleavages which seem so far to be significant are those between men and women (especially in the field of witchcraft), between old and young (in matters of village discipline and perhaps too in witchcraft accusations), and more generally between ordinary, law-abiding villagers and cattle thieves and other criminals. Too little is known about the background of such thieves and brigands to pronounce upon the social and economic roots of their activities. There is little to suggest at present that they fit easily within the category of 'social bandit'.[8] Some of them seem likely to be veterans of the Uganda war, and others have almost certainly obtained firearms from such veterans, but detailed life histories are not yet available. One hypothesis might be that they represent the extreme edge of the criminality of the 1970s which appears to have been generated by attempts to maintain a centrally controlled economy in unfavourable conditions – both internal and external to the country – and whose milder forms consisted of black-marketeering, smuggling, and the like. If this were so, and it may well not be the case, it becomes conceivable that, in addition to the positive response which Sungusungu groups have received from party leaders, both their broad popular base and the cattle thieves and brigands they arose to combat are to some degree the product of the same 'socialist' system.

NOTES

1 This is a collaborative essay which arises from convergent research interests. Ray Abrahams' investigations of the groups concerned form part of his long-term study of Nyamwezi local-level politics and dispute settlement. Sufian Bukurura is an academic lawyer, now training for a Ph.D. in social anthropology, whose interest in the groups was first aroused by the challenge they posed to the formal Tanzanian legal system.
2 There are, of course, also some socialist systems where the party itself has become highly bureaucratized.
3 TANU (Tanganyika African National Union) was the ruling party in mainland Tanzania until 1977, when it joined with Zanzibar's Afro-Shirazi Party to form the CCM (*Chama cha Mapinduzi* – i.e., Revolutionary Party), which has remained in power since then. The possibility of developing a multi-party system in the country is now under consideration.
4 The most obvious failure to live up to these ideals was the forceful implementation of the villagization programme in the 1970s. Cf. Abrahams (1981) for a discussion of this in the Nyamwezi area.
5 A more detailed study of the situation is planned by Bukurura in 1991–92.
6 This comment is reminiscent of Gluckman's (1955) analysis of adaptive certainty in broad legal principles.
7 In Kenya there seems to have been a strong Kanu connection (cf. *Sunday Nation*, 3 Aug. 1986: 13), and in South Africa we have in mind the division between 'vigilantes' and ANC supporting 'comrades'. For America, see Brown (1975).
8 Cf. Abrahams (1987: 196). For 'social bandits' in Africa, cf. Heald (1986), who discusses a connection with vigilantism, and also papers by Austen and others in Crummey (ed.) (1986).

REFERENCES

Abrahams, R. (1967) *The Political Organisation of Unyamwezi*, Cambridge: Cambridge University Press.
—— (1981) *The Nyamwezi Today*, Cambridge: Cambridge University Press.
—— (1987) 'Sungusungu: village vigilante groups in Tanzania', *African Affairs*, 86: 179–96.
—— (1989) 'Law and order and the state in the Nyamwezi and Sukuma area of Tanzania', *Africa*, 59: 356–70.

Brown, R.M. (1975) *Strain of Violence*, New York: Oxford University Press.

Crummey, D. (ed.) (1986) *Banditry, Rebellion and Social Protest in Africa*, London: James Curry.

Ghai, Y.P. (1976) 'Notes towards a theory of law and ideology: Tanzanian perspectives', *African Law Studies*, 13: 31–105.

Gluckman, M. (1955) *The Judicial Process among the Barotse of Northern Rhodesia*, Manchester: Manchester University Press.

Heald, S. (1986) 'Mafias in Africa: the rise of drinking companies and vigilante groups in Bugisu, Uganda', *Africa*, 56: 446–67.

Sabasaba, M. and Rweyemamu, N. (1984) *Exercise of Punitive Powers outside the Judicial Process in Tanzania*, Unpublished LL.B. dissertation, Dar-es-Salaam.

TANU (1971) *Party Guidelines*, Dar-es-Salaam.

Chapter 6

Ambiguities and contradictions in the political management of culture in Zimbabwe's reversed transition to socialism

A.P. Cheater[1]

Socialism, a Western political ideology emphasizing popular democracy and equality, in practice has nowhere yet achieved its ideals. Monolithic and modernizing, modelled on the Soviet experience as prototype, practical socialist agendas in many different countries tried with varying degrees of success to replace allegedly undemocratic and inegalitarian 'traditional cultures' (see, for example, Binns 1979, 1980; Lane 1981). Only in the post-Mao period did the People's Republic of China, in the context of economic reform, declare its intention to create 'socialism with Chinese characteristics', and ease its past onslaught against 'feudal superstition' (Feuchtwang in press; Cheater 1991a).

In Mozambique in the 1960s, as Lan (1985: 208) notes, both FRELIMO and ZANLA (the military wing of the Zimbabwe African National Union, ZANU), as African socialist militants fighting colonialism, accepted the orthodox line that traditional religious beliefs and practices were incompatible with scientific socialism. But later, in the 1970s, and like the Rhodesian Government, ZANLA was to find the spirit mediums (*zvikiro*) useful to its cause, and sought to recruit as many as possible. Those who refused, like many of the chiefs and those identified as witches, were killed as 'sell-outs' (*vatengesi*: Lan 1985: 195). Beliefs in ancestral protection were also common among the ZANLA guerrillas (Lan 1985: xv). After the war, among those who sought ritual cleansing were fighters who had transgressed traditional religious restraints on killing (Reynolds 1990).

The use of spirit mediums in Zimbabwe's liberation struggle had important antecedents, from the first *chimurenga* of 1896–97 (Ranger 1967) to the expression in the 1960s, especially among young men (now the older generation), of cultural nationalism through spirit mediumship (Fry 1976). Yet ZANLA's use of these aspects of traditional Shona religion may have been situational and tactical. After independence in 1980, the new ZANU Government did not involve spirit mediums in the national rituals focused on Heroes' Acre commemorating both those who gave their lives in the guerrilla struggle and those who later assumed state power.[2] These rituals were instead dominated by ZANU (now known as ZANU(PF)) and the state, in conjunction with Christian priests, in a (temporary) resurrection of scientific socialism against traditional culture.[3]

It may be correct that Zimbabwe's socialist revolution lost its way (Astrow 1984); or, indeed, that there never was a revolution, socialist or other. Here, however, I take at face value the commitment in 1980 of ZANU(PF) to those limited socialist objectives reflected in its election manifesto. Even then, however, the party's orientation to socialism was less significant than its nationalist agenda, which was defined against colonialism. ZANU saw socialism primarily as an ideological weapon against the inequalities of colonial racism, but early in 1991 socialism was officially abandoned by ZANU(PF).[4] In this chapter, I shall seek to explain why Zimbabwean socialism self-destructed so quickly, concentrating upon the dimension of culture.

'ZANU'S IDEOLOGICAL BELIEF IS SOCIALISM'[5]

In its 1980 election manifesto, ZANU (1980: 4) claimed that 'the PEOPLE as a whole must come before individuals'. It also claimed to have grown 'from a nationalist political party to a revolutionary vanguard movement'. But in the party's own ranking of its objectives, following the earlier order of rural politicization undertaken by ZANLA (Lan 1985: 127, 201), the promotion of national consciousness and 'cultural welfare' outranked, at third and fourth places respectively, the fifth intention to 'evolve a socialist pattern' of economic reconstruction 'for the common benefit of all the people of Zimbabwe' (ZANU 1980: 3). Concretely, and in addition to demolishing racially differentiated access to health and educational services, these beliefs and objectives translated into the following specifically socialist policies: 'to promote on newly-acquired land the establishment of collective villages and collective agriculture', and to establish state farms 'in respect of certain key products to ensure their large-scale production and provide models' (ZANU 1980: 9). Its other objectives were a mixture of state capitalism and social democracy, but in its 'Thirteen Fundamental Rights and Freedoms' the party did uphold, at number eight, the right of women to 'equal rights with men in all spheres of political, economic, cultural and family life', and the principles of equal work for equal pay and free mate selection for both parties to a marriage (ZANU 1980: 16).

Few of these policy intentions were achieved. Little collectivization occurred, and what occurred achieved little success (Mumbengegwi 1987). Resettlement emphasized individualized plots (Kinsey 1982; 1983), and recently disaffected settlers have 'sold' their state-owned plots held on annual leasehold for thousands of dollars.[6] Few new state farms were created, nor did they or the inherited ones concentrate on 'key products' or act as 'models' (Moyo 1986). Only in the area of gender equality before the law was ZANU's original socialist policy successful. But precisely in this area, success in terms of the law has been problematic in terms of social behaviour, as I shall seek to demonstrate.

In accordance with its self-proclaimed vanguard status ZANU asserted that 'we must not allow the puppets and reactionaries to reap the ripe peaches we have tended. ZANU planted and tended the peach tree. ZANU is, therefore, entitled to reap her peaches' (ZANU 1980: 7). These peaches, encoding state power, have over the past decade stimulated political reliance on elements of neo-tradition diametrically opposed to socialism. Anti-colonial nationalism, plus direct elections based on universal suffrage, precluded Zimbabweans from describing 'bad customs' or 'traditional culture' as 'backward', 'primitive', or 'low-level' and up for replacement. On the contrary, Zimbabwean socialism tried to promote 'tradition', for example in the intention to create 'culture houses' in each district and to train curators at the local university, both of which foundered for lack of money. Zimbabwe's attempted transition to socialism was thus unusual in lacking an explicit emphasis on 'raising' the 'cultural level' of the workers and peasants through the deliberate harnessing of performative culture to the interests of the socialist state (see Mao Zedong 1975 [1942]).

CULTURE AS HISTORICITY

Before proceeding I must define my use of the term 'culture', especially as I have criticized its past abuse, both by anthropology and socialist policy in states that have tried explicitly to manipulate it (Cheater 1988, 1989; cf. Wallerstein 1990a, b). In my view, culture is much more than Geertz's (1973) structures and contexts of meaning or webs of significance spun by human actors. Culture is pre-eminently ideological (Althusser 1971: 241): even when it reflects popular values it is used deliberately as a hegemonic apparatus by various power structures (Gramsci 1985). It is, then, equivalent to what Touraine (1977; 1988) calls 'historicity', encompassing knowledge and other accumulated resources used in the contest between society's ruling and popular classes to control and direct its 'cultural model' (Touraine 1977: 91, 5). I would prefer to be able to use culture only in this Fanonesque sense, as always fluid; always the subject of dispute, as some use its (temporary) meanings to control the behaviour of others; always in the process of *becoming*. However, I indicate older, static referents by 'culture'.

This understanding of culture highlights my problematic: what happens when socialist legal reform creates one set of cultural meanings, politically hegemonic behaviour creates another set (often in the name of cultural nationalism), and the everyday practices of ordinary people construct yet others (at least one of which is denounced by hegemonic politics as the result of cultural imperialism)? These different meanings do not merely conflict: as Fry (1976: 68–106) indicates, they have only situational authority relative to their holders' interests. Where, then, in the traditions of anthropological analysis, can Zimbabwean culture possibly reside? How can it be intentionally managed by the ruling class, as Touraine suggests?

To handle these problems, I divide culture into its relational as opposed to its performative (including material, or 'plastic') aspects. This distinction mirrors those between ideology and practice, structure and organization, content and form, and allows, as Althusser (1971: 241) requires, that aesthetic and material aspects (music, dance, the plastic arts, and so on) form part of culture only through their insertion into 'the system of relations which constitute the ideological'. ZANU(PF)'s conflation of cultural performance and structural relationship has led to its encouragement of traditional performance while attempting to change traditional structures, and to its encouragement of socialist relationships derived from the West while seeking to change the performances of its own Western cultural inheritance.

ZIMBABWEAN 'SOCIALIST' POLICY ON CULTURE

Zimbabwe is culturally polyglot. It has four official languages (including Shona, Ndebele, and Tonga), though English dominates in the cities, the economy, and the official bureaucracies. Its peoples include the indigenous patrilineal Shona- and matrilineal Tonga-speaking peoples, Nguni-speaking black immigrants of the nineteenth century (Ndebele, Shangane), twentieth-century immigrants from most neighbouring states, Hindu and Muslim settlers from South Asia, white settlers from Europe, the United Kingdom and South Africa, and a few Chinese Zimbabweans. Although today Christianity dominates, Judaism, Islam, and Hinduism are also strong, and traditional religious beliefs and practices persist. Among the smaller ethnic communities, boundaries are maintained by the home use of the mother tongue, religious observance, membership of cultural clubs and associations (often with sporting, charitable, and burial functions), and specific types of socio-economic networks.

Speaking to Zimbabwe's polyethnicity, ZANU's 1980 election manifesto wished 'a sense of national belonging' to be made 'a dogma to submerge and destroy tribal, regionalistic, and racial animosity' and 'this diversity of background [to] become more a source of our cultural wealth than a cause of division and mistaken notions of groupist superiority philosophy' (ZANU 1980: 5). The manifesto made no further reference to cultural policy. However, in 1980 the Department of Culture was created and performative culture bureaucratized under state control in the new National Arts Council (NAC). Government apparently desired 'to blend the best cultural heritage from the traditional black Zimbabwean society with foreign models to instil pride in the African past and an appreciation of modern ideas', in 'a cultural compromise which the Government had the duty to supervise for the sake of societal harmony'.[7] Owing to the delicate process of balancing divergent cultural interests, policy remained implicit: an explicit cultural policy was still only in the process of formulation in 1991 (Dube 1991). Its first draft appeared early in 1992.

In the 1980s, implicit cultural policy in Zimbabwe sought to strengthen the performative aspects of traditional African cultures and to create from all of its diverse traditions, via their performative interaction, a new, specifically Zimbabwean, definitely nationalist, and perhaps socialist culture. However, there were clear contradictions between anti-colonial nationalism (emphasizing performative culture) and encouraging the development of a 'socialist culture' for the new Zimbabwean nation by means of performative cultural exchanges (while they lasted) with 'fraternal' socialist countries, the majority of which involved classical music, classical dance, and classical acrobatics, thus vastly expanding the range of locally available classical European entertainment. This presumably unintentional reinforcement of the colonial patterns of cultural domination did not lead to local complaints about cultural imperialism, perhaps because the reciprocation involved Zimbabwe's own classical musicians performing in Eastern European concert halls, and people took pride in this.

Government has not been alone in trying to create a new Zimbabwean performative culture. Private melding efforts, responding to expressed Government desires, have included the incorporation of traditional instruments and ethnomusicology into the programmes offered by the Zimbabwe College of Music; the occasional incorporation of traditional instruments, particularly the *marimba*, into classical concerts; 'outreach' teaching by the National Ballet in working-class black suburbs; and the growth of 'people's theatre'. 'People's theatre' has, however, often targeted both local and national governmental deficiencies. Cont Mhlanga, author of 'Workshop Negative', until 1991 banned from being performed outside Zimbabwe for this reason, recently claimed to regret having written this piece:

> The arts are now financially starved and politicians are suspicious of artists. . . . We are witnessing an increasing reaction from the politicians, and by that they are making everybody afraid of speaking. In the long run, that is not very healthy. If people learn that artists can speak freely, then they too will be able to learn to speak freely. The unity between the African politician and the artist during the time of the struggle needs to be preserved.[8]

Doubtless, cultural officials (see, for example, Chifunyise 1991) would agree with Mhlanga's sentiments. However, both writers and workers have, in creating new cultural forms, assumed their right to structure their own performances, often against the interests of the ruling class identified with the new state (Cheater 1988).

Government itself has concentrated on training schoolchildren in the traditional performative arts; busing adult performers to airports to greet visiting dignitaries; and organizing, as part of the annual independence celebrations, 'galas' extolling Zimbabwe's cultural diversity. These cultural galas are arranged in the main cities by sub-committees representing the Department of Culture and private organizations. Thousands of printed invitations dispatched to individuals of significant rank create a polyglot audience. Performances are carefully planned to display Zimbabwe's diverse sub-cultures for mutual exchange and admiration. Performers, however, offer twists unforeseen by the organizers. 'Traditional' dance groups display themselves as a mixture of colonials and characters from a Western children's television programme. 'Traditional' choral groups combine male and female members in semi-identical modern uniform, and sing songs in impeccably traditional idioms protesting against corruption in contemporary Zimbabwean society. Such creativity is highly appreciated by the elite audiences, though the politicians present as patrons may wriggle uncomfortably.

The contrived artificiality of these cultural events reveals the Government's problem in defining 'culture' as primarily performative, where the meaning is the performance itself (the performance is the message), but where the consumption of performative culture is also taken as a signifier of personal as well as social identity. Performative culture thus substitutes for real knowledge of how others live and think, and enables the hard issues of structural relations in multi-cultural contexts to be avoided. Perhaps for that reason, the Government approach satisfies few social actors in Zimbabwean society, especially those in contention with the ruling class for the control of Zimbabwean historicity, such as the chiefs and the youth.

CULTURE AS LIFESTYLE VERSUS SOCIALISM AND TRADITION AS AESTHETIC

The *de facto* practical emphasis on performative culture, described above, contradicts the explicit understanding of the NAC Director that 'our culture is defined not in theoretical terms but in the ways we live in both the urban and the rural areas'.[9] This understanding endangers the nationalist project in culture, particularly when it forces a recognition that urban lifestyles, especially among the youth, contradict both traditional and austere socialist expectations of appropriately modest demeanour which puts the collective whole before individual interests.

Young black Zimbabweans have, over the past half-decade, recurrently been accused (usually by high-ranking politicians whose own lifestyles are not notably traditional) of having 'abandoned their culture', of being culturally 'handicapped' and 'bankrupt' and of practising 'cultural prostitution', 'cultural suicide', and 'cultural degradation'.[10] They like international pop music, disco-dancing, dreadlocks and other non-traditional hairstyles, and punk clothing. They see all of these as symbolically denying primitivity, which they emphatically reject. They express contempt for local musicians and artists (often working on traditional themes) whose work is 'the last word in mediocrity', who 'just do not measure up' to the expectations of cultural consumers.[11] Increasingly, they also consume alcohol and marijuana. Clearly, their everyday cultural performance threatens not merely the ascetic project of socialism, but also the ease of social control. These young people, whether 'Westernized' or 'rasta', are beginning to defend themselves publicly against charges that they have sold out to (Western) cultural imperialism:

> It is, indeed, true that our own culture and values are fading out of action. ... Indeed the youth have adopted Western norms and values, but then what did you expect? What did you teach us? And what did you raise us to be? ... We were taught and trained to be 'blue-eyed niggers' from table manners to playing rugby and football. Perhaps, someone would like to tell me where I could have learned Shona culture. ...
>
> I refuse to debate whether this is good or bad, or right or wrong – that's just the way it is. It is quite clear that our education is almost completely English. Can we, therefore, be blamed for our pro-Western ways? After all, it is what we were taught. ... We live in a society very similar to that of the West. The parents go to work every day, the children go to school, and the rest of the day is spent watching Western-type television and/or listening to Western-type radio. Occasionally we have Western-type parties, braais [i.e., barbeques], picnics and lakeside holidays. We observe Western-type manners and Christian values. Where are we supposed to learn our own ways in such a Westernised environment? If we cannot learn our ways at school or at home or even in the streets (which, by the way, are also Western), then where shall we learn them? ... I find myself in a state of confusion, my culture is in conflict with my religion and what I consider to be the noble cause of women's liberation. All these conflicts are the result of Westernisation and the tremendous change that our lifestyle has gone through, while our culture has stood still.
>
> (Jaya, 1990: 8)

The accusations of youth's cultural inadequacy have increased in frequency and volume as university students and schoolchildren have become publicly critical of government (Cheater 1991b). They are directed especially against urban youth, and those known as 'the nose brigades' (now indigenized as *nozi*, plural *manozi*), who speak English through their noses like the English themselves. This speech style has come to symbolize the total rejection of 'traditional culture'. This rejection is related, as the above quotation makes quite clear, to class-differentiated educational experiences, but more generally parents are alleged to have lost control over their children. At the same time, the political elders have some difficulty in mobilizing onto their side of this argument, those young people whom the 'noses' call 'SRBs' (Strong/Severe Rural Backgrounds), who have not suffered cultural imperialism to the same degree in their home or educational backgrounds, but who have been exposed to the parastatal radio and television services. Politicians critical of both broadcasting and youth seem to want presented on television not contemporary urban Zimbabwean behaviour (which has great entertainment value to those living it), but idealized representations of what they think should be: 'If you want to perform in Shona, it should be good Shona so that it will set a good example. I am being very critical because people exhibit our own skills, culture, through drama and if what we have seen on ZTV depicts our culture, then I am afraid they [*not* we] have not been good enough', was one ministerial comment.[12] But youth's rejection of the politicians' cultural nationalism is a delightful irony when set against Fry's (1976: 41) remark (concerning what is now the elders' generation of cultural nationalists), that the trance-inducing dance at traditional seances 'was not so different from modern western pop dancing; it was highly expressive and individualistic'!

One is tempted to speculate that, in these arguments about 'culture', young people have little difficulty in identifying at a long distance potential measures to control their own behaviour. As a much older black female Zimbabwean at a conference put the point about her own life and career: 'when you want to do something different, they think of all the logical reasons against it. When they run out of logic, they say "But you can't. It's against our culture"!' Indeed, youthful resentment at falling education standards and extremely high school-leaver unemployment, is probably in the process of crystallizing into a social movement, spearheaded by the university and polytechnic students, in which the cultural argument forms the core of their dispute with the ruling class. When young black Zimbabweans writing in national newspapers use terms like 'blue-eyed niggers', they intend to annoy politicians through colonially inspired satire. They also display a self-mocking confidence in their *colonial* cultural inheritance, which is equally unacceptable to the policitians.

> What baffles [the ruling class] is that in spite of the Presidential concerns which were expressed in no uncertain terms, the youth still cling line, hook and sinker to Western cultures. As if that is not deviant enough, they have the audacity to embark on a collision course with elders who are determined to preserve culture.[13]

If youth is critical of the politicians' stance on 'traditional culture', so too are the chiefs – for diametrically opposed reasons. In 1981, in the name of socialist democracy and state control, the chiefs were stripped of their colonial powers to administer customary law and allocate land (see Cheater

1990). Special skills, described by Seidman (1982), were required to get through Parliament the bill which removed from the chiefs and headmen their former legal obligations in traditional courts. The new courts were riddled with apparently uncontrollable corruption and in 1990 a decision was taken to reinstate traditional courts. However, even those chiefs who form part of the legislature are reported as saying that, whereas the colonialists fully recognized their customary roles, 'our own children thought we were not to exercise our hereditary powers'.[14] This is the context in which problematic structural relations in 'traditional' cultures have been delegated to the chiefs to handle. Together with the police, and in the absence of specific legislation, the chiefs are now expected, under the control of the state, to do the politicians' dirty work, being 'urged to weed out bad customs' within rural society.[15]

GENDER EQUALITY AND 'BAD CUSTOMS'

If traditional performative culture was the subject of nationalist encouragement by Zimbabwe's 'socialist' rulers, specific customs flagrantly contravening socialist ideals had to be confronted and condemned as 'bad'. Most 'bad customs' have to do with the traditional subordination of women to men. As identified recently by one minister,[16] these 'bad customs' include: 'demands by relatives of a dead person for large sums of money before the corpse is buried'[17]; the giving in marriage of young female children to much older men to indemnify the girls' kin for traditional torts and deaths (see Reynolds 1990: 14–15); enforced widow inheritance; the sororate; and the stripping of property from a man's wife and children by his patrikin immediately after his death.

These 'bad customs' all reflect the relational content of Shona culture. They concern rights over people and property involved in bridewealth transactions which contradict socialist equality. But anti-colonial nationalism has precluded any assault on the institution of bridewealth itself.[18] This may be due to the fact that high bridewealth has always been a source of prestige for families of high rank, in the present as in the past. Yet bridewealth generates these 'bad customs' which, through their control of rights over people and their labour, primarily benefit men, who comprise over 90 per cent of the legislative assembly. So securing the passage of gender-equitable legislation through Parliament requires that members of Parliament put their party-political before their cultural interests.

The legal reform of problematic structural relationships has usually taken place without serious explanation of the reason, and occasionally with deliberate intent to mislead. For example, the 1982 Legal Age of Majority Act was outlined correctly to a press conference in English; and then 'explained' to the ZANU(PF) Women's League in Shona as involving no change in parental control, particularly over daughters' sexual behaviour and marriage. In fact this act stripped fathers or guardians of their right to claim damages from those responsible for their daughters' pre-marital pregnancies, and parents of their right to arrange, or forbid, marriages among their offspring over the age of 18 years. It has been the source of considerable popular disaffection, requiring a Supreme Court clarification of its intent, though as yet there has been no move to amend it.[19]

Legal reform favouring gender equality is the one area in which ZANU did keep its 1980 electoral promises (cf. Stewart *et al.* 1990). The state has given adult women control over their own sexuality. It is now they, not their fathers, who can sue for seduction damages. They have the right to choose their marriage partner, to secure financial maintenance from the fathers of children born out of marriage, and personal as well as child maintenance following divorce or a husband's death (previously, accord-ing to customary law, his estate would be inherited by an agnate, whether or not the widow agreed to marry him, widow inheritance being a some-times negotiable custom among most Shona-speakers). Women have obtained rights to a share of the property jointly generated in a marriage, as well as to their own income and property earned during marriage. They are now eligible to own immovable property in their own right, whether married or not. They are entitled to individualized personal taxation (the colonial system was based on the concept of a family taxpayer), and to equal pay for equal work. Gender discrimination in job recruitment has been outlawed, and the Government has announced that it intends to work towards the target of women occupying 30 per cent of all managerial posts in the civil service.[20]

There are, however, certain important rights which women do not yet hold equally with men, including the symbolically significant right, relative to traditional patrivirilocality, to permanent residence in Zimbabwe for a foreign spouse. In practical terms, although employed women enjoy equal pay for equal work, urban women tend to occupy lower-ranked jobs, and therefore earn lower incomes, on average, than men. Rural women still have no formal rights to 'communal' land, while the resettlement pro-gramme was geared to family settlement under a male head. Despite their new legal rights, then, the majority of Zimbabwean women have no inde-pendent access to the means of production. Their continued economic dependence on men in marriage has thus been only marginally affected by gender-blind legislation.

Moreover, as these legal reforms have structurally changed gender relations, so various attempts to re-subordinate women have emerged in public behavioural performances. A steady flow of letters to the news-papers has, for the past decade, quoted St Paul's Letter to the Ephesians in support of their contention that women were born to be subordinated in marriage; that husbands 'manage' their homes, while wives are merely 'workers'. Claiming compatibility with both Christianity and 'traditional culture', more provocative letters (some signed by high-ranking males belonging to the ruling party) have asserted a husband's right to beat his wife regularly and have elicited strongly worded dissent. Running through all of these written performances is the message that liberated women claiming their legal rights may be regarded as unmarriageable, that structural relationships may have changed in the law, but not in social interaction.

Still more striking, perhaps, is the performative re-subordination of women, using the idioms allegedly pertaining to traditional African 'cultures', within ZANU(PF) itself. For the first five years of independence, mixed groups of traditional dancers greeted important state visitors at Zimbabwe's airports. Nowadays, they are separated by sex. When in the mid-1980s President Khomenei of Iran refused to attend a mixed-sex state banquet, the banquet went ahead without him and Zimbabweans fumed publicly about this insult to their female cabinet ministers, among others. But following the Pope's 1986 visit, whenever the state has received visitors or the President has departed or returned home, there has been a phalanx of kneeling members of the ZANU(PF) Women's League on the airport tarmac. Protest against the inappropriateness of such behaviour, especially among socialists, has drawn the response that kneeling is the way women traditionally show their respect in African society. The female members of the households of some members of the Politburo do indeed approach paterfamilias and all male visitors on their knees; for example, when they serve tea. But in most rural and urban households that I personally have entered, the standard pattern is a half-curtsey or brief bob, accompanied by respectful clapping. Kneeling is anathema to educated black women.

Female kneeling, it appears, is encouraged by very high-ranking party and state officials. At an agricultural college's celebrations in late 1989, the State President as guest of honour was presented with a silver tray. The presentation was made, on damp grass under trees, by a young woman, born at the college and herself a secondary school teacher in Harare, who was dressed in a summer suit, stockings and high-heeled shoes. Much taller than the President, she extended the tray in her left hand and her right hand to shake his. He did not extend his hand, nor did he take the tray. He merely looked, unsmiling, into the distance, while two elderly Women's League members, wearing dresses printed with his image, and already on their knees behind him, flapped their hands and hissed '*pasi, pasi*' (down, down). The young teacher looked around, bewildered, for guidance. The college staff looked at one another and then at the ground, obviously embarrassed.[21] With a hard face, the teacher shrugged, and knelt on the wet grass. The President smiled and accepted his tray. A few people clapped raggedly; the majority did not applaud. After the Presidential motorcade had departed in a fanfare of police sirens, the college community, male and female, commiserated with the teacher: 'What can one do? It is not right, we have never done it that way, but what can we do?'

Idioms of patriarchy and kinship hierarchy have also been used in recent years by members of the ZANU(PF) Women's League, against the party's political rivals. In 1989, a Women's League march, led by a female cabinet minister, demonstrated against the formation of the Zimbabwe Unity Movement (ZUM) by Edgar Tekere, himself formerly among the ZANU(PF) top leadership.

> Comrade Mujuru said in African custom the father was the head of a house. If anything went wrong, a child would not complain to the father. . . . 'You will never get a child telling his father to step down because he has failed to run the affairs of the house, but there are always ways of dealing with their problems'. . . . She wondered why most men behind ZUM had failed to manage their homes. 'How can a man who has failed to run the affairs of his house and family lead a nation? How can you let people from outside come to deal with the problems of your country and yet they don't know your culture or the way you live?'[22]

There is clearly a patent contradiction between the past socialist legal reconstruction of gender relations, and recent intra-party behaviour. How should this complex contradiction be explained? One might concur with Martin (1987: 31) that 'Kinship symbolism indeed legitimises authority and commands respect; it also stresses the obligations of those who are in power and reinforces expectations which cannot be discarded, at least not too often'. But even among Zimbabwean parliamentarians of the ruling party, the idiom of fatherhood has been regarded as unsuitable to modern politics:

> Mr Speaker, sir, for those who have a family, you have a counterpart who is your wife. Sometimes your children are grown up and the opposition increases. This is very healthy, it helps you to think, you really govern and you would always learn to do it. You do *not* have to dictate. . . . Let us leave our children with a legacy that they will be proud of. [Or] they will find themselves with no option but to spit on our graves, after we are dead.[23]

The recent disputed political use of the idioms of traditional patriarchy ran in parallel with the new-found ZANU(PF) concern with the 'abandonment' of their 'traditional culture' among Zimbabwean youth. Both may have reflected an attempt, within ZANU(PF) itself as well as in Zimbabwean society more broadly, to establish a politics of consensus as the socialist agenda foundered and dissent (within and beyond the party) increased. Even within the ruling class itself, there has been dispute over the control of Zimbabwean historicity; for example, over the desirability of establishing a one-party state. It is within this context one must set the recent emerging attempt, in classical (national) socialist style, to create a personality cult focusing specifically on the young around the party leader and state President.

CONCLUSION

By examining a mixture of public discourse and ethnographic events, this chapter has tried to explain why the developing trend in Zimbabwean 'socialism' over the past decade was so 'revisionist'. Having started its career in government with a difficult contradiction between its nationalism and its socialism, ZANU(PF) at first used the development of traditional performative culture to divert attention from its socialist attacks on traditional relationships. But following the establishment of an executive Presidency in 1987, ZANU(PF) faced rising criticism of its socialist policies. In this situation, the party came increasingly to emphasise the importance of 'traditional culture', using inegalitarian performance to contradict its previous socialist legal re-structuring of relationships. Selected elements of its original nationalist agenda (focused on the land question) and of 'traditional culture' compatible with patriarchal authority, have been invoked for support. ZANU(PF)'s attempted recourse to the symbols of an allegedly consensual past was clearly related to its desire to retain its 'peaches'. Ultimately, it abandoned socialism as the official party ideology in order to hang on to power. However, not least through its past political (mis)management of cultural issues, the party has alienated many sectors of Zimbabwean society, in particular its pragmatic, youthful electorate, over the future direction in which Zimbabwe's 'cultural model' should be pushed.

Perhaps, as this conflict over the control of its historicity develops further, and contra Martin (1987), Zimbabwe may yet prove to be one African state in which the political manipulation of traditional symbols and idioms of power will not be sufficient to enable socialist politicians *manqu(e)és* to retain control of the state.

NOTES

1 I am most grateful to Peter Fry for a rightfully stringent critique of an early draft of this chapter, and to Rudo Gaidzanwa for later comments.

2 In addition to the national Heroes' Acre in Harare, provincial and district Heroes' Acres have been designated since the mid-1980s, at which re-burials of guerrilla remains (often re-located from mass graves) have become an extremely important ritual focus of waning party solidarity.

3 Folowing the analysis in this chapter, however, I would predict that spirit mediums will very shortly be included in these rituals.

4 *The Herald*, 29 Jan. 1991, p. 3.

5 ZANU (1980: 8).

6 *The Herald*, 28 Dec. 1990, p. 5; 9 Jan. 1991, p. 1. It is a neat irony that those

responsible for 'selling' the land on which they were resettled are those who, in 1980, flatly refused resettlement on a collectivized basis in that area!

7 *The Herald,* 10 Dec. 1990, p. 8.
8 *The Herald,* 31 Dec. 1990, p. 2.
9 *The Herald,* 10 Dec. 1990, p. 8.
10 *The Herald,* 13 Nov. 1990, p. 5; *Sunday Mail,* 25 Nov. 1990, p. 6.
11 *The Herald,* 11 Jan. 1991, p. 11.
12 *Sunday Mail,* 21 Feb. 1988, p. 1; my emphasis and addition.
13 *Sunday Mail,* 25 Nov. 1990, p. 6.
14 *Sunday Mail,* 26 Nov. 1989, p. C8; cf. *The Herald,* 13 Dec. 1990, p. 7.
15 *The Herald,* 6 Nov. 1990, p. 1.
16 Ibid.
17 Although a minority of such persons are the male victims of homicide or murder, the vast majority are females for whom bridewealth payments have not been completed, or even started – in which case the man responsible for the death is required to 'marry the grave' (*kuroora guva*) in a post-mortem payment. See also Hollemann (1975).
18 *The Herald,* 10 Dec. 1990, p. 8.
19 Given youthful disaffection, the legal age of majority (including the right to vote) might in future be raised from its current level of 18 years.
20 *The Herald,* 16 Nov. 1990, p. 13.
21 What prevented me (standing next to the teacher) from intervening was the thought of what the comeback would be on the college principal, a personal friend who had invited me to the occasion. So do we personally learn the precise constraints of relationship, which are usually glossed as 'cultural' and which engender our compliance against both belief and political judgement.
22 *Sunday Mail,* 28 May 1989, p. 1.
23 *Hansard,* 12 Dec. 1990, cols 3070, 3071; my emphasis.

REFERENCES

Althusser, L. (1971) *Lenin and Philosophy and Other Essays,* New York/London: Monthly Review Press.
Astrow, A. (1984) *Zimbabwe: A Revolution that Lost its Way?* London: Zed Press.
Binns, C.A.P. (1979) 'The changing face of power: revolution and accommodation in the development of the Soviet ceremonial system: I', *Man* (n.s.), 14(4): 585–606.
—— (1980) 'The changing face of power: revolution and accommodation in the development of the Soviet ceremonial system: II', *Man* (n.s.), 15(1): 170–87.
Cheater, A.P. (1988) 'Contradictions in modelling "consciousness": Zimbabwean proletarians in the making?', *Journal of Southern African Studies,* 14(2): 292–304.
—— (1989) *Managing Culture en route to Socialism: The Problem of Culture 'Answering Back',* Inaugural lecture, Harare: University of Zimbabwe Publications (1991).
—— (1990) 'The ideology of "communal" land tenure in Zimbabwe: mythogenesis enacted?', *Africa,* 60(2): 188–206.
—— (1991a) 'Death ritual as political trickster in the People's Republic of China', *Australian Journal of Chinese Affairs,* 26: 67–97.
—— (1991b) 'The University of Zimbabwe: university, national university, state university, or party university?', *African Affairs,* 90, 359: 189–205.
Chifunyise, S.J. (1991) 'Highlighting arts events which made impact in 1990', *Sunday Mail,* 6 Jan.
Dube, C. (1991) 'Cultural draft policy has defects', *The Herald,* 12 Jan.
Feuchtwang, S. (in press) 'The problem of "superstition" in the People's Republic

of China', in *Religion and Political Power*, G. Benavides (ed.), New York: State University of New York Press.

Fry, P. (1976) *Spirits of Protest*, Cambridge: Cambridge University Press.

Geertz, C. (1973) *The Interpretation of Cultures*, New York: Basic Books.

Gramsci, A. (1985) *Selections from Cultural Writings*, London: Lawrence & Wishart.

Hollemann, Hans (1975) Address delivered to the Annual General Meeting of the [Tribal Areas of Rhodesia Research] Foundation. Salisbury: 24 Feb. (Typescript held by the Zimbabwe National Archives.)

Jaya, M. (1990) 'Youth should not be blamed for western cultures', *Sunday Mail*, 11 Nov.

Kinsey, B.H. (1982) 'Forever gained: resettlement and land policy in the context of national development in Zimbabwe', *Africa*, 52, 3: 92–113.

—— (1983) 'Emerging policy issues in Zimbabwe's land resettlement programme', *Development Policy Review*, 1(1): 163–96.

Lan, D. (1985) *Guns and Rain*, London: James Currey / Harare: Zimbabwe Publishing House.

Lane, C. (1981) *The Rites of Rulers*, Cambridge: Cambridge University Press.

Mao Zedong (Mao Tse-Tung) (1975 [1942]) 'Talks at the Yan'an (Yenan) Forum on Literature and Art', in *Selected Works of Mao Tse-Tung*, Vol. 3, Beijing: Foreign Languages Press.

Martin, D.-C. (1987) *The Emergence of Original Political Cultures in Africa: The Case of Tanzania*, Pau: Université de Pau et des Pays de l'Adour, Centre de Recherche et d'Etude sur les Pays d'Afrique Orientale.

Moyo, S. (1986) 'The land question', In *Zimbabwe: The Political Economy of Transition 1980–1986*, I. Mandaza (ed.), Dakar: Codesria.

Mumbengegwi, C. (1987) *Continuity and Change in Agricultural Policy*, Dakar: Codesria.

Ranger, T.O. (1967) *Revolt in Southern Rhodesia*, London: Heinemann.

Reynolds, P. (1990) 'Children of tribulation: the need to heal and the means to heal war trauma', *Africa* , 60(1): 1–38.

Seidman, R.B. (1982) 'How a bill became law in Zimbabwe: on the problem of transforming the colonial state', *Africa*, 52(3): 56–76.

Stewart, J. *et al.* (eds) (1990) 'The legal situation of women in Zimbabwe', in *The Legal Situation of Women in Southern Africa*, J. Stewart and A. Armstrong (eds), Harare: University of Zimbabwe Publications.

Touraine, A. (1977) *The Self-Production of Society*, Chicago/London: University of Chicago Press.

—— (1988) *Return of the Actor*, Minneapolis: University of Minnesota Press.

Wallerstein, I. (1990a) 'Culture as the ideological battleground of the modern world system', *Theory, Culture and Society*, 7(2–3): 31–56.

—— (1990b) 'Culture is the world system: reply to Boyne', *Theory, Culture and Society*, 7(2–3): 63–6.

ZANU (1980) *Election Manifesto*, Salisbury: ZANU.

Zimbabwe (1990) *Hansard: Parliamentary Debates*, vol. 17, no. 60 (12 Dec.), Harare: Government Printer.

Chapter 7

Anthropology and the politics of socialism in rural Sri Lanka

Jonathan Spencer

The Democratic Socialist Republic of Sri Lanka may seem an unlikely candidate for inclusion in any assessment of socialism as an anthropological problem. Its political difficulties have attracted the attention of some distinguished anthropologists (Obeyesekere 1984; Tambiah 1986; Kapferer 1988), but usually for quite other reasons, like the intractability of its ethnic problem and the steady growth of political violence. Yet the country has retained the designation 'socialist' in its official title, and most of the different agents involved in recent politics have at some time or another in the recent past thought it appropriate to identify themselves as socialists.

The country designated itself 'socialist' in the early 1970s when a government of the left (led by the Sri Lanka Freedom Party (SLFP)) was in power. The name was introduced as part of a new constitution written by a sometime Trotskyite, itself no small novelty in comparative politics. The government of the time was heavily committed to state intervention in the economy, but spent most of its period in office on the defensive as the economy tottered from crisis to crisis. Eventually it was ousted by a party of the right (the United National Party (UNP)) in 1977. The new government was committed to an 'open economy', which it was thought would encourage native enterprise, and to the swift dismantling of its predecessor's cumbersome corporatist policies. This party has been in power ever since, to the rage of the dwindling band of true believers on the Left, who have busied themselves with intermittent internal warfare and puzzled their supporters with their inability to present a credible alternative to the populism of their rivals.

So far, perhaps, so familiar. But Sri Lanka has its idiosyncrasies too. The UNP, whatever its rhetoric, has kept a strong grip on the country's material resources, and carefully retained the claim to 'socialism' when it rewrote the constitution soon after coming to power. The apparent success of the 'open economy' in the 1980s has to be set against evidence of increasingly violent disaffection amongst the young people of the country. First Tamil youth, and later Sinhala youth, rallied around the flags of linguistic and religious identity in their support for the Liberation Tigers of Tamil Ealam

(LTTE), and the Sinhala youth group the JVP (Janata Vimukti Peramuna), respectively. But these organizations all maintained some, usually rather hazy, aspirations to social revolution. Meanwhile, academic opinion on the country's economy divides fairly neatly between those who see the entire post-independence period as a time of sustained economic failure, and who blame many of the country's current ills on this failure, and those who point out the relative equality in the country's distribution of income, and re-markably high levels of provision of 'basic needs' in areas like health and education. In a way those who hold the latter view face the more uncom-fortable task, because one implication of the 'rosy' interpretation of Sri Lankan political economy is that the failure of political integration may be connected with the state's success in promoting welfare measures and providing for people's basic needs.

I will return to this possibility in my conclusion. First, though, I need to explain just what this chapter is *for*, apart from simply adding another case, another place heard from, in our deliberations. At some point in the early 1970s political anthropology appeared to disappear up a cul-de-sac in which 'the political' was simply identified with 'the instrumental', and the ethnography of politics reduced to ever more virtuosic formal accounts of strategizing and transacting. The major theoretical movements in the an-thropology of the 1970s – Marxism, feminism and symbolic anthropology – were equally indifferent to the study of politics and the public sphere, albeit for very different reasons. Although there has been a great deal of impressive work in recent years on questions of power and domination, many anthropologists are reluctant to associate themselves with the label of 'political anthropology'. Any new political anthropology has to be an anthropology of 'actually existing' politics. It has to concentrate on precise-ly those areas of disciplinary strength which the old political anthropology rather perversely ignored: sensitivity to local knowledge and local meaning, and the interpretation of action in its cultural context. This means looking at questions of political identity as well as patterns of political competition. It also involves taking seriously the imagery of political dis-course as part of people's own self-understandings, instead of reducing it to some narrow calculation of rhetorical effect. We may be more ready to take other people's political ideas seriously when we accept that those ideas share much in common with our own political aspirations. 'Socialism' is a good place to start this process, not least because many anthropologists have, at some time or another, thought of themselves as 'socialists'.

The idea of studying 'political culture' may seem to subsume all these tasks, or at least to indicate the general area of concern. The third part of this chapter investigates images of equality in Sri Lankan society, and could be considered a tentative account of one aspect of Sri Lankan (or Sinhala) 'political culture'. The danger with the idea of a 'political culture' is the temptation it affords to reify the idea of 'culture' in ways which reduce our understanding of political agency, and which also simplify and homo-genize something which is by definition a scene of argument and difference. I am particularly concerned to avoid presenting a picture of Sri Lankan politics as guided by some immanent trans-historical cultural force, not least because such an analysis has the effect of paralyzing and closing off present political possibilities. For example, Sri Lankan politics is suf-fused with images of the past and claims of continuity from the days of kings, to the extent that many observers have been seduced into treating those claims in the present as prima facie evidence of cultural continuity.[1] This sort of appeal to 'culture' is based on a view of cultures as possessing unchanging essences, spirits, or geniuses, and I have argued elsewhere that this view of culture, rooted in European romanticism, is both theoretically incoherent and politically dangerous as a tool for analyzing the politics of modern nation-states (Spencer 1990a).

The obvious alternative is to reintroduce contingency by treating politi-cal culture as a product of a particular political history and to try to understand it as the outcome of specific circumstances. In short, I suggest we follow John Peel and think of culture as 'less a reflection of society, than a reflection on history' (Peel 1987: 112). In the third part of the chapter I give some of the history of peasant–state relations in colonial and post-colonial Sri Lanka, relations which predispose people to accept some versions of political possibility rather than others. A major point here is that political anthropology cannot afford to work in isolation; crucial forces in local politics – in this case the overall pattern of distribution of government resources – may be hidden from local political actors and thus missing from a purely ethnographic account of politics. In the final part I examine the possibilities raised in the deceptively revolutionary politics of the JVP, before returning in the conclusion to the problematic relationship between social welfare and political integration in Sri Lanka.

First, though, I owe my readers some more orientation on the recent history of Left politics in Sri Lanka.[2] After a brief glorious beginning, the parties of the Old Left have steadily declined in significance in post-colonial Sri Lanka. Most have their roots in the politics of the 1930s when elite radicals, some of them recently returned from the heady atmosphere of the London School of Economics, set about the building of a mass socialist movement. In the 1940s the Old Left constituted the main source of electoral opposition to the conservative elite politicians who took over from the colonial power. After the emergence of Sinhala populism as a political force in the mid-1950s, the Old Left was slowly squeezed out of the political frame. Since 1970 the most important forces on the Left have been militant youth movements. In the Tamil north and east of the country the Tigers have employed socialist rhetoric in their campaign for a separate Tamil state. In the south, the JVP led a brief insurrection against the Government in 1971, and a longer and bloodier campaign in the late 1980s.

I will return in the final section to the question of the JVP's 'socialism', but for now it is sufficient to make some general points about its leadership and its message.[3] Unlike the parties of the Old Left, and unlike other Sri Lankan political parties which until recently have remained mostly in the hands of a small 'political class', the JVP leadership comes from the same stratum of Sinhala-educated, ambitious, rural youth as the bulk of its following. Like all the parties of the Left in Sri Lanka, it has had to accommodate itself to the central ideological appeal of Sinhala Buddhist nationalism. Whereas the appeal of Sinhala nationalism caused pain and heart-searching to the Old Left, for the JVP it could be said to represent more of a taken-for-granted part of the political landscape; as early as 1971 their programme was drawing extensively on the nationalist vision of the good life. Both these features – the accommodation with nationalism and the common social origins of leaders and cadres – are apparently shared with the Tamil militants of the LTTE (Hellmann-Rajanayagam 1987). The relative priority afforded to socialism and the national question in these movements is well captured in the words of an LTTE pamphlet:

> If a national race loves its history filled with greatness and its language and culture, its tradition and ancient customs, that we call patriotism. One who discards this progressive patriotism, this love of the nation and calls for cosmopolitanism, is not a true socialist. People like these are bourgeois cosmopolitans.
>
> (Hellmann-Rajanayagam 1987: 74)

CULTURAL CRITICISM AND IMAGES OF EQUALITY

Writing of the prospects for socialism in industrial societies, John Dunn (1984) has isolated a number of crucial components of socialist politics. The most important of these are a cultural critique of things as they are, a vision of things as they should be, and a political programme which promises to effect the transition from critique to vision. This requires the control of state power, and the practical politics of socialism inevitably centre on state intervention in the economy. Dunn also argues that the cultural critique of the distribution of goods and rewards is, and is likely to remain, the strongest component of socialist politics, not least because even the dough-tiest defenders of capitalism find it difficult to invoke the idea of 'justice' and 'fairness' when confronted with capitalism's indifference to the social context of its economic logic:

> As a response to the morally and practically anarchic aspects of capitalist production, socialism is above all else an attempt to reimpose order upon modern social experience through the benign exercise of political au-

thority: to replace the aesthetic, moral and practical anarchy of capitalist production with a new, benign and spiritually compelling order.

(Dunn 1984: 64)

Dunn's identification of this central strength of socialist politics should be particularly attractive to anthropologists as it identifies a fruitful area for ethnographic inquiry.[4] In later sections I shall return to what Dunn sees as the most problematic areas of socialist politics: the practical politics of state intervention in the economy and the long-term vision of an alternative social order in which morality governs economy. First, though, I propose to review some ethnographic evidence on equality and inequality in every-day life in southern Sri Lanka. Sri Lanka lies in a part of the world which has experienced the imposition of crude stereotypes about equality and hierarchy.[5] I therefore need to start with evidence that demonstrates that equality is both possible and valued in everyday life, before assessing how far equality is associated with the ideal of justice in public political criticism.

In a village in eastern Ratnapura District in the early 1980s, I discovered assumptions about equality built into certain everyday patterns of work and association.[6] Most work on the village's paddy fields was still carried out according to the reciprocal labour system known as *attam*, by which cultivators exchanged, with meticulous balance, labour by the day on one another's fields.[7] But by the time of my fieldwork paddy cultivation in this village had become the preserve of a relatively privileged minority of the population. The poor were excluded, as were women, from this embodied equality, while the division of the harvest itself was, of course, quite inegalitarian. Until recently the main agricultural activity was swidden or *chena* cultivation. Again the pattern of work emphasized the equal partici-pation and equal rewards of co-cultivators, this time less structured by gender differences; but again this has to be seen in the perspective of wider relations of dominance and inequality, specifically the claims on the crop of local colonial officials (Spencer 1990c: 104–9). In conversation, a number of people emphasized the *moral* importance of these patterns of working. On new colony land opened up to paddy a few miles away, cash was used for all labour relations, a situation which at least one informant dispara-gingly referred to as 'just like *bisnis* [business]'. In this interpretation, paddy work represented a moral enclave in a wider world of amoral, or immoral, economic activity.

The patterns of paddy and swidden work can be seen as enduring, even embattled, features of past social relations, continued in a changing present. Other egalitarian features were more self-conscious responses to new circumstances. When I went to live there, the village had recently acquired a 'Good Works Society' (*subhasadhika samitiya*). Villagers contributed a small monthly subscription in return for the promise of help at times of emergency (especially funerals). The society was organized by a group of richer villagers (for whom, it should be said, it served as a political resource of sorts), but its members were also drawn from poor and intermediate groups. It met every month at the village temple, and its proceedings were painfully correct in their bureaucratic formality. This initiative, and others like it found in comparable villages all over Sri Lanka, is clearly reminiscent of the Friendly Societies of nineteenth-century Britain (Thompson 1968: 456–69), even though, I suspect, the Sri Lankan organization generally has a shorter life than its Victorian counterpart. In both cases, structures of 'mutuality' (to use Thompson's word) were deployed as protection against the vicissitudes of economic circumstances.

Another, slightly different, response to change is the *sramadana*, 'gift of labour' or collective work party. A group of villagers would assemble for a day's work, for example, cleaning up the grounds of the Buddhist temple or clearing the paths through the surrounding scrub. Some of these occasions were purely local initiatives. At other times, something called a *sramadana* was organized by the village UNP leadership, and the participants were rewarded with government relief supplies. The idea of the *sramadana* has been popularized by the Sarvodaya movement, probably the largest Sri Lankan non-governmental development organization, and its leader A.T. Ariyaratna. The movement has ostensibly Gandhian origins, a commitment to development and self-help, and a line in ruralist rhetoric which goes down especially well with the more romantically inclined members of the aid community, even though Ariyaratna has developed the movement in keeping with the imperatives of Sinhala Buddhist nationalism.[8] Like that nationalism, it employs idealized images of the past to legitimate present practices. This exploitation of selective readings of the past is particularly important, because it appears to give value to rural people's way of life even as it disempowers them: the past is past and can only be actively re-created with outside help. Sarvodaya's vision of rural socialism is just a particularly striking example of a more general phenomenon in Sri Lankan political history: the use by elites of images of the countryside and the rural past in political critique. Such critique characteristically displaces blame for all the ills of the present on the depredations of 'foreigners', while keeping quiet about existing inequities in access to power and resources among Sri Lankans (Samaraweera 1981; Moore 1989). It is the ideological correlate of the 'hidden' sources of state welfarism which I shall discuss later.

More generally, arguments like Ariyaratna's – that Sri Lanka was the home of a socialist order in the pre-colonial past – indicate the dangers of the idea of 'political culture'. At some point Ariyaratna's claims connect up with more academic arguments about the social dimension of Buddhism (for example, Ling 1966), or the Asokan espousal of the 'first welfare state' (Sarkisyanz 1965; cf. Southwold 1983: 116–18). No one would deny that the past, in Sri Lanka as anywhere, can provide models for radical action in the present, but the very frequency of references to past practice in Sri Lankan politics should make us suspicious of the assumption that these indicate a simple continuity between the concerns of the past and the concerns of the present.[9] Even so, the fact that dominant understandings of the past and present lay so much stress on 'equality' indicates that it is a value of proven use in political rhetoric. In a truly hierarchical world there would be nothing to gain from denying the real inequalities of the present, or pointing to the possibility of greater equality in either the past or the future.

But this is something less than the moral critique of present practice which Dunn sees as an almost intuitive response to capitalism. In my own fieldwork I did not encounter any worked-through criticism of local social relations which assessed the suffering of the local have-nots and placed the blame fairly and squarely at the door of the local haves. It is, of course, quite possible that I would have found it just as difficult to locate such a textbook case of class consciousness had I been working in Britain rather than Sri Lanka. Besides, it is naïve to expect moral critique to focus on the local social order, especially when so much that is important comes to the village from outside (a point I pursue below). I did hear grumbling about the different fortunes of rich and poor but this gathered most force when the ills of the poor could be blamed on the avarice of some other group like Muslims or Tamils. I also witnessed at least one exemplary scene of everyday acquiescence when I questioned a poor cultivator about the merchant's loan of his seed grain to be repaid at 100 per cent interest come the harvest. Try as I might, I could not induce the cultivator to describe this as anything other than generosity on the part of the merchant. Similarly, the meteoric rise to fortune of the area's gem-dealers attracted less criticism than might be expected because, according to one farmer I spoke to, 'at least they're our people' (namely, Sinhala, not Muslim or Tamil like the more established wealthy traders in the area).

The most sustained moment of social criticism concerned not the distribution of existing local resources, but the state's distribution of new resources: the allocation of land from a new irrigation scheme. The village arguments that resulted from an attempt to distribute this land in 1984 were dominated by the words *sadhara* and *asadhara*: 'just' and 'unjust', or 'impartial' and 'partial'. James Brow encountered a similar situation in a village in Anuradhapura District in 1983. In his case the problem stemmed from the building of a new 'model village' and the allocation of new housing along political party lines. In both cases, protest took the form of petitions to the Prime Minister in Colombo and appeals to the principle of justice. It also emerged in other ways, particularly through a case of spirit possession in which the villagers were urged, by the deity possessing one of their number, to re-unite as one set of kin and one community (Brow 1988; 1990). In fact, Brow's villagers sent two petitions to the Prime Minister, one claiming that the houses should have been equitably distributed among all the original inhabitants of the village, the other implicitly acknowledging the claims of political party loyalty but asserting that, because of corruption, the houses had not been allocated to the best-qualified Government supporters (Brow 1988: 321). One sees here a tension between the claims of an abstract equity, based in an ideal of local community, and the claims of a more limited equity, based in the implicit rules of the game of political patronage. The two petitions indicate, in their divergence, a tension in expectations about the proper distribution of goods and rewards, but it is a tension which focuses on the state and political relationships, not on the market and more strictly economic relationships.

THE POLITICS OF WELFARISM

There are at least two possible explanations for why people's expectations about the just distribution of material rewards should focus on the distribution of state benefits. The first, based on a strong reading of the idea of political culture, would argue that this demonstrates the continuing force of an old Buddhist political theory in which material prosperity emanates from the centre of the polity (Sarkisyanz 1965; Tambiah 1976; Roberts 1984). Certainly, a number of writers have drawn attention to the ideological importance of the state in colonial and post-colonial Sri Lanka (Moore 1985: 173; Kapferer 1988; Spencer 1990c: 208–31). But this argument obscures as much as it reveals: modern politicians are not divine kings, whatever their pretensions (cf. Kemper 1990). We also need to attend to a much more historically specific argument, based on the peculiar role of the colonial and post-colonial state in local political economy. In this argument people expect the good things in life to emanate from the political centre precisely because that is what their more recent experience has taught them to expect.

Sri Lanka underwent an economic transformation, during the period of colonial rule, far more penetrating than the transformation of the Indian economy. The development of the plantation sector provided the Government with surplus resources, some of which could be devoted to welfare measures. Post-independence governments inherited this situation, and were able to use these resources to finance ambitious programmes of state welfare which were of great benefit to rural dwellers, mostly Sinhala smallholders outside the plantation sector. From the 1930s (when elections based on universal adult franchise were first held) an impressive series of measures was introduced, including universal education, widespread health care (including the near eradication of malaria in the 1940s), and food subsidies. These were originally financed from the plantation sector (Moore 1985: 85–120), although the post-1977 Government has also received extraordinarily high levels of foreign aid.[10] As a result, extremely high levels of basic needs provision have been achieved, despite unremarkable levels of economic growth. Sri Lanka has much higher levels of literacy and life expectancy than other countries with comparable per capita GNP. In such a situation it is not surprising that politicians should try to present themselves as righteous heirs to the kings of old. Nor is it surprising that people should, up to a point, allow them their regal fantasies, especially when the actual source of state largesse is mostly hidden from the electorate, or at best unacknowledged in political argument.

Previous writers have characterized this state of affairs not as socialism but as 'welfarism' (for example, Moore 1985). The state has made occasional attempts at redistributing local resources, most notably through the reform of tenurial relations in the late 1950s and through the creation of a land ceiling in the early 1970s. But land concentration (outside the plantation sector itself) has been less marked in Sri Lanka than its regional neighbours, and these measures have had little impact on the lives of most Sinhala peasants (Herring 1983: 50–84, 125–52; Moore 1985: 50–84). In this sort of situation it is not control of local resources which lies at the base of local inequalities, but control of the inflow of state resources (cf. Alexander 1981: 119–20). Analytic attempts to identify a pattern of local class relations without reference to the state as a source of wealth are futile. That, in the end, is why arguments about economic justice must focus on the state, not on purely local inequalities. It is also why visions of an alternative social order so often treat the existence of the state in something like its present form as a given.

The post-colonial state, though, is encountered not merely as a benign source of material benefit. It is also the symbolic focus of the most important force in the island's politics, Sinhala Buddhist nationalism, and the source of a great deal of regulative legislation which the villagers I knew either ignored or knowingly evaded. Finally, the state makes contact with the average villager not just as an impersonal bureaucratic force, but through personalistic ties with local officials and party bosses. One driving force in the local politics of welfarism is the contradiction between a system rooted in personalistic patronage and a set of rewards which are, by definition, universal or near universal in their reach. This suggests obvious parallels with other socialist economies although Sri Lanka differs in respect of a third component of welfarist politics: local party competition.

With increasing intensity after the 1970 election ruling politicians have tried to make the political party the sole medium for the transmission of government resources to the electorate. In practice this means that jobs, contracts, and other benefits have been in the hands of the local MP, or in some cases in the hands of village party bosses. Party identification is particularly prominent in Sinhala villages, and a great deal of local politics can be summed up in Moore's pithy comment: 'Politics is about who will be employed by the Ceylon Transport Board as bus conductors' (Moore 1985: 210). The diversion of limited goods, like prized government jobs, along the lines of party patronage is resented but generally taken for granted in local politics. Universal benefits, like free education or health care, can hardly be channelled in similar ways. The best a party boss can do is influence the siting of schools and hospitals as 'rewards' for a particular community's support. As many communities are politically split between the major parties, this inevitably benefits both supporters and opponents. The most contentious moments, in a system bound to leave more villagers disappointed than satisfied, occur when politicians distribute goods which are general enough to raise universalist expectations, but nevertheless too few to go round. Thus the distribution of new houses in the village Brow studied led to serious splits, both within the village *and* within the local UNP (Brow 1990). The new irrigated land in the village I studied proved almost impossible to distribute. There were at least 400 local households which considered themselves not just qualified for, but *entitled to*, a share of the land, yet fewer than 100 plots to distribute. Although the allocation showed all the signs of being drawn up by the village's party boss, he argued violently that he was *not* responsible, blaming instead the MP who in turn tried to shift the blame elsewhere. The temporary solution was to abandon the proposed allocation altogether and promise a fresh allocation.

STATE AND REVOLUTION

These are minor hiccups in the workings of the political system. The state's distribution of material resources can, though, be linked in a number of ways to the growth of political violence in Sri Lanka. Between 1956 and 1977 governments were regularly ousted at general elections, not least because they failed to deliver economically. The period of the 'open economy' since 1977 has seen the end of this pattern, partly because of the Government's flexible way with constitutional procedures, partly because of the ineptitude of the main opposition party, and partly because the Government has been seen, to a greater extent than any of its predecessors, to deliver something of what it promised. This is in large part due to the huge amounts of external aid it has had at its disposal. It has been plausibly argued that this source of continuing munificence has actively encouraged the country's rulers to sidestep the usual proprieties of democratic government (Moore 1990). Growing resentment at the Government's abuse of power and an absence of legitimate channels through which to express that resentment were important factors in the second coming of the JVP in the late 1980s.

The flashpoint was provided by the Government's agreement, more or less at gunpoint, to Rajiv Gandhi's proposals to settle the Tamil problem, proposals which were seen by many Sinhala people as a betrayal of the central principles of Sinhala Buddhist nationalism. The first JVP irruption in 1971 was more directly related to popular expectations about the Government's ability to deliver material rewards and it combined millenarian expectations (and styles of action) with more mundane political considerations. The JVP leadership's vision of the new order drew heavily on the cultural capital of Sinhala nationalism. It promised a return to the prosperous days of the Sinhala kings in the wake of the expulsion of the Tamil workforce from the country's tea plantations and the expropriation of those plantations for the benefit of the Sinhala peasantry. The foot-soldiers came from a stratum of rural Sinhala youth, well-educated but under- or unemployed (Obeyesekere 1974). Their intentions were, it seems, sometimes quite straightforward: to secure their 'rightful' share of state employment and state benefits (Alexander 1981). One popular (and possibly apocryphal) tale of 1971 is that the insurrectionaries, having gained temporary control in one area, set about appointing various of their number to the vacant positions in the local bureaucracy – Government Agent, Assistant Government Agent, and so on – thus reproducing the existing structure of the state, with only the personnel changed.

It could be argued that Sri Lanka is a victim of its own success. The post-independence governments' achievements in social welfare provision led to the emergence of a stratum of well-educated but under-employed and politically volatile youth. The 1971 insurrection brought their problems to the top of the political agenda, but government responses ever since have served only to shift the problem, not remove it. The introduction of positive discrimination in favour of rural Sinhala youth in university admissions was seen as discrimination against Tamil youth. The UNP after its election victory in 1977 made efforts to target educated Sinhala youth and win them to its side, but the pattern of party patronage also excluded Tamil youth, who flocked in ever greater numbers to the cause of the Tigers. The Government's inability to deal with the Tigers led, eventually, to Indian intervention and the re-emergence of the JVP as the vehicle for Sinhala youth discontent. This time the JVP seems to have all but abandoned its earlier use of stern Leninist language, subsuming all visions of a new social order under calls for patriotic defence of the motherland. Their idea of an alternative post-revolutionary social order seems to have been as vague as the Tigers' vision of social relations in the new world of Tamil Ealam.[11]

The case of Sri Lanka does not demonstrate that the successful provision of basic needs leads directly to political disintegration, even if it does show – *pace* Gellner (1983: 22) – that 'universal Danegeld' cannot by itself guarantee legitimacy. Throughout the 1980s the Government continued to deliver economic rewards to its followers as the polity disintegrated around it. In this case one needs to explore the specifically political processes by which the Government distributed its resources and how those processes were evaluated, morally as well as materially, by those involved at all levels. It is not the provision of basic needs in general which has contributed to political breakdown, but the specific provision of mass education.

Education produces characteristic kinds of cultural dislocation which require new political answers. More government jobs for the boys and girls could soften that need, but not eliminate it. This is not the place to examine the issue in detail, but it is worth noting that Sri Lanka is not alone in confronting the problem; in recent years the frustrations of educated youth have played a large part in the downfall of governments in both India and Bangladesh.[12]

If one takes seriously Dunn's depiction of the centrality of cultural responses to economic forces in the continued vitality of socialism as a political project – 'the sense that these are not a set of terms on which human beings ought to be expected to live' (Dunn 1984: 63) – the idea of an anthropology of socialism takes on a new urgency, as anthropology has long prided itself on its ability to explore the cultural and moral worlds of other people. The Sri Lankan evidence I have presented, while inconclusive and uneven, suggests that the injustices of state distribution are as likely to arouse 'cultural revulsion' as the injustices of the market-place, while the provision of material goods and services is hardly in itself an adequate response to moral critique, and the imagination of plausible political alternatives is difficult everywhere. By the summer of 1991, the space formerly occupied by the JVP in Sinhala youth and student politics was being filled by a social movement demanding a return to 'indigenous (or national) knowledge' (*jatika cintanaya*) and the replacement of the 'open economy' (*nidahasa artikaya*) with a 'national economy' (*jatika artikaya*). In short the demise of socialist models in Eastern Europe has done nothing to alter the cultural contradictions of rapid political and economic change elsewhere in the world.

NOTES

1 For further discussion of this point, see Spencer (1990d).
2 Because of its early electoral success, which coincided neatly with the onset of the Cold War, more is known about the early history of Sri Lankan socialism than about its later decline. For the first phase (up to the 1930s), see Jayawardena (1972) and Kuruppu (1984); for the early history of the Trotskyist LSSP, see Lerski (1968); for later developments Kearney (1971) and more general works on Sri Lankan politics: for example, Wriggins (1960); Wilson (1979); Jupp (1978).
3 On the JVP in 1971, see Goonetilleke (1975), Wijeweera (1975), Halliday (1975), Obeyesekere (1974), Alexander (1981), Solidarity (1972). For the later history, see Amnesty International (1990a; 1990b), Marino (1989), Chandraprema (1991).
4 For comparative attempts to investigate the cultural critique of capitalist relations, see Moore (1978) and Scott (1976; 1985), both heavily influenced by the work of E.P. Thompson, and Parry and Bloch (1989).
5 Whereas the anthropology of India may be recovering from its earlier stereotypical view of hierarchy (for example, Daniel 1984; Appadurai 1986; cf. Parry 1974, 1979: 314–17; Béteille 1983), Sri Lanka has recently been visited with a bad outbreak of what we might call Late Orientalism (for example, Kapferer 1988,

1989; for a less florid version, see Roberts 1984, 1990; cf. Scott 1990; Spencer 1990a).

6 Fieldwork between 1981 and 1983 was supported by an ESRC studentship.

7 On *attam*, see Spencer (1990c: 110–11); cf. Robinson (1975: 62–80); Knox (1911 [1681]: 14).

8 For a scathing account of Sarvodaya, see Gombrich and Obeyesekere (1988: 243–55).

9 For further documentation of this point, see the papers collected in Spencer (1990d).

10 In 1986 India, with almost fifty times the population, received less than four times more aid than Sri Lanka. With aid making up nearly 9 per cent of GNP, Sri Lanka received the highest per capita aid donations in Asia (World Bank 1988: Table 22).

11 Cf. Hellmann-Rajanayagam (1987); Chandraprema (1991).

12 The problem is by no means unique to South Asia: cf. Hannerz (1987: 554) and Cheater, this volume.

REFERENCES

Alexander, P. (1981) 'Shared fantasies and elite politics: the Sri Lankan "insurrection" of 1971', *Mankind*, XIII (2): 113–32.

Amnesty International (1990a) *Sri Lanka: Amnesty International Briefing*, London: Amnesty International Publications.

—— (1990b) *Sri Lanka: Extrajudicial Executions, 'Disappearances' and Torture*, London: Amnesty International Publications.

Appadurai, A. (1986) 'Is homo hierarchicus?', *American Ethnologist*, XIII: 745–61.

Béteille, A. (1983) 'Homo hierarchicus, homo equalis', in A. Béteille, *The Idea of Natural Inequality and Other Essays*, Delhi: Oxford University Press.

Brow, J. (1988) 'In pursuit of hegemony: representations of authority and justice in a Sri Lankan village', *American Ethnologist* XV(2): 311–27.

—— (1990) 'Nationalist rhetoric and local practice: the fate of the village community in Kukulewa', in J. Spencer (ed.) *Sri Lanka: History and the Roots of Conflict*, London: Routledge.

Chandraprema, C.A. (1991) *Sri Lanka: The Years of Terrror. The JVP Insurrection 1987–1989*, Colombo: Lake House.

Daniel, E.V. (1984) *Fluid Signs: Being a Person the Tamil Way*, Berkeley and Los Angeles: University of California Press.

Dunn, J. (1984) *The Politics of Socialism: An Essay in Political Theory*, Cambridge: Cambridge University Press.

Gellner, E. (1983) *Nations and Nationalism*, Oxford: Basil Blackwell.

Gombrich, R. and Obeyesekere, G. (1988) *Buddhism Transformed: Religious Change in Sri Lanka*, Princeton, NJ: Princeton University Press.

Goonetilleke, H.A.I. (1975) *The April 1971 Insurrection in Ceylon: A Bibliographical Commentary*, Louvain: Centre de Recherches Socio-Réligeuses, Université de Louvain.

Halliday, F. (1975) 'The Ceylonese insurrection', in R. Blackburn (ed.) *Explosion in a Subcontinent*, Harmondsworth: Penguin.

Hannerz, U. (1987) 'The world in creolisation', *Africa*, LVII (4): 546–59.

Hellmann-Rajanayagam, D. (1987) 'The Tamil "Tigers" in northern Sri Lanka: origins, factions, programmes', *Internationales Asienforum*, XVII (1–2): 63–85.

Herring, R. (1983) *Land to the Tiller: The Political Economy of Agrarian Reform in South Asia*, New Haven and London: Yale University Press.

Jayawardena, V.K. (1972) *The Rise of the Labor Movement in Ceylon*, Durham, NC: Duke University Press.

Jupp, J. (1978) *Sri Lanka: Third World Democracy*, London: Cass.

Kapferer, B. (1988) *Legends of People, Myths of State: Violence, Intolerance and Political Culture in Sri Lanka and Australia*, Washington, DC: Smithsonian.

—— (1989) 'Nationalist ideology and a comparative anthropology', *Ethnos*, LIV: 161–99.

Kearney, R. (1971) *Trade Unions and Politics in Ceylon*, Berkeley and Los Angeles: University of California Press.

Kemper, S. (1990) 'J.R. Jayawardene: righteousness and *realpolitik*', in J. Spencer (ed.) *Sri Lanka: History and the Roots of Conflict*, London: Routledge.

Knox, R. (1911 [1681]) *An Historical Relation of the Island Ceylon*, Glasgow: MacLehose.

Kuruppu, N. (1984) 'Communalism and the labour movement in Sri Lanka', in Social Scientists' Association, *Ethnicity and Social Change in Sri Lanka*, Colombo: Social Scientists' Association.

Lerski, G. (1968) *Origins of Trotskyism in Ceylon: A Documentary History of the Lanka Sama Samaja Party, 1935–1942*, Stanford, CA: Hoover Institution Publications 74.

Ling, T. (1966) *Buddha, Marx, and God: Some Aspects of Religion in the Modern World*, London: Macmillan.

Marino, E. (1989) *Political Killings in Southern Sri Lanka on the Brink of Civil War*, London: International Alert.

Moore, B. (1978) *Injustice: The Social Bases of Obedience and Revolt*, London: Macmillan.

Moore, M. (1985) *The State and Peasant Politics in Sri Lanka*, Cambridge: Cambridge University Press.

—— (1989) 'The ideological history of the Sri Lankan "peasantry"', *Modern Asian Studies*, XXIII (1): 179–207.

—— (1990) 'Economic liberalization versus political pluralism in Sri Lanka?', *Modern Asian Studies*, XXIV (2): 341–83.

Obeyesekere, G. (1974) 'Some comments on the social backgrounds of the April 1971 insurgency in Sri Lanka (Ceylon)', *Journal of Asian Studies*, XXXIII: 367–84.

—— (1984) 'The origins and institutionalisation of political violence', in J. Manor (ed.) *Sri Lanka in Change and Crisis*, London: Croom Helm.

Parry, J. (1974) 'Egalitarian values in a hierarchical society', *South Asian Review*, VII (2): 95–121.

—— (1979) *Caste and Kinship in Kangra*, London: Routledge and Kegan Paul.

—— and Bloch, M. (eds) (1989) *Money and the Morality of Exchange*, Cambridge: Cambridge University Press.

Peel, J. (1987) 'History, culture and the comparative method: a West African puzzle', in L. Holy (ed.) *Comparative Anthropology*, Oxford: Basil Blackwell.

Roberts, M. (1984) 'Caste feudalism in Sri Lanka? A critique through the Asokan persona and European contrasts', *Contributions to Indian Sociology* (n.s.), XVIII: 189–218.

—— (1990) 'Noise as cultural struggle: tom-tom beating, the British, and communal disturbances in Sri Lanka, 1880s–1930s', in V. Das (ed.) *Mirrors of Violence: Communities, Riots, and Survivors in South Asia*, Delhi: Oxford University Press.

Robinson, M. (1975) *Political Structure in a Changing Sinhalese Village*, Cambridge: Cambridge University Press.

Samaraweera, V. (1981) 'Land, labor, capital and sectional interests in the national politics of Sri Lanka', *Modern Asian Studies*, XV (1): 127–62.

Sarkisyanz, E. (1965) *Buddhist Backgrounds of the Burmese Revolution*, The Hague: Nijhoff.

Scott, D. (1990) 'The demonology of nationalism: on the anthropology of ethnicity and violence in Sri Lanka', *Economy and Society*, XIX (4): 491–510.

Scott, J. (1976) *The Moral Economy of the Peasant*, New Haven, CT: Yale University Press.

—— (1985) *Weapons of the Weak: Everyday Forms of Peasant Resistance*, New Haven, CT: Yale University Press.

Solidarity (1972) 'Ceylon: The JVP Uprising of April 1971' Pamphlet 42, London: Solidarity.

Southwold, M. (1983) *Buddhism in Life: The Anthropological Study of Religion and the Sinhalese Practice of Buddhism*, Manchester: Manchester University Press.

Spencer, J. (1990a) 'Writing within: anthropology, nationalism and culture in Sri Lanka', *Current Anthropology*, XXXI (3): 283–91.

—— (1990b) 'Collective violence and everyday practice in Sri Lanka', *Modern Asian Studies* XXIV (3): 603–23.

—— (1990c) *A Sinhala Village in a Time of Trouble: Politics and Change in Rural Sri Lanka*, Delhi: Oxford University Press.

—— (ed.) (1990d) *Sri Lanka: History and the Roots of Conflict*, London: Routledge.

Tambiah, S. (1976) *World Conqueror and World Renouncer*, Cambridge: Cambridge University Press.

—— (1986) *Sri Lanka: Ethnic Fratricide and the Dismantling of Democracy*, London: I.B. Tauris.

Thompson, E. (1968) *The Making of the English Working Class*, 2nd edn, Harmondsworth: Penguin.

Wijeweera, R. (1975) 'Speech to the Ceylon Criminal Justice Commission', in R. Blackburn (ed.) *Explosion in a Subcontinent*, Harmondsworth: Penguin.

Wilson, A. (1979) *Politics in Sri Lanka, 1974–1979*, London: Macmillan.

World Bank (1988) *World Development Report 1988*, New York: Oxford University Press.

Wriggins, W. (1960) *Ceylon: Dilemmas of a New Nation*, Princeton, NJ: Princeton University Press.

Chapter 8

Buddhism and economic action in socialist Laos[1]

Grant Evans

Most attempts to evaluate the role of Theravada Buddhism in economic action in South-east Asia have assumed a broadly capitalist context, and some have argued tendentiously for the fundamental compatibility of Buddhist teachings and the values of capitalism (Martellaro and Choroenthaitawee 1987). Paul Cohen, on the other hand, argues that 'Buddhist social ethics . . . are . . . inconsistent with capitalist values', and that its ethic is 'socialistic' (1984: 197). The economic and social issues involved, however, are ambiguous, and this chapter will try to evaluate the role of Theravada Buddhism in the context of socialist development in Laos.

Melford E. Spiro was one of the earliest anthropologists directly to address the issues. The peasants Spiro studied were not 'other-worldly' and did not reject material pleasures. Suffering for them was 'believed to be caused by illness, poverty, dacoits, evil spirits, sorcerers, rapacious government officials, drought, and so on' (1966: 1165). Spiro broadly conceded that Buddhism in the context of Burma does not promote capital accumulation, but he also argued that religion does influence economic action by encouraging a particular form of *spending* rather than saving. Because the religious concerns of Buddhist peasants are primarily associated with rebirth rather than nirvana, the peasant is interested in accumulating merit through charitable deeds. This entails a particular pattern of religious spending, most spectacularly on temple-building. Such spending means that persons can enjoy the fruits of their labour and gain merit into the bargain. To save in the Burmese environment is not rational from the peasants' point of view, argues Spiro, because of government rapaciousness both in the past and the present. As he wrote elsewhere:

> Economic investments . . . are neither very profitable nor very sound. For although the investment potential of the total economy could, in the aggregate, have a crucial influence on Burmese economic growth which in the long run would raise the standard of living of the individual Burman, the savings of the average peasant are too small for his investment returns to increase appreciably his present standard of living. In

addition, he would be deferring known present pleasures for a very risky future pleasure.

(1982: 462)

Thus, in the context of Burma few real economic options were available to the peasant.

Essentially the same conclusions are reached in a number of other studies on Buddhism and economic action: Nash (1965), and Spiro (1966) on Burma; Ebihara (1966) on Cambodia; Pfanner and Ingersoll (1961–62) and Keyes (1983b) on Thailand; and Halpern (1964) on Laos. All of these studies agree that merit-making is the central feature of peasant popular Buddhism, and that it is a spur to economic action because wealth facilitates the making of more merit.[2] Hence a significant portion of the peasant's surplus is directed towards merit-making primarily because there are no 'rational' alternatives. In other words, far from being a drag on economic *effort* because of its 'other-worldly orientation', as Weber (1958) had suggested, Buddhism acts as a stimulus.

Popular Buddhism may also initially act as an inhibitor of private and potentially capitalist forms of accumulation in the villages through the *social pressures* on villagers to make merit, with the attendant redistributive implications and importance for village solidarity. Inevitable attempts to break with these traditional patterns, to abandon or radically transform the 'moral economy' (Scott 1976), have been a frequent source of tension in villages in developing countries. Buddhism has functioned in Thai and Lao villages as a guardian of the moral economy.[3] The process of development has led in Thailand to the emergence of 'rationalist' versions of Buddhism which legitimize a more individualistic road to salvation and provide ideological rationalizations for divergent patterns of economic action (Taylor 1990; Jackson 1989); in underdeveloped Laos such movements are not significant at all. We shall now consider the broader economic and political context in which peasant economic action takes place.

PROBLEMS OF DEVELOPMENT

State-based elites in all developing countries are concerned with the appropriation of the economic surpluses that are generated in their predominantly agrarian societies. Elites in capitalist-orientated countries have attempted to channel some of these surpluses towards the state for investments in infrastructure, including the creation of conditions favourable to the private accumulation of capital. Socialist-orientated development has attempted to channel the bulk of the surpluses into state investments, or into other forms of public investment. Both economic systems have tried, either directly or indirectly, to restrict 'wasteful' practices in the traditional system. For example, customary festivals may be shortened, or denied recognition within the timeframe of modern work organizations – bureaucracies and factories – or even outlawed. In Laos in 1977, for instance, the communist government banned the traditional *boun bang fay* fertility festival, a syncretic 'animist-Buddhist' event held each year just before the monsoon rains. The peasants blamed the following disastrous drought on the banning of the festival, and the reaction was such that the ban was discontinued (Evans 1988: 20–1), but the government continued to promote a work regime that was divorced from the rhythms of the seasons and religion. The party paper *Sieng Pasason* ran an editorial entitled, 'Build a line of conscientiously practising thrift and make it a national habit'. Too much time and wealth was being frittered away: 'Regarding the practice of thrift, it is necessary to save time,' the party paper instructed its readers (BBC 1977; cf. Thompson 1967: 93)

In Laos agricultural cooperatives, ideally, were supposed to be institutions for collectively accumulating capital in the countryside, for applying technological improvements to rice-growing, and for raising standards of living. Yields were to be divided into two parts, a surplus held by the cooperative for reinvestment and payment of taxes, and payments to cooperative members (either families or individuals). Disposal of the former was decided collectively, the latter privately. Income earned by individual cooperative members could be used for religious expenditures. As I have shown elsewhere (Evans 1990), the cooperatives generally were not successful in achieving their aims. This was the result of problems inherent in the organization of the cooperatives, technological incapacity, and the constraints of the wider command-style economy. Inside the cooperatives there were continual disputes over the proportions to be retained for collective investment, and payments to members. These disputes strengthened the feeling among individual peasants that their disposable income, including that available for ceremonial outlays, had been reduced. Outside the cooperatives, restrictions on market transactions lowered the level of activity in the rural economy and led to a general fall in other sources of income.

Yet it is also possible that government restrictions on private economic activity and its promotion of collectives had the paradoxical result of channelling what little peasant surplus there was available into religious activity.[4] In most communist systems religion has been suppressed and the assets of religious institutions nationalized. The outlay on public festivals has been restricted and diverted, back into small domestic celebrations. Besides the purely doctrinaire championing of religious repression by 'militant atheists', the economic logic was to channel unproductive assets and 'wasteful' outlays into economic growth and development. Various Burmese 'socialist' regimes have been an exception to this rule because they did not suppress religion, and in fact propagated a version of 'Buddhist socialism'. The Lao communist government that came to power at the end of 1975 did not promote a doctrine of Buddhist socialism, but neither did it suppress Buddhism. Rather, it attempted to reorganize Buddhism and to bend it to the will of the state.

PROBLEMS OF LEGITIMATION

Buddhism has traditionally been the main source of ideological legitimation for South-east Asian states, but its role has varied historically in each of them (Smith 1979). Until the rise of modern nationalism it legitimised kingships. In Burma it was used to legitimise republican nationalism. In Thailand nationalism, royalty, and Buddhism fused, as they did temporarily in Cambodia until 1970, and in Laos until 1975. Only the Khmer Rouge revolution in Cambodia followed the orthodox Stalinist line of stamping out religion. In Laos, on the other hand, the new communist state displaced Buddhism from its previously pre-eminent legitimizing role, making it a subordinate but nevertheless important element of its nationalist ideology.

The uses of Buddhism as a legitimating ideology in Laos have been discussed expertly elsewhere (Lafont 1982; Bucknell and Stuart-Fox 1982; Stuart-Fox 1984). These sources have shown how the Lao communists reconciled Buddhist doctrine with their own rudimentary Marxism-Leninism, through a focus on relations between the organization of the Buddhist monkhood, the *Sangha*, and the state. They pondered issues such as whether 'other-worldly' Buddhism is compatible with 'materialistic' Marxism. Such doctrinal questions are not unimportant given the leadership role of the monkhood in the country, yet it is interesting to note that monks were less resistant to changes in religious practices than the population at large (Lafont 1982: 157). The 'dialectic of practical religion' (Leach 1968) proved a greater obstacle to change.

In Thailand a strong alliance between the *Sangha* and the state has allowed the promotion of Buddhism as well as quasi-state-sponsored centralizing and intellectual reforms of religion (Keyes 1971). More recent reform movements have sprung from the growing urban middle classes, who have urged further rationalizations of religion, in particular purging Buddhism of its 'folk' superstitions. In Laos, by contrast, neither the state nor the *Sangha* as a bureaucratic body have ever been very powerful, even among the lowland ethnic Lao peasants. The intellectual sophistication of the *Sangha* was low, and the interrelationship between Buddhism and various forms of spirit worship shaded off into pure spirit worship as the limits of both state power and the *Sangha* were reached among the various highland 'tribal Tai'. Practical rather than doctrinaire Buddhism is the norm (Zago 1976).

The relatively weak relationship between the traditional Lao state and the *Sangha* and the latter's lack of intellectual sophistication probably accounts for the receptiveness of the *Sangha* to communist attempts to rationalize its doctrines. Given the modernizing spirit of the communist government and its 'scientific' hostility to superstitious practices, it is perhaps not surprising to find that its general approach was endorsed by Thailand's modernist Buddhists, the followers of Buddhadasa:

> These latter are of the opinion that since 1975, Lao Buddhism has freed itself of those false beliefs that have encumbered the Buddhism of other Indochinese countries. As proof, they point to the prohibition of the spirit cult (worship of *phi*). These monks believe that Lao Buddhism is reverting to the Buddha's original teaching through the labours of the committee of monks entrusted with revision of the scriptures, all of whose distinguished members are men of religious conviction and undisputed spiritual influence. They believe these reforms, once implemented, will permit the Buddha's true doctrine to be understood.
>
> (Lafont 1982: 159)

In fact, communist attempts to curtail 'superstitious practices' failed, as we have already seen in the case of the *boun bang fay*. Moreover, to the degree that the state attempted to control the activities of the *Sangha* it led many people to have greater recourse to the less controllable local spirit cults who, significantly, had been the target of earlier centralization strategies in Thailand. Monks who objected to stricter control in Laos sometimes left the *vats* (a *vat* is a temple or monastery) to become forest monks. The unpredictable movements of some of these monks meant that people came to believe that they could appear and disappear at will and possessed magical powers.

The new government in Laos tried to accommodate Buddhist teachings and morality to certain socialist ideals concerning egalitarianism and work for the common good. The concept of the ascetic, selfless person working for a higher existence is the folk model of a good person in rural Laos, and this model influenced the new regime's concept of the 'New socialist man'. Most ethnic Lao party members remain active Buddhists, and I have observed persons who have held ministerial positions in the Government walking around shirtless in their homes with gold and jade Buddhist pendants dangling around their necks, and this support for Buddhism was not just political expediency.

Speaking to a gathering of monks in late 1976, the then Deputy Premier and Minister of Education, Sports and Religious Affairs Phoumi Vongvichit said:

> The Lord Buddha gave up all his worldly possessions and became an ordinary person with only an alms bowl to beg food from other people. That meant that he tried to abolish classes in his country and to create only one class – a class of morally conscious people. . . . We can see now

that the revolutionary politics practised by the Lord Buddha have the same goals.

(Appendix in Ling 1979: 149)

Variations on this theme were propagated throughout the country by cadres and by monks. The radical monk Khamtan Thepboualy provided a popularization in his *The Lao Sangha and the Revolution* (1975). The monks came to play an enhanced role in post-revolutionary Laos as educators in literacy campaigns which were conducted for older people in the *vats*. This traditional educational role had been declining since the 1950s as secular schools came into existence (Taillard 1974), but the exodus of many educated people after 1975 as refugees threw the regime back into reliance on the monkhood (Lafont 1982). Thus in some respects the role of the *Sangha* was bolstered in the new situation, even though Buddhist teachings were banned from primary schools. The monks also became an important voice for the new regime's policies in the countryside, including the promotion of agricultural cooperatives. The idea of using the *Sangha* in this way was not new. Prior to 1975 various advisers in both Laos and Thailand had sought to involve the Buddhist monkhood in economic development programmes (Niehoff 1964; Boutsavath and Chapelier 1973; cf. Mulder 1973). Modernist reformist Buddhism in Thailand argues similarly for a socially engaged Buddhism (Jackson 1989; Sivaraksa 1985).

In 1976 both pragmatic and doctrinal pressures combined in the government's attempt to forbid ordinary people from supporting monks through daily food offerings. This was part of a campaign against 'parasitism' in a poor and underdeveloped country, and the monks were encouraged to establish gardens and work for their food.[5] The context was one of poor harvests and food shortages during the first years of the regime. There were, naturally, doctrinal objections by Buddhists. Monks were not supposed to be preoccupied with mundane material concerns such as obtaining food, and if they worked in the fields they risked taking life accidentally. However, a much more important popular objection was that by attempting to ban the giving of food to monks the regime was depriving people of an opportunity to make merit. This popular resistance caused a progressive retreat by government and local authorities. First, the authorities said only rice could be offered. Later they attempted to bring the giving of food within the purview of the state by promising in some instances themselves to provide *vats* with rice, or some local authorities attempted to allocate responsibility for the provisioning of monks on a daily basis either to specific families or to small village units (*khum*). Although some communities in Thailand independently organized a similar allocation of responsibility within the village (Moerman 1966: 142), attempts by the state in Laos to regulate the provisioning of the *Sangha* collapsed.

It does, however, seem that in the Lao case the question of whether the monks should help provision themselves or not was less a question of doctrine than necessity. In poorer areas it was not considered outrageous if monks partially provisioned themselves – the alternative being deserted *vats*.[6] Even as late as 1987 some monks (and any nuns present) close to the capital Vientiane cooked for themselves. 'They have adjusted to the new situation', I was told by village officials. From the point of view of the lay person, what was important was the opportunity to earn merit by giving food to the monks on their daily rounds or to the *vat*. Attempts to close off this opportunity to make merit were more important a threat to the villagers than doctrinal reforms.

Much more effective, however, was state disapproval of spending on celebrations or on the upkeep of *vats*. Until the mid-1980s many *vats* needed repairs and those which were only half finished at the time the communists took power stood grey and roofless for fifteen years. To finance or to contribute to the building of a temple earns great merit, and usually only well-off people can afford such outlays. Most of these people left Laos after 1975, and the few wealthy people made a point of not displaying their wealth. Some poorer people said they welcomed a respite from the competitive merit-making cycle, but this is once again in full swing in and around Vientiane.

CEREMONIAL REDISTRIBUTION

Before 1975 surpluses among Lao peasants were often directed into maintaining the *vat*, and ceremonial outlays and expenditures on festivals were a well-established means for redistributing wealth in the villages through the medium of the temple. By contributing to the *vat* the donor acquired both religious merit and social prestige. Merit-making (*het boun*) is fundamental to popular Theravada Buddhism in Laos and in the neighbouring countries. As one man said, 'real Buddhists' are the ones who throw lavish ceremonies. Popular Buddhism is not theologically sophisticated, and it is, by and large, not focused on world renunciation and the ultimate aim of Buddhism, the attainment of *niphan* (nirvana). Most ordinary Lao peasants have a general understanding of the doctrine of *kam* (karma) as a tally of an individual's merit and demerit acquired in previous lives and in the present. Merit is earned by following Buddhist morality and by supporting the *Sangha*, the symbol of Buddhist ideals in the midst of the villagers' everyday life. Karma is not understood as a fatalistic doctrine of predestination, but is something that can be 'worked' on to improve one's chances and well-being both in this life and the next. The most unambiguous and socially registered way of making merit is by giving to the *Sangha* and by holding ceremonies in the *vat*. The doctrine of karma as a kind of fatalism is usually only invoked to help explain events beyond the control of the individual – sudden misfortune, or a windfall of good fortune. However, recourse is made regularly to various spirits and their mediums – *moh dam* and *nang tiam* – to assist with the unpredictable contingencies of everyday life. In fact, popular religion in Laos, as Condominas has demonstrated so well (1970; 1975), is fundamentally Buddhist–spirit cult syncretism.

While the literature on Theravada Buddhism in South-east Asia places great stress on its supposed individualism, merit-making is a profoundly social activity in rural villages. The daily rounds of the monks in the village are not just occasions for individual demonstrations of support for the *Sangha*. They are also highly visible displays of the commitment of the whole community. Furthermore, merit-making of this kind is generally conceived as household support for the *Sangha*. This is achieved through the general belief in merit-transference so fundamental to popular Buddhism in Laos and Thailand (Keyes 1983a). That is, meritorious actions carried out by one person in the household, or a near relative, or a member of the village, can be transferred to another person or persons who can be either living or dead. Key ritual events, such as the induction of monks into the *Sangha* or funerals are occasions on which broader networks are activated to provide support. Thus the son of a poorer family can approach a relatively distant relative to sponsor his entry into the *Sangha*, an act that will earn the donor merit. Throughout Laos religious events are still the principal ones which punctuate the annual cycle of rice-growing. As numerous observers have noted, these festivals provide a moral-religious focus for a village or villages, and are occasions for people from other villages to visit relatives or friends in the host village and for courting. *Bouns* (usually religious festivals) are forms of ceremonial consumption, and they earn merit as well as social prestige for the host. Christian Taillard comments on the importance of these celebrations:

> The dynamic of the *boun* overcomes antagonisms and contributes to the *piep* (good-will) of social life. The individual who accumulates more material goods than others, even at their expense, will then have them redistributed among the community through the *vat*. This levels individual wealth and maintains a socio-economic equilibrium between the various households. By transposing social competition from a material plane to a spiritual plane, the *vat* establishes a new logic of prestige: the more this is striven for the more wealth is redistributed and the more solidarity is reinforced. Thus a dynamic of redistribution is established whereby competition is no longer a problem but in fact reinforces village solidarity.
>
> (1977: 78)

Buddhist ritual and ceremonies dramatize social and economic reciprocity within the village. Thus merit-making in all its forms plays a basic social role in village life, and its disruption threatens to break a vital filament in the social fabric of the village.

One *boun khong bouat* held for the induction of a monk into the *Sangha* in 1982 in a village in my research area just outside Vientiane provides a good example of the ceremonial liquidation of wealth. It was given by an elderly widow in memory of her husband, and her young son was becoming a monk to acquire merit for her. The *boun* itself lasted two days. The first day was taken up with the preparation of the food and gifts to be presented to the *Sangha* at the *vat* the following day, the shaving of the youth's head, well-wishing, and praying. The men prepared a *Phasat* to which money was appended, while women prepared the food and villagers helped in the general preparations. The bulk of the expense fell on the widow, but relatives and friends also made substantial contributions. This particular *boun khong bouat* cost 28,000NK (US$2,800). Matched against the annual earnings of the very highest income-earners in the village, this amounted to approximately five years' cash income expended on one festival. At that time approximately thirty *boun khong bouat* were held in the district (*tasseng*) annually, and considerable wealth was 'unproductively' consumed in socialist Laos, despite government calls for thrift.

Large sums were also spent on the upkeep of religious monuments or the building of new ones. For example, on the far side of a nearby village, a craftsman and his assistant were employed full-time constructing a 6-metre high Buddha adjacent to an existing *vat*. People often said that they did not have as much money for the *vat* as before 1975, and spent what money they had on consumer items. The old headman of another village in the district, who was an active parishioner, complained about the shortage of money because he wished for a better *vat* in his village. Ngai, the head of the cooperative in the same village, claimed that there had been a significant decline in the number of ceremonies related to the agricultural cycle since 1975. Asked if this was due to Government discouragement, he replied that an empty stomach was the main reason, a *boun* could cost up to three or four months of a farmer's income. It appears, however, that after 1975 there was also less social pressure on people to compete for prestige by throwing *bouns*, largely as a result of Government discouragement and because people did not wish to draw the state's attention to any wealth they possessed. By frowning on the 'wastefulness' of religious ceremonies the government may have inhibited a levelling mechanism in the Lao village. After all, it is a common view in Laos and in neighbouring Thailand 'that a rich man should spend his money' (Moerman 1966: 153).

RECIPROCITY AND SOLIDARITY

In Laos the state-socialist context has structured the patterns of peasant economic action. Its restrictions on the private accumulation of wealth and on market transactions ensured that traditional patterns of religious spending continued there. Indeed, the contraction of the market and the

resurgence of the 'natural economy' made villages relatively more aut-
archic and increased the importance of traditional mechanisms of solidarity
such as those centred on the *vats*. It was hoped that the cooperatives would
become the centre of village administration, but they never did. Some
cooperatives displaced the *vat* temporarily as an important centre for
secular village affairs (especially if the cooperative had electricity for meetings at night), but community identity remained fixed on the *vat*, and its
status, rather than that of the cooperative, was considered the primary
index of a village's standing and accumulated merit.

Why didn't the cooperative become a focus for village solidarity? The
reasons are multiple, and elsewhere I have given a detailed analysis of the
contradictions which arose between the peasant economy and the attempts
to establish a collectivized agricultural sector (Evans 1990). The latter
ultimately disintegrated because it tried to rearrange peasant production
without being able to introduce substantial technological improvements.
This not only complicated the peasants' lives unnecessarily but also led to
a fall in production, and to the extent that the cooperatives were economically unsuccessful there was less income available for merit-making. This
added significantly to their unpopularity, although it could hardly be
construed as a fundamental reason for the failure of the cooperativization
programme in Laos.

Would the cooperativization programme been any more successful had
it tried to mobilize Buddhist ideology and practices in order to legitimize
the programme? In the final chapter of my book I discussed the problems
that voluntary cooperatives have in establishing an ideology that will
justify claims made on the individual and the family by the cooperative. In
this regard I suggested that the cooperative was at a disadvantage compared with the peasant household, whose solidarity and claims could be
presented as 'natural' in contrast to the culturally constructed claims of the
cooperative. 'Claims beyond the "natural" ones of kin require different
justifications, such as appeals to community, ethnicity, religious duty,
nationalism, or revolutionary duty. To compete with or supersede the
primordial imperatives of the household these superior claims must be
either compelling or compulsory' (Evans 1990: 216). The socialist Government appealed, of course, to the concept of the 'new socialist man', which
admittedly had been given a light Buddhist gloss, in its attempt to confirm
the cooperatives' superior claims. Yet it is doubtful that state arguments
would have been any more compelling had they upgraded the Buddhist
elements into something approximating a Buddhist-socialist ideology,
primarily for the economic reasons I have outlined very briefly above – cf.
Cohen's (1984) analysis of grass-roots Buddhist attempts at collective action
in Thailand. No doubt the cooperatives could have attempted to integrate
themselves into religious festivals and openly begun collective merit-
making alongside the individual merit-making of its members. However,

just as the failure of the cooperatives to lift peasant productivity under-mined its economic rationality, collective merit-making would have undermined its role as a public accumulator of capital in the countryside and simply duplicated what was already being done by its members. Of course, had the cooperatives been economically successful, then they might have been able to enhance their success by collective participation in merit-making, but that did not happen.

There is a striking homology between the structure of the peasant economy and the structure of merit-making and ceremonial redistribution in the traditional system. Despite Buddhism's other-worldly claims, ordi-nary peasants in Laos and Thailand are not enamoured of poverty and would like to be better off than they are. The organization of the peasant economy does allow good farmers to get ahead both through hard work and through an ability to mobilize the labour of the family and broader kin, and of friends, at crucial times in both the domestic and work cycle. Farmers who do well not only gain respect as good farmers but they are also more able to sponsor merit-making and thereby share their good fortune and acquire prestige as people who have accumulated merit. The rewards for being a good farmer are socially recognized and reinforced by the local community through the medium of the *vat*.

Lao peasant farmers, in trying to balance out their labour requirements seasonally and throughout the domestic cycle of their household, enter into various traditional labour-exchange arrangements, with occasionally some wage-labour at the margin (Evans 1990: chap. 6). Farmers are involved in complex strategic and short-term decisions about the type of reciprocal obligations they can enter into, and these vary according to the composition of the household, its place in the system of village stratification, and so on.

> Not surprisingly labour tends to be mobilized along already existing lines of kinship. Bilateral kin who happen to have neighbouring rice fields are ideal labour-exchange partners, and, of course, for practical reasons neighbours in the field who are not kin are also ideal partners. But, given the importance of the idiom of kinship, attempts will often be made to establish some distant or quasi-familial link.
>
> (Evans 1990: 140)

As Moerman (1966) observes, bilateral kinship allows a wide range of *possible* ties which can be activated or strengthened through social action. The formation of relatively stable labour-exchange groups is one strategy, and these may be reinforced ceremonially. Thus the selection of a sponsor for a *boun khong bouat* may confirm a kinship link which can be used either to form or strengthen a relationship of reciprocity in the paddy fields. These arrangements are designed to stabilize and potentially enhance the peasant farm's productivity. It is a system in which 'rough reciprocity' is designed in such a way that everyone comes out ahead, and therefore this delicately tuned social mechanism is a crucial part of the incentive structure of the peasant economy (Evans 1990: 146–7). Buddhist ceremony and merit-making facilitate these important relationships within the peasant economy and ensure their effectiveness. In this way Buddhism can allow the expression of both private household and broader social interests to be articulated in transcendent terms – precisely the form of ideology that the communist Government was searching for.

Cooperatives, on the other hand, made abstract appeals to the ethics of 'socialist man' and to nationalism – 'building and strengthening the nation' – neither of which strikes any deep chords in Lao villages. They also tried to construct a system of prestigious prizes to reward cooperatives and cooperative members. The cooperatives I studied all had pinned to the wall various certificates emblazoned with the Lao Peoples' Democratic Republic laurel congratulating them on their success in production or their patriotism for selling such-and-such a quantity of rice to the state, and so on. It is fairly easy to understand why these awards did not carry the same aura or prestige as acquired individual merit. The awards were usually held collectively, which meant that they reflected only distantly on each member. As far as I could discern, they reflected most strongly on the cooperative heads and in diminishing amounts down from him in what remains a finely graded hierarchical society. But awards from the state still carry much less prestige in the Lao villages than the awarding of prestige to a person by the local community, which is what happened traditionally through the medium of the local *vat*. The modern state and its system of values is still remote from the world of the villagers in Laos, and while it has clearly gained ground under the socialist regime it is still secondary in the local milieu. If the *Sangha* ever had been put in a position where it could grant merit to the members of cooperatives for selling rice to the state, it is still unlikely that this would have significantly lifted the prestige of these state awards. It is more likely that such a step would have downgraded the prestige of the *Sangha*.

Members of cooperatives were tempted into channelling their funds in traditional ways by sponsoring *bouns*. Cooperative leader Ngai boasted that under the new regime only the cooperatives had large enough yields to throw *bouns*, whereas in the past it was the better-off peasants. Here the head of a cooperative of predominantly landless peasants (see Evans 1990, chap. 5 for details) was dreaming the dream of a traditional well-off peasant. In fact, cooperatives spent little on religious activities. When the cooperative main shed was first completed, monks were brought in and a ceremony was held to bless it. If the 'socialist' peasantry had their way, 'socialist' merit-making would have become integrated into the cooperatives, but what would become of socialist accumulation then?

Cooperatives also threw people together as individuals, expecting them to work as one big happy family. Many peasants complained about this because it robbed them of the ability to make choices about those with whom they would engage in reciprocal labour exchanges. The cooperatives therefore disrupted a crucial element in the incentive structure of the peasant economy, to replace it with, first, moral and political exhortation, and secondly, a work-point 'cash-nexus' incentive structure which had little point to it in an agrarian system in which no basic technological change had been introduced. Ironically, the cooperatives ended up reinforcing 'individualism' through their failure to construct a rationale for transcendent bonds. Hence the cooperatives rapidly collapsed back into the peasant economy as soon as state pressure was eased.

As far as gender relations are concerned, I argued in my book that Lao women had fewer interests in participating in cooperativization campaigns than women elsewhere (for example, in China or Vietnam) because they already had clear access to land, while collectivization was likely to divest them of both ownership and control of land by placing it in the hands of male officials (Evans 1990: 129–33). Furthermore, the promotion of trading cooperatives also threatened the important role of women in trade. In this regard we can suggest that collectivization threatened Lao women's opportunities for merit-making more than it did men's, and in a context where, theologically, they had greater need for merit (cf. Kirsch 1982). This could only have reinforced their reasons for resistance to socialist reorganization of the economy. Significantly, in Laos the trading cooperatives have been no more successful than the agricultural producer cooperatives.

CONCLUSION

In Lao villages the economic role of Buddhism has been complex. Given the importance of merit-making in the traditional system, Buddhism could act as a stimulus to economic action which, however, had as its aim the accumulation of merit not capital. In this sense it discouraged accumulation in the interests of either socialism or capitalism. At a practical level Buddhism was more resistant to intrusive socialist attempts to reorganize the peasant economy because these tried to inhibit merit-making and disrupted religiously mediated bonds of solidarity which were so vital to the peasant economy. Besides the fundamental economic failure of the cooperatives, these institutions were unable to develop substitute bonds of solidarity. Although capitalist developments in the rural economy and reformed Buddhism elsewhere also undermine the moral economy of the villages, these changes operate with a hidden hand rather than a heavy hand, and changes occur piecemeal rather than in one fell swoop. Therefore they engender less uniform peasant resistance than socialism. Under capitalism, gradual changes in relations between villagers are likely to be traced as shifts in individual merit, and so Buddhism is able to act as an ideology which rationalizes the disintegration of the moral economy while simultaneously being used to police it.

NOTES

1 I would like to thank Charles F. Keyes for comments on a draft of this chapter. More information about the fieldwork on which it is based can be found in Evans 1988, 1990.
2 The only dissenting voice is Thomas Kirsch, who argues that women are relatively prominent in village economic action in Thailand compared with men because of 'Buddhist devaluation of economic endeavours in general' (1982: 28). Men are involved in a 'flight from the world'. He does observe that women are more diligent merit-makers than men because of their greater need for merit, but he does not connect this with their economic diligence. Thus, on balance, Buddhism is not important for economic action in Kirsch's argument.
3 I found only one case of a household attempting to free itself from broader community obligations. It took the form of a conflict between the *vat* (temple monastery) and a spirit belonging to a *nang tiam* (female spirit medium). The spirit resided in the house and had a special small room dedicated to it, and it was claimed by this household that the spirit did not like them giving contributions to the *vat*. Consequently they were able to minimize their communal religious outlays. Generally, however, such spirits do not directly compete with Buddhism in this way (Tambiah 1970).
4 Such a response was observed by Spiro in Burma: 'From the traditional Burmese monarchy to the present military dictatorship, confiscation of private wealth has been a consistent policy of almost all Burmese governments . . . these factors alone have served throughout Burmese history to channel savings into religion' (1982: 462).
5 Lafont (1982: 156) notes that similar criticisms had been voiced about the monkhood prior to 1975.
6 Poor areas of Thailand have also faced the same dilemma: 'in some poorer areas, especially the Northeast, the practice of maintaining a *vat* and its resident monks is economically impossible . . . . Life, without institutionalized religion or monks, in this region is a distinct possibility' (Mulder 1973: 9). This was also true for many parts of Laos.

REFERENCES

BBC (1977) Summary of World Broadcasts 5605/B3/2 (Sept. 3).
Boutsavath, V. and Chapelier, G. (1973) 'Lao popular Buddhism and community development', *Journal of the Siam Society*, 69(2).
Bucknell, R. and Stuart-Fox, M. (1982) 'Politicization of the Buddhist *Sangha* in Laos', *Journal of Southeast Asian Studies*, 13(1).
Cohen, Paul T. (1984) 'The sovereignty of Dhamma and economic development: Buddhist social ethics in rural Thailand', *Journal of the Siam Society*, 72.
Condominas, G. (1970) 'The Lao', in *Laos: War and Revolution*, N.S. Adams and A.W. McCoy (eds), New York: Harper & Row.
—— (1975) '*Phi Ban* cults in rural Laos', in *Change and Persistence in Thai Society*, G.W. Skinner and T.A. Kirsch (eds), Ithaca, NY: Cornell University Press.
Ebihara, M. (1966) 'Interrelations between Buddhism and social systems in Cambo-

dian peasant culture', in *Anthropological Studies of Theravada Buddhism*, M. Nash (ed.), Yale University Southeast Asia Studies.

Evans, G. (1988) *Agrarian Change in Communist Laos*, ISEAS, Singapore.

—— (1990) *Lao Peasants Under Socialism*, New Haven, CT: Yale University Press.

Halpern, J. (1964) 'Capital, savings and credit among Lao peasants', in *Capital, Savings and Credit in Peasant Societies*, R. Firth and B.S. Yamey (eds), London: George Allen & Unwin.

Jackson, P. (1989) *Buddhism, Legitimation, and Conflict: The Political Functions of Thai Urban Buddhism*, ISEAS, Singapore.

Keyes, C.F. (1971) 'Buddhism and national integration in Thailand', *Journal of Asian Studies*, 30(3).

—— (1983a) 'Merit-transference in the Karmic theory of popular Theravada Buddhism', in *Karma: An Anthropological Inquiry*, C.F. Keyes and E.V. Daniel (eds), Berkeley: University of California.

—— (1983b) 'Economic action and Buddhist morality in a Thai village', *Journal of Asian Studies*, 42(4).

Kirsch, T. (1982) 'Buddhism, sex-roles and the Thai economy', in *Women of Southeast Asia*, P. Van Esterik (ed.), Center for Southeast Asian Studies, Northern Illinois University.

Lafont, P.-B. (1982) 'Buddhism in contemporary Laos', in *Contemporary Laos*, M. Stuart-Fox (ed.), St Lucia: University of Queensland Press.

Leach, E. (ed.) (1968) *Dialectic in Practical Religion*, Cambridge: Cambridge University Press.

Ling, T. (1979) *Buddhism, Imperialism and War*, London: George Allen & Unwin.

Martellaro, J.A. and Choroenthaitawee, K. (1987) 'Buddhism and capitalism in Thailand', *Asian Profile*, 15(2).

Moerman, M. (1966) 'Ban Ping's Temple: the center of a "loosely structured" society', in *Anthropological Studies of Theravada Buddhism*, M. Nash (ed.), Yale University Southeast Asia Studies.

Mulder, J.A.N. (1973) *Monks, Merit and Motivation: Buddhism and National Development in Thailand*, Center for Southeast Asian Studies, Northern Illinois University.

Nash, M. (1965) *The Golden Road to Modernity*, Chicago: University of Chicago Press.

Niehoff, A. (1964) 'Theravada Buddhism: a vehicle for technical change', *Human Organization*, 23.

Pfanner, D.E. and Ingersoll, J. (1961–62) 'Theravada Buddhism and village economic behaviour: a Burmese and Thai comparison', *Journal of Asian Studies*, 21.

Scott, J.C. (1976) *The Moral Economy of the Peasant*, New Haven, CT: Yale University Press.

Sivaraksa, S. (1985) *Siamese Resurgence*, Bangkok: Sasian Cultural Forum on Development.

Smith, B.L. (ed.) (1979) *Religion and the Legitimation of Power in Thailand, Laos and Burma*, Anima Books.

Spiro, M.E. (1966) 'Buddhism and economic action in Burma', *American Anthropologist*, 68.

—— (1982) *Buddhism and Society: A Great Tradition and its Burmese Vicissitudes*, 2nd expanded edn, Berkeley, CA: University of California Press.

Stuart-Fox, M. (1984) 'Marxism and Theravada Buddhism: the legitimation of political authority in Laos', *Pacific Affairs*, 56.

Taillard, C. (1974) 'Essai sur la bipolarisation autour du *vat* et de l'école des villages Lao de la Plaine de Vientiane', *Asie Sud-est et Monde Insulindien*, 3.

—— (1977) 'Le village Lao de la région de Vientiane: un pouvoir local face au pouvoir étatique', *L'Homme*, 17(2–3) (April-Sept.).

Tambiah, S. (1970) *Buddhism and the Spirit Cults in Northeast Thailand*, Cambridge: Cambridge University Press.

Taylor, J.L. (1990) 'New Buddhist movements in Thailand: an "individualistic revolution", reform and political dissonance', *Journal of Southeast Asian Studies*, 21(1).

Thepboualy, K. (1975) *The Lao Sangha and the Revolution*, Neo Lao Hak Sat Press.

Thompson, E.P. (1967) 'Time, work discipline and industrial capitalism', *Past and Present*, 38.

Weber, M. (1958) *The Religion of India: The Sociology of Hinduism and Buddhism*, Glencoe, IL: The Free Press.

Zago, M. (1976) 'Buddhism in contemporary Laos', in *Buddhism in the Modern World*, H. Dumoulin and J.C. Moraldo (eds), New York: Collier Books.

Chapter 9

The domestication of religion under Soviet communism

Tamara Dragadze

BACKGROUND

The questions I am concerned with are both historical and futuristic. First, what happened to mainstream religions in the USSR after the 1930s when, under Stalin, they were the object of targeted attack? Second, what happens when restrictions are relaxed in the *perestroika* period, and what are the prospects for religion in post-communist society? In seeking to answer these questions I shall be concerned with 'scientific Marxism' as a mode of thought as well as the religious ideologies of Islam and Christianity as found within the territories of what was, until very recently, the Soviet Union. Because there is such ethnographic diversity within this region (for example, Humphrey 1983; Dragadze 1988), I shall restrict the focus to ritual practices accompanying life crises and illness. In exploring this field I draw principally upon Emile Durkheim's classic opposition between 'sacred' and 'profane', and show how it can be applied in contemporary communist and post-communist societies. An important subsidiary theme is the notion of 'rationality', as it used to underlie official militant atheism in the Soviet Union.

For reasons of space it is impossible here to give a full account of communist policies towards religion in the USSR, which undoubtedly shared many features with communist religious policies elsewhere.[1] Among the tasks facing the Bolshevik regime after 1917 was to reconstitute the previous colonies of the tsarist Russian Empire into the Soviet Union. Another task, however, was to mobilize populations into serving a centralized command system whose legitimacy rested on the acceptance of a particular ideology. In my view this ideology was always a botched-up concoction of *ad hoc* measures, with constraints set only by the need to *appear* to adhere to *some kind of* Leninist version of a selection of pronouncements by Karl Marx.[2]

Land and property reform ensured that the economic power base of official religious institutions was destroyed quite soon after the Revolution. A further aim was to destroy religious beliefs that could potentially compete with the ideology of the new state, and a great deal of attention was paid to this aim. The two ways in which this could most rapidly be achieved, apart from the use of direct punitive measures against individuals, were on the one hand to destroy buildings and spaces set apart for religious devotion, and on the other hand to expound militant atheism under the banner of Marx's pronouncement that religion is the opium of the people, with all the means at the state's disposal. Let me turn now to examine the implementation of these policies in the areas where I have conducted fieldwork; namely, the Christian and Muslim populations of Georgia and Azerbaijan respectively.[3]

RELIGIOUS BUILDINGS AND RITUAL SPECIALISTS

Before communist impact, most cultures of the USSR had specific buildings which were set apart for religious worship, where full-time, professional ritual specialists and religious teachers were located in the vicinity, and where particular behaviour by devotees was prescribed. Sometimes due to popular esteem for the quality of devotion displayed in religious worship within the building and its surroundings, and sometimes because of the distinctiveness of its architecture and the history imputed to it, the building tended to acquire an autonomous identity. As is common in the Christian Mediterranean, particular church buildings and their precincts in Georgia were popularly thought to possess divine power deriving from patronage of a particular saint or angel. The term 'popular' implies a unified set of ideas with an unspecified, mass authorship, but it is important to remember that individual interpretations may differ greatly. I was told by some Georgians that the very stones of the buildings were thought to be imbued with divine power, but by others that the presence of any 'angel' was elusive and that its physical location, apart from a vague preference for a given church, could not be defined.

My contemporary informants do not speak with one voice, and one must assume that differing views prevailed before Sovietization as well. In Georgia, village churches were virtually all destroyed and the building materials were used to erect schools, club-houses, or other community amenities. In Ghari village in Ratcha province, the wood of the church was used to build a school. When people kept on coming to touch the school walls and pray, the wood was dismantled again and moved quite some distance away (30 km), for use in the construction of a sanatorium. Where buildings were not destroyed their interiors were vandalized, with icons thrown around and windows smashed.

Among Muslims, certain mosques were imputed with specific spirituality. The burial places of holy men (and of some women, such as the tomb of the mother of Kunta Hadji in Chechnia, in the North Caucasus – see Bennigsen Broxup 1992) were believed to possess the power to channel prayers to divine sources. Particular ritual behaviour in these locations was prescribed, including, for example, appropriate dress and the way people should comport themselves, without ever turning their back to the shrine. The status of the attendants in these buildings was revered; they were the main ritual specialists in Azerbaijani society.[4] One such special location was Bibi Eibat, outside Baku, which had a spring dating back to ancient times, remarkable in its barren surroundings. In the Muslim period this site had become the location of a shrine which was known throughout the country. In 1936 the Soviet authorities dynamited this shrine, covered up the water source with a road, and built on the surrounding land. They argued that the road could not have followed any alternative route, but in reality one suspects that the reasons for the destruction of the shrine and the concealing of the water spring were quite different. Most village mosques in Azerbaijan were either destroyed, ostensibly because the stone was needed to build roads, or deliberately assigned for other purposes, such as a cooperative shop.

Although in both Georgia and Azerbaijan (as well as in Muslim Central Asia) healing and special prayers were often performed by lay members of the public, by those whose main livelihood was derived from other sources, there were also priests and mullahs whose main source of livelihood was derived from religious practice and who were believed to be experts in their profession. In the 1930s many of these were deported as *kulaks* or simply killed, and the ferociousness of this persecution has often been understated by commentators since.[5] A situation was soon created in which there was an absence of professional practitioners. Under threat of punishment, even those religious specialists who remained in the villages were often afraid to practise their skills. Thus, during life crises or religious festivals the people no longer had access to the expertise of professional religious practitioners whose sanctity was believed to set them apart from their fellows. Their special spiritual powers could no longer be invoked. Therefore ordinary people had to adjust, but they were able to maintain their rituals in spite of the absence of sacred buildings and of the personnel which had previously been thought essential for the efficacy of their prayers.

THE DOMESTICATION OF RELIGION

I use the term domestication in two closely related senses. On the one hand, it embodies the idea of shifting the arena from public to private, from outside the home to its interior. On the other hand, it also signifies the harnessing and taming of that which had seemed outside the control of ordinary people. In this case what can loosely be called 'spiritual powers' had formerly been thought to be the domain of specialists, from which non-specialists were excluded through lack of training and sanctity. In such circumstances, domestication implies the attempt to gain more control for oneself. This must imply a shift of the boundary between 'profane' and 'sacred', and it suggests an *enlarging* of the actual mental space of the 'sacred'. This, of course, presents a paradox for the communists. Instead of rejoicing at the demise of official religious structures, they must confront a growth in the relative significance of certain domestic rituals. In comparison with previous practice, the domain of religious observance seemed to become more prominent.

The analysis is underpinned by two implicit assumptions. First, I take it that the need for tapping divine/spiritual power and for intervention in life crises continued unabated in the lives of ordinary people under communism. Second, I assume that the role of communist ideology in the form of atheist propaganda was significant, and had an impact on the way people adjusted to the new environment. The gestalt representations in communist atheism provided the means for lay people to gain sufficient confidence to take on roles previously monopolized by ritual specialists (see Table 9.1).

Table 9.1   Gestalt representations in communist atheist propaganda

'Scientific Marxism'	*'Religion'*
'Rationality'	'Superstition', 'lies'
Full control of destiny	Submission to divine will
Creativity (new rites, new festivals)	Inertia
All-powerful, limitless scope of action	Passivity, humility
Fearlessness	Fearful
Advantage: promise of future wealth and prosperity	Present poverty (all those years of praying in the past got you nowhere)

My extensive research experience in various parts of the Soviet Union suggests to me that there was some internalization by the population of parts of the propaganda of 'scientific Marxism'. On the other hand, this 'communist religion' was not particularly successful in competing for loyalties, since the promises of prosperity did not materialize and contradictions between the alleged rationality of scientific atheism and the irrationality of Stalin's personality cult, as well as the discrepancies between slogans and reality more generally, all eroded popular faith in the infallibility of official propaganda. Let us begin by considering again the case of Islam in Azerbaijan.[6]

The rationale for the destruction of religious buildings and discouragement of religious belief and practice by communists was that people had to be liberated from the hoaxes and illusions that had been foisted upon them by previous power structures. 'Truth' rested in accepting a 'rational' world where the material world alone embodied 'reality'. This in principle implied that humankind had the capacity to control this reality: even death and illness – the main causes for seeking divine intervention – in a bright and hopefully not too distant future would be controlled through 'scientific' means. A boost was given to such reasoning when sacred buildings were destroyed, without immediate catastrophic consequences. For example, I was told that when the shrine of Bibi Eibat was destroyed, some believers had expected a terrible disaster to afflict the whole planet. This did not happen; there was not even an eclipse of the sun. (Nevertheless, I have yet to hear an account of the destruction of a religious building in Georgia or Azerbaijan which was not accompanied by recounting the individual tragedies that afflicted those that carried out the order: premature death, debilitating illness, or some other family misfortune.)

The demise of 'sacred' space had to be absorbed and reinterpreted, not least because a new evaluation of its autonomous powers had to take place. In Azerbaijan, where stones from mosques were used to build roads to walk on, following the initial shame and shock there grew a certain fascination with the possibility of walking on them without enduring subsequent affliction. A shift in parameters took place, which emboldened previously diffident people to attempt ritual practices previously outside their scope and competence. For example, in the Azerbaijani village I have been studying, the increased part played by women is noticeable. Communists saw women as less of a threat and were more likely to turn a blind eye to their 'folk' ways than to those of men. We still do not know enough about how women were able to internalize a rationale that would encourage them to expand their role in religious practices. No doubt they had always played some role in the domestic sphere, as do women in other Muslim societies, but communist conditions gave them for the first time a more central role in the preservation of religious identities.[7] Until recently, it was considered safer and more appropriate for supplication and accompanying rituals of all descriptions to be carried out in the privacy of the home. In Azerbaijan, the cemetery vaults of people thought to have been holy have lately become the focus of religious devotion. Such shrines are mostly tended by women descendants of the holy person commemorated, and their blessings are often specialized: for example one *pir* shrine is considered good for liver disease, another for heart disease, and so on.

In Georgia lay people, sometimes self-appointed, came to undertake some of the ritual activities that used to be performed by priests, not only funeral rites but also those accompanying the ritual sacrifice of sheep on feast days. The running of village affairs was taken out of the hands of the village elders and handed to secular commisars. Often, however, these elders were now called upon to perform religious rituals, at least unofficially. In Ghari village, a tree, always considered holy (Elijah's tree), became the focus of clandestine visits. Indeed, although in the early days villagers had not been indifferent to beginning a new way of life under a communism which promised so many material benefits, as most of these remained mere promises, and as despair over illness and death and the desire for auspicious circumstances for birth and marriage remained as pressing as ever, the performance of old rituals to accompany special events continued. I cannot go into a full discussion of 'tradition' in this chapter, but as so often happens one is faced with a simultaneous increase in ritualistic observances and the disappearance of any knowledge of, or concern with, the underlying theology and moral teaching.[8]

Inside homes, which were always liable to official inspection, areas set aside for ritual were rare, and had to compete for space in usually overcrowded dwellings. When a person prayed over another or consumed ritual foods, it had to be done in the usual living quarters, and it was difficult to exclude other family members. Death rituals were the most significant. Villagers preferred their dying relatives to be brought back from hospital so that they could perform the necessary rituals in secret at home (Dragadze 1988).

In a general way, therefore, without presuming fully to explain the continuance of religious practice, we can trace the development of a shift in emphasis in the division between 'sacred' and 'profane'. The domestication of religion continued in this way until the mid-1980s and the onset of *perestroika*.

LIBERALIZATION AND REHABILITATION

Stalin had begun to loosen controls over religion during the Second World War, as a means of intensifying emotional loyalty to the state. The restoration of holy sites and religious toleration increased slowly thereafter, but resources in terms of manpower and buildings were so scarce that the trend towards increased domestication continued in the manner outlined above. In Armenia, exceptionally, the official church became the focus of renewed national pride and identity. Elsewhere, the farcical aspects of officially sanctioned religious structures persisted. For example, the Muslim magazine *Muslims of the Soviet East* was printed for export in Tashkent in fifty languages, not one of them indigenous (no Uzbek or Tajik versions, for example). In Georgia, religious festivals such as Easter were celebrated in the main cathedral in the capital Tbilisi, but drunken youths would be encouraged by the Government to enter and disrupt proceedings. Pilgrims would flock to particular churches, such as Alaverdi in eastern Georgia, to hold picnics on the site of former village churches; on these occasions the recreational theme usually seemed stronger than any spiritual content.

When Khrushchev allowed the Chechens and Ingush to return to their homes following their deportation by Stalin, they discovered that their family tombstones had been used for pavements. In some cases the writing was still visible, and families concerned were eventually allowed to take them away, to erect them again in the cemetery. For them, as for the other peoples of Caucasia, the period of reconstruction of both national and religious identities began simultaneously and in earnest only under *perestroika*. The Chechens are a particularly interesting case. In deportation, as in other periods of adversity since their conquest by Russia in the nineteenth century, they found succour in their Sufi brotherhood practices. Only recently, however, have they been able to rehabilitate the site of the burial ground of the mother of one of their founders, and openly perform a *Zikr* (male-performed prayer chant and dance) there. Using prayers in their native language, this public display of devotion in 1990 revealed a complex set of concerns, the overriding one being not so much religious identity as the restoration of their national rights.

In other parts of the Caucasus, notably in Armenia and Georgia, religious practice is going through a similar transitional stage. Its public aspects in urban centres where churches have been reopened reflect a drive for reasserting national identity and claiming divine protection for the collectivity of the nation. In Georgia, since the autumn of 1990 when a non-communist government was elected, led by a keenly religious President, Christian images are replacing communist ones, and the President often ends rallies with the cry 'St George is with us!' In Azerbaijan, however, public displays of religiosity have been tempered by the fear of being branded 'Muslim fundamentalists' in an insulting way by the Moscow Government, the Armenians, and, through them, by the entire Western world. The burial service of the victims of the January 1990 massacre in Baku was attended by the Sheikh Al Islam, but he was also accompanied by the Chief Rabbi and a local priest of the Russian Orthodox church. It is possible that religion in the republics with majority Muslim populations is being cynically exploited by the authorities in Moscow as a pretext to justify armed intervention, on the grounds that it is essential to combat 'the ugly face of Muslim fundamentalism'.

In the village I studied recently in Azerbaijan the mosque has yet to be rebuilt, but it does figure in the new plans for village development. The position is very similar in Ghari village in Georgia. In both villages, in different languages and imagery, people have told me time and time again that the erection of a sacred building would attract a spiritual blessing onto the village. They feel it would also provide a meeting place for the community as a whole, the communist-built 'club-house' in both cases having been patronized solely by village youth. The communist attempt at creating a new form of village 'communitas' clearly failed and was unable to establish any deep roots in the societies. Today, the expression of this communitas is linked by most villagers to the recovery of a religious focus through building a place of worship at a suitable site.

These sentiments may be taken at face value to indicate continuity with the pre-Sovietization period. My impression, however, is that at least some attributes of these buildings no longer have meaning for the villagers. One very important new dimension, it appears, is the national symbolism which the villagers now associate with the construction of every mosque or church.[9] In Georgia I have even heard a prayer of supplication emphasizing national identity: 'God bless this *Georgian* boy'. The question of a return of significant numbers of official religious specialists, and the effect this will have on the perceptions and self-understandings of lay communities, is a complex one, and I am not yet ready to speculate on the final answers.[10] A further shift in the boundary between sacred and profane may be expected as some roles are abdicated by the laity in their homes and transferred back to the public arena. It can be predicted with even greater confidence that the idiom of nationalism will strongly colour religious expression throughout the now disintegrating Soviet Union.

CONCLUSION

At the outset I stated that my modest aim was merely to assess the usefulness of applying Durkheim's notions of sacred and profane to the transformations of religious practice that have taken place in the past seventy years in the Soviet Union. Through the study of documents, interviews to obtain retrospective accounts, and observations of current practice over more than two decades, I have concluded that the concept of domestication is a useful one for understanding changes in religious practices under communism. Contrary to 'secularization' ideas, which it must be admitted have not yet been adequately examined in communist conditions, I have preferred to treat the 'degree of religiosity' as a constant. The refashioning of religious life in Georgia and Azerbaijan owes more to the specific impact of communism, with its coercive practices and enforced ideology, than to the march of industrialization. The refashioning is continuing now as these countries seek to consolidate their escape from communist colonial structures, and the most profound influences upon religious practices today would appear to be the nationalist ones. Durkheim's opposition may still prove useful as the successor states in the Caucasus adapt traditional religious symbols to become the new sacred icons of the nation.

NOTES

1 See Walters (ed.) (1988) for a useful survey of the diversity of Christian churches within socialist Eastern Europe. Comprehensive coverage of all religions in these countries has for many years been provided in the journal *Religion in Communist Lands*, published by Keston College.
2 For example, the definitions of the nation advanced by Stalin had to masquerade as Lenin's own: see Kryukov (1989).
3 Although drawing also on fieldwork carried out in Georgia between 1970 and 1973, my main sources for this chapter derive from fieldwork done in 1989–91

in Georgia and Azerbaijan as part of a research project, 'Rural families under Gorbachov in Georgia and Azerbaijan', funded by the ESRC.

4 I emphasize here the setting apart of these buildings in Azerbaijan because it has been argued by some experts on Islam in the USSR that not only can any house serve as a mosque, but that no building ever has special status (T. Saidbaev: personal communication).

5 For example, by Lane 1981.

6 Two-thirds of Azerbaijani Muslims are Shia and one-third Sunni, but for the purposes of this chapter I shall not dwell on their differences.

7 See Sorabji (1989) and Bringa (1991) for detailed investigations of the religious roles of women in another communist Muslim society, Bosnia. In 1979 Tajikistan I was abandoned by my 'minder' as soon as I expressed interest in the ethnography of women: this was taken to be proof of the political insignificance of my project.

8 Hence there was no general recognition of any contradiction when Georgian women never sewed or washed their hair on Sundays for religious reasons, whilst undergoing very frequent abortions.

9 Of course I have to be wary in interpreting what I, as an outsider, am told on this score (the common refrain is 'We must have a mosque because we are Azerbaijanis', or 'We are Georgians so we must have a church').

10 I am currently embarking on a five-year research programme, centred upon the study of rituals, jointly with the Department of Caucasian Ethnography of the Academy of Sciences of the Republic of Georgia.

REFERENCES

Bennigsen Broxup, M. (ed.) (1992) *The North Caucasus Barrier: the Russian Advance Towards the Muslim World*, London: C. Hurst & Co.

Bringa, T.R. (1991) 'Gender, religion and the person: the "negotiation" of Muslim identity in rural Bosnia', Unpublished Ph.D. dissertation, London School of Economics, University of London.

Dragadze, T. (1988) *Rural Families in Soviet Georgia: A Case Study in Ratcha Province*, London: Routledge.

Humphrey, C. (1983) *Karl Marx Collective: Economy, Society and Religion in a Siberian Collective Farm*, Cambridge: Cambridge University Press.

Kryukov, M. (1989) '"Chitaia Lenina": reading Lenin (reflections of an ethnographer on the problem of the theory of the nation)', *Sovetskaya Etnograpiya 4*.

Lane, C.L. (1981) *The Rites of Rulers: Ritual in Industrial Society – the Soviet Case*, Cambridge: Cambridge University Press.

Sorabji, C. (1989) 'Muslim identity and Islamic faith in socialist Sarajevo', Unpublished Ph.D. dissertation, University of Cambridge.

Walters, P. (ed.) (1988) *World Christianity: Eastern Europe*, Keston Book No. 29, Eastbourne: MARC.

Chapter 10

Socialism and the Chinese peasant

Jack M. Potter

With the establishment of the People's Republic of China, the Chinese Communist Party set out to modernize rural Chinese society and to change radically the social lives of Chinese peasants. As members of a quasi-religious revitalization movement, under the charismatic leader Mao, basic-level party cadres struggled to transform landlord-dominated, impoverished, and war-torn 'feudal' Chinese villages into prosperous socialist cooperatives based upon collectivist and egalitarian values, within a new modern, industrialized, socialist state.

The party's programme of revolutionary change in the countryside progressed through three main periods: (1) the initial Maoist period of land reform, social reorganization, and collectivization of the 1950s, which eliminated the old landed elite and established party committees in the countryside, culminating in the enormous Great Leap Forward communes of 1958; (2) the period of Maoist collectivist society, lasting from 1961 through the early 1980s, based upon the 'three-level system' in which the basic levels of organization were the production team, the brigade, and smaller, less radical communes ; and (3) the post-Maoist period, from the early 1980s to the present, during which the Revolution was routinized: agriculture was decollectivized, private internal markets were reinstituted, contacts were re-established with the world capitalist system, temporary labour migration of peasants was permitted for the first time in several decades, and the emphasis in policy was changed from revolutionizing the society to focusing on immediate economic prosperity.

What has been the effect of four decades of revolutionary socialist praxis upon the traditional structures of rural Chinese society? How does present rural China compare to pre-Revolutionary China? Have Chinese peasant society and culture been fundamentally changed? If so, how? If not, what are the continuities, and why have they persisted? What is the changing relation of the peasantry to Chinese society as a whole? Most importantly, how have all these changes affected peasant lives?

Here I present evidence from the results of my fieldwork in Zengbu brigade (now called Zengbu xiang, or 'township'), a rural settlement of over

5,000 people comprising three large single lineage villages and two small hamlets in Guangdong province.

FAMILY, MARRIAGE, AND KINSHIP

Marriage formation has been modified since 1949. Marriages are generally arranged, but not in the sense of the old 'blind marriage', which required the child to accept the parents' choice of spouse without demur. Now, as before, the mother takes responsibility for finding an appropriate spouse, using intermediaries. However, prospective marriage partners may now meet, and a young person may now refuse a prospective marriage partner. The change is to a modified form of arranged marriage, with freedom to meet and freedom to refuse for the parties most concerned. It is considered by the villagers to be a significant improvement.

Now, it is no longer socially impossible for young people to choose marriage partners on their own initiative: this would have been considered indecent prior to 1949. Now, it is permissible to marry a partner from within the same lineage village; this would have been considered incestuous. None the less, most marriages (more than 79 per cent, in 1979–81) are still arranged, and most marriages are still exogamous with respect to lineage and village.

Changes in the status of women are relevant to the understanding of changes in the nature of marriage. The worst abuses of the old system – footbinding, child betrothal, the selling of concubines and maid servants, and polygyny – are legally forbidden. However, some customs relevant to the status of women remain unchanged. The most important of these customs is patrilocal residence after marriage. Since the Revolution, as before, women have not been considered permanent members of their natal families, since the patrilocal residence rule requires them to marry out and become adjuncts of the husband's family rather than the father's.

Simplification of marriage ritual was a revolutionary goal during the Maoist period. The rituals of asking for the hand of a bride, negotiations over dowry, negotiations over the amount of ritual money to be given by the groom's to the bride's family, and the rituals of marriage itself were retained, but there was an emphasis on simplification, rather than elaboration. Efforts by cadres to eliminate the ritual brideprice, the dowry, and elaborate and costly wedding ceremonials during the Cultural Revolution were adamantly and successfully resisted by local women. They argued that large wedding banquets were necessary to cement ties with wider kin, who would be indispensable in times of need, such as serious illness, house-building, weddings, and funerals. As the Maoist collectives assumed increasing importance in people's workaday lives during the 1960s and the 1970s, they began to fulfil functions formerly carried out by relatives, including affines. Team members helped one another with house-building, for example. Under these circumstance the necessity to affirm affinal ties with ritual might seem less urgent. But relations with fellow team members never displaced kinship relationships by marriage.

So, the importance of affinal kinship relationships established between families by the out-marriage of women was maintained throughout the Revolutionary period, and such relationships have been increasingly elaborated in the post-Mao years. Nowadays, the newly prosperous villagers hold elaborate wedding rituals, pay enormous brideprices, and provide elaborate dowries, in order to demonstrate their own wealth and status. There is evidence of the stylistic influence of 'modern' Hong Kong Chinese patterns. For example, a truck is used rather than a sedan chair, to transport the bride from her village to that of her husband. (See the film by Luehrsen and the Potters, *Zengbu After Mao.*)

Some substantive changes were made by the party in improving the status of women in Zengbu during the Maoist period. Prior to 1949, the labour of women was thought of as being at the disposal of the senior male of the household, and the rewards for women's labour were not publicly affirmed. Under Maoism, women were publicly rewarded with work points for their work for the collective. Prior to the Maoist period, indeed throughout Chinese history, women's work was little valued. Under Maoism as well, in the context of reward for labour as a whole, women's work in Zengbu continued to be under-valued and under-rewarded. And women remained responsible for housework, which was 'invisible' and unpaid. Under Maoism, a few women were selected to serve as party cadres, where previously no village leaders had been women. Yet the number of cadres who were women remained low (as of 1985, there was only one woman cadre at the brigade level). As we have said, 'The inequalities between men and women were cultural artifacts so built into Chinese thinking that they were defined as "natural", rather than as social constructs subject to revolutionary change' (Potter and Potter 1990: 96). Village women themselves say that their social position is now better than it was before Liberation, when it was horrendous, but that it is still bad.

The household cycle remains as it was prior to 1949. A young married couple are provided with a dwelling of their own after marriage, but for a year or two they are counted as members of the husband's parents' household, in spite of their separate dwelling, and the structural arrangement takes the form of a patrilocal stem family. The unity of the stem family is symbolized by the pooling of income and the sharing of meals. A formal division of the households is symbolized when a couple retains control of their own income, rather than pooling it with that of the husband's parents, and when they establish separate cooking arrangements. When a second son marries, the family of the first son formally separates from the household of his parents; the second son and his wife, in turn, become part of the parental household and form a patrilocal stem family with it. When the youngest son marries, he and his wife form a patrilocal stem family with his parents, and they do not separate. When the husband's parents die, they inherit the parental house; this is a repayment for having assumed major responsibility for the care of the ageing parents. In Zengbu, there are no joint families (see also Unger and Xiong 1990). (In a joint family, more than one married son lives in the same household with the husband's parents.) Daughters are impermanent members of the household cycle: they marry out and become members of their husbands' families. Household heads are men, with women assuming headship only as widows with young sons or in the absence of men.

Maoist China was one of the most pro-natal societies that has ever existed. The Maoist collectives provided jobs and subsidized rations for all children born, and they provided free house-building land out of the common resources for all male children at marriage. Peasants were motivated to have as many children as possible, not only for cultural reasons, but also to increase the share of the collective earnings and resources which would be received by their own families. Since peasants, unlike urban residents, had no pensions, they had to be supported in old age by their descendants. Care for the aged is a perennial source of anxiety in Chinese thinking. The population of Zengbu almost doubled between 1949 and 1985. This population increase entirely absorbed the increases in agricultural production which had been brought about through capital construction and mechanization during this period of time. Unbridled population growth was a major factor in the failure of Maoist collectivism in China, and the peasants of Zengbu are still living with its consequences. The construction of new houses has absorbed large quantities of what would otherwise have been agricultural land. Valiant efforts have been made by local cadres to bring population increase under control, but popular opposition is strong, little success has been achieved, and absolute increases in numbers are continuing.

Birth planning policy has not changed family and kinship institutions in Zengbu since 1979, and there is little likelihood that it will. The famous one-child policy does not apply to peasants, and has never been implemented in Zengbu. The policy in 1985 was to limit peasant families to two children, if one was a son. A couple was allowed to try four times for a son; but before the fourth child could be born the father had to agree to a vasectomy. With the enormous prosperity of the 1980s, following decollectivization, even this policy has become increasingly difficult to implement.

Zengbu's population explosion has exacerbated chronic and longstanding problems of land and food shortage and environmental degradation; if population is not brought even more firmly under control, ecological disaster will be the inevitable result. Land shortage, and eventual ecological collapse are threats to the peasants which loom as ominously now as they did before Liberation. These fundamental facts have not been changed by the Revolution, and are being exacerbated by the post-Maoist policies of unbridled *laissez-faire* in the exploitation of resources. It is difficult to see how these fundamental problems can be adequately dealt with in the absence of a strong central government and a disciplined political apparatus to enforce rational policies designed to preserve a sustainable future for China as a whole. If the Chinese Communist Party should cease to exist, something like it would have to be reinvented. In the long run, Maoist China provided the governmental framework, although not the appropriate policy, which would be needed to provide a workable solution to these problems; from this point of view, Maoism was potentially capable of providing a better solution to China's long-term problems of over-population and ecological collapse than the post-Maoist system (see also Hinton 1990).

In Zengbu, rights to cultivate household land were allocated to each separate family in the early 1980s during decollectivization. These rights are inherited equally by the sons, and daughters do not inherit. This means that inheritance is as it traditionally was. (Under Maoism, there was no land to inherit, but other rights, such as membership in the collective, were patrilineally inherited in the traditional way.) As of 1985, these rights in household land were being treated by the peasants as private property, although the team retains formal ownership of land. The state retains the right to tax and to collect grain quotas. The current arrangement is reminiscent of the complicated old pre-Revolutionary land-tenure institutions: the state had the right to tax the land, the landlord (usually a lineage ancestral estate, in this part of China) owned the 'sub-surface' of the land – the right to receive rent from it – and the tenants owned the 'surface' of the land – the right to cultivate it. Each of these rights to the land could be pawned, sold, or inherited. It is likely that this will happen again.

During the post-Maoist period there has been a return to the pre-Revolutionary household mode of production in agriculture, and to the old small-commodity marketing economy. With this change, the pre-Revolutionary traditional gender division of labour has returned: women now stay at home and care for the fields and the children; men seek their fortunes working outside the village in more lucrative occupations (Croll 1983: 28–30).

Along with the return to a household mode of production has come an accompanying revival of agnatic kinship ties: the households of close patrilineal kin often cooperate in agriculture, sharing labour during busy times of the agricultural cycle, and exchanging the use of fields. These forms of cooperation replace the collective patterns of cooperative labour characteristic of the Maoist period.

The revival of the household mode of production has also led to a revival of traditional religious and magical beliefs. Since the securities of the collective period have given way to the insecurities, as well as the opportunities, of the post-Maoist period, the peasants of Zengbu now practise traditional religion and magic. Household altars have reappeared, and various supernatural entities are worshipped as they were prior to the Maoist period. Village shrines, temples, and ancestral tombs have been rebuilt, and the villagers practise geomancy and consult spirit mediums to cure illness (see also Huang 1989: 30–1). They worship the traditional deities with the clear and instrumental purposes of furthering success in business, keeping family members healthy, and ensuring the birth of sons, an intensified concern given the birth planning programme discussed above.

THE LINEAGE

In his classic book, *Lineage Organization in Southeastern China* (1958), Maurice Freedman illuminated the nature of the Chinese 'clan' by applying British lineage theory, and models developed by Fortes and other social anthropologists working in Africa, to Chinese social structure. Freedman's work is a testimony to the explanatory power of traditional British structuralism, and a brilliant contribution to the anthropological understanding of rural China. He showed how the differentiated and class-stratified social order of China determined the nature of the Chinese localized corporate lineage, with its assymetrical structure, in which wealth and power were unequally distributed, reflecting the larger society. Wealthy and successful lineage branches symbolized their stratified relationships and strove to assert superiority by establishing branch estates and branch ancestral halls, whose property could be enjoyed only by their descendants. Freedman also showed how the strength of the lineages and lineage segments was directly correlated with the size of the ancestral estates which formed their economic base.

Following Liberation, the lineages of Zengbu were systematically attacked by the party cadres as feudal relics. Lineages were thought of as inherently exploitative because they acted as collective landlords. They were denounced for their inequality and sexism because they gave power to senior men from the richest segments, and as agents of exploitation because they allowed the rich and powerful to exploit the poor and weak. During Land Reform, the landed property of the Zengbu lineages was confiscated, in order to destroy them as corporate groups. Ancestral halls were turned into schools or warehouses, branch ancestral halls were given to poorer villagers as private dwellings, the ancestral tombs were defaced, and public ancestral worship was prohibited. The new collectives were established in Zengbu by deliberately arranging boundaries so that each production team contained more than one lineage segment and each lineage segment was assigned to more than one team. Loyalties to patrilineal kin were to be replaced by loyalties to the collectives and to the state. As I have said:

> The process of living and working in socialist collectives was to modify the peasants' most deeply held values and ideas, and the very structure of their thinking would be revised and re-established on a new basis. . . . New structures were to replace the old: collectives were to replace the lineage. Collective ownership was to ensure economic and social equality, and to eliminate the exploitative class nature of the lineage. Equality was to be established between men and women. . . . Competition was to be replaced by cooperation, and labour was to be fairly rewarded.
>
> (Potter and Potter 1990: 254–5)

On the face of it, the lineages had been permanently destroyed and replaced by the collectives. Yet between 1980 and 1985, ancestral tombs of the apical lineage ancestors of Zengbu's three villages were rebuilt, and ceremonies were held before them on the usual traditional occasions. The Liu lineage of Pondside rebuilt its central ancestral hall. Symbolic expressions of lineage competition, such as the dragon boat races, where each boat is manned by members of a single lineage, were revived as well. The lineages and their symbolic trappings had returned. (Qian and Xie (1991) document a similar resurgence of traditional lineages in Central China.)

This presented an important problem in the anthropological analysis of the Chinese social order. How had lineage structure persisted over four decades, in the face of concerted efforts of revolutionary praxis to destroy it? Plainly, the changes which had been put into effect, although the Chinese experienced them as fundamental and sweeping, were not of a profound enough order to bring about the deeper structural change that was needed. Basic conceptions of the relationship between rights to property, residence rules, and descent, that were characteristic features of the old corporate patrilineages, had persisted throughout the Revolutionary period unchanged and unchallenged. The fundamental structural conception that property should be owned and managed corporately by groups of co-resident, patrilineally related men, which had been the ideational basis for lineage structure, had continued to be the basis for all the socialist collectives designed and implemented in Zengbu by the party since 1949. It could even be argued that when property was transferred from household and lineage ownership to collective ownership, the structural form of the lineage as whole, at the very deepest level, was actually strengthened by the Revolution.

The structural assumptions which were the basis of the traditional lineages had retained amazing power over the minds of Maoist revolutionaries. As the party cadres created socialist collectives in the Chinese countryside, they were impelled by their own unconscious assumptions about the nature of social relationships. They did not question the basic elements of the social life they knew: patrilocality, patrilineality, and corporate ownership of property. Unthinkingly, they created socialist collectives which shared the fundamental qualities of the old order. Once again, material interests of patrilineally related men who owned property in common, albeit under a new collective system, provided a material basis that sustained the traditional pattern in the face of deliberate efforts at planned social change.

The new context did not prevent efforts to challenge the material interests of the patrilineally related men who formed the collective from being resisted. For example, the possibility of matrilocal residence, which had been advocated by the Dongguan county Women's Federation in 1979 as an appropriate way of making the revolutionary changes needed to improve the weak structural position of women, was rejected by the Zengbu cadres. Their argument was the classic one expressing the interests of a strong corporate patrilineal system: they did not want to share their scarce land and other property with in-marrying men. Under the patrilocal residence rule, women born in Zengbu had only three months after marriage to transfer affiliation to the collectives of their husbands. After that time they had no further rights to work and to rice rations in Zengbu, in spite of the fact that they had been born there. If they wished to divorce, they did not retain rights to rejoin the collective. This rule rendered divorce difficult and rare. There had been no revolutionary change at all in the assumption that women were not real members of their own families, lineages, or collectives, but temporary adjuncts, who would marry out and became absorbed into their husbands' kin and social groups. Thus, the new order reproduced the conditions that had placed women in such a weak structural position in the context of the old lineage system, and prevented basic improvements in their status.

It is clear, then, that throughout the Maoist period, from Liberation to the early 1980s, the basic structures of the lineage were preserved, and that in a fundamental sense the socialist collective was a structural simulacrum of the old lineage. Leach comments, in speaking of the relationship between kinship and property in Ceylon: 'Kinship is not a "thing in itself". The concepts of descent and affinity are expressions of property relations which endure through time. . . . A particular descent system simply reflects the total process of property succession as effected by the total pattern of inheritance and marriage' (1961: 11).

The lineages as unitary corporate groups have been reinforced by the rise of the collectively owned rural industries which are a major feature of the economy during the post-Mao period (Fei 1989). Freedman has drawn to our attention the fact that the strength of the south-eastern Chinese lineages, and of their sub-branches was directly related to the amount of collective property they owned (Freedman 1958: 48, 128–32). This remains true (and not simply in the East and South-east; see Unger and Xiong 1990).

The existence of corporate property, in the form of collectively owned rural industries or other enterprises, strengthens the solidarity of the lineages and villages in which it occurs. Throughout China, the absence of such industry results in poorer, weaker, and less solidary lineages.

The management of collectively owned property is carried out according to traditional assumptions for dealing with such matters: property is allocated to individual households, in some cases by competitive bidding, just as lineage property was distributed in the days before Liberation (see Potter and Potter 1990: 267). The traditional lineage village was a competitive arena where fraternally related families competed for power, wealth, and prestige. The return of the household as the basic economic unit under the post-Maoist system recreates this situation, and the competition is resulting in a new process of class differentiation. It is too early to say whether competitive segments within the lineage will build branch halls or create branch ancestral estates. It is not yet clear how much of the specific content of the old lineages will reappear in the newly redifferentiating post-Maoist lineage collectives.

Thus, although there have been surface changes in the lineage system of Zengbu's villagers since 1949, the deep and largely unconscious structural patterns of the lineage have exhibited continuity, a continuity that was never fundamentally attacked by the Revolution, and which is being re-inforced by the post-Maoist policies. The claims of Lévi-Strauss and of Sahlins (1976) that structures have a way of persisting in people's minds over generations in the face of changing historical events are certainly confirmed. Marx's insistence that a society can never be fundamentally changed without changing its economic base is also confirmed.

THE LOCAL ELITE

In Imperial times, the dominant elite in rural Chinese society was the gentry, consisting of degree-holding graduates of the nationwide civil service examinations. The power of the gentry class was derived from the private landlord families and powerful landowning lineages from which its membership was recruited. The gentry represented the landowning families and lineages to the imperial bureaucracy, and furthered the interests of the landowning class, especially in dealings with peasants. The gentry participated in the exploitation of local tenants, sometimes even collecting taxes from them (J. Potter 1968: 22–4). Following the fall of the dynastic order at the turn of the twentieth century (Potter and Potter 1990: 53, 255), the gentry were transmuted into a class of landlords, bureaucrats, and local despots who dominated rural Chinese society. Both the gentry under the imperial dynasties and the landlord-bureaucrat-local despot class of the Republican period were political hinge groups. They mediated between the peasants and the state; their power rested upon a combination of an independent rural economic base and political connections with the ruling government bureaucracy outside the village.

Following the land reform and the destruction of the pre-Revolutionary elite, party members were recruited from the poorest and most oppressed classes of the peasantry, and new party branches were established in the village to carry out the programmes of the new government. A new local elite of party cadres came into being. Throughout the Maoist period this local elite owed its position to political power obtained from membership in and connections to the national party organization; it did not, in the Maoist years, have its own material class base. The Maoist local cadres exerted great power over the peasants. From the point of view of social control, Maoist Zengbu was a kind of bureaucratic feudalism. Beginning in the late 1950s, the peasants were required to labour on behalf of the collective in the villages in which they lived, and under the direction of the local cadres, and were not allowed to seek alternative employment under other auspices or elsewhere (see below). In formal organizational terms the party's power penetrated to the lowest levels in Chinese rural society (Potter and Potter 1990: 270–82).

In spite of their formal political position, however, the rural party cadres of Zengbu were not merely subservient tools of a monolithic and totalitarian system of bureaucratic domination, as other observers have tended to depict them (for example, Siu 1989). The brigade-level cadres in particular were mediators between the peasantry and the higher levels of the state and party bureaucracy. There are numerous examples of circumstances in which local level cadres modified the implementation of party policy as they thought best, or as they were forced to do by the exigencies of local conditions. For example, during the Great Leap Forward, the local party secretary cushioned the peasants from the disastrous consequences he foresaw as a result of the party's requirement that rice be close-planted; he could not prevent close-planting, but he had the peasants plant peanuts and cassava, thus averting starvation. Following the Great Leap Forward, the villagers of Zengbu, under the leadership of their own party secretary, took the initiative in building a breakwater around their low-lying peninsula, so as to secure their fields from floods. This action was taken after state cadres at the commune level, who had previously requisitioned the labour of the people of Zengbu in order to help build embankments for other brigades, reneged on a promise to provide such labour to Zengbu in return. In the early 1960s, the local cadres experimented, not at the state's direction, but on their own initiative, with household production systems much like those now in effect. During the Cultural Revolution, local cadres challenged the pre-eminence of the state-supported Red Guards. During the 1970s, Zengbu cadres openly criticized the restrictive Maoist economic policies which were constraining local prosperity. During the birth-planning campaigns, the local cadres informed the upper levels unambiguously that some of their more radical policies could only be enforced in weakened form, if at all. It is true that cadres were sometimes forced to act against local interests, but they were by no means ciphers, and made active efforts to oppose unworkable policies.

The Chinese political system is best conceptualized, not as an Oriental despotism stronger than society itself, which erodes away all peasant institutions, along the lines proposed by Wittfogel, but as a system of policy bargaining. Under this system, party committees at the various administrative levels negotiate with higher levels over the degree of implementation of central policy. The peasants of Zengbu have some representation of their views, reactions, and interests, as their reaction to policy is transmitted by the local cadres up through the party bureaucracy. The party Central Committee does not have, and never has had, complete and absolute control (Potter and Potter 1990: 271). Throughout Zengbu's recent history there has been a process which we have termed 'bureaucratic segmentation', in which peasants and lower-level cadres try to proliferate levels of decision between themselves and the higher level 'order-givers,' so as to insulate themselves from direct confrontation with the higher levels of the bureaucracy and to allow for bargaining in the implementation of policy – this analysis supports Shue (1988) and Oi (1989) rather than Siu (1989); see Potter and Potter (1990: 79).

In the early 1980s, the post-Mao reforms with their administrative reorganization of the countryside and their attempt to separate economic management from political control threatened the positions of the entire cadre stratum by depriving its members of function and reward. The cadres, however, successfully manipulated the new changes so that they retained power and social position and bolstered them with new-found wealth. For example, local cadres have undertaken to manage the new Hong Kong capitalist factories established in Zengbu, and they receive salaries and bonuses sufficient to provide them with a material basis for their power and prestige. They retain control over the new village and township assemblies, and they have managed to bid successfully for contractual rights over many of the former collective enterprises; see also Huang (1989) and Unger and Xiong (1990). The post-Mao reforms have not destroyed the essential importance of the party cadres, and they still maintain substantial control of the countryside. But in adapting to the post-Mao changes, they have had to transform the nature of their stratum. Formerly, their position and legitimacy was based upon their quasi-religious devotion to the party and the Revolution. During the post-Mao period, as the Chinese Revolution's charisma was routinized, the cadres transformed themselves into a new class of local notables. Allying themselves through business ties and intermarriage with the newly emerging rich peasant class, they now resemble the imperial gentry, or the rural elite of the republican period, in that their power now rests upon local class interests. Now, cadres have their own local material class interests to protect, interests that do not necessarily coincide with the interests of the party or the state.

A CASTE-LIKE SYSTEM OF SOCIAL STRATIFICATION

Building upon traditional cultural and social prejudice against peasants dating back to Confucius, the Chinese Government, beginning in the late 1950s, created a caste-like system that divided Chinese society into two hereditary status groups – peasants and urban residents. Peasants were required to remain in their villages, owed their labour to their collectives, and were required to produce their own rice rations and other food. They were not allowed to move into any urban area, even into the local market town, except under rare and unusual circumstances. This formidable system of social control was enforced by means of the household registration system, and the associated system under which access to rations of food, clothing, and fuel was provided to urban residents. A peasant had no way of buying food and other necessities in the cities in the absence of the ration coupons issued only to urban residents. The system was initially created to prevent a massive influx of peasants into Chinese cities. As a consequence of this system, the inequalities between peasants and urban residents with regard to food, wealth, prestige, education, social organization, and culture were institutionalized. The best that Maoism had to offer was available to urban residents and not to peasants. Urban residents had guaranteed jobs, rations, health care, good education, and old-age pensions; peasants enjoyed none of these advantages.

Classification as a peasant or as an urban resident was inherited from one's mother; if she was a peasant, one inherited peasant status; if she was an urban resident, one inherited urban status. Intermarriage was rare, as few urban residents would want to marry a peasant. As Sulamith Potter (in Potter and Potter 1990: 312) has put it:

> This system is an extraordinary one. . . . It is a deliberately created system of birth-ascribed status, in the context of a modern socialist state, enforced by bureaucratic methods rather than by custom. It is a system which, in spite of being based on birth ascription, is intended to be temporary rather than perpetual. It is a system in which status is inherited from the mother, in the context of a social order that has always been characterized by strongly patrilineal institutions.

The conditions created by these regulations produced a kind of bureaucratic feudalism that is reminiscent of European serfdom. Social mobility for peasants or their children was defined out of existence. Once the regulations governing peasant status were instituted, peasants could leave the village only as a consequence of rare opportunities provided to army veterans, party members, or scholars of exceptional ability. This was a highly significant change in the nature of the social order, created by the Revolution. Needless to say, for the highly competitive and ambitious people of Zengbu, this took most of the zest out of life. There was no way to better one's own situation except in the context of one's collective (S. Potter 1983).

In the post-Maoist years this caste-like system has been bent but not as yet broken. From the peasant point of view, the most significant reform has been that the collective has relinquished its control over the peasants' labour power. (This is a more significant reform than the distribution of collective land to the households: the peasants cannot make much money on these miniscule plots under any form of social organization.) During the Maoist period, when the team controlled the peasant's labour, if a peasant worked either for another collective unit or on an individual basis (as did a village seamstress who sewed clothes for fellow-villagers), wages were paid to the team and not to the peasant. The peasant was then credited not with money, but only with the appropriate number of work-points for that category of labour; this all but eliminated individual incentive. The only situation in which peasant labour was at the peasant's own disposal, aside from housework, was the cultivation of the household's garden plots. With the dismantling of the production teams in the early 1980s, the peasants of Zengbu controlled their own labour for the first time since the Revolution. They could grow whatever crops seemed likely to be the most profitable on their fields; they could become pedlars in the local market economy, now freed of restriction; they could bid a tractor from the team and go into the hauling business, and so on. They were also free to seek employment in towns and cities. (Many urban factory managers have hired peasants because they constitute a cheaper work force and receive no benefits, such as pensions.) In formal terms the caste-like system is still in operation, but some migration to find work is now possible. However, temporary peasant migrants are still legally peasants, and do not have permanent rights to reside in town, or to grain coupons and other rations, or to other perquisites of urban residents (see Fei 1989). They purchase their own grain on the open market or bring it from home. (The demand for grain by non-legal residents of cities has turned the grain-rationing coupons of China's urban residents into a second currency system.) Peasants can be forced to return to their villages at any time if the Government decides to tell them to do so.

Peasant migrants from the poorer interior mountain regions of China are also flooding into the more prosperous rural regions, to work as farm labourers and employees. Zengbu in 1985 had a large resident population of migrants from northern Guangdong province. These migrants worked in the local factories or did the lower-status agricultural work for Zengbu villagers, while the latter became wealthy working in the new Hong Kong factories.

Labour mobility allowed under the post-Mao reforms has thus eliminated some of the harsher aspects of the caste-like system for peasants. However, the system itself is still very much in existence, and legal status as an urban resident is tremendously desirable to peasants. It is rumoured that peasant troops who agreed to put down the Tiananmen demonstrators were motivated to do so by the promise of legal urban resident status.

CONCLUSION

Over two-thirds of the villages of Zengbu welcomed the post-Mao reforms. During the post-Mao period, in this most prosperous part of China – although not necessarily in the more disadvantaged regions; see Unger and Xiong (1990) and Hinton (1989) – many of the peasants have become prosperous beyond their wildest dreams. Hundreds of young unmarried women work in the new export factories which are jointly operated by Hong Kong capitalists and local collectives. Other peasants work as pedlars, construction workers, and haulers, and many have sought work elsewhere in the province, some in the special Shenzhen economic zone on the Hong Kong border. They are using their new-found prosperity and social freedom to resurrect their traditional social, cultural, and ritual practices. Over four decades of revolutionary experience, the fundamental goals, values, and view of the world of the peasants of Zengbu have not changed at all. The major goal in life for village families is still to get rich and to raise their status *vis-à-vis* the other members of their lineage villages. They wish to secure good marriages for their children, to build new houses for their sons, and to live out a culturally ideal old age in comfort, surrounded by their descendants. Probably some residue of revolutionary goals and Utopian dreams remain in the minds of the cadres and some of the young people – but not much. It has all been overwhelmed by the post-Mao prosperity.

Although there was much surface flux and change in Zengbu over the thirty-six years between 1949 and 1985, what impresses me most is the remarkable continuity. There have been reforms but not basic changes in marriage patterns; family and kinship patterns remain much the same; the lineages changed on the surface but the deep structural features persisted throughout the Maoist period. The more shallow symbolism displayed by tombs, ancestral halls, and dragon boat races has reappeared in the post-Maoist period. Traditional religious and magical beliefs have returned, and their content and meaning do not appear to have changed. My conclusion is that in spite of three decades of revolutionary efforts at change there has been remarkable continuity in Zengbu social structure and culture – especially at the deepest structural level – and that there has been a flood-tide return of traditional culture and society during the post-Mao period.

In the post-Mao period, Western cultural models arriving via Hong

Kong are increasingly influential. They are brought in by visiting relatives, by technicians in the Hong Kong factories who come to live in the village, and by television. The pattern of cultural influence that began before the Revolution, and was temporarily interrupted by it, has been resumed.

The influence of the world capitalist system is brought to bear, as well. The adoption of Western-style industrialization in the context of the capitalist world market, emanating from Hong Kong, may prove far more productive of social change, particularly concerning of social mobility and urbanization, than the manipulation of peasant social organization ever was.

REFERENCES

Croll, E. (1983) *Chinese Women Since Mao*, London: Zed Books.

Fei Hsiao-Tung (1989) *Rural Development in China: Prospect and Retrospect* Chicago: University of Chicago Press.

Freedman, M. (1958) *Lineage Organization in Southeastern China*, London: Athlone.

Hinton, W. (1990) *The Great Reversal: The Privatization of China: 1978–1989*, New York: Monthly Review Press.

Huang Shu-Min (1989) *The Spiral Road: Change in a Chinese Village Through the Eyes of a Communist Party Leader*, Boulder, CO: Westview Press.

Leach, E. (1961) *Pul Eliya, A Village in Ceylon*, Cambridge: Cambridge University Press.

Luehrsen, T., Potter, J.M. and Potter, S.H. (1988) *Zengbu After Mao, A Video Documentary*, Eugene, OR: New Dimension Media.

Oi, J.C. (1989) *State and Peasant in Contemporary China: The Political Economy of Village Government*, Berkeley: University of California Press.

Potter, J.M. (1968) *Capitalism and the Chinese Peasant: Social and Economic Change in a Hong Kong Village*, Berkeley: University of California Press.

Potter, S.H. (1983) 'The position of peasants in modern China's social order', *Modern China*, 9: 465–99.

Potter, S.H. and Potter, J.M. (1990) *China's Peasants: The Anthropology of a Revolution*, Cambridge: Cambridge University Press.

Qian Hang and Xie Weiyang (1991) 'The coresidence of patrilineage members and present lineage activities in our country's peasant villages', *Quarterly Journal of the Shanghai Academy of Social Sciences*, 3: 157–64. (In Chinese.)

Sahlins, M. (1976) *Culture and Practical Reason*, Chicago: University of Chicago Press.

Shue, V. (1988) *The Reach of the State: Sketches of the Chinese Body Politic*, Stanford, CA: Stanford University Press.

Siu, H.F. (1989) *Agents and Victims in South China: Accomplices in Rural Revolution*, New Haven, CT: Yale University Press.

Unger, J. and Xiong, J. (1990) 'Life in the Chinese hinterlands under the rural economic reforms', *Bulletin of Concerned Asian Scholars*, 22(2).

Chapter 11

Ethnic relations, economies of shortage, and the transition in Eastern Europe[1]

Katherine Verdery

The collapse of communist party rule in Eastern Europe and the Soviet Union has been accompanied by severe ethno-national[2] tensions throughout the region. Ceauşescu was barely in his grave before Romanians and Hungarians began spilling one another's blood and that of Gypsies (Roma); the Czech and Slovak parts of 'Czecho-Slovakia' began their post-communist history by quarrelling over a hyphen; the former entities 'Yugoslavia' and the 'Soviet Union' have ceased to exist as such, owing to seemingly irreconcilable differences among their nationalities; and anti-Semitism is on the rise throughout the region, even in places such as Poland where Jews are almost non-existent.

Only those external commentators who knew little about the region saw this as something new (or, more often, as a resurgence of something old). Those with more experience knew that far from disappearing, ethno-national tensions had persisted and perhaps even intensified under socialism. This fact, and some of the reasons for it, are important to bring out in any discussion of the prospects for 'transition' during the 1990s and beyond. In this chapter I suggest why ethno-nationalism was in certain ways 'built into' the organization of socialism, manifesting itself differently in different countries but fully absent from none. My account is partial, inasmuch as its research base is Romania, a non-federated type of polity. The forces encouraging nationalism in the federations – Yugoslavia, the Soviet Union, and perhaps Czechoslovakia – thus require comment beyond what I offer here. None the less, my account offers at least a start at thinking about ethno-nationalism in the socialist context, with implications for its place in post-socialist societies.

My arguments are primarily of a macro-systemic, structural kind, even though I recognize that ethno-national sentiments are also lodged in persons, as aspects of self-conception, and manifest themselves in micro-interactions. Emphasizing the systemic element as opposed to the interactional, the psychological, or the micro-level, helps to clarify ethnicity's particular place, or role, in particular social orders, thereby enriching the significance of the micro-level data that ethnographers more commonly gather. In my view, for the Romanian case it is precisely the *peculiarities of socialism* that make national identity there interesting. My argument in this chapter is that the organization of the socialist political economy as an 'economy of shortage' (Kornai 1980) created a potentially central role for ethnic sentiment, both within the population at large and within important sectors of the intellectual and political elite. This role was actualized more visibly in some countries and in some periods than in others – Ceauşescu's Romania was the most marked example[3] – but it was possible everywhere, and this conditioned future politics throughout the region.

In what follows, I briefly outline two general features of socialism's political economy, drawing upon models from Hungarian and Romanian economists and sociologists.[4] I discuss the 'economy of shortage' and processes of bureaucratic allocation, explaining how each was connected with national identity. My examples come from Romania, a somewhat extreme case with respect to the issue being discussed, but I believe the argument is relevant – with modifications – elsewhere as well. Because these models no longer apply as such to Eastern European societies, I use the past tense, even though versions of 'real socialism' continue to exist in other parts of the world.

THE ECONOMY OF SHORTAGE

In their formal economic organization, socialist systems were built on the principle of redistribution, rooted in 'appropriational movements toward a center and out of it again' (Polanyi *et al.* 1957). Legitimating ideologies emphasized centrally coordinated planning for the general welfare and the promise of employment for all. All types of producing units – ranging from shoe factories to universities – had to compete for funds from the centre, to be distributed according to social priorities that were centrally determined.

Among those social priorities were several (such as the commitment to full employment and state subsidy for a wide variety of goods) whose cumulative result was what Hungarian economist János Kornai (1980) has called 'soft budget constraints'. Those firms that did poorly would be bailed out – that is, most socialist systems lacked a concept of bankruptcy. Financial penalties for what capitalists would see as 'irrational' and 'inefficient' behaviour – excess inventory, over-employment, over-investment – were minimal. In consequence, socialist firms did not develop the internal disciplinary mechanisms supposedly characteristic of most firms under capitalism. Because of this, and because central plans (ratcheted upward every year) usually exceeded what could be produced, firms learned to hoard materials and labour. In 'bargaining' over their production plans, managers overstated both their material requirements for production and their investment needs, in hopes of having enough to meet targets. Any manager encountering bottlenecks in production or failing to meet targets could always claim that he could meet the plan with more investment. Processes of this sort went on at every level of the system: from small firms up to the largest steel combines and on through progressively more inclusive segments of the economic bureaucracy. At each level, manager-bureaucrats were padding their budgets. Thus, socialist systems had expansionist tendencies that were not just inherent in growth-orientated central plans but were *generated from below*.

The result of bargaining between centre and lower-level units and of hoarding by enterprises in relation to the centre was an 'economy of shortage'. Hoarding at all levels froze in place resources needed for production somewhere else; all producing units wanted more inputs than they could get. Shortages were sometimes relative, as when sufficient quantities of materials and labour for a given level of output actually *existed*, but not when and where they were needed. Sometimes shortages were absolute, owing to the non-production that resulted from relative shortage (or the export of items needed locally, as in 1980s Romania). Because what was scarce and problematic in socialist systems was *supplies*, rather than *demand*, as in capitalist ones, Kornai calls socialist systems *supply-* or *resource-constrained* systems (as opposed to *demand-constrained* capitalism). This systemic contrast accompanies another: whereas demand constraints pose for capitalists the problem of *selling* and thus put a premium on 'salesman-ship', supply constraints pose, rather, the problem of *obtaining* and thus put a premium on what we might call 'acquisitionsmanship'. The cause of supply constraints was not some planning error but the investment hunger inherent in the conditions of socialist planning. The combination of insatiable investment demand and expansionist tendencies was the main reason for the incessant growth in the productive forces during the early phases of socialism.

In summary, socialist systems had a characteristic form of competition, intrinsic to the way the political centre set up the economy. The competition was for access to resources in a social order characterized by endemic shortage. The more highly centralized such a system was – the more it resembled Romania or the Soviet Union rather than Hungary or Yugoslavia, for example – the more severe the shortage was, and the more active the competition was likely to be. Devices for alleviating it included a variety of personalistic ties, which enabled people to avoid having to queue for goods and thereby facilitated acquisition. Western writings on socialist systems generally called such arrangements 'corruption' or 'nepotism'. I propose that another way of alleviating shortage was to sharpen ethnic boundaries. In its most exclusive form, this expels competitors from the networks that would supply a shortage economy.

The literature on ethnicity is rife with mentions of 'competition for resources' as one of the motivations of ethnic group mobilization and/or conflict. My aim in discussing the concept of an 'economy of shortage' is to show precisely what kind of competition was specific to these orders, a competition in which ethnic identity might prove relevant. This kind of competition might emerge at two somewhat different levels. In those socialist systems based on a federal structure for which nationality was the federating principle (such as the Soviet Union, Yugoslavia, and Czechoslovakia after 1968), ethno-national mobilization might occur much as it does in other systems in which political interest is mobilized on sectional, ethnic grounds to influence the distribution of state-allocated goods – such as in the United States, with blacks and Hispanics (or homosexuals or regional interests) mobilizing to influence central policy. The main difference between examples of that type and the nationally federated socialisms is that in the latter, ethno-national mobilization was the *only* form of political interest-group activity that could be engaged in with some legitimacy, even if within certain strict limits. The political centre initiated and sought to control all other organizations, so as to prevent organized challenge from below. When a system of that sort begins to *de*centralize and to encourage more initiative from lower-level units, the chief such units that have the organizational history and experience to respond are ethno-national ones. This is particularly true where, as in Yugoslavia and the Soviet Union, the national principle had been actively institutionalized in the socialist polity from the very outset. The result is the scenario of the Soviet Union from 1985 to 1991: entire regional communist party structures or major factions in them adopted anti-centrist positions, calling into question the country's very existence. A major issue for them was this: By what principles and according to what nationality's rights are scarce resources to be appropriated and distributed?

Although one could find elements of this scenario in socialist countries that were not federated,[5] it was chiefly the federations that exhibited it. Common to both federated and non-federated socialisms, however, was a second level at which I think ethnicity functions in relationship to an economy of shortage. Whether or not ethno-national groups had an effective *sectional* existence (that is, a meaningful political life *as groups*), in circumstances of severe shortage ethnic identities potentially served like personalistic ties: when goods were short, they went preferentially to members of one's own group.

The likelihood that identity would work in this way was enhanced if national values had entered importantly into official rhetoric, as was true in Romania. Ceaușescu's emphasis on Romanian national values, on Romanian history (at the expense of that of the national minorities), on a Romanian path to socialism, and so on made national identity much more publicly salient than it was in Hungary, for instance, where the party leadership assiduously suppressed such discourse. Shortages in Romania grew increasingly worse during the 1980s – chiefly because the party leadership was exporting virtually everything that was saleable abroad and was leaving citizens to fend for themselves on all fronts, whether for food, for clothing, for hair dye, for fertilizer, for raw materials needed in a factory, or whatever. It was precisely during these years that Germans I knew began to complain of a resurgence of hostility from their Romanian neighbours, and that one heard hitherto non-existent reports of Romanians beating up Hungarian youths, and vice versa.

Let me give a concrete example to show how ethnicity might work in regulating shortage. In Transylvania, where the mix of nationalities is greatest, one sometimes finds ethnic occupational specializations (quite common in multi-ethnic settings). In the city of Cluj, for instance, where I spent most of my time in 1984–85 and the summers of 1987 and 1988, hairdressing is almost wholly in the hands of Hungarians. Several of my middle-aged Romanian women friends began showing up rather often with their hair visibly grizzled at the roots, a lapse in self-presentation wholly out of keeping with their usual style. Finally one of them threw herself on my mercy and begged me to get her some hair colouring through my embassy channels. She complained that with the many restrictions on hot water and on imports of virtually everything, including hair dye, her beautician could no longer service all the regular customers but only special friends. I do not claim that in all such circumstances every Hungarian beautician served only her *Hungarian* friends; some of them might have treated a few Romanian friends with their few bottles of dye, as well. It is, none the less, a commonplace that in situations of historical ethnic antagonism, such as that between Romanians and Hungarians in Transylvania, the likelihood is high that special friends *will* be Hungarians, and that Romanians will feel excluded *as Romanians*. Moreover, other factors – to be suggested below – that had heightened the salience of ethnic identity in Romania made it a very ready means of excluding competitors for the resources that an intensified economy of shortage had made unusually scarce.

The problem with the 1980s in Romania was that shortage had become so pervasive that virtually no one with a desirable good was going to have enough of it to exchange with more than a fraction of those interested in having some. Clerks in bookstores got fewer copies of interesting books, not enough to set aside for all the people they usually 'helped' in this way. Restaurants and food stores received so much less food that waiters and sales girls simply could not service all their usual back-door clients and still have anything at all for the public. Petrol stations had so little petrol to give out that service station attendants could now boast of intimate friends even among persons in relatively high places, so much in demand was their product. Collective farms vied with one another to obtain from their county agricultural centres even a fraction of the herbicides and fertilizers necessary to producing the ever-larger harvests demanded of them. State subsidies to 'cultural' institutions such as museums, libraries, publications, and so on were being reduced, necessitating layoffs of personnel; two Hungarian friends at the library where I usually worked complained that their Romanian co-workers had become less cordial towards them, and they were now concerned for their jobs. Under these circumstances, social networks of exchange and service had to constrict. Allocating along the channels of ethnic similarity became one possible result.

It is important to note that although the parameters of the processes I am describing were set very much by the state – the central planning, the ever-rising targets, the ever-increasing shortages, the constant export of goods, and the cessation of imports – the response I am describing is very much at the level of everyday interaction. I suspect that it was often not even conscious – that is, beauticians did not necessarily say to themselves, 'I'm going to save my Clairol for Hungarians only,' and Romanian library workers facing staff reductions did not necessarily suggest getting rid of the Hungarians first. Some of the exclusionary effect of ethnic identity emerges 'naturally' from restricting one's services to one's closest associates, who in this situation (as I suggested above) are more likely to be of one's own ethnic group.

This tendency might be fed and rendered more conscious if one picked up one's newspaper and read lines like the following, written by Romanian poet C.V. Tudor and published in a magazine (*The Week*) that at the time had a weekly circulation of about 100,000,[6] exceeded by only one other such publication:

> We love the Communist Party for realizing that a nation can build itself only through the people of its localities *who have been born here for hundreds and thousands of years* [i.e., not Hungarians, Germans, Jews, or Gypsies] and who do not abandon the front of work when things get tough [i.e., not Germans, emigrating in record numbers]. The Party knows that the highest honours should go not to visitors eager for gain, clad in foul-smelling tartans [a pun on a Romanian word for Jews], Herods foreign to the interests of this nation. . . . As [nineteenth-century Romanian poet] Eminescu rightly said, 'A floating population [i.e., Jews and Roma] cannot represent the stability of institutions, cannot represent the deep-rooted sentiment of the idea of the state, of harmony and national solidarity'.
>
> (*Săptămîna* 1980; emphasis added)

Intellectuals like the author of those lines were contributing in their own way to sharpening ethnic ideology, enlivening it for a larger audience, who might find it an unconscious part of their service to clients on another day. What were some of the forces motivating such an intellectual's performance?

BUREAUCRATIC ALLOCATION AND NATIONALIST INTELLECTUALS

Alongside the economy of shortage, socialist systems like Romania's had characteristic processes tied to their nature as redistributive bureaucracies. I have described above how organized shortage produced horizontal competition among units at all levels in the system, including individuals as well as enterprises of production, service, and distribution. My examples so far having emphasized the lower levels, I now focus on similar processes of competition higher up, among segments of the bureaucracy, or among units that wanted *allocations from the central budget*, rather than the specific goods in short supply that I discussed above.

Redistribution, Eric Wolf reminds us (1982: chap. 3), is not a type of society so much as a class of strategies implemented through a variety of means. Redistributors must accumulate things to redistribute and, at the same time, build 'funds of power'. A redistributive logic locates power in the hands of those persons or – in the socialist case – bureaucratic segments that dispose of large pools of resources to redistribute. Socialist bureaucracies consisted of segments and segments within segments. For instance, the Romanian state bureaucracy (as distinct from the *party* bureaucracy) included the Committee for Socialist Culture and Education, under which were found museums and publishing houses, each with different sections (fiction, history, electronics, and so on). Also part of the state (as opposed to the party) bureaucracy was the Ministry of Education, to which the various universities and research institutes were subordinate. A few research institutes were subordinated instead to the Ministry of Defence or to the bureaucracy of the party, such as its Central Committee. That is, several people engaged in a single kind of activity, such as historical research, might be pursuing their work under the auspices of different bureaucratic segments: in museums under the Committee for Culture, or in research institutes under the Central Committee or the Ministry of Defence, or in university departments under the Ministry of Education.

All of these segments needed funds; in centralized systems like Romania's up to 1989, most or all of their funds came from the centre. Since units at all levels overstated their budgets and hoarded resources, it is no surprise that claims upon the state budget from its various bureaucratic segments were always much bigger than the central budget could support. Therefore, segments competed to get the attention of central planners for their particular request or endeavour, much as departments in a university try to get the attention of their dean or provost for extra money for this or that. Within any given bureaucratic segment, people such as directors of publishing houses or research institutes or heads of university departments had to come up with arguments that would ensure them a sizeable allocation at the expense of their competitors at the same level of segmentation. These processes of bureaucratic competition were not unique to socialism, as my example of university deans makes clear: what was unique to socialism is that this was *the major* form of competition at the system level, in the absence of the market-based competition that was largely (if differentially) suppressed in most of these societies.

Throughout the bureaucracy, then, there was rampant competition to increase one's budget at the expense of those roughly equivalent to one on a horizontal scale. In the redistributive systems common to literature in anthropology, chiefs redistribute goods to their followers, just as socialist bureaucrats allocate social rewards.[7] The limits on a chief's power, as on a socialist bureaucrat's, come from the power of other chiefs to siphon followers away by giving – or creating the impression that they *can* give – bigger and better feasts or more generous loans. Like chiefs in such redistributive systems, socialist bureaucrats were constantly under pressure not to be outdone by other bureaucrats: they had continually to strive for influence, amass more resources, and raise the standing of their segment of the bureaucracy.

Within this context, social actors at all levels had to justify why they, rather than some other actor or unit, should receive allocations. This was true of enterprise managers, local administrative officials, government ministers, editors of publishing houses, individual authors or scholars – that is, the principle was pervasive. Understanding it is fundamental, for only if the basic form of competition is seen in these terms (rather than in terms of competing 'cultural capitals', for instance) can we make sense of the various claims upon resources for cultural production, and this is essential to understanding how ethno-national ideologies might enter into the heart of the politicking that went on among intellectuals and the bureaucrats of culture.

Persons seeking an allocation from the centre, whether they were individual supplicants or agents of their bureaucratic segment, stood much chance of success only if they couched their appeal in a language congenial to the central allocators. Central allocators in socialist systems were responsive to some sorts of language and not to other sorts. Since they too had to justify their own decisions to a top party leadership claiming to rule in the name of Marxism-Leninism, appeals couched in the language of socialist equity were generally a better bet, say, than appeals invoking efficient production or higher profits – notions not privileged within these systems' ideologies until the late 1980s. Appeals invoking social progress for all had greater chance than those that invoked developing the talents of a few gifted persons. In Romania of the 1970s and 1980s – and, I would argue, more covertly in other Eastern European countries – it proved increasingly gainful to appeal to national values.

The appeal to national values had little to do with socialism *per se*. In the Romanian case, it conformed, rather, to the evident personal sympathies of the party leadership. But these sympathies were themselves part of a broader project of 'homogenization' characteristic of all socialist states,[8] a project in which effacing deviations from the ideal 'socialist man' was all too readily conflated with effacing difference of *any* kind, including ethnic and national difference from the dominant national group. Within such a homogenizing environment, appeals to national values – that is, ethno-national ideology – became a valuable means of building budgets. Although this was visibly the case in Romania, I suspect that the appeal to national values formed a significant part of behind-the-scenes bargaining in other Eastern European countries as well.

The outcome was what we might call contests over *representativeness*, which is to say that different claimants justified their claim by saying that their project, or their version of a project, was *more representative of the true national values* than someone else's project or someone else's version. For example, Romanian literary critics of the 1980s argued bitterly over whether Romanian novels must, or need not, focus on values of 'the folk,' seen by some as the true repositories of the Romanian national character. Some critics such as C.V. Tudor, quoted above, defended national values by expelling aliens (Hungarians, Roma, Jews, Germans) from the state and by defining 'Romanianness' through indigenist values. Others promoted a definition of Romanianness as European. For both groups, definitions of national identity split the Romanian population itself into 'good' and 'bad' Romanians, meriting inclusion or exclusion in the contest for bureaucratic attention. The result of their arguments might be greater subsidies or eased censorship for one publication (the indigenist *Week*, say) at the expense of another (such as the pro-Western *Literary Romania* or *Twentieth Century*).

Contests over representativeness were particularly common, I believe, in the sphere of cultural production. That is, an argument to get funds on the grounds that one's work supported Romanian national values best was more likely to make sense for the director of a publishing house, say, than for the head of a salami factory or a steel mill (although even the latter could argue that their enterprises were essential to maintaining *national independence*, and thus to defending national values). Here are two examples of the sort of thing I have in mind.

First, a man I know used to head one of the larger publishing houses for academic books. He explained to me in very self-satisfied terms how he had 'captured' the job of republishing the corpus of Romania's most prolific historian, N. Iorga – whose output included an astounding 1,003 volumes and 12,000 articles. When I began to commiserate, he made it clear that this was in fact a real coup, since the budget accompanying this editorial task was huge, and it had not been easy to secure the contract. Among his arguments had been that Iorga is a 'national treasure', an endless source of national values that should be made available to Romanians in current editions.

Secondly, the same C.V. Tudor mentioned above wrote a long diatribe that was part of a larger attack on the literary critics who produced school manuals (Tudor 1981). He complained about the selection of past writers whom the existing manuals were emphasizing, and he called into question whether these were really the best, the most representative, of Romanian literary values. This complaint was part of a mammoth agenda to overturn the group then dominating the Writers' Union; it included allegations that, for example, the 'wrong' kinds of writers got the literary prizes, and certain works of 'unquestioned national value' appeared in tiny press runs while trash about Baudrillard and Lévi-Strauss was rotting unsold in bookstores in editions of many tens of thousands. (This kind of complaint constituted a claim not only for a different relationship to censorship and to the budget but also for sizeable allocations of *paper* – an item in extremely short supply.) Literary critics, then, fought in print about whose idea of Romanian literature was the 'correct' idea, so that they could become more central to the institutions through which Romanian culture was produced and to the privileges that this entailed.[9]

The importance of this point – that the form of competition most common to producers of culture was contests over representativeness – is that precisely the category of people who had the most influence over what was disseminated throughout Romanian society were likely to be making arguments in the language of national values. A dispute between two heads of salami factories and their superior would probably not make it into the pages of magazines like *The Week*, to be read by hundreds of thousands of people; but an argument by a contributor to that magazine arguing against some other literary critic's definition of Romanian identity certainly did. Representativeness was part of what was at issue in other parts of the essay by Tudor from which I quoted briefly above.

To make my point in a somewhat over-simplified way: one result of the nature of bureaucratic competition in Romania was that intellectuals and other producers of culture, the chief fashioners of social ideologies, came to emphasize the language of national values more than other sorts of appeals (such as, perhaps, socialism). This made it all the more likely that ideas about ethnicity would enter into the daily behaviour of hairdressers, petrol station attendants, waiters, those who procured materials for factories, and all those others trying to cope with extreme shortage.

ETHNO-NATIONALISM AND THE TRANSITION

The two organizational points I have emphasized above – the shortage economy and the nature of bureaucratic competition – both clearly suggest how ethno-national ideology and ethnic sentiment might have persisted and even intensified under socialism. They show that, far from having been made socially irrelevant, as Marxism-Leninism anticipated, and far from having been put into the deep freeze for four decades, as today's comments about the 'resuscitation of inter-war nationalism' suggest, national senti-ment had considerable room to flourish during the socialist period. The visibility of its flourishing and the spheres of social life in which it was manifest differed from one case to another. In all of them, however, ethno-nationalism was actively reproduced at one or another point in the operation of socialism and in people's daily experience within it – the experience of intellectuals and other producers of culture, of fashionable women with greying hair, of people standing in bread lines much longer than the supply of bread, of store clerks hiding goods from Hungarian customers to save for their Romanian friends, of office-workers cooling out their non-Romanian office-mates, of collective-farm heads berating their villagers for not contracting a pig 'as if you weren't even a Romanian'.[10] Whether national sentiment 'went public' depended partly on the inter-ethnic environment in which people experienced these realities, but the *potential* of ethnic exclusiveness in situations of shortage remained con-stant.

For these reasons one might anticipate that appeals to ethno-national identity will have a place in post-socialist Romania, as well as in other countries of the region. It will be some time before these economies stop being shot through with shortages – that is, before queues for goods are reduced by income differentials and the differentiating effects of targeting different market sectors. Devices that were important in coping with short-age before will not cease to be relevant just because Ceauşescu or Honecker or Jaruzelski is no longer in charge. Although post-socialist states are drastically cutting state subsidies for culture, these will continue to be significant in the support of writers and publishing houses – and their diminution makes claims of representativeness even more urgent, as people fight for the small subsidies that remain. The defence of 'national values' can also be expected to enter into the marketing of culture, as well, in another form: that of protectionist arguments in favour of promoting cultural products that are *local*, in preference to those from the West. Such cultural protectionism, in a nationalist language, also characterized earlier periods of imperfect market economies in the region (see Gheorghiu 1985).

In a context in which national ideology already has solid purchase, for the reasons I have suggested, there are additional determinants of its perpetuation in post-socialist politics. One relates to the consequences of electoral politics in enclaves where national minorities outnumber the dominant national group. Creed (1990) argues, for example, that during 1989–90 the worst conflicts between Bulgarians and Turks occurred in heavily Turkish regions of Bulgaria, where elections would sweep Bulgar-ian politicians from power. Deletant (1990) has made a comparable argument to explain ethnic conflict in the Hungarian-dominated region of Tîrgu Mureş in Romanian Transylvania. In both cases, to speak of resuscitated ethnic tensions is less accurate than to speak of *new* threats that ethnic differences pose to local politicians – many being hangers-on from the former regime.

A second reason why ethno-nationalism might be expected to remain an active element in post-socialist societies stems from one of the central characteristics of the 'logic' of socialist systems. As systems based on bureaucratic redistribution, they were driven by a logic that strove to maximize redistributive capacity – see, for example, Fehér *et al.* (1983); Campeanu (1988) – but this in turn was buttressed by its obverse: the destruction of resources and organizations *outside* the control of the apparatus. Because a social actor's capacity to allocate resources is relative to the resources held by other actors, power at the centre would be enhanced to the extent that the resources of other actors could be disabled.[11] Other foci of production had to be prevented from posing an alternative to the central monopoly on goods. Sociologist Jan Gross, in his analysis of the Soviet incorporation of the Polish Ukraine in 1939 (Gross 1988), helps to fill out this idea. Calling the Soviet state a 'spoiler state', Gross argues that its power came from incapacitating actual or potential loci of organization, thus ensuring that no one else could get things done or associate for purposes other than those of the centre.

As a result, the intermediate space between state and households was cleansed of all independent organizations, anything not controlled by the state – the kinds of organizations that so heavily populate the space of Western societies and that many refer to with the term 'civil society'. Trade unions, nationality councils, women's organizations, churches (where possible), social services, and all manner of other associations were either attached to the state, locked in a struggle of cooptation with it, or placed under severe pressure from it. Hence the significance of those few feeble independent organizations formed during the 1970s and 1980s – such as Czechoslovakia's Charter 77 and VONS, Hungary's SZETA (for aid to the poor), and various peace movements, Romania's short-lived SLOMR (free trade union) and Goma movement in support of Charter 77, Poland's KOR and, most spectacularly, Solidarity – all of them subject to constant persecution. That the destruction of such independent organizations was indeed imperative, from the 'system's' point of view, is clear from the catastrophic consequences that followed from their persistence – and from that of Solidarity, above all.

I believe this is specifically relevant to ethnic relations for the following reason. With the fall of communist party rule, ethno-national resentments flare up in an environment maximally unpropitious to managing them, an environment devoid of any intermediate institutions for channelling ethnic sentiments, for settling disagreements peaceably, or for offering alternative means of expressing one's grievances. To institutionalize ethnicity is not necessarily to defuse it, of course – often precisely the contrary – but it can sometimes none the less help to prevent excesses of the sort now occurring, for example, in Romania. There, the only association formed to articulate the concerns of Transylvania's Romanians appears to have been either actually formed by or instantly penetrated by former Secret Police operatives, who use the organization in part to embarrass and destabilize the government in Bucharest.[12] Had there existed independent ethnic organizations with their own stable memberships, programmes, and goals, perhaps such speculation by those shadowy figures the 'revolution' disempowered would be more difficult. The efficacy of these suspect nationalist associations is, moreover, directly related to the under-development of alternative political organizations.

If, as most anthropologists believe, the history of institutional forms influences their future development, then at least some of Eastern Europe's once-socialist societies are strongly predisposed toward ethno-national conflict. Its roots are not to be sought primarily in 'age-old enmities' or in the ethnic relations of the 1930s, contrary to the opinion of many observers. As this chapter has sought to show, national ideology and national sentiments were amply fortified by the political economy of socialism itself.

NOTES

1 This chapter summarizes the argument made in Verdery (1991a). A somewhat fuller version of the present essay, but not focused on the question of nationality, can be found in Verdery (1991b). Many persons contributed to my thinking on the questions addressed here, and I acknowledge with gratitude not only this collegial assistance but also the two research grants that supported my work: a fellowship from the Woodrow Wilson Center in Washington, DC, and three International Research and Exchanges Board grants for research in Romania.

2 I use the cumbersome term 'ethno-national' since some of the groups in question might accept the label 'ethnic' but many think of themselves rather as 'nationalities'. Incorporating both possibilities in my label is preferable to a lengthy definitional exercise, which I see as unnecessary to my purposes here.

3 One of the most common explanations for this fact among political scientists was that the Romanian regime, incapable for one or another reason of generating support for itself by any other means, 'used' nationalism to legitimate itself. I think this sort of understanding is misguided – or at best, quite incomplete – for it assumes that the major problems facing all political regimes centre on legitimation: on the creation of the consent of the governed, a peculiarly *Western* political concern. I also believe, but will not further elaborate the argument here, that one reason the Romanian party talked the language of national identity so much more visibly than some of the other East European party leaderships was that it was virtually *forced* to do so by the institutional embeddedness of the national discourse, in a context in which Marxism had been very feebly developed prior to the Second World War (see Verdery 1991a: chaps 1, 3).

4 The principal inspirations for the model I present are Campeanu 1988; Fehér *et al.* 1983; Konrád and Szelényi 1979; and Kornai 1980. Fuller discussion can be found in Verdery 1991b.

5 In Romania, for example, ethno-national groups were supposedly accorded

proportional representation in governing bodies such as the National Assembly, the party, and the Central Committee. This practice made nationality salient in politics and contributed to such things as politicization of the census.

6 For a population of 22 million, that means about one copy per 200 persons or per 100 adults, leaving out the 2 million Hungarians who would not have been reading this magazine.

7 Clearly, socialism's bureaucracies were *not* comparable with redistribution in chiefdoms, yet some of the insights generated from study of the latter may be instructive in examining the former.

8 Several forthcoming papers by Gail Kligman show this process extremely well for Romania. The subject is also taken up in Lefort 1986: chap. 8.

9 See Verdery 1991a: chap. 5, for fuller discussion of this example.

10 This was the language in which the mayor of the village in which I worked in 1985 berated a peasant for not contracting a pig to the collective farm.

11 An alternative solution, characteristic above all of the Hungarian strategy in the mid to late 1980s, would be to *co-opt* other foci of production, rather than to disable them. Good examples are the formation of VGMKs in Hungarian factories (Stark 1989) and the restoration of share-cropping in collective farms.

12 For a more extended argument to this effect, see Deletant 1990. Similar points emerge also from Verdery and Kligman 1992, although without specific reference to the national question.

REFERENCES

Campeanu, P. (1988) *The Genesis of the Stalinist Social Order*, Armonk, NY: M.E. Sharpe.

Creed, Gerald (1990) 'The bases of Bulgaria's ethnic policies', *The Anthropology of East Europe Review*, 9(2): 11–17.

Deletant, D. (1990) 'Convergence versus divergence in Romania: the role of the *Vatra Românească* movement in Transylvania', Manuscript.

Fehér, F., Heller, A. and Márkus, G. (1983) *Dictatorship over Needs: An Analysis of Soviet Societies*, New York: Basil Blackwell.

Gheorghiu, M.D. (1985) 'La stratégie critique de la revue "Viaţa Românească" (1906–1916)', in Culture and Society, Al. Zub, (ed.), pp. 127–36. Bucharest: Ed. Academiei.

Gross, J.T. (1988) *Revolution from Abroad: The Soviet Conquest of Poland's Western Ukraine and Western Byelorussia*, Princeton, NJ: Princeton University Press.

Konrád, G. and Szelényi, I. (1979) *The Intellectuals on the Road to Class Power: A Sociological Study of the Role of the Intelligentsia in Socialism*, New York: Harcourt, Brace, Jovanovich.

Kornai, J. (1980) *Economics of Shortage*, Amsterdam: North-Holland Publishing Co.

Lefort, C. (1986) *The Political Forms of Modern Society: Bureaucracy, Democracy, and Totalitarianism*, Cambridge, MA: MIT Press.

Polanyi, K., Arensberg, C.M. and Pearson, H. (1957) *Trade and Markets in the Early Empires*, Glencoe, IL: Free Press.

Saptamîna (1980) Idealuri, *Saptamîna* (5 Sept.): 1.

Stark, D. (1989) 'Coexisting organizational forms in Hungary's emerging mixed economy', in *Remaking the Economic Institutions of Socialism: China and Eastern Europe*, Victor Nee and David Stark (eds), pp. 137–68. Stanford, CA: Stanford University Press.

Tudor, C.V. (1981) 'Cine îi educă pe dascăli', *Saptamîna* (4 Dec.): 7.

Verdery, K. (1991a) *National Ideology under Socialism: Identity and Cultural Politics in Ceauşescu's Romania*, Berkeley and Los Angeles: University of California Press.

—— (1991b) 'Theorizing socialism: a prologue to the transition', *American Ethnologist*, 18(3): 419–39.

Verdery, K. and Kligman, G. (1992) 'Romania after Ceauşescu: post-communist communism?' in *Eastern Europe in Revolution*, I. Banac (ed.), pp. 117–47. Ithaca, NY: Cornell University Press.

Wolf, E.R. (1982) *Europe and the People Without History*, Berkeley and Los Angeles: University of California Press.

Chapter 12

Gypsies, the work ethic, and Hungarian socialism

Michael Stewart

In our country the government and the party have decided that everyone must have a registered work-place, that everyone will get their wages from their work-place. It is said that what these people do [Gypsy women scavenging for discarded industrial produce] is 'usury', they practise 'usury' with these goods.

(Manual labourer employed at
municipal rubbish tip, March 1988)

The regimes of 'actually existing socialism' in Eastern Europe did not just fall, they were pushed. Beset as they were by internal contradictions, they might yet have staggered on through another generation were it not for the capacity of ordinary people to conceive of an alternative life and struggle to achieve it. Despite repeated efforts to shore up these systems through egalitarian social and economic policies, they never achieved more than momentary legitimacy. Most commonly the governments of the region were met with active as well as with passive resistance to their efforts to reform society. This case study of Gypsy responses to Hungarian social policy provides one image of the sources of popular resistance to the massive experiment in social engineering undertaken by the socialist governments of the Soviet bloc.[1]

For some twenty-five years from 1961 the Hungarian Socialist Workers' Party (communist) led a vigorous campaign to assimilate the near half-million Gypsy population into the Magyar working class. The aim of the party was to eliminate totally all traces of Gypsy lifestyle and behaviour. This was to be done by removing the conditions which it was thought reproduced Gypsy identity and community, in particular un- and under-employment of Gypsy adults.

The Gypsy assimilation programme formed an important plank in the overall social policy of the Hungarian regime for a number of reasons. Gypsies formed the largest single ethnic minority in Hungary. The largest part of this minority was living in conditions of shocking poverty.[2] The state, which was committed to modernization under conditions of social equality and was attempting to renew its socialist pledge after the political disaster of 1956, had to be seen to act.[3] In the context of Stalinist social theory, modernization would be achieved by mobilizing the greatest possible social cohesion and directing this to achieving certain centrally defined goals. When unity is all, then variation (economic, social, political, even cultural) between sections of society is not a source of dynamism but rather threatens conflict and division. The economic, social, and cultural distinctiveness of the Gypsies, a distinctiveness which had been sustained in apparently autonomous Gypsy communities throughout the first decade of socialist rule, appeared greater than that of any other group in society and as such ideologically embarrassing. By 1961 the time had come to put an end to the Gypsies' waywardness.

The result of the assimilationist campaign was, however, more or less the opposite of that intended. Gypsies were as prominent in Hungarian society in 1985 as they had been in 1960. Even worse, as an unintended consequence of its economic policies it seemed as if the communist regime had inaugurated a veritable 'time of the Gypsies'. The state had managed to create conditions in which, in popular imagination at least, being a Gypsy seemed the most viable way to survive the privations and humiliations of a planned economy.

The issues raised by these events concern more than the historical analysis of a single socialist society. First, similar Gypsy policies were pursued in several other socialist societies of Eastern Europe with comparable results.[4] Secondly, socialist governmental practice, both East and West, has been blighted by its use of the state as the source of social reform. The revival of capitalist radicalism in the 1980s derived in part from the way 'bottom-up' social processes, notably the market, were harnessed to its cause. The spectacular failure of top-down redistributive social justice which I will describe here was rooted in a theory of social change and of the relation between intellectuals and the people which characterizes much of socialist discourse all over the world. If the socialist project or anything like it is to be renewed, the hard lessons of cases like this will have to be learnt.

THE CAMPAIGN TO ASSIMILATE GYPSIES IN SOCIALIST HUNGARY

The campaign to assimilate Gypsies into the Hungarian working class, lasting from 1961 to 1985, began with the adoption by the political committee of the party of a resolution, 'On the various tasks connected with the improvement of the Gypsy population's position' (Mezey 1986). The crux of this resolution was a decision that Gypsies were neither an ethnic group nor a nation.[5] 'Cultural' factors did not play a significant role in the reproduction of Gypsies as a distinct population and any attempt to 'turn [the Gypsies] into a nation' by encouraging separate language teaching and the like would be misguided (Bán and Pogány 1957: 6). Gypsy nationalist programmes were therefore reactionary, as they 'preserve the separateness of Gypsies and slow down the process of assimilation' (Mezey 1986: 241). All forms of Gypsy self-organization and expression were to be discouraged as likely to encourage a nostalgic and unnecessary attachment to ways of the past.[6]

Instead, the existence of Gypsies was attributed to the nature of the feudal and then the capitalist division of labour. Gypsies were characterized less by a culture than by a 'way of life' marked out by behavioural traits such as scavenging, begging, hustling, dealing, and laziness. These were the product of their exclusion from the society and the economy of the past, and lay at the root of their otherness. Gypsies had been sustained by the feudal division of labour in which they had played an important role. They had then lost their social importance as capitalist industrialization rendered their skills redundant. By 1960 Gypsies seemed no more than a 'survival' of a defunct way of life. The task therefore was to end the conditions which had produced the Gypsy way of life and thereby ensure their disappearance as a separate population.

As the communist reformers saw it, the social effects on Gypsies of profound infrastructural changes offered the possibility at that moment in the early 1960s that 'the Gypsy problem' could be solved once and for all. Due to changes in the mode of production initiated at the end of the nineteenth century and continued in the early socialist period, the relation of Gypsies to the majority society had changed and become diversified. First, there were those Gypsies who were no longer really Gypsies at all, that is 'the assimilated' (*beilleszkedett*), who had 'reached the average economic and cultural level of the population, given up the Gypsy lifestyle and for the most part live dispersed. Thirty per cent of Gypsies fit into this category.' Gypsies 'in the process of assimilation' also made up 30 per cent of the total, 'liv[ing] in hovels on separate settlements at the edge of towns and villages, working for the most part only occasionally; their cultural level is really low.' Finally there were the non-assimilated (half-settled or wandering (*vándor*) Gypsies of whom 'a significant part have absolutely no work, avoid respectable jobs, live day by day, or sponge off society. They frequently change houses and live at the lowest cultural level; most of them are illiterate. Forty per cent of Gypsies belong in this group' (Mezey 1986: 240; my translation).

It was the lifestyle of this last group which expressed *the* Gypsy way of doing things in its most explicitly anti-socialist form. Of all aspects of their 'low cultural level', it was their rejection of permanent engagement in waged labour in favour of the freedoms of self-employment which marked them out. When their economic activities involved craft labour (such as blacksmithing or music-making) this was not in and of itself socially objectionable to communist officials. But when this shifted into 'wheeling and dealing' (*kupeckedés*), its social character changed. Thus a Gypsy offering to mend a peasant's fence might be tolerated as performing a useful function, but if during his work he noticed, say, a machine in the yard and offered to buy it (in order later to sell it at a profit), this would reveal his tendency to 'avoid respectable jobs and sponge off society'. Such wheeling and dealing was only a more active and developed form of those behavioural traits such as begging and laziness which were associated with Gypsies' exclusion from the old division of labour.

The aims of the party were that 'the Gypsies should not live in permanent houses separately from the rest of the population, that they should be permanently employed, their health conditions be improved and their cultural level raised' (Mezey 1986: 242). Once the Gypsies were put to work, their 'level of civilization' would rise to a socialist standard and even they would understand the need to leave behind them their anti-social customs. In this process, work discipline, decent housing, and educational achievement would all go together and, as each improved, so Gypsies would become barely distinguishable from other members of Hungarian society.

The uncompromising assimilationist campaign attained greatest intensity in the late 1970s at the very time when Gypsy intellectuals had begun to challenge its assumptions and moral basis.[7] These spokespeople argued that Gypsies constituted an ethnic group and as such should be granted certain rights of self-expression. Though these campaigners managed gradually to enlarge the arena for legitimate Gypsy self-expression, the state maintained its assimilationist campaign in the field I discuss in this chapter – the organization and representation of labour.[8]

Before moving to consider this in more detail I should point out that, just as the party in its own terms acknowledged that Gypsies were not a unitary or homogeneous population, I should do the same in sociological terms. To put matters most simply, neither from the point of view of social morphology nor from that of mores (*morales*) did Gypsies form a single group. Consequently, the results of the socialist state's policies among them were not the same for each group. It can, however, be fairly generalized that none of the Gypsy populations entirely surrendered either their 'way of life' or their distinct identity, nor were any of those who tried the assimilationist road able to shrug off the stigma of Gypsy descent.

Of no group was this more true than the Vlach, Romany-speaking Gypsies. These Gypsies were thought by ordinary Hungarians and officials alike to represent the 'worst' of the Gypsies. As such they were subject to the greatest pressure to give up their communities and 'integrate' into Magyar society. Yet when I lived with such Gypsies in 1985–86 in the agrarian town of Gyöngyös in northern Hungary, they virtually flaunted their distinctive identity, and their communities were flourishing.

FROM THE TOP DOWN: THE SOCIALIST WORK ETHIC

Among the various methods of the assimilation campaign it was the plan to set all able-bodied Gypsies to socialist waged work, which was put at the heart of official initiative. This focus on labour corresponded to the three-tiered categorization of Gypsies listed above. The first group was effectively proletarian; the second group would become such if given the chance; the third (with whom the Vlach Gypsies were associated) comprised those who refused regular work, living instead from hand to mouth. By trading in horses and making money in other shady deals the Vlach Gypsies, it was thought, were able to earn a living without sweat or effort. To communist ideologists this looked suspiciously like exploitation of the labour of the 'productive workers'. According to their reading of Marx's labour theory of value, Gypsy traders were creating no new value and therefore must be living off the value others had produced. They were, it was said, 'practising usury' (*üzérkednek*). Money 'won' thus would, moreover, be spent 'easily' rather than accumulated for future productive use. Trading would therefore never provide a solid basis for an increase in wealth, health, education, and general well-being, but could only encourage renewed bouts of profligacy.

The experience of socialist labour was offered as a positive contrast to the image of the carefree but outmoded Vlach Gypsy lifestyle. The integration of these Gypsies into the socialist labour force would remedy their wanton way of life, since by working Gypsies would regain the self-respect they had lost with the elimination of their old craft occupations and discover for the first time the rewards of consistent effort as part of a social group or collective. Their 'level of civilization' would thus be transformed.

There was more to the party's theory than a kind of techno-economic determinism. Their policy differed from previous attempts to assimilate the Gypsies because the socialist construction of 'labour' involved more than mere commodity exchange. Working was the duty of all citizens, and, excluding exceptional conditions, Hungarians had no right not to work. Under 'actually existing socialism', as Swain has noted (1985: 6) 'labour power has to be purchased since all members of society are expected to work; and it cannot be relinquished simply because of inadequate demand or low profitability' (1985: 6). Labour power was not a separable part of the human person which one could choose to part with or not according to market conditions. Within official ideology, labouring was *the* activity which constituted one as a full member of society. The nation was conceived as being composed of a 'working people' (*dolgozó nép*), and so it was not primarily as citizens that Hungarians achieved full social status but as workers in the process of social reproduction. In capitalist economies exchange is the stressed and most salient activity in social reproduction. Under actually existing socialism this emphasis was inverted.[9] The key image was that of the 'productive' (*termelö*) work-place, such as a factory, which produced for the nation. The concrete labour of each person was thus directly part of the total effort of the Hungarian people.

Because work was itself a socially orientated activity rather than a private one enabling a person to lead a social existence in leisure hours, 'working' in a factory was invested with a moral efficacy that is alien to a capitalist economy. By labouring in a factory, the worker was directly 'building our socialist society'. Physical work was thought to have the uplifting qualities which Westerners are more likely to associate with intellectual or artistic effort. Hence the work-place Socialist Labour Competitions were marked not only in terms of output per brigade but also according to the brigades' cultural and social activities. There was no ontological difference between these expressions of sociality and increasing productivity. It was in such a context that the then Communist Party daily could proudly emphasize as late as 1987 that 'communist Hungary has got away from the idea that "work is something unworthy and degrading"' (*Népszabadság*, 20 Aug. 1987).[10]

By making workers out of Gypsies it was thought that the 'effect of the collective' (*a kollektiva hatása*) would gradually lead them out of their anti-social habits. Because working in a socialist factory was morally exalting, the Gypsies would experience its discipline as a value to be extended to their non-working lives. They would thus 'grow up' from their child-like attachment to the sudden and spectacular earnings of the 'dealer' (*kupec*) and the profligate consumption that went with that lifestyle.

Communist theorizing, rooted as it was in the naturalistic and positivist interpretations of Marx developed by Kautsky and Lenin (see Kolakowski 1978: 40–3; Lichtheim 1961: 244–58), assumed that the reform would have relatively straightforward effects. The realization of the obvious financial benefits of work as well as the experience of the work process itself would transform Gypsy consciousness from its individualistic, petty-bourgeois and short-term orientation to a proletarian, collective, long-term one.

FROM THE BOTTOM UP: GYPSY INTERPRETATIONS OF LABOUR

So much for this social reform seen from the top down. How did Gypsies experience this policy and how did they interpret it? From the point of view of the party twenty-five years into the reform, it could seem in 1986 that many of its goals had been achieved. In the town where I carried out my research less than 14 per cent of Gypsy men had been in work in 1964.[11] By 1976 the figure had risen to 75 per cent and, by 1983, 92 per cent of able-bodied Gypsy men were in permanent employment. Even more significantly, it was clear that Vlach Gypsies had indeed realized the financial benefits of working. I was often told by Gypsies in approving terms, 'We all work now', and equally commonly, I was told how in the old days when there was no waged labour (Romany: *butji*) Gypsies lived in an unbeliev-able poverty. Waged labour had patently become an essential part of the lives of the Gypsies – to the extent that Gypsy feasts and parties (which celebrate Gypsy autonomy and distinctiveness) are most commonly or-ganized to coincide with pay-day.

However, it was also obvious that the Gypsies, far from giving up their 'traditional' way of life, their communities, their trading in horses, antiques, and other goods, and their occasional craft-work, were in fact using their waged labour to subsidize these irregular activities. These were still the ones that they valued, that they held to express the essence of the good life. I have discussed several aspects of this resistance to change elsewhere.[12] Here I want to focus on how Gypsies interpreted the experience of work and thereby resisted taking on the communist ideology of labour.

Contrary to communist party theory, Gypsies came to the experience of 'socialist wage-labour' not with a *tabula rasa* resulting from their exclusion from previous production systems but with a complex set of repres-entations of work and how non-Gypsies conceive of work. Gypsies first tried to make sense of their waged work in socialist factories in terms of these ideas.

Communist theory had supposed that Gypsies had lived excluded from pre-socialist society. The reality was that, although often residentially separated, excluded from the bars and denied kinship ties with most peasants, Gypsies in 'traditional' Hungarian villages were in more or less constant contact with the Magyar population through providing cheap labour for better-off peasants (see, for example, Fél and Hofer 1969; Havas 1982b). Through such contact, the dominant ethics of peasant Magyars were certainly familiar to Gypsies. The kind of ethical system I am referring to is that described in rich detail by the ethnographers Fél and Hofer for one north Hungarian village as the proper peasant (*rendes paraszt*) world-view. Though peasant life varied enormously in pre-socialist Hungary (Hann 1980: 17–18), this kind of ethic was widely shared (see Kiss 1981 [1939] for an extended presentation).[13]

The foremost features of the peasant ethic can be summarized as a commitment to achieving economic self-sufficiency and personal auto-nomy through hard, physical labour on the soil of one's ancestors, avoiding as far as possible any dependency on others and any involvement in monetary or market dealings (Stewart 1988: 273–7). The elements I bring to the foreground here are the representations of labour and trade. Labour for the proper peasant was the source of all value – labour conceived as 'self-denying, careful and efficient work' on one's land (Fél and Hofer 1969: 274). Being able to sustain hard work with the aim of self-enrichment was one of the qualities that made one a true peasant. The peasants talked of the pleasures of those months of the year spent toiling out in the fields, (1969: 58), and the villagers were so proud of their ardour that they claimed to have a reputation for it even among the migrant workers of Budapest where most people disappeared in the anonymous crowd (1969: 348). Herdsmen employed by the villagers who 'earn all [their money] with a whip' – that is to say, without effort (1969: 240) – were thought to have dubious moral standards and be prone to fritter away their wealth on drink and women.[14]

The prolonged and regular character of peasant labour was also significant. Among proper peasants, 'sudden affluence is viewed with suspicion and is regarded as more or less irregular', possibly linked to malicious magic (1969: 249). Poor peasants who made their money in 'games of chance', such as animal trading, were seen as unrespectable and different in nature from the man who lived from his landed property, since the demand on the market 'for bold and shrewd action is alien to the customary activities of rural farming' (1969: 233). Indeed, any involvement in affairs of the market was thought to be alien to the peasant ideal (cf. Kiss 1981 [1939], and Bell 1984). One way this was evoked was the idea that food bought on the market, especially bread, was less filling than that produced by one's own labour.

Gypsies, who worked for peasants, performing dirty jobs around the yard as well as providing labour at the bottlenecks of the yearly cycle, could not have been unaware of these ideas, which peasants, we can be sure, then as now proudly and loudly articulated. As Okely has argued, wherever Gypsies live they have defined themselves in contrast to the dominant population (Okely 1983: 78). In pre-socialist Hungary, I suggest, it was in contrast to the proper peasant ethic that Gypsies had to establish their own identity. Being landless and without other means of production, the Gypsies defined themselves as 'sons of the market' (Romany: *foroske save*), people who lived off their wits, their ability to talk and deal with different sorts of people through their trading. Attachment to land and place, accumulation of wealth for investment, and autonomy via self-sufficient production were all rejected by the Gypsies. Instead, they constructed an image of autonomy and liberty through being able to imagine 'evading the law of reciprocal exchange' on the market (Stewart 1992).

It was precisely this sort of self-definition, with its suggestion to their ears of usurious exploitation by a middleman, which the communists hoped to abolish by setting the Gypsies to work. But when Gypsies were drawn into the socialist labour force it seemed to them that the non-Gypsies were once again trying to persuade them to give up their way of life. As far as the Gypsies were concerned, they were being offered the same alternative as in the past: elevation through labouring for others. What difference to the Gypsy whether the advocate of labour be a peasant or a communist boss? Indeed, the Romany word for non-Gypsy, *gazo*, had traditionally meant 'peasant', and when I asked for a gloss on it in 1985 Gypsies were insistent that its meaning had not changed. My informants were perfectly happy with the implication that all non-Gypsies, including party bosses, teachers, factory managers, and fellow-workers were in some sense 'peasants', since they all displayed the essential qualities of the peasant world-view.

By reinterpreting communist labour ideology in this way Gypsies were not performing an ideological sleight of hand. On the contrary, they understood all too well the implications of communist rhetoric. The point is that they were not being offered Marx's philosophical/anthropological view of labour, but rather an amalgam of a naturalistic reading of the labour theory of value and a pre-socialist work ethic. The resulting Stakhanovite image of labour owes more to medieval ideas of labour as the creation of matter than it does to Marx (see Gurevich 1985). It is in this light that one should read the comment by the ordinary Hungarian worker whose words preface this chapter. His comment on the 'usurious' practices of Gypsies reflects the widespread view that dealing and scavenging are ways of making money without labour, without producing anything. This was the ethic against which Gypsy culture had been traditionally organized, so it is understandable that they continued to view it with suspicion when it was re-presented by the state in socialist guise.

But the Gypsies' interpretation of communist ideology as 'proper peasant world-view' re-hashed tells only half the story of Gypsy resistance to assimilation. Gypsy interpretation of the socialist work ethic was not an intellectual matter, the result of a clash of two ideologies. To put this in anthropological terms, the history of the confrontation between Gypsies and communists was not a case of Gypsy ideology encompassing the challenge posed by the 'event' of socialist transformation, as a Dumont-type analysis might suggest. Just as significant as ideological opposition to 'labour' was the individual Gypsy's (constructed) *experience*, which taught him or her that whatever the rhetoric of the state, it was not via labouring that people got on in socialist Hungary. In other words, it was also because of their experience of working as socialist wage-labourers that Gypsies rejected the socialist construction of labour. No matter how hard the socialist state tried to persuade them that socialist labour was fulfilling, Gypsies were not convinced by their experience in factories that the life of a wage-labourer was the most attractive way to live in socialist Hungary.

I have argued elsewhere (Stewart 1990) that the nature of the work process in a socialist factory was not one to induce the kind of qualities associated with a work ethic. Gypsies were often employed on jobs where they were not strictly needed, where their labour was in effect superfluous. Once Gypsies were at work, far from enjoying the beneficial 'effects of the collective', they experienced the kind of semi-organized chaos that many commentators on socialist factories have described (Kemény 1978; Burawoy 1985). They experienced, as did other Hungarians, both urban and rural, the way in which personal ties with one's bosses ensured access to good jobs and a good position in the internal factory or farm division of labour. Because of the way socialist production lines were organized, the labour force tended to be split between a core group of workers who kept production going, and who re-designed jobs when the machines broke down or the standard materials were unavailable, and on the other hand a peripheral group of workers who simply did what they were told (Kemény 1978). The core workers were better rewarded by the factory managers, who necessarily colluded with this internal factory hierarchy. The qualities required of such core workers included an ability to get on well with the bosses and with workers in charge of key areas of the factory such as the stores (Ladó and Tóth 1988: 525). Even outside this core group, an ability to hustle from the bosses and foremen allowed one access to a regular and high salary (cf. Haraszti 1971). Only through personal contacts, not through ability or diligence as a worker, could one hope to achieve a position of influence in the socialist production line. In other words the skills of the wheeler-dealer which Gypsies had to use in their ideologically illegitimate self-employed activities were the very ones needed for success in the world of the socialist factory or farm.

An ethnography of a collectivized village near Gyöngyös shows how salient these concerns were to other ordinary Hungarians at this time. One peasant told Peter Bell that 'now the people [Magyars] are Gypsy' (1984: 294). By this he meant that in the socialist world the way to get on was through 'carrying on like a Gypsy' (*cigánykodás*). Bell defined this as 'worming oneself into the good graces of the leadership through ingratiation, two-facedness, betraying fellow workers, flattery, holding back complaints, granting sexual favours, or, expressed metaphorically "licking upward and spitting (or kicking) downward"' (1984: 253–4). Of the people who ran the village's cooperative farm it was said, 'they don't do any work; they just order people around' (1984: 170). Members of the farm believed that job allocation and access to privileges depends on 'standing close to the fire' (1984: 247). Whatever the real situation (and Bell showed that a new, strict, cooperative chairman replacing a corrupt one may have altered behaviour without upsetting the ideological stereotypes) it was thought that in this world it was not a person's labour that advanced him so much as his contacts. As a common saying put it, 'I'm too busy working to earn any money'.

One consequence of this situation was that stealing from the factory or cooperative became legitimate among the workers, who re-named it using the verbs for 'obtaining' (*szerezni*) or 'bringing' (*hozni*) (Bell 1984: 183; cf. Marrese 1981: 59–60 for industrial parallels). There were daily reports in the press, books published, and even films made on the lack of work discipline, on the theft of collective property, the moral corruption that accompanied hustling in all spheres of life. There was a definite shared sense that the lot of the modern Hungarian was that of the dealer and the hustler, that is, of the Gypsy.[15]

Cruelly, Gypsies themselves were rarely well placed to achieve regular, let alone high, salaries in their waged work. They entered the labour market as un- or semi-skilled workers and were given tasks peripheral to the main production processes. In a word, they continued to provide cheap labour for the dirty jobs. For them it was easier to try and construct an image of themselves as autonomous persons in relation to their traditional occupations of horse-dealing, scavenging, and trading on the unsupervised market, where they were constrained only by their ability to find a buyer in need, and not by their ability to curry favour with those in power. In such markets they could at least symbolically realize their ideal of autonomy (Stewart 1992).

This rejection of proletarianization was, of course, only reinforced by the nature of the reforms introduced gradually in Hungary from 1968 onwards, as a result of which various forms of private business and trade were tolerated. Though Gypsies were rarely involved directly in such enterprises, the reforms opened up a space in which Gypsies could operate more or less legitimately. So 'dealing' continued to be the ideal for Gypsy youth. If they could get permission to set up as a 'small manufacturer' or 'trader' (*kisiparos*), the road to wealth was open to them. The few Gypsies in Gyöngyös who had cars, to take just one example of conspicuous wealth, had just such permits and had made their wealth as dealers and traders.

REPRODUCING GYPSIES

The communist reformers between the 1960s and 1980s believed that they were making an entirely original and unprecedented offer to the Gypsies of Hungary. For the first time Gypsies were to be given the chance to participate as full members of society, as members of the class that was nominally in charge of production. Central to the success of the state's policy was the general attempt by communists across the whole society to create an ideology within which labour had a positive social value.[16] Yet, to take one example of the scale of failure on this front, the state was never even able to repeal laws enforcing registered work on all citizens – laws which had originally been passed as a means to curb the black market after the war. Matters declined so that in the mid-1980s forced labour itself was reintroduced for people avoiding waged labour. Such legislation only worsened the image of manual labour.

Throughout the socialist period labour continued to be tainted by the negative connotations it had in the capitalist past, and the very rhetoric within which communists tried to give expression to their morality soon acquired the taint of old forms of thought and speech. In its representations of labour, trade, and morality official communism paralleled widespread popular ideas, and gradually the two merged into a sort of hybrid, a hybrid to which, of course, the Gypsies had a practised aversion.[17]

Communist theory had also (wrongly) assumed that Gypsies traditionally lived outside class society, and that this lack of integration explained the profound differences in attitude and material culture between Hungarian peasants and Gypsies. In fact, it was the form of integration of Gypsies into class society which had made them different. During the communist period this was still the case: if Gypsies resisted assimilation it was because of the forms through which they were integrated in the socialist political economy. Even some of the longest-term wage-labourers I knew in Gyöngyös were heavily involved in horse-dealing and maintained the ideal of dropping wage-labour if possible.

Why did communist bureaucrats have such misleading expectations of the ease with which Gypsies would change their outlook? First, they were used to working with a *tabula rasa* theory of post-revolutionary cognitive change, and secondly, they held a positivist theory of consciousness for those parts of the collective consciousness which had not been wiped clean. I take these related points in order.

Communist theory of social change, like any revolutionary theory, conceived of radical social transformation in terms of creating a clean break from the past among those whose lives were to be changed. Only after such a rupture could the communists impose their scientifically derived formulae for a good social life, uncorrupted by the false consciousness induced by class society. Like other revolutionary regimes, the communists had to create the world afresh in order not to be weighed down by the inertia of the past. The peculiarity of the communist efforts concerning Gypsies was that it was thought that nothing had to be done to wipe their slate clean, since there was nothing on it in the first place. Gypsies had lost their place in the social division of labour decades previously; they spoke an unwritten language, lacked any religion or even any apparent social organisation, and appeared to lack all the qualities that make up nations (different groups appeared not even to acknowledge their identity with one another). They thus presented a blank board waiting to be written on (Guy 1978; cf. Erdös 1960, 1961).

Secondly, in so far as Gypsies did clearly have some ideas and shared representations, these could be explained as expressing in a straightforward, utilitarian fashion their material interests. If Gypsies saw themselves (as to some extent they did) as scavengers and beggars, it was assumed this was because they could only make their living in this fashion. The crucial representation of their mode of livelihood which the communist reformers hoped to change bore no simple relation to the Gypsies' material practice. For many decades, if not centuries, Gypsies in Hungary had in part depended on wages, while representing their mode of money-making as scavenging, begging, and dealing. If Gypsy images of dealing presented an accurate picture of their practice of wealth creation, then as these activities became less important economically to them, so would the idea that Gypsies are, by definition, dealers, beggars, and so on. However, because the representation and the practice were not straightforward reflections of each other, a change in the actual process of reproduction did not alter, in any direct way, the representation of that process. When communist social planners argued that there was no more than a 'lag' between cultural and economic change, between base and superstructural transformation (for example, Báthory 1983: 9), they only showed how little they knew about Gypsy culture. In fact, because the Gypsy way of imagining reality was ideologically sealed from material practice – in a fashion which it would take another essay to describe – it persisted more or less unscathed by communist attempts to breach it.

The failure to create the *tabula rasa* led the communists in time to a necessary engagement with the ideas people actually held. In this engagement communist theory almost always lost out to local knowledge, or adapted itself in a surprisingly plastic fashion to the contours of popular consciousness. This might be attributed simply to opportunism, of which there are plenty of examples in communist politics (one thinks of the use of anti-Semitism throughout the Soviet dominion – Fejtö 1974: 295–9), but I would argue for a less reductive, less transactional explanation. Perhaps it was precisely the idealist notion that communist theory was derived scientifically, that is a-socially, which allowed the consequent collapse into its opposite, abandoning even a critique of local models in favour of their total assimilation. Hungarian communism had been derived in an intellectual and social refuge from the world (the internal development of scientific Marxism on the one hand and the conditions of emigré life in Stalin's Moscow on the other). As far as the people of Hungary were concerned, both Magyar and Gypsy alike, socialism had never begun from a critical engagement with their ideas, their dreams, and their needs.

NOTES

1 Research was funded by an Economic and Social Research Council grant. I would also thank the London School of Economics for help with the initial writing up of this research (Stewart 1988).

2 During the twentieth century, Gypsy disadvantages altered, but their status as the most multiply disadvantaged population in Hungary was reproduced in new forms. Gypsies had made up one-quarter of all agricultural wage-workers prior to the war and would therefore have been eligible for land in any land reform. But when this came in the wake of the liberation in 1944–45 they were left out of the redistribution (Donáth 1979: 117; Kozák 1983: 114). Then, as agricultural land was collectivized in the 1950s, the main traditional source of Gypsy income dried up: low-paid agricultural wage-work for peasants was now no longer feasible for most Gypsies. At the same time, trading became impractical as there were no markets in agricultural produce or livestock (Fél and Hofer 1969:

352) and the state pursued an active campaign against all forms of marketing. Moreover, factories were still swamped by peasant labour recently liberated from the land, so that in 1960 at most 30 per cent of all adult Gypsies had regular waged work (Kozák 1983: 115), with fairly predictable consequences for the economic well-being in a society with no unemployment benefits.

3 Communist parties throughout the Soviet dominion were adopting Gypsy reform policies at this period inspired by the example of the CPSU which had woken up with a fright to its own Gypsy problem in the early 1950s (see Bán and Pogány 1957).

4 In all the socialist countries of South-eastern Europe the 'Gypsy question' had a salience equivalent to the 'immigrant' question in some North-west European countries.

5 A good, accessible source for ideas current at this time in communist theory is Erdős (1960, 1961).

6 The importance of this question is connected with the rights enjoyed by the officially recognized 'national minorities'. Unlike other Eastern European countries, the rights of these minorities were genuinely exercised in Hungary (possibly because, having few members, they posed little threat to the state). The rights were jealously guarded, and when, many years ago, a delegation of Gypsies was encouraged to attend a plenum meeting of representatives of the other national minorities, the latter refused to enter once they heard of the proposed Gypsy presence (János Báthory, personal communication).

Guy, analyzing Czechoslovak data, provides the best discussion in English of the conjunctural and practical reasons for the communist parties' rejection of national minority status for Gypsies (1978: 129–60). He also discusses communist theory of nationality with respect to the Gypsy question (1978: 700–23).

7 This provides a powerful example of the way public debate was constrained by the 'leading role of the party' under 'actually existing socialism'. It was only after there had been debates within the party about the application of the terms 'assimilation' and 'integration' (one word had previously been used in Hungarian: beilleszkedés; see Herczeg 1976) to the recognized national minorities that Gypsies were able to raise publicly similar questions in relation to their (unrecognized) ethnic group.

8 In the mid-1980s a new phase of Gypsy–socialist state relations began, characterized by a growing contradiction between official attempts to continue the assimilationist policy and officially tolerated Gypsy efforts to resist it. At this stage a place was allowed for expressions of Gypsy culture as a kind of residue. Those parts of 'old, traditional' Gypsy culture which were thought to stem from lumpenization or exclusion from the previous class-based modes of production (extended family, sharing wealth, gambling, scavenging, begging, and so on) would pass away once Gypsies were given work. Thus it was said that the Gypsy with a fixed job and a home in the town will 'present no special problems'. As the Gypsies become settled wage-workers and indistinguishable socially from the Magyars, so harmless elements of their culture (dress, songs, and so on) would become folklore, a colourful reminder of the past. Gypsies would be workers from Monday to Friday and on the occasional communist Saturday (days of labour 'freely' given to the state towards, for instance, Nicaraguan solidarity), but on Sundays and holidays they would re-live their past in folk performances and the like, becoming Gypsies again for a day.

9 In order to bring out the difference, let me caricature reality a little. In England, the general public get a sense of the condition of the economy from daily reports on the state of the Stock Exchange, whereas on a Hungarian news report one was

more likely to hear about rises or falls in output in a branch of agriculture or industry. Such a difference in the rituals which surround 'the economy' reflected a view of social reproduction which stressed production and not exchange as the decisive moment.

10 Compare Le Goff's comment about early modern Europe: 'Before as well as after the Industrial Revolution, social classes which had risen owing to labour hastened to deny their working roots. Labour has really never ceased to be a sort of mark of servility' (1980: 121).

11 There are no separate figures for Vlach Gypsies. One may assume that they were less involved in waged labour than other Gypsies.

12 Most fully in Stewart 1988; in reference to Gypsy ideology: Stewart 1989; in reference to trade: Stewart 1992.

13 Fél and Hofer themselves point out (1969: 38) that the 'proper peasants' only ever formed a minority in the village which they studied but they provided an ideal according to which other 'less successful' villagers strove to live.

14 Cf. Kiss (1981 [1939]: 287): 'easily earned money naturally goes with a rash life-style'.

15 János Kenedi (1986) has suggested various functional reasons for the scapegoating of Gypsies, noting the particular ambiguity towards hustling among Hungarians (1986). It seems to me that he over-stresses the particularly Hungarian aspects of this: Gypsies are similarly salient in Romania, Czechoslovakia, and even Russia.

16 See Humphrey for similar Soviet evidence of this (1983: 159–70, 228–58, 300–16, 354–8).

17 In a recent work Nee and Stark identify changes in the theorization of communist societies away from notions of monolithic totalitarianism towards theories which allow and account for the evolution and transformation of socialist systems (1989: 3–8). In the light of the evidence presented in this chapter, one could take their argument one stage further and suggest that one of the important variables in socialist societies has been the way particular elements of the general socialist ideological complex took root in differing environments. For example, communist egalitarianism found welcoming soil in Czechoslovakia, while the rest of the ideology fell on stony ground (Holy 1992). In Hungary and Romania (Kideckel, forthcoming) attitudes to labour, trade, and the moral economy constituted the elements which took firmest root.

REFERENCES

Bán, G. and Pogány, G. (1957) A magyarországi cigány helyzetéröl ('The situation of Hungarian Gypsies'), Budapest: Ministry of Labour cyclostyled document.

Báthory, J. (1983) 'A "cigánykérdés"' ('The "Gypsy Question"'), in L. Szegö (ed.) Cigányok, honnét jöttek – merre tartanak? ('The Gypsies, whither have they come – where are they headed?'), Budapest: Kozmosz, pp. 8–24.

Beck, S. and Gheorghe, N. (1981) 'From slavery to co-inhabiting nationality: the political economy of Romanian Gypsies', Unpublished paper presented to the Symposium on the Social Anthropology of Europe IUAES Intercongress, Amsterdam.

Bell, P. (1984) Peasants in Socialist Transition: Life in a Collectivised Hungarian Village, Berkeley: University of California Press.

Burawoy, M. (1985) The Politics of Production, London: Verso.

Cliff, T. (1974) State Capitalism in Russia, London: Pluto.

Donáth, F. (1979) *Reform and Revolution: Transformation of Hungary's Agriculture, 1945–1970*, Budapest: Corvina.

Erdös, K. (1960) 'Le problème Tsigane en Hongrie', *Etudes Tsiganes*, 6(3): 1–10.

—— (1961) 'Remarque sur le problème Tsigane en Hongrie', *Etudes Tsiganes*, 7(2): 8–13.

Fejtö, F. (1974) *A History of the People's Democracies*, Harmondsworth: Penguin.

Fél, E. and Hofer, T. (1969) *Proper Peasants. Traditional Life in a Hungarian Village*, Chicago, Aldine: Viking Fund Publications in Anthropology, 46.

Gurevich, V. (1985) *Categories of Medieval Culture*, trans. G. Campbell, London: Routledge and Kegan Paul.

Guy, W. (1978) 'The attempt of socialist Czechoslovakia to assimilate its Gypsy population', Unpublished Ph.D. thesis, University of Bristol.

Hann, C. (1980) *Tázlár: A Village in Hungary*, Cambridge: Cambridge University Press.

Haraszti, M. (1971) *A Worker in a Worker's State*, Harmondsworth: Allen Lane.

Hart, K. (1986) 'Heads or tails? Two sides of the coin', *Man*, 21(4): 637–56.

Havas, G. (1982a) 'Foglalkozásváltási stratégiák különbözö cigány közösségekben' ('Strategies for changing occupations in different Gypsy communities'), in M. Andor (ed.) *Cigány Vizsgálatok*, pp. 181–202, Budapest: Müvelödési Kutató Intézet.

—— (1982b) 'Korábbi cigány foglalkozások' ('Previous Gypsy occupations'), in M. Andor (ed.) *Cigáany Vizsgálatok*, pp. 161–80, Budapest: Müvelödési Kutató Intézet.

Herczeg, F. (1976) *A MSZMP nemzetiségi politikája* ('The policy of the Hungarian Socialist Workers' Party on the national minorities'), Budapest: Kossuth.

Holy, L. (1992) 'Culture, market, ideology and economic reform in Czechoslovakia', in R. Dilley (ed.) *Contesting Markets*, Edinburgh: Edinburgh University Press.

Humphrey, C. (1983) *Karl Marx Collective: Economy, Society and Religion in a Siberian Collective Farm*, Cambridge: Cambridge University Press.

Kemény, I. (1978) 'La chaine dans une usine hongroise', *Actes de la Recherche en Sciences Sociales* (Nov.).

Kenedi, J. (1986) 'Why is the Gypsy the scapegoat and not the Jew?', *East European Reporter*, 2(1): 11–14.

Kideckel, D. (forthcoming) *The Solitude of Collectivism: A Romanian Region before the Revolution*, Ithaca, NY: Cornell University Press.

Kiss, L. (1981/1939) *A Szegény emberek élete* ('The life of the poor'), Budapest: Gondolat.

Kolakowski, L. (1978) *Main Currents of Marxism*, vol. II, Oxford: Clarendon Press.

Kozák, I. (1983) 'A cigányok a társadalmi munkamegosztásban' ('The Gypsies in the social division of labour'), in L. Szegö (ed.) *Cigányok, honnét jöttek – merre tartanak?* (The Gypsies, whither have they come – where are they headed?'), Budapest: Kozmosz, pp. 102–22 (written in 1979).

Ladó, M. and Tóth, A. (1988) 'In the shadow of the formal rules', *Economic and Industrial Democracy*, 9(4): 523–33.

Le Goff, J. (1980) *Time, Work and Culture in the Middle Ages*, (trans. A. Goldhammer), Chicago and London: University of Chicago Press.

Lichtheim, G. (1961) *Marxism: An Historical and Critical Study*, London: Routledge and Kegan Paul.

Marrese, M. (1981) 'The evolution of wage regulation in Hungary', in P. Hare, G. Radice and N. Swain (eds) *Hungary, A Decade of Economic Reform*, London: Allen & Unwin, pp. 63–76.

Mezey, B. (ed.) (1986) *A magyarországi cigánykérdés dokumentumokban, 1422–1985*,

('The Hungarian Gypsy question through documents, 1422–1985'), Budapest: Kossuth.

Nee, V. and Stark, D. (1989) 'Towards an institutional analysis of state socialism', in *Remaking the Institutions of Socialism: China and Eastern Europe*, Stanford, CA: Stanford University Press.

Nove, A. (1983) *The Economics of Feasible Socialism*, London: Allen & Unwin.

Okely, J. (1983) *The Traveller-Gypsies*, Cambridge: Cambridge University Press.

Stewart, M. (1987) 'Brothers in song: the persistence of Gypsy identity and community in socialist Hungary', Ph.D. thesis, University of London.

—— (1989) '"True speech": song and the moral order of a Vlach Gypsy community in Hungary,' in *Man*, 24(1): 79–102.

—— (1990) 'Gypsies, work and civil society', in C. Hann (ed.) *Market Economy and Civil Society in Hungary*, London: Frank Cass.

—— (1992) 'Gypsies at the horse fair: a non-market model of trade,' in R. Dilley (ed.) *Contesting Markets*, Edinburgh: Edinburgh University Press.

Swain, N. (1985) *Collective Farms Which Work?* Cambridge: Cambridge University Press.

Szegö, L. (ed.) (1983) *Cigányok, honnét jottek – merre tartanak?* ('The Gypsies, whither have they come – where are they headed?'), Budapest: Kozmosz.

Chapter 13

The end of socialism in Czechoslovakia

Ladislav Holy

In Czechoslovakia, socialism has been replaced politically by liberal democracy, whilst economically it is in the process of being replaced by the swift introduction of private ownership of the means of production and by the free market. This momentous change is the result of the 'velvet revolution' which took place at the end of 1989. Undeniably, change in the Soviet Union and, more importantly, the revolutionary changes in other socialist countries had their effect on the events in Czechoslovakia at that time. If nothing more, they indicated to the Czechs that change was possible and that it would not be resisted from the outside as it had been in 1968. However, changes do not happen merely because they are possible. They have to be carried out by people who have an interest in instigating them.

As every revolutionary worth his salt knows, the pre-condition of a successful revolution is widespread dissatisfaction of the masses, who can then be politicized and mobilized for action in the name of the envisaged change for the better. By this textbook formula, conditions in Poland in the 1980s and in the Soviet Union in the late 1980s and early 1990s were probably more conducive to revolutions than was ever the case in Czechoslovakia before November 1989. Opposition to the regime in Czechoslovakia was weak in comparison with other socialist countries. It was centred in a number of 'independent initiatives', of which the oldest and best-known was Charter 77. Although the number of 'independent initiatives' had been steadily increasing in the run-up to 1989, it remains doubtful whether this increase was matched by any increase of actual persons actively involved in their activities. The most characteristic feature of the 'independent initiatives' was the considerable overlap of their membership; prominent Czechoslovak dissidents were often involved in more than one 'initiative'. Moreover, active involvement remained limited to a small circle of intellectuals who lacked the support of the working class. This was a fact of which they themselves were very well aware:

> When the friends from Polish Solidarity, whom we meet occasionally at
> the Czech–Polish border, ask how many people Charter 77 has behind

it, I feel like answering that if there are millions of people behind Solidarity, only millions of ears stand behind Charter 77.

(Vaclav Havel, in *The Times*, 12 August 1988)

Yet, a little more than a year after Havel expressed this rather pessimistic view, a revolution took place. After the students who demonstrated in Prague on 17 November 1989 were brutally beaten up by the police, they declared an indefinite strike in which they were immediately joined by actors and musicians.[1] The day after the demonstration not a single theatre played in Prague, and very soon thereafter all theatrical and concert performances came to a halt throughout the country. The declaration of the students' and actors' strikes was followed by daily mass demonstrations in Prague, which were eventually attended by an estimated 750,000 people (in a city with a population of 1,200,000). The demonstrations soon spread to other cities and towns. Ten days after the students and actors in Prague went on strike, a general strike in protest against the rule of the communist party took place. According to a published survey, about half of the population of the country actually stopped work for two hours on 27 November and a quarter of the population joined in nationwide demonstrations. Ten per cent of the workforce did not take part in the strike in order not to jeopardize essential services, and only 20 per cent did not strike for other reasons (either because they did not want to, or because they were afraid of dismissal and other reprisals from their managers and local party secretaries). Two days after the strike, the Federal Assembly (the Parliament) abolished the article of the Czechoslovak constitution which enshrined the leading role of the communist party, and the communist chairman of the Federal Assembly resigned. The new cabinet formed on 3 December consisted of 15 communists and 5 non-communists. Further mass demonstrations followed, and under the threat of another general strike the new Government survived for only seven days. On 10 December the communist President swore in a new 'government of national understanding', which consisted of nine communists and eleven non-communists. Following this act, he resigned. In January, the Prime Minister and one of the Deputy Prime Ministers resigned their Party membership, thereby reducing the number of communists in the cabinet to seven out of twenty. On 28 December, Alexander Dubček was elected chairman of the Federal Assembly, and on 29 December the Federal Assembly elected Vaclav Havel as President of the Republic. The phrases expressing allegiance to socialism were left out of his constitutionally prescribed oath by mutual agreement of all concerned.

A number of Western political commentators looked in disbelief at this revolution, led by actors and a playwright, as if it were in itself some kind of absurd theatre. Yet, the change which this revolution brought about was not only faster than the transition anywhere else in Eastern Europe but, with the possible exceptions of East Germany and Hungary, it was also much more radical. Elections held in June 1990 were contested by twenty-three political parties and movements and resulted in the formation of a coalition governemnt of the Civic Forum and Christian Democrats. The Government vigorously pursued its policy of privatization and transition to a free market economy.

How, then, can one explain the paradox that the most successful revolution in Eastern Europe was one which defied all textbook formulas and one which was started by students and led by intellectuals who had no support from the masses when they embarked on their political gamble? I want to argue that this paradox is only apparent; it arises through conceptualizing politics in terms of a narrowly defined discourse of political scientists, commentators, and pundits. Such specialists see politics simply as the pursuit of group or sectional interests which exist somehow independently of any particular culture. The politics they talk about is, however, always and everywhere a process embedded in cultural contexts. Cultural premisses and assumptions, which in themselves are not seen as 'political', inevitably influence the shape and form of political action in the narrower sense. Once one starts seeing 'politics' as an aspect of the cultural system in Czechoslovakia, the seeming paradox of the recent revolution disappears. In this chapter, I shall sketch some of the specifically Czech cultural conceptualizations[2] which affected the course of the 'velvet revolution', whilst focusing on two main questions: first, why was the revolution started by students, actors, and other intellectuals? Secondly, why was the publicly expressed opposition of intellectuals to the communist regime so swiftly followed by the masses?

STUDENTS

An important instrument of communist propaganda before 1989 was the unceasing comparison of the achievements of socialist Czechoslovakia with the pre-war capitalist Czechoslovak republic. Socialist Czechoslovakia emerged from this comparison as greatly superior to the pre-war capitalist system: full employment and universal education were guaranteed, and medical care and old age pensions were available to everyone. Socialism could also draw support from statistics giving the number of cars, bathrooms, radio sets, and other gadgets per family. This elementary trick of comparing the past with the present and then presenting it as a comparison of one contemporary social system with another may have enjoyed at least partial success as long as there were enough older people around able to enliven such statistics with narratives of their personal experiences of the horrors of the depression years of the 1930s.[3] Such narratives re-emerged again in the form of letters of old communist party members to the party newspaper *Rude Pravo* in the early months of 1990 as arguments against privatization and the introduction of an economic model based on market principles. The crucial point is that it is personal experience of this kind which gives credence to the statistics employed by the official propaganda. Statistical figures are remote from experience. Reality, as it is understood by the people themselves, can only be apprehended through 'experience close' concepts. Although undoubtedly the proverbial pattern according to which the values of one generation are denied by the next one played some role, the main reason for the politicization of young people in Czechoslovakia lies in the fact that their life experience was quite different from that of their parents, and certainly their grandparents. Most of those involved in the demonstration on 17 November and in the subsequent student strike were not even born in 1968, and few could remember it personally. Their personal experience was limited to post-1968 Czechoslovakia, and they compared it not with the Czechoslovakia of the past but with its contemporary neighbours to the West. In comparison with their counterparts there, they felt deprived. They were prevented from travelling, from playing and listening to the music they liked, from reading books and looking at pictures they liked, from hearing more than one view in the course of their education, and even from choosing freely whether or not to believe in God.

Another factor impelling young people to rebel against the state was the complete failure of the regime to force the population to toe the socialist line. Although leading dissidents were given prison sentences after 1968, the main forms of controlling dissent were economic. Dissidents were prevented from getting employment appropriate to their qualifications and could at best earn their living in menial jobs. Writers, journalists, actors, and even priests were employed as stokers, unskilled labourers, lumbermen, or – in exceptional, particularly fortunate cases – taxi drivers. One of the most effective means of forcing potential dissidents to give up their subversive activity was the impact of repression upon their children. Irrespective of their academic achievements, they were denied access to higher education. It is one thing to engage in political opposition against the regime and suffer in consequence; it is another to engage in such opposition in the knowledge that one's children will suffer as well. There is no doubt that using children as hostages was the most effective means of breaking down the widespread popular opposition which followed the invasion by Warsaw Pact countries in 1968 (Simecka 1984). Young people in 1989 were free from this particular kind of pressure. Of course not only they themselves but their parents too could have suffered for their actions. But while it is difficult to justify morally the punishment of innocent children for actions of their parents over which they had no influence, it is not so difficult to accept the risk of punishment for the parents as a result of the actions of their children. After all, it was precisely the inactivity of the parents' generation which had got the country into the mess in which it found itself. The possible punishment of the parents, unlike that of the children, was not a punishment of the innocent.

ACTORS

The small circle of dissidents who stood in active opposition to the regime objected particularly to the systematic persecution of scholars, journalists, writers, poets, musicians, pop-singers, and other artists who had declared their open support for the reforms of 1968 and were unwilling to gain the regime's favour by publicly revoking their 'ideological mistakes'. The active dissidents formed only a tiny minority of the country's intelligentsia, but this small circle comprised virtually all leading Czech and Slovak intellectuals, among them many of those who had contributed to the high international profile of Czechoslovak cinema, drama, and literature in the 1960s. Those who did not emigrate (as did Kundera and Forman) were banned, forced to survive in menial occupations, and from time to time imprisoned (like Havel himself). Their creativity was pushed underground. The result was that hardly a novel, film, or play of any significance was published or performed in Czechoslovakia after 1968. In the words of Heinrich Böll, Czechoslovakia became 'a cultural Biafra'.

The Czech conceptualization of the nation and its relationship to the state are key elements in my argument. The self-image of the Czechs, perpetually invoked in all possible contexts and marshalled to motivate practical action, is the image of a highly cultured and well-educated nation. At present this image motivates what the Czechs describe as their 'return to Europe', which they generally perceive as the ultimate goal of their revolution. They have always detested being classified as East Europeans, and are always ready to point out that Prague in fact lies west of Vienna. For the Czechs, Eastern Europe consists of the Soviet Union, Romania, Bulgaria, and possibly Poland, but Czechoslovakia itself is part of Central Europe. It is common to describe it as lying in 'the heart of Europe' or even as *being* 'the heart of Europe'. The Czechs use the concept of *kulturnost* (a noun derived from the adjective 'cultured') to construct a boundary between themselves and the 'uncultured' East, into which they were lumped after the communist *coup d'état* in 1948. They see their proper place as being alongside the civilized, cultured, and educated nations of Western Europe. The idea of 'the return to Europe' dominated the election campaign in June 1990 when virtually every political party presented itself to the voters as the party best-qualified to lead Czechoslovakia into Europe.

The systematic creation of a cultural desert in post-1968 Czechoslovakia was thus perceived as a gift of the state to a people whose self-image is that of a highly cultured and well educated nation. The persistence of rigid censorship and the systematic persecution of anybody expressing a thought which deviated from the official line were seen by intellectuals as the state's betrayal of the very nation to which it nominally owed allegiance. The state's cultural policy pushed the intellectuals into resisting its power in the name of the nation of which they formed a part.

Actors joined the students in the strike not because their grudge against the state was any greater than that of other intellectuals, but simply because they, together with musicians, were the only intellectuals who could strike effectively. One would hardly notice a writer or poet on strike in the solitude of his study. Of all intellectuals the actors were the most visible – and this brings me to the second question, the question of what exactly made the strike so effective.

MASSES

The idea that a strike in the theatres of London's West End could possibly topple the British Government, when neither miners nor ambulance drivers could come anywhere close to it in the 1980s, is clearly laughable. The strike of actors in Prague theatres, however, not only spread like wildfire to all the theatres and concert halls in the country (and was emulated by other entertainers, such as footballers, who refused to play their scheduled league matches) but was followed within ten days by a nationwide general strike. With hindsight, it is clear that the general strike could have followed even earlier. The intellectuals who led the revolution were cautious in estimating the impact of their own action on the masses, and thought that at least ten days were needed to rouse them from their lethargy. Their caution derived from their awareness that, in contrast to Poland and Romania, the Czechs and Slovaks were not suffering any significant economic deprivation. In spite of its technological backwardness, the Czechoslovak economy was in better shape than any other in the Soviet bloc, and one obvious source for widespread popular opposition to communist rule was therefore missing. The intellectuals were also very well aware that their specific grievances could hardly be sufficient to motivate the population at large. Most people even did not know who the leading intellectuals were. When Havel first addressed the mass rallies, most people perceived him as one of 'those mysterious dissidents'. When he later emerged as the only serious candidate for the Presidency, Czech newspapers hurriedly printed articles explaining who he was. Many puzzled cooperative farmers and factory workers believed that if he really was the world-famous playwright he was suddenly made out to be, his plays would surely have been staged in Czechoslovakia and they would have heard about him before.

But whatever one might say about the cultural and educational level of those who expressed such views, they too were Czechs. They too saw themselves as members of a cultured and well-educated nation. What they resented as members of this nation was not the persecution of a few intellectuals, but the affront which they felt when they had to obey orders from those who knew not only less than they should have known in their leadership positions, but often less than those whom they were supposed to lead. The image of those in authority as blithering idiots was all-pervasive and an endless source of popular jokes. The Civic Forum skilfully exploited these feelings when it broadcast the secret recording of the General Secretary's impromptu speech to the district party secretaries. The grammatically incorrect and syntactically incoherent speech of the man who had formerly been the most powerful man in the country itself drove the point home without any need for further comment. The crowds of ordinary people who listened in the street to this broadcast roared with contemptuous laughter, displaying in this way their own *kulturnost*. The message was: less cultured nations would shoot you, we laugh at you.

What gave the velvet revolution its impetus was the general feeling in the country that on 17 November state repression had reached an unbearable level. People's self-perception as a cultured and well-educated nation played a significant role in fostering this general feeling. The 'uncultured' use of brutal force by the state against the 'cultured' and peaceful demonstrators made it clear that the Czechs had a state unbefitting a cultured nation. In an open confrontation between intellectuals and future intellectuals (students) with uncultured and uneducated power, the masses would have to be on the side of the cultured and educated.

Various other aspects of Czech culture were also influential at this juncture. References to Czech history recur not only in much political commentary but also in everyday political discourse. By constantly referring in this way to their history, the Czechs tell themselves who they are. They do so by projecting contemporary ideas and values into their narratives of the past, thus creating myths which are then in turn invoked for legitimation purposes. One of the important myths which the Czechs create when narrating their history is the myth of a nation whose leading personalities have always been intellectuals. The 'father of the country', King Charles IV, is remembered primarily as the founder of the oldest university north of the Alps. The most important Czech martyr, Jan Hus, was a professor at this university. The Hussite movement owed its authority mainly to the fact that the Czech people were led by preachers 'with better knowledge of the scriptures than the Pope himself'. A tiny group of Czech intellectuals kept the Czech language alive in the nineteenth century and managed to bring the Czechs into the fold of modern European nations. A university professor, a high-school teacher, and an astronomer were the founding fathers of the Czechoslovak republic in 1918. All the many components of this myth together provided a charter for action. In the confrontation between intellectuals and the power of the state in 1989, the myth helped to sway the nation to the side of the intellectuals.[4]

The political impact of the actors' strike derives to a great extent from the fact that these notions of Czech nationhood and Czech history are encapsulated in the symbol of the National Theatre. Even those with only a smattering of knowledge of Czech history know two things about the National Theatre. The first (not, in fact, historically accurate) is that the National Theatre, by keeping the Czech language alive, was instrumental in the survival of the Czech nation in the period when the Czechs were unsuccessfully fighting for their political rights as a nation within the Austrian monarchy. The second (likewise dubious in terms of historical fact) is that the theatre's construction was made possible only by the financial contributions of ordinary people at a cost of considerable financial sacrifice and that, after a fire in 1881 before construction was completed, it was rebuilt in record time exclusively through such contributions. The words 'Nation to itself' emblazoned above the proscenium remind every-body of this remarkable dedication to the national cause. The story of the building of the National Theatre is one of the most important national myths, and, in consequence, the theatre itself is one of the most important symbols of the Czech nation and, after Prague castle, probably the most frequently visited site. Few Czechs have never visited the National Theatre. It is popularly known as 'the golden chapel', a name which suggests that this building serves more as a national shrine than as a venue for theatrical performances. Although the actors' strike did not start in the National Theatre, the fact that the actors of the National Theatre immediately joined it was of the utmost importance. The fact that the National Theatre was not playing was seen as an unmistakable sign that the nation's situation was critical.

One must, however, look beyond the actors' strike and examine other myth–symbol complexes to explain the politicization of the masses. Like other previous demonstrations, that held on 17 November 1989 was timed for a symbolically significant day, the fiftieth anniversary of the closing of all Czech universities in 1939. This day marked the execution of nine students and the deportation of some 1,200 into concentration camps as a reprisal for students' demonstrations against the Nazi occupation of Czechoslovakia. These 1939 demonstrations took place during the funeral of Jan Opletal, a student who had been shot dead by the Germans during a pro-Czechoslovak demonstration on 28 October (a national holiday com-memorating the foundation of the republic). In comparison with earlier demonstrations in 1989, that called for 17 November was different in two respects. First, it was authorized by the city authorities after they had agreed with the students on the route for their march. Secondly, the police and what later appeared to be specially trained anti-terrorist units brutally assaulted the students. As all possible escape routes were blocked by the police themselves after the students were told to disperse, it seems clear that the purpose of the police attack was not so much to disperse the demonstration as to teach all possible demonstrators a lesson once and for all.[5]

The demonstration on 17 November was the culmination of a large number of demonstrations, none of which articulated any specific political demands formulated by the independent initiatives. They did not even demand the legalization of these initiatives. In none of the pre-November demonstrations were there calls for the Government's resignation, change in the party's leadership, or the party's relinquishing its monopoly of power, or change of the whole political system. The only demand the demonstrators expressed explicitly was in chants for 'Freedom' and 'Give us freedom!' The demonstrators relied heavily on the display of nationalist symbols. In addition to their choice of venues and timing, which both had strong nationalist connotations, the participants sang the national anthem, carried national flags, and wore ribbons in the national colours. They encouraged bystanders to join them by shouting 'Czechs come with us!'. The police who confronted the demonstrators with truncheons, tear-gas, dogs, and water cannon were greeted as 'Fascists' and 'Gestapo'. One commentator missed the point when he suggested in an underground newspaper that the demonstrators might as well have shouted 'communists', for beating up opponents was not a prerogative of fascists but an integral part of communist political culture (*Listy*, 19, 2 (1989): 16). The true meaning of the abuse directed at the police was expressed by a participant in one of the demonstrations, when he described it euphemistically as 'assuring the police that they were not Czechs' (*Listy*, 19, 1 (1989): 44).

NATION, STATE, AND FREEDOM

The demand for freedom, the only demand the demonstrators articulated, was thus expressed in the context of strong nationalist emotions and was understood by the demonstrators and the Government alike as an anti-government protest. Nationalism, government, and freedom are thus intertwined and feed on one another. In invoking this package of inter-related notions, the demonstrations were clearly expressing a specifically Czech cultural construction of the relations between nation and state. Although the concept of the Czech nation as a community of people speaking the same language and sharing the same culture crystallized only during the period of the national revival in the nineteenth century, the Czechs now conceptualize this community as a natural entity that has existed from the dawn of time. Until the beginning of the seventeenth century, the Czech nation had its own state, the Czech kingdom. The suppression of the uprising of the Czech nobility against the centralizing and absolutist tendency of the Habsburg monarchy at the beginning of the seventeenth century effectively meant the end of the sovereignty of the Czech state. The centre of political power moved from Prague to Vienna, and for the Czech nation there followed 300 years of 'darkness', 'oppression', and 'suffering'. The founding of the independent Czechoslovak state in 1918 was hailed as the liberation of the nation after 300 years of Habsburg rule. Freedom of the nation was seen as the major achievement of the political change – freedom in the sense of the nation being the master of its own collective destiny. For the Czechs, freedom is the core symbol of a nation enclosed within its own state, and the calls for freedom in the demonstrations of 1988 and 1989 were invocations of this symbol.

If this interpretation is correct, why then should people who have their nation-state rally behind 'freedom' and other nationalist symbols, and, even more importantly, why should their action be seen as anti-state? The question can be reformulated as, why is the nation opposed to the state? The answer lies in the logical implications of 'freedom' as the central ideological construct and core symbol of the relations between the nation and state. One of the implications is that the nation is free not just when it has its own state but when that state is an instrument for the management and channelling of the nation's interests. The ultimate interest of the nation is, of course, its continued independent existence. All this is contained in the notion that the Czech nation has always been there, even in the centuries of darkness and oppression when it was not free and lacked a state to manage its interests. One can start to understand why it was not felt to be free in the pre-November days, in spite of having its own state, when one looks at the political rituals and symbols employed by the communist party. These did little to engender a perception of the Czechoslovak state as an organization for the pursuit of national interests. The two most important slogans displayed all over the country were 'The Soviet Union – our example' and 'With the Soviet Union for ever' (the popular attitude to these was expressed as usual in a joke: 'With the Soviet Union for ever but not a day longer'). It is no wonder that in the spring of 1980 it was widely rumoured in Prague that Czechoslovakia was to be fully incorporated into the Soviet Union as one of its republics (Gellner 1987: 126). Likewise it is no wonder that the communist system itself is widely seen as something alien to the national interest.

If, in the Czech conceptualization, the state is seen as the political instrument of the nation's freedom, the state has to guarantee both the freedom of the nation as a whole and the freedom of all its constituent parts. A nation-state cannot be repressive. If it is repressive, it is not a state which serves the nation's interest. In this context of notions it is logical that the demand for freedom was expressed in overtly nationalistic terms and eventually pitched the nation against the state. As the police were the visible instrument of the state's repression, it was logical that they were seen as standing outside and against the nation. This view was strongly reinforced every time the police took action against demonstrators who were waving national flags, singing the national anthem, and invoking other nationalist symbols. When on 17 November police brutality became all too clearly visible, and reminiscent in a way of what German fascists had done fifty years earlier, the tension between the nation and the state escalated into an open revolt of the people against the state.[6]

Repression is the opposite of care and compassion, and the socialist state had devoted a considerable amount of propaganda to presenting its caring image. It did this mainly through stressing its role as the guarantor of a social security system available to all citizens. Now, in the Czech cultural conceptualization care is a primarily feminine trait, and therefore the cultural construction of gender relations in Czechoslovakia also influenced interpretations of the events of 17 November. The pattern of gender relations is underpinned by a few basic assumptions about femininity. Its defining features are motherhood and the socialization of children. Maternal sentiments are culturally assumed to be grounded in female nature. As something given in nature, they are not open to manipulation by culture and society, for culture and society can only accommodate the givens of nature. They cannot go against them. The result is a strong cultural affirmation of a 'naturally given' association of women with the domestic domain (which allows the woman to hold the purse and be responsible for the running of the domestic economy), and of the 'naturally' determined gravitation of women towards caring professions in the public domain (more than 90 per cent of teachers are women, and women outnumber men in the health service not only as nurses but also as doctors). To give birth, to bring up children, and to be caring are the culturally assumed main characteristics of womanhood. All the activities of the Czechoslovak Union of Women were built on this conceptualization of womanhood, with motherhood as its central image.[7]

Mother, as a symbol with all its connotations, enters into the construction of the nation despite the fact that there is no semantic equivalent of the word 'motherland' in the Czech language. For the Czechs, their country is their 'homeland' (*domovina*) or *vlast* (a noun etymologically connected in at least one of its senses with the verb *vlastniti* – to own; Macura 1983: 162), and this makes it different from all other countries (*zeme* – lands). Unlike the terms 'fatherland' and 'motherland', the term *vlast* has no semantic association with parenthood. Its parental role is, however, made explicit by being referred to as *matka vlast* (*matka* – mother). Through this metaphor, the country (*vlast*) is construed as a life-engendering entity. It is a mother to every individual Czech, and all Czechs are its children (building upon this metaphor, one of the independent initiatives called itself the 'Czech children'). In the same way as one is born into a family and one's personal identity – signified by one's name – is established at birth, one is also born into a nation. Like one's personal identity, one's national identity is primary and one belongs to a nation in the same way that one belongs to a family. Both are preconditions for human existence. Neither the family nor the nation is made up of autonomous individuals, but rather individuals come into being as parts of the family and the nation. Through the metaphor of the mother country, Czechs remind themselves that each individual has two mothers: as a member of the family one has a biological genetrix, and as a member of the nation one has a symbolic genetrix.

If through the metaphor of the mother country the nation is construed as a life-engendering entity, the state – construed as the guardian of the nation's interests – cannot but behave in a caring – namely, motherly – way. It certainly should not repress members of the nation, the metaphorical children of the mother country. If it does, it has alienated itself from the nation, it has betrayed it. On 17 November 1989 the socialist state was not just beating up its citizens, the metaphorical children of the nation. It was beating up actual children – young people who were 'the future of the nation', in other words, those who would physically assure the nation's continued existence.

As with many other cultural premisses, those which motivated the perception of the events of 17 November were largely taken for granted and not an object of explicit discourse. Their existence can only be inferred from the explicit discourses into which they feed as verbally unformulated assumptions underlying their logic. One such explicit discourse has a direct bearing on the events of 17 November, and this is the discourse concerning the leadership of the Czechoslovak Union of Women after this date. The then leadership of this organization expressed its regret about the severity of the police action. It did not, however, condemn the police outright, but described the repression as 'disproportionate' to the task of maintaining public order at the demonstration. This formulation outraged the rank and file members, who saw in it the betrayal of the maternal feelings of the women whom the Union was supposed to represent. The leadership was forced to resign and the Union did not survive the crisis. At its next congress it dissolved itself and was replaced by a number of new independent women's organizations.

CONCLUSION

The revolution in Czechoslovakia was triggered on 17 November 1989, when the socialist state, in using violence against students (young people – our children) in a demonstration for which it itself gave permission, showed that it had betrayed the nation. The nation's outrage against the state was given visibility and shape by intellectuals (mainly actors) and students who were in the forefront of the popular revolt. This revolt highlighted not an opposition between socialism and democracy – as stressed by Western commentators – but an opposition between totalitarianism and freedom.

Demands for an end to the communist party's monopoly of power and for the creation of a democratic political structure were articulated by diverse groups of intellectuals and students at a meeting in one of the

Prague theatres on 19 November. The opposition of the independent initiatives to communist power had always been formulated in terms of a demand for respecting the citizens's legal rights. It was therefore appropriate that the organization now founded to co-ordinate the opposition to communist rule was called Civic Forum. Its spokesman – Vaclav Havel – addressed the demonstrators on 21 November, and subsequently presented the Forum's demands to the communist government and led political negotiations with it.

It was due to Civic Forum that the conflict between the nation and its state was eventually redefined as a conflict between citizens and the state. Civic Forum's political demands for the creation of a democratic political structure were embraced by the people when it became clear that this was the way to achieve their main objective: the replacement of the hated state. Democracy entered on the coat-tails of a more general desire to bring relations between the nation and state back into line with a culturally constituted ideal. I would suggest that in the context of the cultural construction of these relations, the questions of the specific form the government should take were initially quite secondary. (Of course they came to the forefront eventually, for one cannot avoid the task of creating tangible structures for the expression of all cultural relations.)

What the Czechoslovak Revolution expressed was something deeper than political dissatisfaction. It was the expression of a dissatisfaction with a situation in which the relationship between nation and state was defined in such a way that one could not talk about the one through the other. The 'political' crisis was precipitated by an event which highlighted this culturally unacceptable conceptualization of the nation–state relationship. The Civic Forum's policy document, published on the eve of the November general strike, spoke of a deep moral, spiritual, ecological, social, economic, and political crisis in the country. In my view, the document is right to put the political crisis last and the moral crisis first, for the ultimate crisis lay in the symbolic order, and it was this crisis which precipitated the political change.

NOTES

1 Although I have been in Czechoslovalia several times since 1986, I observed the events of November 1989 and the pre-November demonstrations at a distance. My account is based on reports in Czechoslovak official and underground press and mass media. *Kronika sametove revolues* (A chronicle of the 'velvet revolution'), published by the Czechoslovak Press Agency, provides a useful summary of events between 17 November and 10 December 1989.

2 In this chapter, I am specifically concerned with *Czech* cultural conceptualizations. The revolution started in Prague, but it spread immediately to Slovakia and the leading Czech intellectuals sought actively to engage their Slovak colleagues in the common cause. The reasons for dissatisfaction with the com-

munist regime were to some extent different among the Slovaks than among the Czechs; and the Slovaks' differing expectations of post-socialist arrangements are at the root of the contemporary tension between the Czechs and Slovaks. However, I am not qualified to comment on Slovak cultural conceptualizations and their effect on the political process in Slovakia.

3 Similar personal experiences of unemployed miners' hardships in the 1930s were used to sustain the morale of British miners striking in the 1980s against pit closures.

4 The rallying of the masses behind the intellectuals was of course considerably facilitated by television. It was significant that the students were first joined in the strike by actors, and that the actors were seen as the main representatives of the intellectuals. The actors who openly rebelled were not unknown dissidents but men and women whose names and faces were known from television screens. This gave them visibility which no dissidents could hope to match.

5 The massacre, as it was later referred to, occurred on one of Prague's major streets when the students were marching through in an attempt to reach the city centre, instead of ending the demonstration at the cemetery on the outskirts of Prague as had been agreed with the authorities. One theory advanced during the later parliamentary inquiry into the events of 17 November was that the students were actively encouraged to march onto the city centre by provocateurs from the ranks of the police and that the massacre was planned by the police right from the start. There is good evidence which supports this view.

6 It was no wonder that one of the representatives of Charter 77, who were normally very careful to check the accuracy of their information, reported to the world press that a student had been killed by the police during the demonstration. The logic of the situation made the rumour of a death entirely plausible to every Czech.

7 The new Government in 1990 abolished celebrations of International Women's Day and reinstituted Mother's Day. This change met with no opposition, as if the people were saying; 'Correct, what right does a woman have to be venerated unless she is a mother?'

REFERENCES

Gellner, E. (1987) *Culture, Identity and Politics*, Cambridge: Cambridge University Press.
Kronika sametove revoluce, (1990) Prague: Ceskoslovenska tiskova kancelar.
Macura, V. (1983) *Znameni zrodu: ceske obrozeni jako kulturni typ*, Prague: Ceskoslovensky spisovatel.
Simecka, M. (1984) *Obnoveni poradku*, London: Edice Rozmluvy.

Chapter 14

'Socialism is dead' and very much alive in Slovakia

Political inertia in a Tatra village[1]

Peter Skalník

The sudden demise of socialism and of the unconstrained rule of communist parties in Central Europe was something nobody could predict. The November 1989 revolution in Czechoslovakia was mainly the work of urban masses (see Holy, this volume) and it was at first hardly understood and welcomed in the countryside. Especially in Slovakia, people were suspicious and doubted its meaning. Under the long rule of a Slovak president, Dr Gustáv Husák, their living standards had improved steadily and there was little for them to complain about; even the Government's policy towards the Roman Catholic church had softened during the 1980s. But to understand what ordinary rural people in Slovakia really felt about the revolution and the direction their society has taken since 1989, there is no better method than a close examination of a particular community.

In 1991 the northern Slovak village of Šuňava could still create an impression of prosperity. From a distance it forms a long string of mostly recently built houses, with some as yet unfinished large houses on the outskirts suggesting considerable affluence. There are two churches and at each end of the village one can see the large and well-equipped agricultural centres of the Unified Peasant Cooperative Šuňava. The village is surrounded by rolling fields, meadows, and forests, with a breathtaking view of the nearby high Tatra mountains. It is accessible on three paved roads and lies only 6km from the E85 highway, and 9km from the train station. Frequent bus connections allow villagers easy access to the regional centres, and also to the High Tatra national park.

Out of 421 permanently inhabited houses in 1980, more than half were built after 1961 and three-quarters after 1946. All of these houses are classified, with the exception of the presbytery, as family houses, and were built by the families themselves, with the help of relatives and friends. The more recent houses tend to be large and comfortable, many have interior toilets and central heating, and almost all have television (including many colour), refrigerators, and washing machines. A significant number of households own private motor vehicles. According to data from the last census taken in 1980, out of 1,742 permanent residents in the village, 910 were economically active. More than three-quarters of these worked out-side the village, mostly in nearby light industries, building, and communications. Only 16 per cent of the working population found jobs in the village, mostly in the Unified Peasant Cooperative, and the 1991 census will probably show even less local employment, because the cooperative laid off some employees recently.

In 1970 when I started my fieldwork the upper and lower hamlets constituted two separate villages. Their inhabitants espoused a different mentality and differed also in costume and dialect. The rate of intermar-riage was surprisingly low in spite of the negligible distance between the settlements. My fieldwork revealed that the hamlets had experienced cen-turies of cooperation and rivalry, in the course of which differential treatment by the state had played a significant role. What united them was their 100 per-cent adherence to the Roman Catholic religion. The hamlets were almost equal in population, but Lower Šuňava had more than twice the average hectares of land and was less socially differentiated than Upper Šuňava. Prior to the twentieth century all the Šuňavians were very poor mountain peasants dependent on relatively infertile soils, on which they grew potatoes, barley, rye, flax, and hay for their animals. Cattle and sheep farming boosted local income, as did forest exploitation.[2]

The long isolation of the two Šuňavas, and indeed of the entire Tatra region, came to an end with the construction of a railway which in the latter part of the nineteenth century connected eastern and western parts of today's Slovakia. Industrial and tourist development followed, though not enough to prevent many Šuňavians from emigrating to North America. Some emigrants used to send remittances to their families back home, others returned with their savings and bought more land or built better houses. Even today some households still receive American benefits, or profit from American inheritances. The hamlets were drawn more directly into industrialization from the mid-1930s when the Bata shoe company built a factory for artificial silk in Svit, a town a mere 10km from the villages. Later a sock-making factory and other industries followed, and these offered employment to many Šuňavians.

The seizure of power by the communist party of Czechoslovakia in 1948 led to many changes, including the closing of the borders and an end to emigration. The subsequent drive towards accelerated industrialization in Slovakia and the collectivization of agriculture caused many workers to adopt the lifestyle of the 'peasant-workers'.[3] Regardless of low soil fertility, the communist state imposed very high compulsory delivery quotas of milk, meat, and other products, which could not be met by Šuňavians. It goes without saying that state prices for these quotas were extremely low. In 1950 communist provocations climaxed in the arrest of the village priest and eighteen others, whilst about 200 villagers were forcibly transported to Svit, where they were interrogated and beaten. Five persons were sentenced to prison terms, and a further fourteen were kept in detention for nine months without any trial.

This event, mainly affecting Lower Šuňava, caused its inhabitants to become hostile to outside influences, and only about half of all landowners eventually succumbed to the pressure to establish a cooperative. Both hamlets were starved of funds and their public facilities were badly neglected. In 1968–69 the verdicts of the political trials of 1950 were declared invalid and the persons concerned rehabilitated, though they received no compensation. (This was partly because the reform movement of the time was aborted following the Soviet-led invasion and subsequent introduction of totalitarian rule.) A film made about the 1950 resistance and its aftermath was seized and never transmitted. In Upper Šuňava, the communist agitators were more successful and a cooperative was founded, with all except three landowners participating. The village leadership was able to attract more public funds for its development. By the early 1970s, during my fieldwork, a special act was passed which declared the land remaining in private hands to be mismanaged: the owners either had to join the cooperative, or see their land taken away and incorporated into that of the cooperative. This law opened the way for unification of the hamlets, for which the district administration and the communist party had been pressing.

One might have expected that by 1974, when the two hamlets successfully merged into a unified Šuňava and the two cooperatives merged, they would be ready to shed the burdens of the querulous past. For example, with subsidies from the state and the cooperative a multi-purpose three-storey administrative building and a spacious cultural house were built and other new development projects were undertaken by the communist-led council of the village. Modern shops and some pubs were opened in all parts of the village. However, the new unified village did not receive the status of 'stredisková obec' – that is, a village 'with prospects of development'. As a result, state funding of public projects was limited and family housing projects were discouraged through refusing building licences and loans. The state urged Šuňavians to build new houses in a larger settlement nearby, but this was considered totally unacceptable, not least because the population of this town was predominantly Protestant. Šuňava villagers resented this discrimination and continued building large modern family houses without permits and loans, sometimes living for years in their new houses without road access, and with a makeshift, illegal electricity connection. The new housing projects required broader building plots than the available private garden land provided, which led to lively transactions in local real estate. The price of plots has exceeded the officially approved figures many times over. Many land disputes arose, in which the village leadership tried to mediate, sometimes successfully and sometimes not.

POLITICAL LEADERSHIP IN ŠUŇAVA

In my opinion, the nature of leadership provides the key to understanding this village in the twentieth century. Šuňava leadership patterns followed those of the country as a whole, through the historical vicissitudes of the country. The political regime has already changed five times during this century, and each attempt at revolutionary change at the state level demanded from the villagers, and especially their leadership, an ability to read these changes (or their promises) well, in order to reap benefits for the village community and the survival of the same leaders.

The 'traditional' political culture of the Šuňavians was informed by a kind of 'big-man'syndrome. Informants agree that those who drank heavily were generally considered powerful. Candidates seeking the support of the electorate during the last years of Hungarian rule used to throw coins to the people. Family cliques stood behind every individual's attempt to gain public office. During the democratic Czechoslovak Republic (1918–38), local competitors for office joined the village branches of nationwide political parties, such as the Republican (also known as Agrarian) Party, and the National Socialist Party. In addition, the nationalist Slovak People's Party gradually gained influence in this period. The criteria of property and individual merit were important in the election of the official village leadership; but even more important was where the support of the heavy drinkers was directed. The democratic process was only superficially implemented and internalized in the village community.

This political culture was abrogated during the period of the Slovak Republic (1939–45). For the first time young men assumed executive offices in the villages, in alliance with the forces of the one-party state. This practice continued after the war. Some of the agents of the war-time 'coup' on the part of village youth joined the post-war democratic parties with the same fervour as they had joined the nationalists before. But shortly afterwards the communists imposed their rule in Šuňava violently in 1950, and after this recruitment to the village leadership was not left to chance. Even though the chairman of the local branch of the National Committee (council) was always a local man, and sometimes not a party member, the secretary was a communist appointee. His voice was politically decisive, and yet this office was several times filled by persons who were not natives of the village. Communist organization in Šuňava was still very weak after 1950, comprising only a few members. The party cells at the plants at Svit were required to 'help' and 'strengthen' the party at Šuňava during the 1950s and 1960s. This deepening penetration of communism into village politics did not eliminate alcohol as a political tool altogether, but relegated it to a subsidiary role. The hegemon was the communist party which from outside of the village decided who was suitable to be its leader.

It seems that the direct involvement of outside bodies in Šuňava's internal politics diminished after the hamlets merged in 1974. The last fifteen years of 'actually existing socialism' in the united village gave some scope to leaders of various personality types, some of them problematic. For example, one recent chairman who led the village for ten years was an alcoholic, but he was none the less regarded as an expert in solving neighbourhood disputes. His successor was a woman, who led the village principally through an instinct for balance between various family factions, combined with her influence among members of the middle and older generations of villagers. She was said to have joined the communist party because of her ambition to gain the chairman's job. The village party cell was for years led by a man who joined the party at 40, just after the purges in 1970. At each election the list of candidates was carefully prepared by the local party, ratified at district level, and voters had virtually no choice except to approve the candidates proposed.

THE IMPACT OF THE 1989 REVOLUTION

The 1989 change of political regime (see Holy, this volume) was welcomed by an overwhelming majority of the citizenry of Šuňava, who expected justice to be meted out for crimes committed during the communist dictatorship and hoped for economic prosperity combined with guaranteed political and religious freedom. They immediately enjoyed complete freedom of religious practice, previously *de facto* denied to public servants, especially teachers. A small group of supporters of VPN (Public Against Violence) formed in the village under the leadership of a man who had married into the village twenty years earlier. An electrician in one of the nearby factories, he had never been a party member and was known for regularly helping out with electrical installations in the Šuňava churches. The problem was that the VPN group soon closed its ranks to potential members and assumed a comparable exclusivity to that practised by the communists before them. The latter disappeared from the scene almost entirely.

The policy of leniency towards present and former communists adopted by the new Czechoslovak President and the civic movements which took power in the country meant that in this village the chairman of the National Committee continued to exert influence. For a year, an uneasy balance of power prevailed between the representatives elected at the 1986 elections (pseudo-elections, like all others in the communist period) and the VPN members who were supported by a few adherents of the newly emerging Christian Democratic Movement. As a result, in the local elections held on 23–24 November 1990 there was no real competition for seats in the new council. In fact, there were only three candidates in excess of the number to be elected, a pattern strongly reminiscent of electoral practices under communism, which had also on occasion allowed for a few people on the local list not to be elected.

The stalemate on Šuňava's political scene was also evident in the complete absence of candidates for the new position of *starosta* (mayor). That election had to be postponed. Eventually the village VPN leader stepped forward as a candidate, promptly followed by the former National Committee's chairman, who had by then left the communist party. A new date for the election was fixed, but the outgoing chairman was disqualified on procedural grounds (she had some invalid names and signatures on the citizens' support sheet which was required for nomination by the election law). She and her large group of supporters, many of them relatives, then shifted their support towards another counter-candidate who, though in principle supporting a similar political programme to that of the VPN candidate, canvassed under the slogan of indigenous leadership. Although the VPN candidate won convincingly, villagers felt disgusted by the pre-election intrigues and frictions. The disqualified candidate lodged a complaint through the courts, which took months to investigate and brought no satisfaction to her in the end. The election also reminded the village of its former division into two halves. Not only were there two separate polling stations, one in the Lower hamlet and one in the Upper, but the rival to the VPN candidate received a majority of votes cast in his native Lower hamlet, whilst the VPN candidate was the overwhelming choice of the Upper hamlet.

The economic reform, launched in Šuňava as elsewhere in Czechoslovakia on 1 January 1991 with dramatic price increases and sad prospects of a steady decline in living standards, has seriously discouraged many supporters of the new regime. People now openly recall the 'advantages' of the previous system. They point out that not only were prices low under socialism, but (for example) housing projects were heavily subsidized by the state. An even more serious threat is that posed by the industrial restructuring in the region. Socialism, in the eyes of many villagers, offered social securities which are now being phased out, and ordinary people are very much afraid of the future. Older villagers refer to the impending fulfilment of Sibyl's prophecies of the end of the world, sometimes connected with the end of the millennium. Others fear that the possible demise of nearby industries and cooperatives might throw the village back into the misery and backwardness of the pre-industrialization era.

It is obvious that the new village council will not be able to carry out its ambitious programme of public projects without financial support from the state budget. But these funds are scarce, and it is therefore doubtful whether the council will be able to maintain its present level of support. It can play a popular role through the rehabilitation of victims of the communist regime, and the restitution of property, especially the collectively owned forests, meadows, and pastures which had been appropriated by both the state and the agricultural cooperative. Those imprisoned without trial and those whose property was confiscated have initiated legal action to obtain full redress. The problem is that their grievances touch only old people or the fortunate heirs of some rich deceased. Most young people are more interested in new public projects, such as sewerage, better access roads to their houses, regulation of the village stream and the like, for which there will be little or no funds unless they can be raised locally from taxes. However, any increase of taxes will be unpopular in the present climate of general economic pauperization.

The situation is further complicated by the grim prospects of the Unified Peasant Cooperative. The new Land Act which is presently under preparation in the Federal Assembly seems likely to spell the destruction of this 'achievement of socialism'. Either the cooperatives will be dissolved from above, or power will revert to the original landowners whose holdings were appropriated to form the cooperative, irrespective of whether these former owners or their heirs are actually members of the cooperative. The intention is, of course, to put right wrongs committed by the communists, but in practice it may lead to a disaster because these former owners are in no position to resume private agricultural enterprise. At this stage it looks as if socialist agricultural cooperatives are the only option if the country does not want to jeopardize its food production, but Šuňava's cooperative can hardly hope to survive even if there is no move to change its ownership structure. In the socialist period, because of its less fertile soils the cooperative used to receive substantial 'differential bonuses' from the state, payable on each litre of milk or each kilogramme of meat or grain produced. This subsidy is already diminishing and is likely to disappear altogether. In addition, if it survives at all the cooperative will certainly have to pay rent to the ex-owners for the land it took from them in the past.

Privatization has been designated by the Government as the only viable alternative to the previous socialist economic order, and its prospects in the villages like Šuňava are depressing outside the agriculture sector too. In several decades of industrial employment Šuňavians learned only how to carry out the directives of political and technocratic elites. The overwhelming majority of the villages are unskilled workers who put all their savings into their houses and small-scale food production around these houses. They have no capital resources available today, and even if they did they lack know-how, a willingness to risk funds, and any basis for trust between possible partners. Perhaps when people start losing jobs in industry and have to fall back on the village for their livelihood, then they will start seriously considering private enterprise. At least in their large houses and yards they have plenty of space available for business activities, unlike the inhabitants of the overcrowded cities. By June 1991 only three or four villagers have launched small private shops or pubs. Those who were planning to buy existing shops or pubs were their current managers or their family members, whose capital may well have derived from their use of state property for personal objectives. A few lucrative kiosks in the village were owned by an outsider whose fortune was also of dubious origin. The big privatization of large enterprises, which is to start early in 1992 through coupons obtainable for a nominal price by every adult citizen, seems unlikely to attract many supporters in Slovakia, at least judging from those who have registered claims in the early months.

CONCLUSIONS

Šuňava is, in 1991, more than a year after the official political fall of 'actually existing socialism', still fully in its grip. Its political culture is still based on particularistic group solidarities – namely, kinship and friendship – rather than open democratic competition. Villagers, accustomed to passivity and fear during communist rule, do not realize their rights and duties as citizens in the public sphere. As elsewhere in Czechoslovakia, elements of civil society are weak, and anyone seeking public office is initially suspected of pursuing his own selfish interest, most likely of a material nature. In economic terms, everyone in Šuňava is dependent on income from state-owned or cooperative employment and they do not try to extricate themselves from this dependence. People do not yet realize that the days of sheltered employment and social guarantees are now over. Only time will tell whether Šuňavians will embrace the 'spirit of the free enterprise' exhorted by the new authorities, or instead join those calling for a return to the social and economic organization of the socialist period.[4]

The Šuňava case should help us to understand that the ideals of liberty sound empty to people who grew up and lived their whole lives in conditions of 'actually existing socialism'. This socialism stressed material security and consumption above everything else. The villagers seem to cherish lower prices more than democratic political values, because the latter have so far been associated only with economic decline, security problems, immorality, and so on. Spiritually, the Šuňavians remain prisoners of the egalitarian demagogy of socialism. If economic decay should deepen, it may eventually render such people receptive not only to the revival of leftist political programmes, but also to other extremist political movements, such as fascism and chauvinist nationalism. For the time being, socialism in the pseudo-benevolent form it came to assume remains very much alive in Šuňava and elsewhere in Czechoslovakia.

NOTES

1 The fieldwork for this chapter was carried out in Šuňava between January and June 1991, and was partly financed by the Slovak Ethnographical Society. It is a sequel to the main corpus of fieldwork which took place in 1970–76. During this

period I visited the village on thirteen occasions, spending more than six months there in total. The research of the 1970s was financed by the Institute of Ethnology at the Comenius University in Bratislava, my employer at the time, and the Slovak Ethnographical Society. I am grateful to these sponsors for their financial assistance, as well as to my former colleagues in Bratislava and to Mihály Sárkány (Budapest) and C.M. Hann (Cambridge) for their comments.

2 After the abolition of serfdom in Hungary (to which Slovakia belonged before 1918), the forests were administered collectively by groups of co-owners (Skalník 1979, 1982, 1986).

3 Comparative discussion of 'peasant-workers' and 'worker-peasants' is available in Franklin 1969 and Hann 1987. See also the special number of *Sociologia Ruralis*, 1983 and Pine, this volume.

4 It has yet to be seen how villagers will respond to the nationalist propaganda of vocal cultural elites in Slovakia, calling for either 'confederation' of the existing state or for complete Slovak independence. Some villagers said to me tersely that those who won the 1990 elections are sure to lose the next ones.

REFERENCES

Franklin, S.F. (1969) *The European Peasantry: The Final Phase*, London: Methuen.

Hann, C.M. (1987) 'Worker-peasants in the three worlds' in T. Shanin (ed.) *Peasants and Peasant Societies*, 2nd edn, Oxford: Blackwell.

Skalník, P. (1979) 'Modernization of the Slovak peasantry: two Carpathian highland communities', in B. Berdichesky (ed.) *Anthropology and Social Change in Rural Areas*, The Hague: Mouton.

—— (1982) 'Community studies and the limits of representativeness: a socio-ecological discussion on mountain communities', in H. Mendras and I. Mihailescu (eds) *Theories and Methods in Rural Community Studies*, Oxford: Pergamon Press.

—— (1986) 'Uneven development in European mountain communities', *Dialectical Anthropology*, 10 (3–4): 215–28.

Chapter 15

'The cows and pigs are his, the eggs are mine'

Women's domestic economy and entrepreneurial activity in rural Poland

Frances Pine

Complete equality between men and women before the law and in social life; a radical reform of marriage and family laws; recognition of maternity as a social function; protection of mothers and infants. Initiation of social care and upbringing of infants and children (creches, kindergarten, children's homes, etc.). The establishment of institutions that will gradually relieve the burden of household drudgery (public kitchens and laundries) and systematic cultural struggle against the ideology and traditions of female bondage.

(From the programme of the International Women's Secretariat of the Comintern, under Clara Zetkin, Moscow, 1924)

The best thing is to keep your land and your women; if you must lose one, better to lose the women and keep the land.

(Polish peasant man, highland village, 1979)

Poland, with its awkward and recalcitrant peasantry who stubbornly refused collectivization and its flourishing, indeed almost dominant 'second economy',[1] was in many ways the maverick state of socialist Eastern Europe. The profligate Gierek years saw the creation of a massive national debt. Hungry for hard currency, the Government allowed and even encouraged the growth of a black market which extended to every possible commodity and service. Throughout the 1970s in Poland, the vast discrepancy between official policy and actual practice was openly acknowledged in all but the highest official circles. As I was often told by the villagers in the highlands where I did research, '*Tutaj nic nie jest wolno, ale wszystko jest możliwe*' ('here nothing is allowed but everything is possible').

This chapter is concerned with the position of Polish peasant women in the south-western highlands during the later years of the socialist regime, when nothing was permitted but everything was possible. Specifically, it focuses on the complex strategies devised by women in their pursuit of economic security, and the ways in which these often entailed delicate balancing acts between obligations, time, and labour in the domestic economy, the state sector, and the ubiquitous 'second economy'.

There can be no doubt that the lives of the peasantry, and particularly the lives of peasant women, changed enormously in the years between the establishment of the socialist regime in 1947 and its demise in 1989. That the dreams of early socialist feminists, such as Clara Zetkin and Alexandra Kollantai, envisaging a world marked by total equality at work, collective responsibility for domestic labour and child care, and equitable partnership and free choice within marriage, were not realized even in the early post-Revolution years in Soviet Russia is perhaps not surprising. What is striking is that, despite the fact that in Poland, as in other Eastern bloc countries, legislation, extremely progressive by Western European standards, to protect and support women in areas such as work and safety, family and marriage, and health care and maternity, was initiated in the mid-1950s, its practical application was minimal, particularly in rural areas (Sokolowska 1963; Jancar 1978; Pomian 1989). Clearly, the 'revolution from the top' did not extend fully to women, who remained for the most part definitely at the bottom. Kolankiewicz and Lewis state this bluntly:

> most of the burden of decreasing living standards is shouldered by women, who make up 51.2 per cent of the population. It is women who have to stand in queues for goods in short supply; it is also they who serve their irate sisters in retail outlets. . . . They had to cope with the decline of . . . communal feeding and cleaning facilities which raised the hours spent on housework and shopping to 7.5 *per day* on average. This was aside from the time spent at work, where they earned at best 30 per cent less than their male counterparts, although figures are apparently so shameful that official statistics do not provide a breakdown by sex.
>
> (1988: 60; my emphasis)

In rural Poland, women's labour has a particular developmental cycle, which corresponds with life stages characterized by early marriage, repeated child-bearing and the demands of child-rearing, and a labour-intensive and highly flexible agricultural economy and market network. The types of paid work available to rural women, the labour demands of the family farm (especially when male waged labour entails long absences from home), and the social demands of caring for children, the ill and the old, combine to create a certain pattern of female economic activity. This pattern, I would argue, is characteristic of rural underdevelopment generally and not of Polish socialism in particular; what we witness is not so much the socialist government's failure to integrate women fully into the labour market, although this is certainly one aspect of the problem, as the difficulty of changing women's situation and lives when the economy is backward and when there is no social or cultural context for questioning gender ascriptions. In Poland, for various cultural and historical reasons including the very powerful position of the Roman Catholic church, there is enormous ideological stress placed upon the family and upon a woman's role within it as mother and nurturer (cf. Siemieńska 1987; Holy, this volume). That this does not coincide with the realities of many women's lives is clear. Women are certainly nurturers and carers, but face-to-face relations between women and men within the family are often brutal, male alcoholism and domestic violence are common, and the family often represents anything but a 'safe place' or haven.

For peasants particularly, socialism often represented the 'enemy other', manifested in the state which had the potential to invade their lives at any moment. In contrast to this state, the family, centred in popular representation more around the nurturing mother than the patriarchal father, could be seen as protecting and caring for its members. For the peasantry, the ideological value placed on the family is reinforced by the fact that it is the productive and reproductive centre of social and economic life. The ideology of gender within the family often masks the fact that in terms of both agricultural labour and waged work, women are not 'different but equal' but are subject to mutually exclusive, unequal systems of constraints. While all peasants can be seen in some ways as disadvantaged in relation to national social and economic hierarchies, women's association with the family economy and lack of consistent integration into external economic structures is decidedly more marked.

Three factors particularly can be seen as militating against the integration of regional groups of peasants into the national economy. First, economic development in Poland was uneven during the socialist period, and the rural areas lagged far behind urban centres in health care, education, and work opportunities. Secondly, while collectivization programmes in the other Eastern bloc countries transformed agrarian conditions, or at least provided alternative labour and authority structures to those of the peasant family farm, less than 20 per cent of Polish agricultural lands were collectivized, while the rest remained in the hands of peasant farmers. This meant that erosion of the authority of the senior generations, and particularly of the senior men, occurred far more slowly in rural Poland than in other parts of Eastern Europe. Thirdly, Poland's history of partition from 1772 until 1918 meant that many peasants identify far more strongly with their villages and regions than with any idea of the nation. Whereas the post-war generation of children, educated under the state system, have a strong sense of Polish history, albeit through a socialist lens, the sentiments which they learn at home are often strongly anti-state. Particularly in regions such as the southern mountains, which have for generations been peripheral and isolated, the state is regarded with hostility. Villagers may take instrumental attitudes in their dealings with state bureaucracy, but they also harbour deep resentment towards powerholders whom they see as having failed to develop agriculture adequately. Many retained a deep suspicion that the final aim of the Government was to collectivize their land. Although state-supported 'agricultural circles', equipment cooperatives, and distribution networks were all used extensively by the peasants during the socialist period, and certainly facilitated what little growth took place in the agricultural sector, the peasant farmers rarely let go of the idea that these organizations were really just a ploy, masking or preceding further concerted attempts towards state control and ultimate collectiviza-tion.[2]

The pattern which emerged was one in which peasants participated instrumentally in both the agricultural and waged sectors of the state economy, but gave priority to their local systems of reciprocity and cooperation, which revolved around established authority structures and divisions of labour based on the small family farm. Many peasants worked for wages in the state sector in order to supplement their inadequate agricultural income. In the region in which I did research, however, the second economy provided more, and more flexible, economic oppor-tunities for the peasants.

My argument here is that the integration and participation of women and men in these three sectors, the domestic economy and family farm, the state waged sector, and the second economy, were uneven. Women's economic careers, although straddling the three sectors, were rooted most firmly in the domestic organization associated with traditional peasant farming. I want also to suggest that in the Podhale region where I worked, and possibly in other regions as well, the family provided both in fact and in ideology an alternative and often oppositional social structure to the state. In so far as the peasants in this region rebelled against socialism, they did so through the 'everyday acts of resistance and rebellion' characteristic of peasants everywhere rather than through any coordinated or planned political strategy (Scott 1985). These acts of rebellion, predominantly played out in subversive social behaviour and small gestures of economic sabot-age, locate the family and the wider net of kinship and neighbourhood relations as the source of resistance from below. It is in these spheres of family, kinship, and domestic economy that the agency of women is most vividly expressed.

ETHNOGRAPHIC BACKGROUND

The Podhale lies in the south-western foothills of the Polish Carpathians, a breathtakingly beautiful area of gentle slopes and valleys leading up to the formidable peaks of the High Tatra Mountains. The people of the Podhale are the Górale, or highlanders, a distinct ethnic group of shepherds and subsistence farmers with a reputation for innate wisdom, autonomy, and wild and colourful behaviour.[3]

Until as late as the 1960s the peasant villages of this region were poor and isolated. Partible inheritance had led over generations to extreme fragmentation of fields and dwarfing of holdings. By the beginning of the twentieth century, the largest peasant farms were about 25 ha, while the average size was nearer to 2 ha. Peasants supplemented their subsistence farming with activities such as carpentry, weaving, knitting, and basketry, and midwifery and bone-setting within the village; with the sale of eggs and cheese at the local market, and with sporadic migrant labour, sometimes as far afield as Budapest. Members of the poorer families worked as day labourers on the farms of the wealthier villagers, and on the local estates, and young girls were sent into domestic service. On the whole, however, the village economies centred on subsistence farming, and agricultural production was based on the extended family, often encompassing two or three separate households, and on reciprocal labour exchanges between kin and neighbours. The household and agricultural divisions of labour were based on age and gender, and although in reality the practical boundaries were flexible, ideal female and male spheres were clearly demarcated. At the head of the farming household stood the senior couple, the male *gazda* and the female *gospodyni*, who exercised considerable moral and economic authority over junior members. The *gospodyni*, however, was responsible primarily for domestic management and organization of female and child labour, while the overall running of the farm was seen as falling under the encompassing authority of the *gazda* (see Pine 1988).

When the socialist regime took power in Poland in 1947, it inherited a country ravished by war, with a rural economy which had been severely under-developed even before the destruction of the war years took its toll. The Government immediately embarked upon a programme of intensive industrial development. Attempts to collectivize farm lands were eventually abandoned in the face of massive peasant protest and refusal to deliver goods, but this only meant that even more resources were invested in industrial development at the expense of agriculture (see Pine and Bogdanowicz 1982; Hann 1985; Kolankiewicz and Lewis 1988). In the area of the Podhale which I am discussing here, there was never a consolidated attempt to collectivize. The land is too poor, the terrain too rugged, and the climate too harsh to support a thriving agricultural sector. Rather, small enterprises were built, such as a shoe factory and a ski factory, and the region was also developed for tourism, to absorb the overspill of tourists from the long-established alpine resort town of Zakopane. Communications with the rest of the country improved as roads were built and bus and train services extended. This in turn enabled the villagers to travel to and from town to work in the local factories, and to take advantage of the demand for goods and services created by the growing influx of tourists. By the 1970s acute deprivation had become on the whole a thing of the past, yet the memory of poverty remains strong to this day. The peasants' attachment to their land and distrust of government officials and local administrators are rooted in this remembered past of exclusion and deprivation.

The village in which I have done research is small for the area, with a population of about 800, and a total household count of about 160. Today it has a shop, a school, a post office, a tourist hostel, a bar, and a new church and cemetery. The market town Nowy Targ is about 10 km from the village. Nowy Targ is the site of an historic periodic market, which every Thursday draws huge crowds both of local farmers and market women buying and selling livestock, tools, food, crafts, and wool, and of tourists from all over Poland who come to buy these commodities or to seek out such rare bargains as amber necklaces, coral earrings, fine old shawls, and gold rings. Nowy Targ is also the local *gmina* (local government area) headquarters, accommodating the court, police station, secondary school, technical colleges, and the communist party headquarters. There is a wide range of both state and private enterprises in the town, providing employment for local residents and for many of the inhabitants of outlying villages. Just outside Nowy Targ are the factories built during the post-war industrialization drive. These factories are also places of employment for village women and men (Pine and Bogdanowicz 1982).

The village itself lies in a remote valley, which has been accessible by road and rail only since the 1950s. Its economy is still primarily agricultural. Less than 10 per cent of the village households are without farmland, and even members of most of these households work regularly in the fields of their parents or siblings. From the late 1950s the groundwork was laid for the economic development of this village. Agricultural production and distribution improved somewhat with the development of Agricultural Circles to manage and distribute farming machinery, and cooperatives for purchasing local produce (in this area primarily milk). Men from most households joined the Circle and contracted to provide the state distribution centres with milk and, in rare cases, beef, and pork. Farming production itself remained highly labour-intensive and unmechanized, and the division of labour continued to be based on gender and generation divisions within the extended family, and patterns of cooperation and reciprocal labour with close kin.

For the majority of village households, however, farming alone could not provide a sufficient income. By 1977, when I first went to the village, many adults, both female and male, derived more of their income from activities outside farming. While many villagers worked in the state sector, either in one of the local factories or in the service and less frequently the administrative sectors, the most lucrative income sources were found in the legal, semi-legal, and straightforwardly illegal second economy. Here activities ranged from petty commodity production and sale, self-employed building and carpentry, to illicit currency deals, smuggling, and black market trading. A further economic dimension was added by the pattern of wage-labour migration to the United States.[4] By the late 1970s the most affluent village families were those from which one or more member had gone to work in Chicago, staying with kin for two or three years and working, often illegally, to earn dollars to finance a big new house in the village, suitable for accommodating tourists.

DIVISIONS OF LABOUR

Many adult villagers are involved in all three economic spheres. Nearly all villagers, from the very young to the very old, work in the fields during planting, hay-making, and harvest, and take some role in the day-to-day chores of running a farm. Most men and women of the post-war generations have worked in the state sector, often part-time or temporarily, as factory hands or other unskilled workers, less commonly full-time, and permanently in the service sector or in administrative posts in town. Finally, it would be hard to find a villager with no contact with the second or informal economy, be it an occasional expedition to the market to sell eggs and cheese, a regular provision of some service such as driving, or seasonal work such as private building. In each of these three spheres, principles of gender and age can be seen to underpin the divisions and organization of labour. I would also argue that the gender divisions of the domestic and farming economy, and the ideologies of male and female which relate to the family and the domestic group, can be seen as extending into the division of labour outside family farming, particularly into the second economy.

Within most village households various economic activities are pursued, which together make up the household economy with farming as the priority. Both women and men are involved in every stage of agricultural production, but clear distinctions are made about spheres of work. Women are associated with the house and the farmyard, and are responsible for cooking, for feeding both the people and the livestock, milking the cows, and gathering the eggs. Men are responsible for maintaining the buildings, for slaughtering animals and preparing meat and sausage, and for looking after machinery and tools. Just as women are associated with the house and its immediate proximity, men are associated with the outside, with the fields and the woods, and with the work that is carried out there. Women and children rake hay and help to bring it in, weed fields, plant and pick potatoes and other root vegetables, and gather and bundle grain. All household members except the very young and the very old or infirm participate in threshing. Men work with horses, tractors, and machines, turning and fertilizing the soil, ploughing, and sowing grain and cutting hay. During the most intensive times of agricultural work, planting potatoes, hay-making, and harvest, men, women, and children work together in the fields, often with the help of kin and neighbours. At these times, labour is exchanged between households, and male and female labour is separately accounted and balanced.[5]

Both women and men market farm produce. Men, however, are usually the ones who take the main responsibilty for delivering quotas of produce to the distributive cooperatives, and organizing the private sale of livestock at markets, and of meat to private sources. Women market small amounts of produce on an occasional basis; they take eggs to market, make and sell cheese and butter, and during the summer months gather and sell mushrooms and berries.

Villagers themselves see farming as a household enterprise, and rarely acknowledge, at least overtly, conflicts of interest between men and women in terms of production. The farm is usually owned jointly, and women as well as men own individual fields and property. They do, however, clearly recognize the different male and female spheres. Male work is seen as important, female work as subsidiary. This was put clearly to me by one 60-year-old woman, who said, 'The farm is ours. The cows and pigs are his; the eggs are mine.' While both women and men are equally necessary to, and involved in, all phases of agricultural production, their roles are ascribed different values, and women's work is viewed, by themselves and by men, as practically and economically less significant. The difference between the value of a cow and the value of eggs is a measure of this.

A small number of farms specialize in dairy or meat production, and have no household members working outside agriculture, and a few very old couples, without any resident children, survive solely by subsistence farming. Most adults, however, also work in other fields at some point in their lives. Their earnings are on the whole channelled back into the household economy, although young single men and women may only give part to their parents or senior kin, and keep the rest for their own use, particularly saving up for marriage. Most villagers follow one of two patterns after leaving school; they either begin to work for the state, or they are apprenticed to close kin and begin immediately to work in the second economy.

What interests me here is not so much the different sorts of jobs that men and women do as the way in which gender distinctions are maintained in the different economic spheres. Patterns of male waged labour and work in the second economy are determined largely by the need to generate income above that which can be obtained from farming, and by the demands of farm work, which vary greatly according to season. During the summer and early autumn the demands of agricultural labour are most demanding, and take priority over other work. Men who work in the state sector organize their holidays around these peaks, or negotiate shifts which allow them to spend much of the day in the fields. Work in the informal sector, which is often organized on an irregular, highly *ad hoc* basis, may be suspended during these times. During the slack agricultural months, however, men are free to work as drivers, to haul timber, and to take on building contracts. This work is quite highly paid. It involves long hours away from home, and often out of the village. Male workers are recruited in much the same ways that agricultural labour is organized. As in farming, a man may work alone, or with a son or brother, for small jobs, but for larger work, such as building contracts, a team is recruited through ties of kinship, neighbourhood, and friendship, with individual members recruited on the basis of skill or access to tools and machinery. Although social ties are essential in recruitment, such work is strictly accounted and conducted like a business enterprise. In this it is different from farming; most farm labour involving members of other households is arranged in terms of strictly calculated, balanced reciprocity. Elsewhere the work is contractual, and men are usually paid in cash by their employers. This pattern of alternating agricultural labour with paid work continues throughout a man's life, mitigated obviously by the availability of work and by the developmental cycle of the farm labour force.

Women's working lives unfold differently. Just as male work is largely organized around the needs of the farm, the work of women must accommodate the demands of the domestic household. This does not mean that women's non-farming labour is not also affected by the farming cycle; it is, and, like men, women who work for the state arrange their free time and their shifts around planting, haymaking, and harvest. Other factors, however, also influence the ways and the areas in which women work. The majority of young village women go to work in the state sector after leaving school, either on the factory floor or in the service sector, waitressing, cleaning, or working as shop assistants. This work is, as the the quotation from Kolankiewicz and Lewis on p. 228 indicates, extremely badly paid. It has, however, several advantages for women, which are directly connected to their household responsibilities. First, state employment brings with it rights to health care and pensions. For women, this involves sixteen weeks' paid maternity leave, and an option of up to three years unpaid leave. Second, waged work in the state sector is viewed as relatively undemanding. It is often extremely hard work, but no more so than either farming or domestic labour. And while farm work and domestic labour must be done well, and involve great personal commitment to the general well-being of the family, state work is viewed with detachment, with little emphasis placed upon good performance or productivity. Finally, work in the state sector is seen as badly organized, which ironically makes it flexible in terms of women's time. Often with the collusion of the managers, women take turns leaving work to stand in queues for food and scarce consumer goods, to negotiate and exchange with other women the 'under-the-counter' goods and produce which might be available at the workplaces of each, and to sell and exchange both farm produce and any number of goods and services to which they might have access through their families and kin. In some cases, the workplace provides opportunities for petty pilfering. One woman, for example, worked for the state weaving cooperative, and whenever possible smuggled home with her a ball of the high-quality wool used in tapestries and clothes, which she could then sell, or use in her own private weaving. The important point here is that women view state work totally instrumentally. They feel no moral obligation to the state, and no compunction to work well or to be productive. This frees them to take advantage of facilities available, and to use the workplace as the location for a variety of tasks necessary for daily home life, and deals aimed at helping the domestic economy.

The maternity benefits offered by the state also make such work attractive to young married women. A common pattern is for a woman to work for the state until the birth of her first child, and then take the paid leave to which she is entitled, during which time she helps on the farm, and often works with other female household members knitting, weaving, or sewing, or making cheese for sale. Most women return to paid work at the end of this period, but after the birth of her second or third child a woman is more likely to remain off work for the full three-year period. Many women do not return to wage-labour, finding it too much to accommodate with the demands of domestic labour and child care, particularly when their participation in second economy dealing becomes more time-consuming and financially rewarding. Some women return to state work when their older children become able to care for younger ones; others continue to divide their time between the daily farm and domestic work required of them, and some type of 'informal' activity.

WOMEN'S WORKING LIVES

Women's labour on the farm and in the house, revolving as it does around the daily care and nurture of people and livestock, ties them consistently far more closely to the farm and the village than does that of men. Some women, despite this, become successful market women who travel as far afield as Crakow and Warsaw, selling wool, sheepskins, and cheeses in the railway and bus stations, or on the street in the main squares. A few women are known to be involved in smuggling, usually of highland sheepskins and foreign gold and currency, and to travel routes which take them across national borders and even as far as Turkey. Still other women go abroad, usually to Hungary or Czechoslavakia, to work on short contracts. All women I knew in these categories were either young and unmarried, or were well into middle age with grown, married children among whom was a resident daughter or daughter-in-law capable of taking over the daily running of the farm and household. The only exceptions to this pattern are a few young women, with children, who have gone to America for one or two years to work; their children were left in the care of their own mothers, who may or may not have been members of the same household. The important point here, I think, is that wage-labour in North America is so extraordinarily lucrative,[6] and so difficult to arrange, that normal constraints and obligations cease to apply when such an opportunity presents itself.[7]

Women who travel extensively, however, are the exception. Most women try to find ways of earning money which are compatible with the demands of the farm and the family. On the whole, they do what they are best at, with the people with whom they are used to working. The tourist industry in particular provides an extension of existing domestic roles for women, and a range of jobs and services which can coexist with child care and farm work. Networks of female kin and affines, who provide the basis for women's cooperative activities in agriculture and in elaborate domestic work such as cooking for a wedding or a christening, are also central in developing labour pools, marketing networks, and distributive channels for goods and services. Sisters and sisters-in-law drop in on one another in the evening, and sit together in the kitchen with their young daughters, chatting and knitting sweaters to sell. Little girls are taught to knit by their mothers and sisters when they are 6 or 7; often by age 8 or 9 they are knitting for sale, sitting up late at night, exchanging gossip with their elder kinswomen to the fast clacking of needles. If pressed for time, several girls and women may work on one sweater, one knitting the front, another the back, and two others the arms. The sweaters, if not commissioned by a particular tourist, are taken by one of the women to sell on the Nowy Targ market, or passed on to a market woman, who collects from various village women before market day and sells their produce, either paying them by the piece or on commission.

Women with modern two- or three-storey houses, often paid for with American dollars, let rooms to tourists who come to ski in the winter and to relax in the clean mountain air in the summer. Many such women do not register their rooms with the local tourist board; although they risk of being caught and fined, they also avoid paying taxes, and can choose their own guests and regulate their own prices. Tourists tend to return to the same family, and to bring various friends over the years. If the village woman lacks room for the friends in her own house she passes them on to a sister, sister-in-law, or daughter. Villagers often become very friendly with tourists, while at the same time viewing them quite instrumentally, and incorporating them into their network of *znajomy*, acquaintances who can do one favours. Much as the tourists are passed around the female kin circle, so are the opportunities and potential for asking favours which the tourists offer shared among kin. One village woman who is a wonderful cook started a small private restaurant in her own house. When her 'own' tourists started to bring their friends and she needed to expand, she trained her cousin to be her assistant, and began to employ her young daughters, as well as the daughters of sisters and cousins, to wait on the tables. This organization of female kin labour is identical to that which would be orchestrated at a *wesele*, the elaborate two-day Górale wedding feast. The labour network was simply transposed into a seasonal, money-making enterprise.

In certain families the women serve illicit vodka in their basements, drawing custom from village men as well as from tourists. Others sell milk, eggs, and cheese to the tourists, and occasionally try to interest them in buying an article of clothing sent from America, or gold or jewellery from some more questionable source. They sell the tourists sweaters or wool, offer them sheepskin coats in the winter months, and generally provide them with whatever services they appear to need, and even some they had not anticipated.

These types of female entrepreneurial activity mediate between the world of the household and of kinship, and the outside world of strangers. The work can be seen as using the same skills, and as based on the same ideologies of correct female work, as female labour in the farming household. However, it takes place outside the spheres of farming and household subsistence, and involves payment for service or product. The women use their networks of kinship and affinity to produce and sell their goods to the outside economy, or to bring the outside world in, in the form of tourists. The tourists are certainly not totally incorporated into the internal world of the village, the household, and the kin networks; but they are welcomed into the household and provided with many of the services with which women also provide their families. They are also given part entry to the world of female kinship, although whether the tourist is valued as a person or as an economic asset is not always absolutely clear.

Women's reasons for working for the state are practical and pragmatic, and the work they do there, as I have already discussed, is seen as neither important nor worthwhile. State-sector employment is outside the constraints of morality which temper economic relations between co-villagers and productive relations within the family and the household. Although it could well be argued that, particularly in relation to maternity benefit, the socialist system implemented policies which allowed women more choice and control over their work than they had had previously, the women themselves do not perceive this. They see the state as producing the scarcities, the queues, and most of the factors which make their lives so hard – fair exchange, then, that those involved in waged work in the state sector should use that time and those workplaces to cope with the problems of daily life.

Female family and kinship networks, centred in the household and extended out into an intricately wrought complex of relationships, form the basis for women's cooperative production, exchanges of support and services, and sale and distribution of produce. It is interesting to compare female networks with the agricultural circles and cooperatives established by the state but run by male peasants; in terms of the organization of production, distribution, and marketing, there are marked similarities. To some extent, kinship can be seen as providing an alternative basis for economic organization to that of the state. The household is the focus of morality for the Górale villager; it is the place in which work is perceived as being part of one process, and in which, despite legitimate hierarchies of age and gender, common interest is assumed. Within the household, by word and by example, children are taught an ambivalent attitude to the state. On the one hand, they are told that if they want to 'get on', they must be polite to teachers, speak only in 'clean' Polish, behave humbly in front of priests and bureaucrats, and generally conform to society's ideas of good, and civilized, behaviour. On the other hand, they continually witness other kinds of behaviour. The moment visiting priests or officials leave, the villagers drop their appearance of humility, and start turning them into figures of fun. They mimic them accurately and mercilessly, parodying an affected 'elegant' accent, pretending to mince along on high heels in the snow, and telling stories of the priests' wandering hands, or the villas owned by the priests' sons in the mountains. Children see their parents using the Górale dialect to communicate in front of strangers, and using house names instead of surnames in address and identity to provide a cloak of anonymity in a private language and naming system that the outsider cannot penetrate. They hear tales of how, as children, their parents were sent to steal kindling from the estates of wealthier villagers or the gentry, and how they were whipped and beaten if caught. At the same time they see their mothers returning from work with wool smuggled out of the factory, and their fathers turning up with loads of coal which have some-how gone astray from their intended destination. The implicit parallels are clear. They are taught to protect their own information and that of those close to them, to run and alert people working in the fields if police come into the village, and to combine their polite deference to priests and bureaucrats with an alert but totally guarded reticence. These strategies effectively locate loyalty, morality, and interest first in the household and family, and second within the village. They identify the enemy 'other' as the powerful outsider: the landed gentry or rich peasants of old, the priests, and the contemporary state officials. It is largely from their mothers, and from listening to the talk of their mothers and their female kin, that children receive these teachings.

CONCLUSIONS

The failure of the Eastern European socialist regimes to win the hearts and minds of the people is now indisputable. For the Górale, as for other isolated, peripheral groups of peasants (cf. Kligman 1988), the socialist state represented only one more stage in a long history of opposition and subversive action against the 'outside'. In fact, many aspects of villagers' lives improved during the socialist period. Health care, education, and opportunities in waged labour all lagged far behind the urban areas, but were a marked improvement on what formerly had been available. Ironically, collectivization, which the villagers feared and most often cited as the reason for their anti-state sentiments, was never much of a threat in the mountains. The socialist regime failed, however, either to implement any policies to develop private agriculture, or to provide the kind of work which would allow villagers in such unproductive regions as the Podhale to move permanently away from agriculture. For women particularly, work in the state sector was limited, and conditions arduous and unrewarding.

Consequently, the central role of the family farm, and the gender divisions within it were never seriously threatened. The house, centred on the family and particularly the mother, continued to play a vital role in the village economy and to be the primary source of social identity and value. Because conditions in the state sector were so poor for women, they used the state economy and policies only at the times that served them best. For most women, work continued to be associated with the house and farm, and to be organized through networks of female kinship. Their ability to transform these into flexible entrepreneurial strategies for dealing with the external economy made their lives somewhat easier during the years of shortage.

I stated at the beginning of this chapter that the developmental cycle of female labour, which creates for women a constantly interrupted pattern of conflicting needs and obligations, can be seen as much as a symptom of under-development as of socialism gone wrong. Studies from Africa and from Latin America have stressed comparable balancing acts to those that Górale women perfected in the post-war years. It remains to be seen whether the post-socialist Government commitment to rapid conversion to a free market economy will help or hinder rural women. Current trends of rising unemployment[8] and factory closures, and increasingly vocal arguments in the press and from the Government itself that women should be 'allowed' to return to the home and look after their families, all suggest that that there will be a marked decline in female participation in the structured workforce. It seems likely that for many rural women, waged work opportunities will diminish rapidly, and their dependence on informal earnings, small-scale marketing, and home-based industry will increase. This in turn suggests that rural Poles may turn inward again, relying more and more on production for subsistence, and looking increasingly to village-based ties of kinship and neighbourhood to provide a safety net in times of deprivation. For the Górale, many of these networks are already firmly in place. Whether the skills of survival they have developed over the years will continue to serve them well in what appears to be a climate of increasing polarization between rich and poor, and between urban and rural areas, remains to be seen.

NOTES

1 The term 'second economy', referring to economic activity which is not included in the state or cooperative sectors, has a wide range in Eastern Europe. In addition to the legal private sector, it extends to illicit and illegal activities throughout the economy, and is used in much the same way as the term 'informal economy' in the anthropological discussion of non-socialist societies. For comparative material, see Grossman (ed.) 1987, and Hann (ed.) 1990.
2 For a comprehensive discussion of Polish agriculture at this period, see Galeski 1972.
3 Field research was carried out in 1977–79, 1981, 1984, and 1989. I am grateful to the Social Science Research Council for funding the 1977–79 research, and to the Economic and Social Science Research Council for funding the 1989 research. Additional support was received in 1977–79 and 1981 from the British Council, and in 1977 from the Central Research Fund of London University.
4 The first mass migrations of Górale to North America occurred during years of famine in the late nineteenth century, and continued until America closed its doors to European migrants in 1915. More limited migration persisted throughout the first half of this century. It stopped only during the first two decades of the socialist regime and was reactivated after Polish travel restrictions were partly lifted in the 1970s.
5 Labour is ranked, with adult male labour being the most valued, followed by that of women, and then of children. If a household sends only women and children to a neighbour's threshing party, they in turn will receive only female and child help when their turn comes. Old women who live alone are at a particular disadvantage here, as whatever help they give to neighbours is likely to be reciprocated with a minimal team of perhaps one woman and one child. The old woman's choice is either to work for as many neighbours as possible, exhausting herself and neglecting her own fields, in order to accumulate enough 'credit' for her own harvest, or to hire day labour, which is usually viewed as a highly unreliable option.
6 In 1979, average savings over a two-year period in Chicago were $20,000, then equivalent to about 2,600,000 zlotys at the unofficial exchange rate, or about twenty years of above-average earnings in Poland. Moreover, during the 1970s and 1980s many goods, particularly motor vehicles and building supplies, were only easily available for hard currency.
7 In the 1970s and 1980s both Polish passports and American visas were quite difficult to obtain, and often involved a great deal of time, expense, and manipulation of connections. It is my impression that female applicants with young children were favourably viewed by both Polish and American authorities, as it was assumed that they were certain to return to their children.
8 At the time of writing in November 1991, official unemployment is 2 million of whom over 53 per cent are women.

REFERENCES

Galeski, B. (1972) *Basic Concepts of Rural Sociology*, Manchester: University of Manchester Press.

Grossman, G. (ed.) (1987) *Studies in the Second Economy of Communist Countries*, Berkeley: University of California Press.

Hann, C.M. (1985) *A Village Without Solidarity: Polish Peasants in Years of Crisis*, London: Yale University Press.

—— (ed.) (1990) *Market Economy and Civil Society in Hungary*, London: Frank Cass.

Jancar, B. (1978) *Women Under Communism*, Baltimore, MD: Johns Hopkins University Press.

Kligman, G. (1988) *The Wedding of the Dead: Ritual, Poetics and Popular Culture in Transylvania*, Berkeley and Los Angeles: University of California Press.

Kolankiewicz, G. and Lewis, P. (1988) *Poland: Politics, Economics and Society*, London: Pinter Press.

Pine, F. (1988) 'Kinship, marriage and social change in a Polish highland village', Ph.D. thesis, University of London.

Pine, F.T. and Bogdanowicz, P.T. (1982) 'Policy, response and alternative strategy: the process of change in a Polish highland village', *Dialectical Anthropology*, 7(2).

Pomian, A. (1989) *Polish Independent Press Review 6*, Munich: Radio Free Europe Research.

Scott, J.C. (1985) *Weapons of the Weak*, New Haven and London: Yale University Press.

Siemieńska, R. (1987) 'Women in social movements in Poland', *Women in Politics*, 64 (Winter).

Sokołowska, M. (1963) *Kobieta Pracująca*, Warsaw: Wiedza Powszechna.

Chapter 16

'Working class' versus 'ordinary people'

Contested ideas of local socialism in England

Susan Wright

In 1985 John Gyford produced a slim volume which crystallized discussion about recent changes in local socialism, or at least, the kind of society the Labour Party was trying to create through local government in England. He set up a contrast between 'Labourism' and 'the New Urban Left'. This distinction hinged on the ways in which the old guard and the New Left conceptualized the relationship between 'council' and 'people'. I will argue that, more than this, the New Left tried to construct 'people' differently. They rejected Labourism's certainty that they were working for the 'working class' and introduced a confusing array of alternative constructions.

In this chapter, after examining Gyford's distinction in more depth, I will trace the development of Labourism in Teesside, its vision, its policies, and political practices. The New Left responded to the crisis of unemployment in the late 1980s with an alternative vision of local socialism. Using a case study, I will show how in one of the old heartlands of Labourism, now experiencing 20 per cent male unemployment, in a contest between the New Left and the old guard, the latter has managed to retain the definition of the public as 'the working class', and keep to its established political practices.[1]

LABOURISM AND THE NEW URBAN LEFT

Gyford is careful to distinguish Municipal Labourism from an earlier Municipal Socialism of the late nineteenth and early twentieth centuries. In the latter, Labour local municipalities ran utilities (water, gas, and transport) as income-generating concerns and provided more generous redistributive welfare services than other councils, like public assistance benefits, maternity care, welfare services, and education (Gyford 1985: 5). These traditions of using local government to achieve some measure of socialism were devalued in the inter-war period. The road to socialism was thought to lie in Labour Party control of national government. Attention turned towards nationally planned provision of services which were large-scale, cost-effective, efficient, and distant from the local electorate and consumers. Local government's role was to carry out local redevelopment on a similarly large scale, with the efficient use of resources for a public good that they determined.

It is this new phase of Labour activity in local government that Gyford calls Municipal Labourism. It is characterized by the high-rise housing block. Comprehensive redevelopment 'too often became associated with the enforced and resented destruction of familiar places and of established patterns of employment, recreation, friendship and neighbourliness' (1985: 7). The Labour Party was not alone in promoting the insensitivities of centralized planning, but major improvements in welfare and standards of living that they achieved came to be perceived by their beneficiaries as oppressive: they were a means through which the state had increased control over their lives. Municipal Labourism established a distance between councillors and 'the people' and 'could display a certain heavy-handed paternalism. . . . Usually it did the right things *for* people; but sometimes it could do the wrong things *to* people; and only rarely had it previously discussed either of those things *with* people' (1985: 10).

The people for whom councillors were working were the 'working class'. Through trade unions and the Labour Party, it was assumed that Labour councillors represented working-class views, implicitly male and in waged production, and that they and their agenda of employment, transport, and housing were the stable basis of 'real' politics. This assumption even underlies academic analyses of the local state. Even though empirically, workers in capitalist production were the declining base of Labour's traditional support (Hindess 1971), Saunders (1984) calls political struggles based on anything else unstable and interest-based, as if those based on male workers are not. The New Urban Left shifted away from conceptualizing local government as acting in the interests of the 'working class', with its male breadwinner image.

The New Left was not homogeneous, and Gyford's characterization draws heavily on London experience. He associates it with gentrification of the inner city. Members of new local government and welfare-state professions, trained in the period of community action against municipal redevelopment, moved into old streets of Camden and Islington that had avoided redevelopment by Municipal Labourists. Informal New Left networks became active in feminism, anti-racism, single issue, anti-nuclear, and environment campaigns. Those who joined the Labour Party sought to give it new impetus by making links with these 'fragments' (Segal *et al.* 1979). Boddy and Fudge (1984) say the impact of academic work on their visualization of 'the state' should not be under-estimated.[2] It was no longer seen as a unitary body in league with, and creating the conditions for, capitalism. It became an 'arena' where capitalism, patriarchy, and racism were often in conflict and produced contradictory policies which left 'space' for action on local economic development, community action, equal opportunities, anti-nuclear, and other issues.

In the early 1980s a New Left came to power in several local councils in England. They sought in different ways to redefine the traditional Labour local government 'working-class' agenda and represent a wider range of interests. Some tried to mobilize popular support for local government services against central government cuts and reactivate people's involvement in politics in the process. Some concentrated on making services more accessible through decentralization of their administration; others combined this with an attempt at participatory democracy through neighbourhood forums. Some felt local government should become a base for community campaigns, and its resources should be used to enable people to 'gain more control of their own lives'. As the agenda widened, so the 'people' appeared in different contexts as 'public', 'citizens', 'clients', 'consumers'. Increasingly, a new phrase tried to embrace them all: 'ordinary people'. This phrase stood in place of 'working class' and suggested a closeness between people and the activists, professionals, or politicians in local government. It simultaneously set activists apart as 'unordinary', and another distance was created.[3] This distance was reflected in political debates among the New Left about how to achieve 'empowerment' of ordinary people. In attempting to break down Municipal Labourism's distant relations between the 'council' and the 'people', the new urban Left set up a new relationship between 'activists' and 'ordinary people'. But the vagueness of the replacement term, 'ordinary people', represented the confusion about how to cope with the variety of interests that competed for this new political space.

After the 1983 elections, when Labour lost control of many councils, Massey (1983) suggested that in the remaining Labour authorities, Old Labourism dominated the regions, while new alliances of the Left controlled cities. In broad terms this was true, but there is a danger of treating these as pure types. In some authorities, younger councillors drew on ideas of the New Urban Left but did not share all its characteristics, and exerted some influence on old Labourists, whilst not having overall control. Such is the case in the North-east councils on which my research is based. The next stage of my analysis is to trace the development of Labourism in the North-east region and examine the form of the New Left or, in local parlance, 'Young Left', before taking the focus in closer to examine the contest between these two ideas of local socialism within a small town.

MODERNIZATION IN TEESSIDE

Residential clearance and the redevelopment of high-rise housing blocks were only one aspect of a much wider modernization process in the 1960s, of which Teesside was the prime example. In 1962, unemployment in the

North-east was twice the national average. The Conservative Government appointed Viscount Hailsham as Minister of the North. He made his famous 'flat cap tour' and drew heavily on ideas of Labour councils in his plan for the North-east (Board of Trade 1963). Its vision of the modernization of the region became the basis of a political consensus encompassing all parties, central and local government, trade unions and capitalists. It recommended that consultants should draw up a comprehensive plan for Teesside. Hailsham's definition of the problems and suggested solutions were carried forward by the Labour Government of 1964. They informed the resulting *Teesside Survey and Plan* and all subsequent plans, through to the 1972 Structure Plan.

The first priority for modernization was industry. Parts of the mining industry were identified as incapable of modernization and would close. Shipbuilding would be restructured to see if it could survive international competition. But two industries on Teesside, steel and chemicals, were the key to the Government's attempt to make sectors of the national economy internationally competitive. They were considered dynamic growth industries, and there would be state support to modernize production. Local authorities were to facilitate the assembly of new and extended sites. Water authorities built controversial new reservoirs to guarantee the necessary supplies for industry. Teesside was identified as the dynamic motor for industrial growth in the region that would achieve full employment. Even if some jobs were lost in the process of modernizing steel and chemicals, it was thought that employment would be secure for the future in those industries. In addition, on green-field industrial estates and reclaimed land, new industries would be brought to the area to diversify employment.

Secondly, not only would industry be modernized, but so would the urban form. State support would cover the cost of the new road network which was necessary to service the industry. The town centre of Middlesbrough would be demolished and a new shopping complex built. This would give the area an appropriate modern image, bring in the services necessary to support thriving industry, and further diversify employment. Thirdly, the settlement pattern would be modernized. Labour would move from redundant mining villages to Teesside, and the settlement pattern would be reshaped accordingly. Mining villages were expected to die out. In Teesside, new estates were to house the influx of workers for the steel and chemical industries and to rehouse people living in substandard, city centre housing.[4] In moving from street houses to semi-detached council houses, old communities would be broken up but families would benefit from having clean houses which were sufficiently large to take the new white goods and consumer items associated with the 'modern' lifestyle.

In short, old historical forms of industry, built space, and social relations would be cut through, and modern forms constructed as from new. The aim was for Teesside to grow from 480,000 in 1969 to 704,000 in 1991, with the creation of 120,000 new jobs (Wilson and Womersley 1969: summary). The pollution and dereliction would be cleared up so that people could enjoy their surroundings and a healthy lifestyle. The plan projected comprehensive changes at breathtaking speed. To implement them, eight councils were amalgamated into one large authority in 1968 capable of making strategic decisions for the whole Teesside area. In the general reorganization of local government in England in 1974, an even larger county council and a second tier of smaller district councils were set up.

In these larger authorities, councillors were no longer making decisions for areas small enough for them to know and be known. This was made worse by the emphasis on 'strategic' thinking in councils which emphasized space rather than people, and development in the sense of buildings rather than social relations. Councillors tended to be either wedded to planning and its vision and mission of modernization, or to decry the new profession of planners whilst still engaging in clearance and redevelopment. These extremes of attitude were found among members of both parties, and both shared an approach that Gladstone identified in Teesside and called 'getting things done':

> 'Getting things done' depends on an argument that goes as follows. The first priority is to bring jobs to the area; bringing jobs to the area depends on being able to attract employers; being able to attract employers depends on their attracting bright young executives. And this in turn depends on being seen to do 'prestige' projects which 'get you in the twenty-first century'. And this is largely a matter of building large-scale city-centre developments and a system of urban motorways.
>
> (1976: 50)

The effect of 'modernizing', 'thinking big', and 'getting things done' in such a large and remote authority was, as Gladstone goes on to illustrate, to limit and control public information and comment on proposals that affected them. This attitude to decision-making was defended on the grounds of professionalism or with the political argument that councillors were representatives elected to make decisions that were right for the people – even if those people disagreed and protested. Although not peculiar to the Labour Party, this politics of modernization, using local government to carry out large-scale redevelopment with 'efficient' use of resources for a public good that they determined, can be considered one of the prime ingredients of Labourism (Gyford 1985).

THE OUTCOME OF MODERNIZATION

Through the 1960s, Teesside was booming. Blue-collar wages were among the highest in the country; it seemed that growth and full employment might be possible. A continuous process of modernization of steel and chemicals was subsidized through the Government's regional programme. Local authorities prepared sites for them and built new housing estates. It was intended that modernization would be accompanied by diversification of the economy and employment. It is difficult to establish why this failed. Sadler provides evidence of one agreement between ICI and the Government to prevent other large firms that would compete for male labour from setting up in the area, and another arrangement with Eston Urban District Council to allocate its new housing to ICI Wilton (1990: 334–5).[5] These are two factors in a complicated process, the results of which were that large firms which might have diversified male employment did not set up in the area. Teesside was made dependent on the fortunes of two firms.

This was not the subject of dispute at the time. Hudson explains the political context:

> The alliance between the major chemical and steel companies, the trades unions whose members found or retained employment with them as fresh capital flowed in and the local councils many of whose members were employed by these companies, was an extremely powerful one. It cut across class boundaries in a vigorous promotion of one conception of what Teesside's future ought to be.
>
> (1986: 23)

This 'one conception' of what was good for Teesside lasted into the 1970s. ICI's and BSC's vast holdings of land meant that there was restricted space for the development of oil-related industries in Teesside.[6] Local authorities, trade unions, and capitalists, with funding from central government and the European Community, 'reclaimed' a bird migration site of international importance for this purpose. Conservationists' protests were rejected with the slogan 'jobs not birds'. It was not until the late 1970s that the county council first began to leave the alliance of industry and unions and began to emphasize the cost of capital-intensive and land-extensive development which created only 2–6 jobs per acre.

Labour had held that this cross-class conception of what was good for the region was 'in the interests of the working class'. Contrary to its initial impression, this phrase connotes a politics of modernization which was not based on consciousness of the interests of workers defined by their position in the system of production. It also sounds neutral, as if what is in the interests of the working class benefits all people in that class position. It was, however, highly gendered. The modernization policies of continuous investment in capital-intensive heavy-industry plants, using large tracts of land, with heavy environmental costs, was to secure 'men's jobs'. State policies which were 'in the interests of the working class', while appearing neutral, affected men and women differentially.

Manufacturing industry that would compete for ICI and BSC's male workers might be discouraged from entering the area, but firms with jobs considered suitable for women were welcome. They solved another problem for heavy industry. In the heyday of the unions' emphasis on the need for a male breadwinner to earn a family wage (Land 1980), increased housing rents in new council houses and the cost of a 'modern' standard of living put pressure for higher wages on heavy industries. This was alleviated by providing 'women's' employment.[7] Between 1958 and 1975 half of the new manufacturing jobs and most of the new service jobs in the new town centre and in local government were filled by women – although service-sector employment only ever reached two-thirds of that aimed for in the *Teesside Survey and Plan* (Hudson 1989: 366). This employment enabled women to supplement household income so that they could afford the higher cost of living and the expenditure on so-called labour-saving devices which were supposed to ease women's dual or triple roles in household management, community organizing, and waged employment.

While modernization was intended to cut away historical forms, as part of the process, gender relations were entrenched in what was considered 'traditional'. In the return to 'normal' after women had done even the heaviest jobs in the steelworks during the Second World War, there was a strict demarcation between what was considered a man's job and a woman's job.[8] Both might be in manufacturing, but men's jobs were in 'heavy' industry and women's jobs were in 'new' factories. Men's labour was associated with established trade unions; women's labour was 'green', meaning they had never previously been in waged labour and were not unionized. Men's work was organized in a three-shift system whereas women's jobs were timed around the men's shifts to enable them to be home with a dinner cooked, ready for the husband's arrival. Men's and women's jobs were associated with different levels of pay; and women's jobs were characterized by insecurity, being part-time, casual, or temporary. The policies to diversify employment in Teesside were implemented in such a way as to protect the status of male labour and their trade unions and entrench a strict gender division of work.

RESTRUCTURING AND RECESSION

When the recession started in the mid-1970s, the modernized industry of the North-east was shown to be weak. Central government had been trying to operate on a notion of a 'national economy'. Local authorities had been using ideas of regionalism. Meanwhile capitalists ceased to work within either regional or national frames. They had been restructuring capital internationally. What had become important was not just whether industrial activity was 'modern', but where a plant fitted into the international division of labour (Massey 1984). Firms distributed their functions across the globe. Massive state investment to modernize Teesside's steel and chemicals industries had been used to specialize in very vulnerable sectors.[9]

Modernization had been accompanied by a concentration on branch plants of firms based elsewhere. State support had not been used for the diversification necessary for a self-sustaining regional economy. If, before the modernization programme in the 1960s, Teesside was considered a peripheral region in the United Kingdom, in the 1970s it became a global outpost in a new international organization of capital.

The recession revealed the problems. From 1975, first the Labour and then the 1979 Conservative Government cut back state support for industry. First to go were the 'new' industries which mainly employed women on industrial estates. Gradually, all the major industries were affected: shipbuilding, steel, chemicals, and even the new oil-related industry. Modernization policies had already worsened the employment problem. Between 1965 and 1976 capital investment in 'old' industries in Cleveland had displaced 34,000 workers, while 'new' industry on industrial estates had created only 11,400 new jobs. The effect of the recession on this industrial scene was that in 1974–77 male registered unemployment doubled to 8.2 per cent. By 1981 it was 18 per cent, with 66,000 redundancies in that year alone. In March 1985 it peaked at 22.5 per cent. It remained the highest in mainland United Kingdom at over 20 per cent for the rest of the 1980s, with half of the 44,000 people in question unemployed for more than a year.

The concern in the village where I began fieldwork in the mid-1980s was that school-leavers might never get a job and earn a wage. This is borne out by the figures. Of those who left school in Cleveland county in 1985 only 9 per cent went into permanent employment, 46 per cent were on Youth Training Schemes. Of those on such schemes in 1983/84 only 35 per cent had a job by January 1985 (the national figure was 60 per cent) (Foord et al., n.d.). YTS managed the transition from school to unemployment, not from school to work, and the situation continues. Even those who still had a job felt the impact of high unemployment. Around a core of well-paid, permanent male employees at ICI and BSC is a penumbra of men who are taken on for peak work-loads and whose employment is insecure, short-term, sub-contracted, and non-unionized. However, Foord et al. (ibid.) indicate that the distinction between women's work and men's work is still maintained. Men are not taking jobs traditionally done by women as the wages are considered too low for a man. Similarly, Morris (1985) suggests that the domestic division of labour, whereby women do almost all daily domestic work, has not changed under conditions of high male unemployment.

THE COUNTY COUNCIL'S RESPONSE TO HIGH UNEMPLOYMENT

In twenty years, Teesside had gone from boom to bust, from the epitome of Harold Wilson's 'white heat of new technology' to Britain's unemployment blackspot with the greatest area of derelict industrial land in Western Europe (2,000 acres in 1974, according to Hudson 1986: 13). By the late 1970s it was becoming clear to some people in the local authorities that high levels of fixed capital investment, underwritten by central government regional policies and supported by local authority land-use policies was associated with environmental problems and rapidly rising unemployment. The local authorities tried to use their resources to promote the local economy but their role and ability to intervene in the local economy and society were being curtailed. Central government began to marginalize local authorities by setting up other agencies to take over certain of their functions.

In February 1986 a Task Force of five civil servants with direct access to ministers and a £1 million budget from central government was sent to Middlesbrough. They set up projects to work with public- and private-sector and community groups on 'enterprise' and skills training. In October 1986 the formation of four Development Corporations, one to be based in Teesside, was announced at the Tory Party Conference. An appointed committee of ten, mainly men in business and property development, took over local authority planning powers on land adjacent to 10 miles of the River Tees. Central government promised them a budget of £160 million to redevelop the land 'single-mindedly' over six to seven years, seemingly without regard to equity issues. The Manpower Services Commission, through a centrally appointed board, greatly expanded its schemes for unemployed people in the county. Community Programme places doubled in August 1985. The voluntary sector took great advantage of the availablility of 'jobs' and finances to cover support costs to develop environmental and care schemes. Those changes represented a shift in the balance of power and resources away from the county council to the private and voluntary sectors.

In the mid-1980s, whilst the national Labour Party (Kinnock 1985) spoke of 'the enabling state' in opposition to Thatcherism's 'roll back of the state', some county council officers and councillors in Cleveland began to look in new ways at the role of the council in the county. It was estimated that unemployment would remain at around 20 per cent into the next century. What was needed was jobs, but local government could not counter the effects of international movements of capital and central government policy through autonomous development. It was argued that high unemployment would remain and its social effects should be addressed. In areas with high unemployment the council's research unit produced a stark picture of poverty, lack of self-esteem, lack of community activity, and a lack of knowledge of available support for unemployed people (Smith 1986). An informal network of officers and councillors began to look for ideas from authorities with New Left programmes. A number of small projects were pursued jointly with the churches and with voluntary organizations. One of the major concerns was to discover how to turn a 'dependency culture' into an 'enterprise' one and build a social basis for future economic development. The thinking is captured in the resulting *Unemployment Strategy*:

> For all people in Cleveland there is dependency on a narrow economic base and a few large firms. . . . For the unemployed, already victims of dependency, new aspects of social and economic dependency operate, involving the government, through Social Security and MSC, and local government through social services and concessions. This leads to a sense of powerless and hopelessness.
>
> (Cleveland County Council 1987)

The first sentence here signals a clear move away from the Labourist argument that to support the interests of the 'few large firms' is to protect jobs and therefore is in the interest of the working class. The strategy also moved away from other aspects of Labourism. Instead of a comprehensive plan devised by experts in their definition of the people's best interests, the council was to respond to unemployed people in a way that empowered them. It was argued that instead of bringing unemployed people into contact with bureaucracies in a way that controlled them, the council's resources should be used to foster initiative and enterprise. This could be through supporting community action or through involving clients in the design of services. This discussion revealed that unemployed people did not have the resources to exercise their rights as citizens, and their problems were not reaching the council through the traditional routes of pub- and club-based Labour Party and work-based trade unions. Other categories of people who had been outside waged employment were seen to be similarly disempowered as citizens and as the public. There were few alternative local organizations through which communities could be reinvigorated and people could become more active in 'gaining control of their own lives'. The county council recognized that it could not remedy these problems alone; it would have to collaborate with other agencies and the voluntary sector. Instead of the simple 1960s image of a council responsible for its people within its area, this introduced a far more complicated picture of a council in an arena of organizations with different relations to the public.

Here were many of the themes Gyford (1985) identified in the New Urban Left. As they widened the agenda from the traditional issues labelled 'working class', the relationship of the council to people became very complicated. Those who were at first called 'unemployed' soon came to be constructed as clients, consumers, the public, citizens, the community, and voters. They were held together in the overall aim to use council resources to empower 'ordinary people'. It was planned to do this by having community development teams in four Action Areas working on the above agenda. From the bottom of the council's hierarchy at the interface with people, they were to feed their perspective on council operations to a central team of officers who would create the necessary changes in the way the council worked.

The development of this Unemployment Strategy was taking place in a council where the old guard had all the chairs but two to three members of each committee considered themselves new 'Young Left'.[10] Despite being in a minority, they were hard working and committed to different aspects of the empowerment vision of local socialism represented by the Unemployment Strategy. It was formally adopted in April 1987 and was fully operational eighteen months later. Subsequently, a new Labour leader took over with the support of the Young Left. His emphasis is on efficient delivery of a high level of services, and it seems that the Young Left's agenda with its complex array of relations between the council and different constructions of 'people' may be narrowed down to one: the modelling of the council on the retailing image of people as consumers.

CONTESTED IDEAS OF LOCAL SOCIALISM IN PRACTICE

A history of Labourism can be traced in the settlement pattern along one valley in the rural part of the county. Here also, different visions of socialism are being contested currently. The valley contains three settlements. On one side is a market town. On the opposite bank and on the valley floor are two villages which sprang up in the nineteenth century when the mining and steelworks were developed.

In terms of voting behaviour, like most of the county, this area is marginal. One current councillor was the first Labour councillor on the Urban District Council in the 1950s. He worked hard to get more Labour candidates on the council, and by the 1960s Labour had control. He became wedded to the large-scale planning and modernization ideas. He was on the cross-party organization for industrial development in the region in the 1960s. He consistently holds that his aim is to create jobs, and that to do this there has to be financial support for companies, industrial sites, a good road network, and a modern image for the area that will attract executives.

From the late 1960s various bodies, including the larger county council, made plans to redevelop the area. The mines, which had been the rationale for the location of the villages, had closed. The future of the steelworks was uncertain. Men commuted to work in heavy industry on Teesside, but there was very little work for women. To attract industry, an industrial estate was to be built on the edge of the market town. The valley was too steep for industrial traffic, so one plan was to fill it (using the 'unsightly' shale heaps), and to take a new road across and connect it with the new network planned for Teesside. The two villages in the valley were now redundant, and the plans proposed the demolition of nearly all of one, but only half of the one on the bank as it was divided by the boundary between two councils. Their 'unfit' terraces were to be demolished and the people relocated to a modern council housing estate attached to the market town. When, in 1973, the public were at last consulted on these plans, there was an outcry. The Urban District Council commissioned its own consultant and modified the plans, aiming to rebuild rather than demolish the village on the valley floor. But even when this was announced, it caused uproar.

Implementation of the plan continued during the period when local government was reorganized and the new distict council took up responsibility for the sub-standard housing in the villages. The leader of the Labour group on the district council was upset that all he got for recognition of rural problems was a bad name in the press. His power base was in the urban area. Each of the councillors from the hitherto separate and small rural council areas seem to have related to the leader individually as clients to a patron, seeking approval and funding for plans for their area. In return, the councillor was expected to keep control of his ward, so that no public outcry should occur over council plans. On top of the impetus against active public participation that came from the new professionalism of planning and the political ideas of representative democracy, this was an added incentive for practices to build up whereby councillors tended to constrain local initiatives and dampen anything which could be construed as dissent.

This is illustrated by an incident in the village on top of the bank, where the plan was to demolish half of it. In the 1970s some terraces were taken down to accommodate the new road. (They managed to regrade the road without filling the valley.) A further terrace was demolished as 'substandard', leaving a grassed gash through the village. Villagers hoped that the site would be used to build old people's bungalows. In the late 1980s, the green gash remained, but the problem for elderly people was getting worse. The village has only two- or three-bedroomed houses. If a person needs a bungalow, they have to move to another village, quite a distance away. In their own village, they are almost always looked after by children or friends; isolated in a new village, in story after story that I heard, they could not cope on their own again, they became mentally disturbed, or they just suddenly died. Women in the village argued they should be able to look after their own elderly relatives, and they should not be 'sent out of the village to die'.

The women raised a petition and sent it to the district council. As the district council no longer had resources to build houses itself, the request was passed to a housing association. A year later, the housing association presented its plans in a full day consultation in the village hall. The plan was for mainly highly quality three-bedroomed houses. One after another, people came into the hall and, on seeing the plan, explained that what was wanted was old people's bungalows. They told the housing association officers about the petition. The officers explained that district council officers had advised them that the need was for better, quality houses to attract executives to the area who would bring jobs.

At tea-time the Labour councillors arrived. They clustered around the modernization advocate, who was known to have worked hard and with integrity all his lifetime to bring jobs to the area and to do what was best for the working class. He tried to explain that these plans were best for the area. The women respected him, but clearly disapproved: they said that they wanted the one building site in the village to be used for old people's bungalows. He became very angry. He talked about holding things up and getting things done. He got out his diary and explained to the women that these plans would go to committee in a few days time and they had gone to a lot of trouble to get them approved before the housing association regulations changed. After that there would be little chance of getting this kind of project funded in future. The choice was to accept the plans or lose the opportunity. The women did not concede. The housing association officer interceded by saying his association tried to ensure they did what the people wanted. The green gash remains.

This councillor is utterly consistent in pursuing the principles of modernization and the Labourist style of political practice that flows from that. He holds to the cross-class consensus, even in the recession, treating it like a cloud which, in time, will surely lift, and then there will be a response to his unstinting attempts to get industry and jobs to return to the area. He says he is working for the best interests of the working class, even if they disagree. The most important way to promote their interests is to keep in power, and, whereas for the good of the region he will work cross-class and cross-party, in the market town he works adamantly to promote Labour and put down the Conservative and latterly the Green opposition.

In the 1980s, the market town began to attract young professionals who were prepared to commute to work on Teesside. Some joined the Labour Party and one became the county councillor. A struggle ensued in the Labour Party branch. New members wanted to increase the membership by holding discussions on current issues and finding out about what was going on in the council. According to reports I have heard, at every attempt the Labourist councillors have responded by using the rule book to stretch the business part of the meeting through the allotted time. There is no time for discussions, and many members cease attending these branch meetings.

Into this setting came the Unemployment Strategy Action Area team of three community workers. Nobody in the party or the town knew they were coming until they saw advertisements for the posts in the newspaper. The adamant modernizer, when he heard that an Unemployment Strategy was to address the social problems of unemployment, immediately proclaimed that it would do nothing to create jobs. Even before the team started work, the traditional Labourist agenda was reasserted. The team has been working on local service provision and, especially in the vast housing estate, enabling women to express their demands and improve facilities in their area. This raises gender issues. In the above account of the old people's bungalows in my fieldwork village I indicated that the petition was raised by women, and it was mainly women who attended the public meeting. This may look like 'political activity', but locally it is classified as women's work for their family, part of their caring and domestic roles. 'Politics' is for men, and women should not have to put up with it.

The gender divisions that have been identified in this chapter come together at this point. Labourist industrial policy is based on a distinction between men's work and women's work, with clearly differentiated wages and conditions associated with each. The domestic distribution of income in such households is now well documented (Pahl 1983; Morris 1984). The idea that the male 'breadwinner' should have money for his own private use, whereas the wife's money is for household management, seems to survive into unemployment. What seems not to have been noticed before is the impact that this domestic distribution of income has on community organizing and local politics.

Women's role of family carer in this fieldwork village is not confined to work in the house. Besides caring for relatives and neighbours, it concerns running children's activities, an old people's luncheon club, and social afternoons, geared especially at unemployed people, in the village hall. These activities are all run by women and funded out of their housekeeping (via bingo and coffee mornings and other fund-raising events). Family caring is women's public activity, but it is a different public space from that controlled by men. Men occupy their own space in the village, notably the Working Men's Club, and 'political' talk is confined there, in the men-only bar.[11] The boundaries around male space and men's concerns are maintained with frightening severity (Wright 1986). The housing association public meeting was on women's own ground in the village hall, but even so, many who had been in the forefront of organizing the campaign were reticent, and the speaking in the final confrontation with the male councillors was done by only a few women. To engage those who are involved in community activities in the reinvigoration of local politics, as the Unemployment Strategy set out to do, is to threaten this male control of 'public' space. This uncovers the gendered nature of the old agenda which had been in the interests of the apparently neutral 'working class'.

If the work with women is perceived as a threat, in other cases the work of the team is hardly noticed. The words 'empowerment', 'helping people get more control of their lives', and 'involvement in the community', are used with approval by people in the town. But ideas about developing new relations between the council and different categories of 'people' seem to be too complex to communicate clearly. None of the politicians, even of the Young Left, have taken up the principles of the Unemployment Strategy and promoted them as an alternative vision of local socialism. The county councillor who is in the new administration and presumably supports its emphasis on services to the consumer, is reputed to hold that the Unemployment Strategy is a waste of money. In a nice involution of the different ideas of local socialism, he is said to have argued that the money would have been better spent sending a delegation to Japan to attract a branch plant to the area.

CONCLUSION

In this chapter I have identified two principles of local socialism which suggest different Labour political practices and contain different visions of how local social relations should be organized. For some people, these are recognized as stark alternatives at the level of principles. The adamant modernizer in my case study maintains a consistent stand on principles, policies, and political practice. This seems to be rare. The example of the county councillor above indicates how the ideas weave in and out of one another in arguments. Others seem to use the whole range of ideas as an available repertoire without acknowledging the different versions of local socialism that lie behind them.

The analysis of industrial development and of the causes of unemployment in this chapter suggests why modernization has failed to achieve its aims. The cross-class consensus seems not to have benefited 'the working class', and that phrase, contrary to the assumptions of some sociologists, does not connote politics based on class conflict. Rather, it stands for a traditional Labourist agenda which, while appearing neutral, is strongly gendered.

In the case study, the clash over bungalows versus executive housing indicated the gulf between women's definition of what was needed to deal literally and metaphorically with death in their community, as against the Labourist politicians' and planners' external imposition of a definition of 'development' which they claimed to be in the villagers' best interests. The women, although not powerless, in that they resisted this imposition, have not yet been able to make the council act on their definition. The alternative New Left agenda with its aim of empowerment of people in their relations to authorities, in terms of being citizens, consumers, and members of the public, has not yet been conveyed clearly in principle or in practice. It has been marginalized as the antics of community workers. In the contest between different local socialisms in this locality, even in the face of high unemployment, the old guard has managed to retain the definition of the public as the 'working class' and to keep to its established political practices.

NOTES

1 This chapter is based on research conducted in one- to three-month periods each year from 1985. It includes an ethnography of an ex-mining and steel village,

archival research on policies affecting the mining villages since the 1960s, interviews with officers and councillors on 'community development' in all its various meanings, and in particular, annual interviews to plot the development of the county council's Unemployment Strategy. I am grateful to Cleveland County Council for funding my attachment to its Research and Intelligence Unit from January to December 1991 in order to make an evaluation of the Unemployment Strategy.

2 Main influences were Miliband (1969), Cockburn (1978), and subsequent feminists, for example, Eisenstein (1981), Franzaway *et al.* (1988), Walby (1990).

3 Edwards (1991) explores another way in which the phrase 'ordinary people' is used in relation to class.

4 The *Teesside Survey and Plan* identified 40 per cent of Teesside's housing as sub-standard. It recommended that 28,000 dwellings should be cleared and a further 30,000 rehabilitated.

5 There was a similar agreement to protect the National Coal Board's labour in the Durham coalfields. Alternative male employment was safely steered away from existing sites of heavy industry and into new towns and industrial estates elsewhere in the region: 46 per cent of new firms were located in eight such sites between 1961 and 1973 (Hudson 1989: 364).

6 In 1970 steel and chemicals had 6,000 acres, half the industrial land in Teesside, much of it undeveloped (Hudson 1986: 6).

7 Some firms providing 'women's' manufacturing work were established alongside heavy industrial plant, clearly making a differential between men's and women's jobs and wages. An example is the KP Crisp factory, which was set up alongside ICI Billingham.

8 My fieldwork confirms Price's (1987) analysis of women's involvement in steel production in nearby Consett.

9 The problems in Teesside were not caused by under-investment. From 1975 to 1979, new investment in Cleveland's manufacturing industry (mainly oil, chemicals, and metals) was £11,800 per employee, five times the national average (Cleveland County Council 1980). In that period the area received a quarter of the national total of Regional Development Grant payments (Foord *et al.*, n.d.). This state support had not created diversification of employment: in 1965, 79 per cent of manufacturing employment was in heavy industry, and in 1984 the figure was 74 per cent. In 1971, 40 per cent of all manufacturing plants in the Northern Region were branch or subsidiary plants of industries based elsewhere (Hudson 1989: 365). In the most successful new town in the region, Washington, in 1980, 20 per cent of the manufacturing jobs were lost within the space of six months (Hudson 1989: 373).

10 They called themselves 'Young Left', and although they drew on many ideas from the New Urban Left, did not share their characteristics. The New Urban Left were from welfare-state professions; the Young Left in Cleveland were, like the old guard, in manual employment or unemployed, and only eight out of forty-eight councillors seem to have a professional qualification. They were predominantly male (only five women councillors), and all were white.

11 The domestic distribution of income is reflected in the resource bases of these two institutions. In 1985 the village hall raised sufficient to cover its weekly running costs of £45, whereas the annual surplus on the bar account alone in the Working Men's Club was £42,300.

REFERENCES

Board of Trade (1963) *The North East: A Programme for Regional Development and Growth*, Cmnd 2206, London: HMSO.

Boddy, M. and Fudge, C. (eds) (1984) *Local Socialism?*, London: Macmillan.

Cleveland County Council (1980) *The Case for Urgent Action to Meet Cleveland's Growing Unemployment Crisis*, Report No. Y14, Cleveland: Research and Intelligence.

—— (1987) *Unemployment Strategy*, Cleveland.

Cockburn, C.(1978) *The Local State*, London: Pluto.

Edwards, J. (1991) 'Idioms of bureaucracy and informality in a local housing aid office', Paper given to the GAPP Anthropology of Organisations Conference, Swansea (4–6 Jan.).

Eisenstein, Z. (1981) *The Radical Future of Liberal Feminism*, New York: Longman.

Foord, J., Robinson, F. and Sadler, D. (n.d.) *The Quiet Revolution: Social and Economic Change on Teesside 1965–1985*, Durham University, a Special Report for BBC North East.

Franzaway, S., Court, D. and Connell, R. (1988) *Staking a Claim: Feminism, Bureaucracy and the State*, Cambridge: Polity.

Gladstone, F. (1976) 'Teesside: sprawl gone mad', pp. 35–56 in F. Gladstone, *The Politics of Planning*, London: Temple Smith.

Gyford, J. (1985) *Politics of Local Socialism*, London: George Allen & Unwin.

Hindess, B. (1971) *The Decline of Working Class Politics*, London: Granada.

Hudson, R. (1986) *Formulating and Implementing Local Authority Modernisation Policies in Teesside since 1964*, Middlesbrough Locality Study, Working Paper No. 7, University of Durham.

—— (1989) *Wrecking a Region*, London: Pion.

Kinnock, N. (1985) 'It can be done, it must be done', Speech to Labour Party Conference, Bournemouth, London: Labour Party.

Land, H. (1980) 'The family wage', *Feminist Review*, 6.

Massey, D. (1983) 'The contours of victory . . . the dimensions of defeat', *Marxism Today* (July).

—— (1984) *Spatial Divisions of Labour*, London: Macmillan.

Miliband, R. (1969) *The State in Capitalist Society*, London: Weidenfeld & Nicolson.

Morris, L. (1984) 'Redundancy and patterns of household finance', *Sociological Review*, 32: 492–523.

—— (1985) 'Local social networks and domestic organisations: a study of redundant steel workers and their wives', *Sociological Review*, 33: 327–42.

Pahl, J. (1980) 'Patterns of money management within marriage', *Journal of Social Policy*, 9: 313–35.

—— (1983) 'Allocation of money and the structuring of inequality within marriage', *Sociological Review*, 31: 237–62.

Price, K. (1987) 'What did you do in the War, Mam? Women steelworkers at the Consett Iron Company during the Second World War', pp. 178–95 in C. Creighton, and M. Shaw (eds) *The Sociology of War and Peace*, London: Macmillan.

Sadler, D. (1990) 'The social foundations of planning and the power of capital: Teesside in historical context', *Environment and Planning D: Society and Space*, 8: 323–38.

Saunders, P. (1984) 'Rethinking local politics', pp. 22–48 in M. Boddy, and C. Fudge (eds) *Local Socialism*, London: Macmillan.

Segal, L., Rowbotham, S. and Wainwright, H. (1979) *Beyond the Fragments*, London: Merlin.

Smith, E. (1986) 'Living with unemployment', *Northern Economic Review*, 13: 2–17.

Walby, S. (1990) *Theorising Patriarchy*, London: Blackwell.

Wilson, H. and Womersley, L. (1969) *Teesside Survey and Plan*, Ministry of Housing and Local Government, London: HMSO.

Wright, S. (1986) 'Gender divisions in village voluntary activity', Paper to the Meeting of British Sociological Association/Leisure Studies Association, Teesside Polytechnic (Oct.).

—— (1989) *Discourses on Local Government*, Sussex University, Papers in Urban and Regional Research, No. 71.

—— (1991) *The Context within which the Unemployment Strategy was Devised*, Evaluation of the Unemployment Strategy, Paper No. 2, Research and Intelligence Unit, Cleveland County Council.

Name index

Subject index